Julia Maurer

Relationships between Foreign Subsidiaries

GABLER RESEARCH

mir-Edition

Herausgeber / Editors:

Prof. Dr. Andreas Al-Laham
Universität Mannheim,
Prof. Dr. Johann Engelhard
Universität Bamberg,
Prof. Dr. Michael Kutschker
Universität Eichstätt, Ingolstadt,
Prof. Dr. Profs. h.c. Dr. h.c. Klaus Macharzina
Universität Hohenheim, Stuttgart,
Prof. Dr. Michael-Jörg Oesterle
Universität Mainz,
Prof. Dr. Stefan Schmid
ESCP Europe Wirtschaftshochschule Berlin,
Prof. Dr. Martin K. Welge
Universität Dortmund,
Prof. Dr. Joachim Wolf
Universität Kiel

In der mir-Edition werden wichtige Ergebnisse der wissenschaftlichen Forschung sowie Werke erfahrener Praktiker auf dem Gebiet des internationalen Managements veröffentlicht.

The series mir-Edition includes excellent academic contributions and experiential works of distinguished international managers.

Julia Maurer

Relationships between Foreign Subsidiaries

Competition and Cooperation in Multinational Plant Engineering Companies

Mit einem Geleitwort von Prof. Dr. Stefan Schmid

RESEARCH

Bibliografische Information der Deutschen Nationalbibliothek
Die Deutsche Nationalbibliothek verzeichnet diese Publikation in der
Deutschen Nationalbibliografie; detaillierte bibliografische Daten sind im Internet über
<http://dnb.d-nb.de> abrufbar.

Bibliographic information published by the Deutsche Nationalbibliothek
The Deutsche Nationalbibliothek lists this publication in the Deutsche Nationalbibliografie;
detailed bibliographic data are available in the Internet at http://dnb.d-nb.de.

Dissertation ESCP Europe Wirtschaftshochschule Berlin, 2011

1. Auflage 2011

Alle Rechte vorbehalten
© Gabler Verlag | Springer Fachmedien Wiesbaden GmbH 2011

Lektorat: Marta Grabowski | Jutta Hinrichsen

Gabler Verlag ist eine Marke von Springer Fachmedien.
Springer Fachmedien ist Teil der Fachverlagsgruppe Springer Science+Business Media.
www.gabler.de

Das Werk einschließlich aller seiner Teile ist urheberrechtlich geschützt. Jede Verwertung außerhalb der engen Grenzen des Urheberrechtsgesetzes ist ohne Zustimmung des Verlags unzulässig und strafbar. Das gilt insbesondere für Vervielfältigungen, Übersetzungen, Mikroverfilmungen und die Einspeicherung und Verarbeitung in elektronischen Systemen.

Die Wiedergabe von Gebrauchsnamen, Handelsnamen, Warenbezeichnungen usw. in diesem Werk berechtigt auch ohne besondere Kennzeichnung nicht zu der Annahme, dass solche Namen im Sinne der Warenzeichen- und Markenschutz-Gesetzgebung als frei zu betrachten wären und daher von jedermann benutzt werden dürften.

Umschlaggestaltung: KünkelLopka Medienentwicklung, Heidelberg
Gedruckt auf säurefreiem und chlorfrei gebleichtem Papier
Printed in Germany

ISBN 978-3-8349-3191-7

Vorwort der Herausgeber

Für viele Unternehmen ist es heute unerlässlich, sich auf ausländischen Märkten zu betätigen. Ein erfolgreiches Management der Internationalisierung stellt Unternehmen allerdings immer wieder vor neue Herausforderungen. Die Herausgeber beabsichtigen mit der Schriftreihe mir-Edition, die vielfältigen und komplexen Managementanforderungen der internationalen Unternehmenstätigkeit wissenschaftlich zu begleiten. Die mir-Edition soll zum einen der empirischen Feststellung und der theoretischen Verarbeitung der in der Praxis des Internationalen Managements beobachtbaren Phänomene dienen. Zum anderen sollen die hierdurch gewonnenen Erkenntnisse in Form von systematisiertem Wissen, von Erklärungen und Denkanstößen sowie von Handlungsempfehlungen verfügbar gemacht werden.

Diesem angewandten Wissensverständnis fühlt sich seit nunmehr 50 Jahren auch die in über 40 Ländern gelesene internationale Fachzeitschrift mir – Management International Review – verpflichtet. Während in der Zeitschrift allerdings nur kurzgefasste englischsprachige Aufsätze publiziert werden, soll der breitere Raum der vorliegenden Schriftenreihe den Autoren und Lesern die Möglichkeit zur umfänglichen und vertieften Auseinandersetzung mit dem jeweils behandelten Problem des Internationalen Managements eröffnen. Der Herausgeberkreis der mir-Edition wurde 2008 um weitere renommierte Fachvertreter des Internationalen Managements erweitert. Geblieben ist jedoch die Herausgeberpolitik für die mir-Edition, in der Schriftenreihe innovative und dem Erkenntnisfortschritt dienende Beiträge einer kritischen Öffentlichkeit vorzustellen. Neben Forschungsergebnissen, insbesondere des wissenschaftlichen Nachwuchses, können auch einschlägige Werke von Praktikern mit profundem Erfahrungswissen im Internationalen Management einbezogen werden. Wissenschaftliche Sammelbände, etwa zu Tagungen aus dem Bereich des Internationalen Managements, sind ebenso sehr gerne in der Reihe willkommen. Die Herausgeber laden zu Veröffentlichungen sowohl in deutscher als auch in englischer Sprache ausdrücklich ein.

Das Auswahlverfahren sieht vor, dass die Herausgeber gemeinsam über die Veröffentlichung eines für die Reihe eingereichten Werkes entscheiden. Wir freuen uns auf Ihre Manuskripte und hoffen, mit dieser seit langer Zeit renommierten Schriftenreihe die wissenschaftliche Diskussion und die praktische Lösung von Problemen des Internationalen Managements weiter zu stimulieren.

Andreas Al-Laham, Johann Engelhard,
Michael Kutschker, Klaus Macharzina,
Michael-Jörg Oesterle, Stefan Schmid,
Martin K. Welge, Joachim Wolf

Preface of the Editors

Nowadays, it is essential for a multitude of companies to engage in foreign markets. However, the successful management of internationalization processes constantly poses new challenges. By publishing the book series "mir-Edition", the editors attempt to provide academic guidance on the manifold and complex requirements of international business activities. The book series' purpose hence is twofold. Firstly, the "mir-Edition" is to provide empirical assessment and theoretical elaboration on the phenomena which can be observed in international management practice. Secondly, the findings obtained are to be made available in the form of systematized knowledge, explanations, thought-provoking impulses as well as recommendations for further courses of action.

For the past 50 years, the international journal "mir – Management International Review", which is read in more than 40 countries, has seen itself committed to promoting an understanding of international management as an applied academic discipline. As of now, the journal only publishes articles in English. The wider range of the existing book series ought to give authors and readers the opportunity to deal with the various problems of international management in a comprehensive and thorough manner. The editorial board of the "mir-Edition" was extended in 2008 through the addition of renowned experts from the domain of international management. Yet, the established editors' policy for the "mir-Edition" of presenting innovative work to a critical audience, which support the scientific advancement, has remained unchanged.

Besides the academic contributions of young scholars, the editors also welcome the relevant works of practitioners, who possess a profound knowledge in the area of international management. Furthermore, edited volumes, collecting for instance presentations held at conferences in the field of international management, are invited for publication. The editors explicitly welcome books both in the English and the German language.

The selection process stipulates that the editors jointly decide on the publication of any book manuscript submitted for the series. As editors of this well established and renowned book series, we are looking forward to receiving your manuscripts and we hope to further stimulate the academic discussion and to provide applied solutions for the challenges in the area of international management.

Andreas Al-Laham, Johann Engelhard,
Michael Kutschker, Klaus Macharzina,
Michael-Jörg Oesterle, Stefan Schmid,
Martin K. Welge, Joachim Wolf

Foreword

International business (IB) and international management (IM) literature has researched headquarters-subsidiary relationships in detail for many decades. As a consequence, we have substantial knowledge on how headquarters manage subsidiaries. In recent years, IB and IM research have also started to explore how subsidiaries gain voice and attention. The literature on subsidiary roles has helped us to shift our focus away from a pure center-periphery view to a multi-center view of the Multinational Corporation (MNC). However, so far, not much research emphasis has been given to horizontal relationships between foreign subsidiaries, although these linkages are important for the MNC. For instance, in some cases, foreign subsidiaries of a specific MNC cooperate or have to cooperate with each other to reach their goals. In other cases, foreign subsidiaries of the same MNC compete or have to compete with each other.

The present work by Julia Maurer has the objective to shed light on various forms of cooperation and competition between foreign subsidiaries. I am convinced that this is a highly important endeavor since, so far, IB scholars have neither conceptually nor empirically analyzed this research area in detail. While some scholars, such as Li/Ferreira, Birkinshaw/Lingblad or Luo, have started to investigate the field and while they have tried to identify factors influencing cooperation and competition, the present book is the first to offer a systematic conceptual and empirical approach. I see three major contributions of Julia Maurer's research. First, there is the conceptual contribution of presenting a very rich and systematic framework for analyzing intersubsidiary relationships. The framework is useful to IB and IM research in summarizing previous findings and in structuring future research. Second, Julia Maurer applies this framework to a particular industry, the plant engineering industry. She demonstrates the usefulness of the framework for empirical analysis and practice. Third, Julia Maurer combines the framework with Bartlett/Ghoshal's typology of international, multinational, global and transnational firms. This helps her to identify whether the strategic orientation of a firm has an influence on intersubsidiary relationships. By using a case study approach in a transnational industry – the plant engineering industry – Julia Maurer can fill an important research gap in IB and IM literature.

The research can be characterized by a mix of descriptive, explicative and normative objectives which are very well linked to interesting and intriguing research questions. The results are presented in a structured and systematic way. The approach chosen by Julia Maurer is innovative; it shows that a theoretical research interest is not in conflict with practical relevance. I am sure that Julia Maurer's work will not only be helpful for future research; it should also be read by managers who want to gain an insight into subsidiary-subsidiary relationships. Management can and should actively and deliberately influence subsidiary-subsidiary relationships. Admittedly, it is not only top-management at headquarters' level who is and who should be involved in this important task.

Berlin, May 2011   Stefan Schmid

Preface

This research was triggered by my desire to explore a specific topic in the International Business (IB) field from both a managerial and an academic perspective. For this endeavor I decided to temporarily interrupt my diversified, fast-paced work as a management consultant and return to my alma mater – meanwhile ESCP Europe Wirtschaftshochschule Berlin – to write my thesis as part of the European Doctoral Programme in International Management.

First and foremost, I would like to thank Prof. Dr. Stefan Schmid, Chair of the Department of International Management and Strategic Management, for facilitating this step by already having offered me upon completion of my graduate degree that his doors would be open if I ever decided to take a leave of absence from consulting in order to pursue a dissertation project. His immediate enthusiasm for the topic of intersubsidiary relationships enhanced my motivation to embark upon this research, his continuous inspiration and support enabled me to bring it to a successful end. I always valued his tenacity and intellectual rigor, coupled with openness and trust.

I am also obliged to Professor Pervez Ghauri, Department of Management, King's College London, who not only agreed to act as second reviewer for my thesis, but already gave direction to the research at a very early stage by providing valuable comments on a paper submitted within the context of an annual IB conference. Professor Ghauri always gave me the impression that he had an honest interest in the progress and success of my research project.

The empirical part of this research is based upon interviews with top executives in four leading large-scale plant engineering companies. Given the interviewees' managerial responsibilities it is far from self-evident that they took the time to discuss my questions in detail and provide profound insights into the complex intersubsidiary relationships in their company. I would like to thank each and every one of them for making such a significant contribution to this research project by sharing their comprehensive knowledge and experience.

A thank you also goes to my fellow doctoral students at the Chair of International Management and Strategic Management, with whom I share fond memories of joint international conferences, research colloquia and informal conversations and who always treated me as part of their group.

Finally, I would like to thank my family for their unconditional support and backing throughout the time of my dissertation – and beyond. Particularly without my parents' significant help in taking care of our little son I would not have been able to complete this challenging project. It is thus to my parents that I dedicate this dissertation.

Frankfurt, June 2011   Julia Maurer

Overview of the Contents

1 **Introduction** 1
   1.1 Problem Definition and Relevance 1
   1.2 Case Example and Implications 3
   1.3 Research Setting 6
   1.4 Research Questions 8
   1.5 Methodological Approach 14
   1.6 Structure of the Research 16

2 **Analyzing Intersubsidiary Relationships** 18
   2.1 Delineation of Intersubsidiary Relationships 19
   2.2 Types of Intersubsidiary Relationships 23
   2.3 Origin of Intersubsidiary Relationships 29
   2.4 Contents of Intersubsidiary Relationships 36
   2.5 Classification Scheme for Intersubsidiary Relationships 62

3 **Explaining Intersubsidiary Relationships** 65
   3.1 Approach to Theory Selection and Discussion 66
   3.2 Benefits and Drawbacks of Intersubsidiary Relationships 67
   3.3 Theoretical Perspectives 74
   3.4 Contingency Approach 109
   3.5 Influencing Factors 120
   3.6 Summary and Implications 137

4 **Intersubsidiary Relationships in Project Marketing of Plant Engineering Companies** 139
   4.1 Plant Engineering 139
   4.2 Project Marketing 142
   4.3 Models of Intersubsidiary Relationships in Project Marketing 164

5 **Link between Strategic Orientation and Intersubsidiary Relationships** ... 177
   5.1 MNC Strategic Orientation as a Key Influencing Factor 177
   5.2 Propositions on Intersubsidiary Relationships 186

6 **Empirical Study and Findings** 198
   6.1 Research Methodology: Case Studies 198
   6.2 Research Methods 203

6.3 Review of the Research Approach 215
6.4 Scope and Comparability of the Case Studies 218
6.5 Empirical Findings on Company A 221
6.6 Empirical Findings on Company B 233
6.7 Empirical Findings on Company C 251
6.8 Empirical Findings on Company D 274
6.9 Summary and Implications 296

7 Contributions, Limitations and Implications for Future Research 306
7.1 Contributions to IB Research 306
7.2 Managerial Implications 311
7.3 Limitations and Implications for Future Research 313

Appendices 319

References 329

Contents

Figures XXI

Tables XXIII

1 Introduction 1
   1.1 Problem Definition and Relevance 1
   1.2 Case Example and Implications 3
   1.3 Research Setting..6
   1.4 Research Questions...8
   1.5 Methodological Approach 14
   1.6 Structure of the Research 16

2 Analyzing Intersubsidiary Relationships 18
   2.1 Delineation of Intersubsidiary Relationships 19
   2.2 Types of Intersubsidiary Relationships..23
      2.2.1 Competition 24
      2.2.2 Cooperation..25
      2.2.3 Coopetition...27
      2.2.4 Independence 28
   2.3 Origin of Intersubsidiary Relationships 29
      2.3.1 Headquarters-Led Relationships..30
      2.3.2 Subsidiary-Led Relationships..32
      2.3.3 A Note on Formal and Informal Relationships.........................34
   2.4 Contents of Intersubsidiary Relationships 36
      2.4.1 Objects of Competition 36
         2.4.1.1 Choice of Categories..37
         2.4.1.2 Resources 38
         2.4.1.3 Charters 40
         2.4.1.4 Customers...43
      2.4.2 Objects of Cooperation..45
         2.4.2.1 Choice of Categories..46
         2.4.2.2 Resource Sharing 48
         2.4.2.3 Knowledge Sharing 50
         2.4.2.4 Split of Work..60
   2.5 Classification Scheme for Intersubsidiary Relationships 62

3 Explaining Intersubsidiary Relationships 65
3.1 Approach to Theory Selection and Discussion 66
3.2 Benefits and Drawbacks of Intersubsidiary Relationships 67
3.3 Theoretical Perspectives 74
3.3.1 Transaction Cost Economics 75
3.3.1.1 Key Terms and Concepts 75
3.3.1.2 Relevant Areas of Application 76
3.3.1.3 Implications for Intersubsidiary Relationships 80
3.3.2 Resource-Based View 86
3.3.2.1 Key Terms and Concepts 87
3.3.2.2 Relevant Areas of Application 88
3.3.2.3 Implications for Intersubsidiary Relationships 92
3.3.3 Network Approaches 96
3.3.3.1 Key Terms and Concepts 97
3.3.3.2 Relevant Areas of Application 98
3.3.3.3 Implications for Intersubsidiary Relationships 101
3.3.4 Complementary Theoretical Perspectives 102
3.3.5 Interim Conclusion 106
3.4 Contingency Approach 109
3.4.1 Historical Development 110
3.4.2 Concepts and Methods 111
3.4.3 Critical Assessment of the Contingency Approach 114
3.4.3.1 Methodological Criticism 114
3.4.3.2 Content-Related Criticism 115
3.4.4 The Contingency Approach in IB Research 117
3.4.5 Research Implications 119
3.5 Influencing Factors 120
3.5.1 Determinants of Interunit Competition 121
3.5.2 Determinants of Interunit Cooperation 124
3.5.3 Determinants of Interunit Coopetition 127
3.6 Summary and Implications 137

4 Intersubsidiary Relationships in Project Marketing of Plant Engineering Companies 139
4.1 Plant Engineering 139
4.2 Project Marketing 142

4.2.1 Definition and Delineation 142
 4.2.2 Scope of Activities 144
 4.2.3 Traditional Focus: External Relationships and Transactions 146
 4.2.4 Research Gap: Internal Relationships and Structures......................... 149
 4.2.5 Starting Point: Process-Oriented Industrial Marketing 150
 4.2.6 The Project Marketing Process 151
  4.2.6.1 Basis and Contribution 152
  4.2.6.2 Project Acquisition.. 154
  4.2.6.3 Project Execution 160
 4.3 Models of Intersubsidiary Relationships in Project Marketing 164
  4.3.1 Mapping Responsibilities and Relationships 164
  4.3.2 Headquarters-Led Independence.. 171
  4.3.3 Subsidiary-Led Independence... 171
  4.3.4 Headquarters-Led Cooperation 172
  4.3.5 Subsidiary-Led Cooperation 173
  4.3.6 Headquarters-Led Competition 173
  4.3.7 Subsidiary-Led Competition 174
  4.3.8 Headquarters-Led Coopetition 175
  4.3.9 Subsidiary-Led Coopetition 175

5 Link between Strategic Orientation and Intersubsidiary Relationships 177
 5.1 MNC Strategic Orientation as a Key Influencing Factor 177
  5.1.1 The Integration-Responsiveness Framework 178
  5.1.2 Bartlett and Ghoshal's Typology of Multinational Companies............... 179
   5.1.2.1 Conceptual Typology 180
   5.1.2.2 Empirical Investigation 183
   5.1.2.3 Research Implications 185
 5.2 Propositions on Intersubsidiary Relationships... 186
  5.2.1 Scope and Contents of the Contingency Framework 187
  5.2.2 Intersubsidiary Relationships in Multinational Companies................... 188
  5.2.3 Intersubsidiary Relationships in Global Companies 191
  5.2.4 Intersubsidiary Relationships in International Companies 192
  5.2.5 Intersubsidiary Relationships in Transnational Companies 194
  5.2.6 Summary of the Propositions 196

6 Empirical Study and Findings 198
6.1 Research Methodology: Case Studies 198
6.2 Research Methods 203
6.2.1 Data Collection: Interviews 203
6.2.2 Data Analysis: Thematic Coding 209
6.3 Review of the Research Approach 215
6.4 Scope and Comparability of the Case Studies 218
6.4.1 Strategic Orientation 218
6.4.2 Intersubsidiary Relationships 218
6.4.3 Discussion of Intersubsidiary Relationships 219
6.4.3.1 Review of the Propositions 219
6.4.3.2 Additional Influencing Factors 220
6.4.3.3 Developments and Their Managerial Implications 220
6.5 Empirical Findings on Company A 221
6.5.1 Strategic Orientation 221
6.5.2 Intersubsidiary Relationships 222
6.5.2.1 Competition 222
6.5.2.2 Cooperation 225
6.5.3 Discussion of Intersubsidiary Relationships 229
6.5.3.1 Review of the Propositions 229
6.5.3.2 Additional Influencing Factors 231
6.5.3.3 Developments and Their Managerial Implications 232
6.6 Empirical Findings on Company B 233
6.6.1 Strategic Orientation 233
6.6.2 Intersubsidiary Relationships 236
6.6.2.1 Competition 236
6.6.2.2 Cooperation 238
6.6.3 Discussion of Intersubsidiary Relationships 245
6.6.3.1 Review of the Propositions 245
6.6.3.2 Additional Influencing Factors 247
6.6.3.3 Developments and Their Managerial Implications 248
6.7 Empirical Findings on Company C 251
6.7.1 Strategic Orientation 252
6.7.2 Intersubsidiary Relationships 255
6.7.2.1 Competition 255

    6.7.2.2 Cooperation 257
  6.7.3 Discussion of Intersubsidiary Relationships 268
    6.7.3.1 Review of the Propositions.. 268
    6.7.3.2 Additional Influencing Factors 270
    6.7.3.3 Developments and Their Managerial Implications 271
 6.8 Empirical Findings on Company D 274
  6.8.1 Strategic Orientation.. 275
  6.8.2 Intersubsidiary Relationships 281
    6.8.2.1 Competition 281
    6.8.2.2 Cooperation 284
  6.8.3 Discussion of Intersubsidiary Relationships 291
    6.8.3.1 Review of the Propositions.. 291
    6.8.3.2 Additional Influencing Factors 293
    6.8.3.3 Developments and Their Managerial Implications 294
 6.9 Summary and Implications 296
  6.9.1 Strategic Orientation.. 297
  6.9.2 Intersubsidiary Relationships 298
    6.9.2.1 Review of the Propositions.. 298
    6.9.2.2 Additional Influencing Factors 302
    6.9.2.3 Developments and Their Managerial Implications 303

7 Contributions, Limitations and Implications for Future Research............... 306
 7.1 Contributions to IB Research 306
  7.1.1 Analyzing Intersubsidiary Relationships 307
  7.1.2 Explaining Intersubsidiary Relationships 307
  7.1.3 Industry and Functional Insights.. 308
  7.1.4 Empirical Insights 309
 7.2 Managerial Implications... 311
  7.2.1 Conceptual Elements 311
  7.2.2 Empirical Findings 312
 7.3 Limitations and Implications for Future Research 313
  7.3.1 Conceptual Issues... 313
  7.3.2 Methodological Issues... 315

Appendices 319

References 329

Figures

Figure 1:	Level and Units of Analysis	20
Figure 2:	Types of Intersubsidiary Relationships	24
Figure 3:	Types of Competition by Subjects and Objects	38
Figure 4:	Types of Cooperation by Subjects and Objects	48
Figure 5:	Classification Scheme for Intersubsidiary Relationships	64
Figure 6:	Benefits and Drawbacks of Intersubsidiary Competition and Cooperation	73
Figure 7:	The Contingency Approach as a Scientific Program	112
Figure 8:	Internationalization Strategies of Selected Industries	141
Figure 9:	Simplified Overview of the Project Marketing Process	153
Figure 10:	Overview of Project Acquisition Phase	159
Figure 11:	Overview of Project Execution Phase	163
Figure 12:	Legend to Project Marketing Models	166
Figure 13:	Project Marketing Models – Part I: Independence and Intersubsidiary Cooperation	169
Figure 14:	Project Marketing Models – Part II: Intersubsidiary Competition and Coopetition	170
Figure 15:	Contingency Framework of Intersubsidiary Relationships	188
Figure 16:	Category Scheme for the Analysis of Intersubsidiary Relationships	211
Figure 17:	Exemplary Project – Company A	227
Figure 18:	Exemplary Project – Company B	241
Figure 19:	Exemplary Project – Company C (Technology)	259
Figure 20:	Exemplary Project – Company C (Global EPC Business)	265
Figure 21:	Exemplary Project – Company D	285

Tables

Table 1:	Determinants of Intrafirm Competition according to Birkinshaw/ Lingblad (2005)	123
Table 2:	Antecedents of Organizational Knowledge Sharing according to Zhao/Luo (2005)	126
Table 3:	Influencing Factors for Cooperation and Competition among Foreign Subsidiaries according to Li/Ferreira (2003)	129
Table 4:	Determinants of Cooperation among Foreign Subsidiaries according to Luo (2005)	131
Table 5:	Determinants of Competition among Foreign Subsidiaries according to Luo (2005)	132
Table 6:	Factors Affecting the Establishment of an Internal Market for Charters according to Cerrato (2006)	136
Table 7:	Factors Affecting the Establishment of an Internal Market for Knowledge and Competencies according to Cerrato (2006)	137
Table 8:	Bartlett and Ghoshal's Typology of Multinational Companies	182
Table 9:	Summary of Propositions – Competition and Cooperation by Type of Company	197
Table 10:	Review of Propositions for Company A – Expected and Actual Level of Intersubsidiary Competition and Cooperation	230
Table 11:	Additional Influencing Factors for Intersubsidiary Competition and Cooperation – Company A	232
Table 12:	Review of Propositions for Company B – Expected and Actual Level of Intersubsidiary Competition and Cooperation	245
Table 13:	Additional Influencing Factors for Intersubsidiary Competition and Cooperation – Company B	248
Table 14:	Review of Propositions for Company C – Expected and Actual Level of Intersubsidiary Competition and Cooperation	268
Table 15:	Additional Influencing Factors for Intersubsidiary Competition and Cooperation – Company C	271
Table 16:	Review of Propositions for Company D – Expected and Actual Level of Intersubsidiary Competition and Cooperation	291

Table 17:	Additional Influencing Factors for Intersubsidiary Competition and Cooperation – Company D	294
Table 18:	Summary of Propositions – Expected Level of Competition and Cooperation by Type of MNC	298
Table 19:	Summary of Results – Actual Level of Competition and Cooperation by Company	299

1 Introduction

This introductory chapter is intended to provide a condensed overview of the underlying research project and is structured as follows: In section 1.1 the overall research problem is defined and its theoretical and practical relevance outlined. In section 1.2 a case example is used to make the research problem more tangible and to discuss some possible implications. The research setting, i.e. the industry and functional focus of the research, is presented in section 1.3. In section 1.4 the key research questions are formulated, including a brief discussion of their relevance, investigation procedure and inherent challenges. The methodological approach of the research is addressed in section 1.5. Finally, section 1.6 provides an overview of the structure of the research, i.e. the contents of each chapter.

1.1 Problem Definition and Relevance[1]

In today's global economy, many firms have their value-creating activities dispersed across various countries and regions. According to their respective business models, many multinational corporations (MNCs) consider the direct and immediate host-country presence through legally independent engagements as vital for their economic success. Therefore, they establish or acquire (foreign) subsidiaries to carry out or bundle activities.[2] How these foreign subsidiaries are managed by headquarters, which tasks they fulfill and what their position in the overall organization is can vary considerably, though. International business (IB) scholars have conducted a considerable amount of research on both headquarters-subsidiary relationships (for example, Baliga/Jaeger 1984; Gates/Egelhoff 1986; Gupta 1987; Martinez/Jarillo 1989; Birkinshaw/Morrison 1995) and subsidiary roles (see Schmid et al. 1998; Schmid/Kutschker 2003; Schmid 2004 for overviews).

However, so far not much attention has been given to the **horizontal relationships between foreign subsidiaries,** although these linkages are known to play an important role, for example, in the internal development and utilization of knowledge (Bartlett/Ghoshal 1998: 69, 105-106; O'Donnell 2000: 543; Luo 2005: 72; Matsuo 2005). Network approaches to the MNC typically consider such linkages, but suggest

---

[1] This section largely corresponds to Schmid/Maurer 2011: 55-56 and Schmid/Maurer 2008: 1-3 (Chapter 1).
[2] In this research the term 'foreign' subsidiaries is used to underline the importance of units located outside the MNC's home country. However, there is no reason to exclude national subsidiaries from the analysis.

them to be mainly cooperative (Perlmutter 1969a: 14; Hedlund 1986: 22; White/Poynter 1990: 98; Doz/Prahalad 1991: 147; Bartlett/Ghoshal 1998: 102). Pooling resources, sharing knowledge or dividing work packages among international locations may all be means of achieving competitive advantage. Business practice shows that subsidiaries can also compete with one another – for resources or recognition, for responsibilities or charters, for business or customers (Birkinshaw 2001b: 113). Subsidiaries may also experience a state of 'coopetition', in which they simultaneously, or sequentially, compete and cooperate with their peers (Brandenburger/Nalebuff 1996; Luo 2005). In the plant engineering industry, for example, foreign subsidiaries may initially compete for customer responsibilities and subsequently cooperate by contributing their particular expertise to the overall project. It can be observed that even companies operating in the same industry and pursuing very similar business models differ significantly in terms of competition and cooperation between their subsidiaries.

Up to now these multifaceted relationships between subsidiaries have been more of a 'black box' to academics in the IB field – and in many aspects even to practitioners. Intrafirm competition, for example, is described as a "real but often under-recognized phenomenon" (Birkinshaw/Lingblad 2005: 684). Most scholars treat competition, cooperation and coopetition as interfirm phenomena (for example, Porter 1980; Lado et al. 1997; Dowling/Lechner 1998; Bengtsson/Kock 2000; Dagnino 2002; Ullrich 2004). The few authors who do take an internal stance tend not to account for an international dimension. Rather than looking at competition and/or cooperation between foreign subsidiaries, they dedicate their research to functions, teams or business units. The complex relationship between globally dispersed subunits certainly merits investigation, though.

Although some IB scholars have tried to identify factors influencing intersubsidiary (or interunit) competition and cooperation, their propositions have not been explored empirically (Li/Ferreira 2003; Birkinshaw/Lingblad 2005; Luo 2005; Li et al. 2007).[3] It was only recently that Harzing and Noorderhaven called for more consideration of intersubsidiary relationships in empirical investigations (Harzing/Noorderhaven 2006: 212). In doing so, they reinforced an appeal that Ghoshal and Bartlett had formulated about fifteen years ago: "The investigation of the lateral network relations among the different subsidiaries can open up avenues for [...] fine-grained analysis of both the causes and consequences of horizontal interdependencies and synergy"

---

[3] An exception is Zhao/Luo 2005 who explore the antecedents of intersubsidiary organizational knowledge sharing.

(Ghoshal/Bartlett 1990: 620). Walley adds to these demands by explicitly encouraging formal investigations and empirical research in the field of internal coopetition (Walley 2007: 25).

The call for empirical investigation of intersubsidiary relationships highlights both the theoretical and the practical relevance of the topic. Only if MNC managers develop a thorough understanding of how subsidiaries actually interrelate and can possibly interrelate, can they take purposeful action in this respect. Intersubsidiary competition and cooperation may also have an impact on other variables – for example, on technology transfer. Managers to whom such transfer is important need to evaluate the behavior of their subsidiaries to align strategy, structure and social relationships to the desired ends (Li et al. 2007: 26-27). The research aims at providing managers at both the corporate level and the subsidiary level with an awareness of the strategic options and opportunities related to intersubsidiary relationships and, consequently, with an informed basis for decision making.

1.2 Case Example and Implications

The research was triggered by the observation of a very particular **phenomenon** in the large-scale plant engineering industry. Plant engineering companies mainly provide engineering, procurement and construction (EPC) services related to the individual, project-based development of technologically complex industrial production facilities. Examples are power plants, chemical plants, petroleum refineries, steel mills and cement works. The latter have in common that – although combining known and proven technologies – their design and implementation tends to be customized and thus unique (Allers 2002: 361). It is their service-driven business model that distinguishes EPC providers from manufacturing companies of the capital goods industry. Most projects transcend national borders, leaving the plant engineering industry inherently international. While many leading companies have their headquarters in the USA, Europe, Japan or South Korea, they maintain an extensive network of foreign subsidiaries (Allers 2002: 363). The aforementioned projects typically require the (combined) resources and capabilities of more than one national unit. This raises the question of how foreign subsidiaries of multinational plant engineering companies actually interrelate. Based on an initial exploration of business practices, the companies appear to differ in the amount of intersubsidiary competition and cooperation they foster in the acquisition and execution of large industrial projects. The following (fictitious) case example illustrates a possible, yet slightly exaggerated manifestation of intersubsidiary competition and suggests the related scope for cooperation. The chosen phenomenological approach not only highlights the overall relevance of the topic, but also allows the key research objectives to be deduced.

Case Example

An internationally renowned plant engineering company is serving the global market via its four subsidiaries in Germany, the USA, the Czech Republic and China. A German customer now plans to build a petrochemical plant in South Korea and announces a public tender for the development and execution of the project. All four subsidiaries take notice of this tender and are interested in placing a bid. Each of them finds itself particularly qualified for different reasons: The German subsidiary looks back on a long-standing, trusted relationship with the client and only recently accompanied a project of similar scope – albeit with a different technical focus. The U.S. subsidiary, on the other hand, emphasizes its expertise with the technical requirements of this very specific project and refers to the U.S. Export-Import Bank's willingness to provide financial guarantees. Given that numerous external competitors are also vying for the contract, the Czech subsidiary advertises its ability to come up with a very attractive offer due to the lower price level in Eastern Europe. A tradeoff in terms of quality is refuted, as the Czech subsidiary received significant 'coaching' from its German sister company following its foundation ten years ago. Finally, the Chinese subsidiary sees itself as the preferred provider due to its geographic and cultural proximity to South Korea. Given the public interest in the petrochemical industry, access to key decision makers and an understanding of the country's political and economic arena are particularly important. The Chinese subsidiary also employs two experienced Korean project managers.

The main question resulting from this brief case example is how the company deals (or should deal) with the depicted situation. First of all – in terms of unity and credibility – it seems unlikely that the parent company would let its subsidiaries approach the customer in open **competition** to one another. Although such market-oriented behavior remains a theoretical option (Phelps/Fuller 2000: 227; Birkinshaw 2001b: 119), in practice the rivalry for participation in the tender will most likely be settled internally. The parent company's role can vary significantly here. It could decide to restrict competition between subsidiaries altogether and assign geographic, customer-oriented or competence-based responsibilities in advance. In the above example, the Chinese, German or U.S. subsidiary, respectively, would then be allowed to participate in the tender. Such a hierarchical solution would, however, forego the benefits of internal competition – and possibly those of cooperation. Alternatively, the company could choose an intermediate approach, allowing (or even advocating) competition but finding a way of settling it internally. This could either be done by defining a more or less formalized application and selection procedure (request for proposal) or by relying on informal arrangements between subsidiaries.

In addition to managing internal competition, the parent company may want to foster a certain degree of **cooperation** between its subsidiaries. The combination of dispersed resources and capabilities could prove to be a significant competitive advantage in the bidding process for such a large-scale project. In the example, the German subsidiary could take the lead in developing the project together with the client, drawing on the U.S. subsidiary's support in technical matters. The Czech subsidiary could contribute competitively priced labor for the design and subsequent engineering phase, whereas on-site responsibility in the execution phase could be given to one of the Korean project managers from the Chinese subsidiary. Since the client has the right to know who he will be dealing with in the course of the project, the planned division of labor is typically spelled out in the engineering contract. Therefore several agreements between subunits already have to be reached in the acquisition phase. Again, the parent company can take a more or less active stance in guiding subsidiary behavior. First, headquarters could leave this decision completely up to its subsidiaries. Unless cooperation was an integral part of corporate culture, it would most probably be triggered (only) if individual subsidiaries expected to benefit from such an approach. Second, the parent company could impose cooperation by fiat, i.e. dictate on a general or case-specific basis which subsidiary is to account for which part of the project. Third, subsidiaries could receive financial or non-financial incentives for cooperation. A parent company would possibly choose this approach to enhance knowledge exchange between its subsidiaries.

These first thoughts on how companies can or may deal with the situation depicted in the case example highlight the variety of approaches companies can take to the international division of labor and the related intersubsidiary relationships. They illustrate that nowadays it is difficult for foreign subsidiaries to operate independently of one another. Such interdependencies are not only difficult to separate from configurational considerations (compare to the discussion in subsection 2.4.2.4); they may even provide a basis for decision making: While competition between subsidiaries may facilitate the identification of 'ideal' locations for individual tasks, cooperation may open up avenues for splitting work packages. Of course, resulting cost savings on the operational side need to be weighed against additional costs on the organizational side. The latter may be incurred directly through coordination activities or indirectly through dysfunctional elements of either competition or cooperation. It therefore seems that a great deal can be gained from MNCs being aware of how their foreign subsidiaries relate or could possibly relate to one another.

1.3 Research Setting

As suggested by the case example, the research sets out to explore the intersubsidiary relationships prevalent within the project acquisition and execution activities of multinational plant engineering companies. Adopting such an **industry focus** is justified by three reasons: First, the phenomenon of market-oriented competition and cooperation between subsidiaries is not relevant in all industries. Especially where the need for national differentiation and responsiveness is very high – e.g., in the food industry (Frese 2005: 507) – subsidiaries tend to be characterized by a high level of national independence (Bartlett/Ghoshal 1998: 56; see Meffert 1986: 694 and 1990: 98 or refer to Figure 8 in section 4.1 for a classification of industries according to their need for global integration versus national differentiation). Second, an industry focus allows approaching a scarcely examined phenomenon from one angle before creating additional complexity. In order to detect certain relationships and regularities one needs to be able to draw comparisons between companies. The more similar and stable the economic environment is, the easier it is to draw conclusions regarding company-specific factors like management practices. Third, concentrating on a specific industry has some pragmatic advantages for carrying out the research. In order to arrive at meaningful results, it is important that the researcher knows her research site very well. She needs to have a solid industry and company knowledge and be able to gain access to firm representatives for data collection. Of course this does not mean that analogies to other industries are foregone – quite the contrary is the case: It is an explicit objective of this dissertation to arrive at certain industry-transcending conclusions regarding the investigation, occurrence and management of competition and cooperation between foreign subsidiaries.

Its inherent internationality, project-based division of labor and strong marketing/sales orientation make the large-scale **plant engineering** industry a particularly interesting target for investigating intersubsidiary relationships. Interdependencies between globally dispersed units are particularly relevant in industries that have been international for a long period of time. For the plant engineering industry the challenges stemming from internationalization go beyond the mere establishment of international presence. Having maintained international activities for more than 100 years, the main question for most plant engineering companies is where to allocate which parts of the value chain in order to hold their ground in the competitive global market (Allers 2002: 361; for a definition and discussion of configuration as the geographical allocation of value chain activities see Schmid/Grosche 2009: 4-5). It is in the nature of the business that plant engineering companies need to be highly international and secure business from abroad. On the demand side, the large contract value and long economic plant life limit the number of domestic orders placed in a given period of time (Schiller 2000: 13; Gleich et al. 2005: 183). International demand for large plants is high and has experienced a shift to emerging markets (Schwanfelder 1989: 15-16; Königshausen/Spannagel 2004: 1127). On the supply side, increasing cost pressures drive plant engineering companies to leverage global project execution and outsource certain value-creating activities to subsidiaries in low-cost countries. While historically the industry had been export-oriented, maintaining a local presence and collaborating with international partners has become indispensable for fulfilling local (content) requirements (Schwanfelder 1989: 15-16). Also, the technical complexity of large-scale industrial plants typically exceeds the capabilities and resources of a single provider (Schiller 2000: 11; Königshausen/Spannagel 2004: 1127-1128). Multinational plant engineering companies frequently find themselves acting as main contractor or consortium leader (Backhaus/Voeth 2007: 308). Recall, however, that the focus of this dissertation is on relationships within the MNC, not on those established with external partners (suppliers, contractors, government agencies, etc.). The project business allows (or requires) companies to re-define the optimal division of labor on a case-by-case basis (VDMA 2007: 29). Nevertheless, for one and the same MNC one would expect a similar pattern of intersubsidiary relationships across projects, i.e. a greater or lesser degree of intersubsidiary competition and/or cooperation.

The research is geared towards the market-oriented side of intersubsidiary competition and cooperation. Since plant engineering companies do not (or rarely) engage in production activities, they direct all efforts to providing the best individual solution to their customers. One would expect the ways in which subsidiaries interrelate to correspond to this goal. The research sets out to reveal and explain intersubsidiary relationship patterns in the sales and marketing activities of multinational plant engineering companies. More specifically, the focus is on **project acquisition and execution**, which are summarized under the term 'project marketing' (see subsection 4.2.1) and constitute the core business of plant engineering companies (Engelhardt 1977: 26; Heger 2000: 14; Königshausen/ Spannagel 2004: 1128; Backhaus/Voeth 2007: 310).

Interunit relationships within the sales and marketing organization have received relatively little attention in academic literature. On the cooperative side, it has mainly been the interaction between marketing and other business functions such as research and development (R&D), engineering, manufacturing, and purchasing that has been analyzed (see Hillebrand/Biemans 2003: 736 for an overview). Special attention was also drawn to cross-functional teams (Parker 1994). On the competitive side, upstream activities such as R&D, production and procurement have attracted greater interest. But rivalry there tends to center on superior technologies, sites or internally assigned procurement quotas (see, for example, Crookell 1986; Phelps/Fuller 2000; Birkinshaw 2001a; Frese 2005: 268 and the case examples in Birkinshaw/Lingblad 2001: 36); with the exception of the development function, a customer interface hardly exists. The lack of research on the market-oriented side of intersubsidiary relationships is surprising given that ultimately all products and technologies – regardless of whether they are developed and produced in-house or procured externally – reach the customer through the sales of an integrated plant. Finally, compared to other functions, the international sales and marketing organization is typically characterized by a fairly high degree of operational decentralization (Turner/Henry 1994: 426; Bartlett/Ghoshal 1998: 111-112). In their study of relationships between competitors, Bengtsson and Kock found that "competitors cooperate with activities far from the customer and compete in activities close to the customer" (Bengtsson/Kock 2000: 418). Although this statement is directed towards interorganizational relationships, there is likely to be some truth in it on the intraorganizational level. If rivalry was indeed more common in downstream than in upstream activities, this would provide an additional incentive for investigating sales and marketing-related intersubsidiary relationships. Contributions that offer insights into a cooperative design of industrial project acquisition are no less difficult to find.

1.4 Research Questions

The **three main objectives** of this research are: (1) to identify different types and manifestations of intersubsidiary relationships, (2) to investigate how and why these relationships vary among companies belonging to the same industry, and (3) to assess developments that have taken place over time and their managerial implications.

The core of the research is dedicated to finding an explanation for different manifestations of competition and cooperation between foreign subsidiaries. So far, only a few scholars have tried to identify factors influencing intersubsidiary (or interunit) relationships, but their propositions have not been investigated empirically (Li/Ferreira 2003; Birkinshaw/Lingblad 2005; Luo 2005; Li et al. 2007; an exception is Zhao/Luo 2005 who explore the antecedents of intersubsidiary organizational knowledge sharing).[4] It is only intuitive to expect patterns to differ by industry and function, as suggested by authors identifying environmental determinants (Birkinshaw/Lingblad 2005: 679-680). But interestingly the prevailing levels of intersubsidiary competition and cooperation can be observed to also differ among corresponding activities of firms operating in the same industry. Explicit propositions on the link between a company's strategic orientation – as a key influencing factor – and its intersubsidiary relationships are developed and then tested empirically. In line with the case example, the research focuses on project marketing activities of multinational plant engineering companies. As noted above, noticeable differences exist in the amount of intersubsidiary competition and cooperation these companies foster (or tolerate) in the acquisition and execution of large industrial projects.

The above objectives result in **three specific research questions**. Although delineating the research focus at such an early stage means anticipating some results of the literature review, this approach proves very helpful for guiding the research process and enabling the reader to follow it. Each of the three questions outlined below is complemented by a brief discussion of its relevance, implied investigation procedure, expected results and impending challenges. Key terms and constructs such as intersubsidiary competition and cooperation, strategic orientation, project marketing and plant engineering are defined and specified in subsequent chapters.

Research Question 1: Which alternative models exist for the acquisition and execution of large industrial projects with particular respect to competition and cooperation between foreign subsidiaries? (→ Primarily descriptive goal)

---

[4] Birkinshaw and Lingblad (2005) analyze competition between units of the multi-business firm. They do not explicitly refer to MNCs and their foreign subsidiaries, but these may be interpreted as a special case of the phenomenon under investigation. Li et al. (2007) capture many of the ideas originally developed by Li/Ferreira (2003), which is why mostly only references to the earlier publication are included.

Since the phenomenon of competition and cooperation between foreign subsidiaries has only been examined very scarcely, an initial 'inventory' of its manifestations marks an important starting point for further analysis. The goal is to identify **alternative project acquisition/execution models** pursued by multinational plant engineering companies, which differ in terms of the prevailing intersubsidiary relationships. These models can be sketched by adopting a process view and then mapping subsidiaries' (and headquarters') involvement in each core activity and/or decision. Whereas the existing literature on plant engineering and industrial marketing provides quite an informative basis for defining a typical project acquisition and execution process (Backhaus/Günther 1976: 257-264; Engelhardt 1977: 25-26; Bretschneider 1980: 61; Blessberger 1981: 63-75; Schwanfelder 1989: 18-25; Heger 2000: 14; Königshausen/Spannagel 2004: 1128-1141; Backhaus/Voeth 2007: 309-311), very few references are made to where responsibilities are allocated. The aspired models therefore need to be derived in a logical manner. This can be done by first mapping the project acquisition and execution process (short: project marketing process, for a definition see subsection 4.2.1) in its entirety and simplifying it to focus on key steps. Responsibilities are then assigned to subunits by means of a matrix, combining the core process steps and decisions on the horizontal axis with the relevant subunits on the vertical axis. Without going into too much detail at this point, solid or empty circles may indicate a subsidiary's responsibility for or support of a particular process step; and color schemes can be used to illustrate different objects of competition and cooperation. In order to provide a complete picture, the role of the parent company needs to be taken into account. As will be shown later, intersubsidiary relationships can either be headquarters-led or subsidiary-led – an important differentiation that should be reflected in the models.

The derived models – and particularly their depicted form of illustration – ultimately serve as a basis of analysis in the empirical study. The goal is to identify a limited number of distinct models rather than account for all possible variations. A total of eight models seems sufficient to capture headquarters-led and subsidiary-led independence, competition, cooperation and coopetition between foreign subsidiaries (for a distinction of these types of relationship see section 2.2). The models do not have to be mutually exclusive but should be collectively exhaustive in the sense that they reflect the basic manifestations of intersubsidiary relationships in the marketing of large industrial projects. A certain degree of simplicity is needed to convey a message and to link the models to their influencing factors – as is aspired with the second research question. Conversely, it is anticipated that the constellations found in practice will be more complex and deviate from the simplified models. The derived models should be thought of as a schematic summary or aggregation of the prevailing relationships. They guide a systematic approach to reviewing projects within the empirical investigation by encouraging researchers and managers alike to think in certain categories and to review certain issues.

Research Question 2: How does a company's strategic orientation influence the relationship between its foreign subsidiaries, as reflected in alternative project acquisition/execution models? (→ Primarily explicative goal)

This question is motivated by the desire to understand why companies operating in the same industry and pursuing very similar business models choose very different set-ups for their project acquisition and execution. Why does one parent company foster intersubsidiary competition by issuing internal requests for proposals while another prefers to avoid redundancies by assigning responsibilities in advance? And why do the subsidiaries of one company cooperate intensely with each other, for example, by sharing information on customers or technology, while those of another company prefer to operate single-handedly?

As will be shown, some scholars have tried to identify factors that influence the level of competition and/or cooperation between foreign subsidiaries (Li/Ferreira 2003; Birkinshaw/Lingblad 2005; Luo 2005; Zhao/Luo 2005).[5] Although, with the exception of Zhao and Luo (2005), none of these propositions have been investigated empirically, it can be assumed that the determinants of intersubsidiary relationships are manifold. The influencing factors identified by the authors cited above can roughly be divided into two groups: **'external' and 'internal' factors**. While the external factors comprise industry, market and environmental characteristics, the internal factors refer to aspects of a company's strategy and structure. Considering that this research focuses on a particular industry, the companies in question can be assumed to encounter very similar external factors. Certain differences may exist based on a company's international presence or due to company-specific external shocks (such as a sharp decline in sales or a hostile takeover). This research will try to recognize such outliers but will not make an issue of them.

Given the industry focus, it is mainly internal factors that are expected to account for cross-company differences in acquisition/execution models and intersubsidiary relationships. The most convincing argument relates to a company's strategy,

---

[5] Again it needs to be noted that Birkinshaw and Lingblad (2005) refer more broadly to interunit competition in the multi-business firm. Many of their ideas, however, are transferable to the particular case of intersubsidiary competition in MNCs.

especially if structural characteristics such as (de)centralization or normative integration (Li/Ferreira 2003: 13-17; Birkinshaw/Lingblad 2005: 680-681) are considered to reflect strategic objectives. It was only recently that IB scholars were encouraged to investigate how parent-level characteristics or strategic attributes influence the level and pattern of intersubsidiary knowledge sharing (Zhao/Luo 2005: 91). Bartlett and Ghoshal propose a link between a company's overall strategic orientation and its organizational model in their typology of multinational companies (Bartlett/Ghoshal 1998: 55-60; also see Kutschker/Schmid 2006: 539-540). Based on a company's response to the demands for globalization, localization and innovation, they distinguish between international, multinational, global and transnational companies (Bartlett/Ghoshal 1998: 15-20; Harzing 2004: 45-48; Bartlett et al. 2007: 203-206). Although their organizational focus lies on the vertical relationship between headquarters and subsidiaries, it can be assumed that the horizontal relationship between subsidiaries is similarly impacted by a company's strategic orientation. In other words, it is a company's **strategic orientation** that should tip the scales towards more or less competition and cooperation between foreign subsidiaries. Occasional hints at this contingency can be found in literature, but propositions remain vague and lack empirical investigation (Li/Ferreira 2003: 10-13; Luo 2005: 72, 87). Drawbacks are linked to the fact that the cited authors look at the MNC in its entirety and do not account for any functional particularities; nor do they refer to a particular taxonomy or typology, leaving the strategy concept somewhat ill defined. Their choice of words does, however, suggest that they were inspired by Bartlett and Ghoshal's typology of multinational companies.

A main goal of this second research question is to establish explicit **propositions** on the link between Bartlett and Ghoshal's archetypes of multinational companies and the intersubsidiary relationships that characterize their project acquisition/execution models. By the line of argument the research follows a contingency approach. The independent variable is a company's strategic orientation, which, according to Bartlett and Ghoshal, can be international, multinational, global or transnational. The dependent variable is the intersubsidiary relationship as reflected in the acquisition/execution models identified in the context of the first research question. The hypothesized 'combinations' are then tested in practice, resulting in case studies of companies with distinct strategy (and organization) models. Given that even a typology as prominent as Bartlett and Ghoshal's has hardly ever been subject to empirical investigation (for two attempts see Leong/Tan 1992 and Harzing 2000), it is important to define a convincing yet practicable approach to the typification of participating MNCs. Respecting (top) managers' time restrictions, it was decided to adhere to Bartlett and Ghoshal's own criteria and to not exceed their level of detail.

The goal is to provide a rich description of both strategic orientation and intersubsidiary relationships in the companies analyzed, thus seizing the opportunity of illuminating an underresearched phenomenon.

Despite its proposed impact, a company's response to the demands of globalization, localization and innovation will hardly constitute the only (strategic) determinant of intersubsidiary relationships. The investigation of propositions will thus be complemented by the exploration of additional influencing factors, which may be considered on a supplementary basis or used to guide future research. Strategic determinants may include a company's preferred sales approach (proactive versus reactive), its subsidiary-related growth strategy or the intensity of innovation. Company history, corporate culture and management philosophy constitute more general aspects.

Research Question 3: Which managerial implications can be derived from any developments in the concerned companies' strategic orientation and/or intersubsidiary relationships? (→ Partially normative goal)

This question takes the insights gained from the previous two questions one step further by trying to assess the suitability and success of different strategic orientations and project acquisition/execution models – and possibly the 'fit' between them. If there has been (or is expected to be) a significant change in a company's prevailing orientation or model, this can be assumed to be a deliberate management decision (compare Bartlett/Ghoshal 1998: 33-34; also see, for example, Putnam/Mumby 1993; Werder 1999 on the rationality of management). It is insightful to have managers comment on how the rules of the game have changed, why an existing strategy or certain types of intersubsidiary relationships are no longer perceived as adequate and what they expect from a new approach. By taking a **dynamic perspective**, i.e. looking at past, present and future scenarios, important conclusions can be drawn regarding the suitability and success of individual strategies or acquisition/execution models in certain business environments. These conclusions are also expected to be of particular interest to managers, especially if they go beyond the scope of their own company. Typically, managers who value the opportunity to reflect upon developments and discuss which options make the most sense are inclined to contribute to such research. On an academic level there may be support for Bartlett and Ghoshal's underlying proposition that organizations move from one model (or strategic orientation) to another in manifold ways as situations change (for example, Bartlett/Ghoshal 1998).[6] Compared to the previous two research questions, this last one is rather open-ended. Results depend on the types of development that have taken place (or are expected to take place) and managers' willingness to share their personal assessments and experiences.

By addressing the above three questions, this research wishes to contribute to an enhanced understanding of intersubsidiary relationships and their managerial implications. The results are valuable to academics interested in a holistic view of the MNC and to managers assessing their strategic and organizational action parameters.

1.5 Methodological Approach

As illustrated above, the motivation for this research stems from the observance of a very particular phenomenon: the (potential) competition and cooperation between the foreign subsidiaries of multinational plant engineering companies. A phenomenon can be described as a "fact of occurrence that appears or is perceived, especially one of which the cause is in question" (Allen 1990: 893). Correspondingly, the purpose of this dissertation is not only to explore and describe which shapes the phenomenon can take, but to explain its manifestations by investigating influencing factors and managerial implications. Despite including deductive elements in this pursuit, the primary logic of the research is inductive: Propositions are established based on the observation of facts rather than the application of a known premise (Ghauri/Grønhaug 2005: 16).

As suggested in the previous section, the applied **methodology varies by research question**. The first question will be answered by logically deriving alternative project acquisition and execution models. Especially given the particular focus on intersubsidiary relationships, these models need to be based on common sense and industry expertise rather than abstract theories. The second research question departs from theoretical contributions and results in the empirical study. As the literature review has shown, several scholars have set out their propositions as to which factors influence intrafirm competition and cooperation, some of them even referring directly to an MNC's strategy (Li/Ferreira 2003: 10-13; Luo 2005: 77-79, 87). When tracing their argumentation, it is necessary to evaluate to which extent it is applicable to the functional and industry focus chosen for this research. The goal is to

---

[6] For a discussion of the types and dynamic spectrum of strategic orientation see section 5.1.2.1.

arrive at very specific propositions regarding the link between a company's strategic orientation and the prevailing project acquisition/execution model. These propositions incorporate the key elements of Bartlett and Ghoshal's typology of MNCs and related literature. It is essential to pick up any hints the authors themselves provide on competition and cooperation between foreign subsidiaries and to complement these arguments with other substantial theories.

As noted above, part of the second research question is the empirical investigation of the developed propositions. **Case studies** are used to examine the expected links between a company's strategic orientation and the project acquisition/execution model it employs. This qualitative approach is the most appropriate because it allows profound insights into a complex and underresearched phenomenon as well as the practices of individual companies (Hussey/Hussey 1997: 66; Yin 2003: 13). Theories will be generated in the process of trying to establish causal links between variables (Eisenhardt 1989).

The companies for investigation are chosen from the large-scale plant engineering industry. Per se they can either be independent single-business firms or a strategic business unit of a conglomerate. Prerequisite is that they maintain operations in multiple countries. There are no explicit rules as to how many cases should be studied (Miles/Huberman 1994: 30; Yin 2003: 51; Ghauri/Grønhaug 2005: 119). For this particular research it seems appropriate to analyze four companies (or cases), each ideally pursuing a different type of strategy: international, multinational, global or transnational. In practice such **theoretical sampling** is not all that simple: The number of leading large-scale plant engineering companies is limited; the latter do not necessarily correspond to 'pure' types, and their managers have to be willing to participate in the empirical study. Within the case studies, the primary focus is on subsidiaries engaged in project marketing activities. These activities range from customer relationship management to project acquisition and execution. Whether these subsidiaries also cover additional value chain activities is of minor importance. The main unit of analysis is the relationship between (foreign) subsidiaries, as observable in the acquisition and execution of large industrial projects. Overall, one can speak of a "multiple case (embedded) design" (Yin 2003: 39).

The case study approach is carried forth to the investigation of the third research question. A dynamic perspective is now adopted, which corresponds to Eisenhardt's interpretation of the case study as "a research strategy which focuses on understanding the dynamics present within single settings" (Eisenhardt 1989: 534). Resulting in the identification of managerial and organizational implications, the third research question is the most practice-oriented. It requires a certain amount of openness and involvement on the part of management.

This leads directly to the **methods for data collection**. Within each case, **interviews** were conducted at both headquarters and subsidiary level. Being semi-structured, they provided enough flexibility to respond to newly arising issues and to adapt to the interviewee's willingness to provide information on a sensitive topic. Interview partners mainly included board members, heads of sales/operations, subsidiary managers and project managers. Involving key informants from both headquarters and local entities is important in order to get a comprehensive picture of the prevailing relationships. In order to assure the quality of the research, the interviews were recorded and transcribed. For the same reason they are selectively complemented by other methods of data collection (Hussey/Hussey 1997: 140; Yin 2003: 86, 97-98): Company documents such as organizational charts, presentations and annual reports serve as additional – albeit mainly confidential – sources of evidence (compare to section 6.3).

1.6 Structure of the Research

The structure of the dissertation follows the logic of the research questions. Building upon this brief introduction, in **Chapter 2** the 'groundwork' for analyzing intersubsidiary relationships is laid. After delineating the level of analysis, competition and cooperation are introduced as the two main types of intersubsidiary relationship. Headquarters and subsidiaries are differentiated as their potential origins and the main objects of competition and cooperation are identified. The chapter concludes by integrating these findings in a comprehensive classification scheme for intersubsidiary relationships.

Transcending the descriptive character of the previous chapter, **Chapter 3** is dedicated to explaining intersubsidiary relationships. Triggered by the analysis of benefits and drawbacks of intersubsidiary competition and cooperation, alternative theoretical approaches to the topic are evaluated. Given that most theories fall short of explaining why intersubsidiary relationships differ across firms even within the same industry, a contingency approach is identified as the most promising conceptual framework. This conclusion is supported by the review of existing studies on factors influencing intersubsidiary competition and/or cooperation.

Chapter 4 narrows the focus to intersubsidiary relationships in project marketing of plant engineering companies. It includes an introduction to both plant engineering and project marketing and addresses the first (primarily descriptive) research question by presenting alternative models of intersubsidiary relationships within the delineated setting.

In **Chapter 5** the second (primarily explicative) research question is addressed by establishing the proposed link between an MNC's strategic orientation and its intersubsidiary relationships. Based on previous theoretical insights and a review of Bartlett and Ghoshal's typology of MNCs, explicit propositions are developed regarding the relationship between a company's strategic orientation and the competition and/or cooperation between its (foreign) subsidiaries.

Chapter 6 is dedicated to the presentation of the empirical findings. Prior to the investigation of the propositions, case studies are outlined as the chosen research methodology. Interviews are presented as the main method of data collection, and thematic coding is introduced as the pursued method of data analysis. Following a review of the research approach according to defined quality criteria, case studies on four large-scale plant engineering companies yield insights into strategic orientation, intersubsidiary relationships and the implied link between the two. The developed propositions are compared to the results obtained from the interviews. Findings on the third (partially normative) research question are also discussed in this chapter.

Finally, the contributions and limitations of this dissertation as well as some avenues for future research are outlined in **Chapter 7**.

2 Analyzing Intersubsidiary Relationships

As a basis not only for this study but also for future research in the field it is useful to start out with a systematic approach to analyzing intersubsidiary relationships (see Fong et al. 2007: 54 and similarly Luo 2005: 80-81 for this appeal). The goal is to provide a general overview of the characteristics and dynamics of the phenomenon and to reflect upon their implications for the underlying research project. Given that few contributions on intersubsidiary relationships exist, such 'groundwork' is necessary before attempting an explanation of the phenomenon. This chapter is structured as follows: First, a delineation of intersubsidiary relationships is undertaken by setting out the relevant level of analysis and providing some basic definitions (section 2.1). Second, competition and cooperation are presented as the two main types of relationship, with coopetition representing a combination of both (section 2.2). Third, headquarters and subsidiaries are identified as the origins of intersubsidiary relationships (section 2.3). Fourth, the relevant contents or objects of competition and cooperation are outlined (section 2.4). Finally, the types, origin and contents of intersubsidiary relationships are integrated in a holistic classification scheme (section 2.5).

Before proceeding to section 2.1, it is worth noting that all of the above aspects build a foundation for addressing the three research questions. First, they provide a framework for describing the kind of relationships that prevail between subsidiaries in the plant engineering industry and for reducing the project acquisition/execution models to a few key characteristics. Second, they delineate the possible manifestations of the dependent variable, i.e. the facets of intersubsidiary relationships that are expected to vary with a company's strategic orientation. Third, they offer a systematic approach not only to discussing developments together with managers, but for helping the latter identify and assess the levers available for shaping intersubsidiary relationships. By specifying relevant relationship patterns in advance, an arbitrary selection of questions can be avoided (Burt 1983: 67). The resulting classification scheme for intersubsidiary relationships helps researchers to structure the findings from past, present and future work. At the same time it demonstrates managers the amplitude of strategic options they have in promoting and/or facilitating intersubsidiary relationships.

2.1 Delineation of Intersubsidiary Relationships[7]

The study of intersubsidiary relationships is located at the intraorganizational level. The focus is on what happens within the boundaries of the MNC, not between an MNC and its external environment – the latter including competitors, suppliers and customers (for a differentiation of internal and external network partners and their influence on the development of critical capabilities within foreign subsidiaries see Schmid/Schurig 2003; for an investigation of the importance of a subsidiary's external embeddedness for its role as a center of excellence see Andersson/Forsgren 2000). At the same time, the level of analysis exceeds that of the individual in the corporate context. Foreign subsidiaries – or, more specifically, the relationships between them – are the main unit of analysis. This can be taken literally, since subsidiaries represent a certain type of organizational 'unit'. Other organizational units would include divisions or business units, functional areas or administrative departments.

Birkinshaw defines a **subsidiary** as "any operational unit controlled by the MNC and situated outside the home country" (Birkinshaw 1997: 207). According to his definition, the term 'foreign subsidiary' would be tautological. In this research, however, it is deliberately used to emphasize the international dimension of the research. In fact, the concept is even broadened to include subsidiaries located in the MNC's home country. Especially given the industry and functional focus of the research, it is difficult to justify why national subsidiaries should be excluded from the investigation (just consider conglomerates that frequently bundle product- or customer-specific activities in national subsidiaries). The decisive factor is that the MNC as a whole conducts business in a number of international locations. As is the case with any other unit, subsidiaries are made up of individuals – managers and employees who interact on a daily basis. In IB research, a subsidiary is often treated as a **collective actor**, a term that seems particularly appropriate when referring to organizations or subunits as units of analysis (Cook 1977: 63). Figure 1 illustrates the depicted level of analysis.

---

[7] This section largely corresponds to Schmid/Maurer 2011: 57-58 and Schmid/Maurer 2008: 3-5 (Chapter 2).

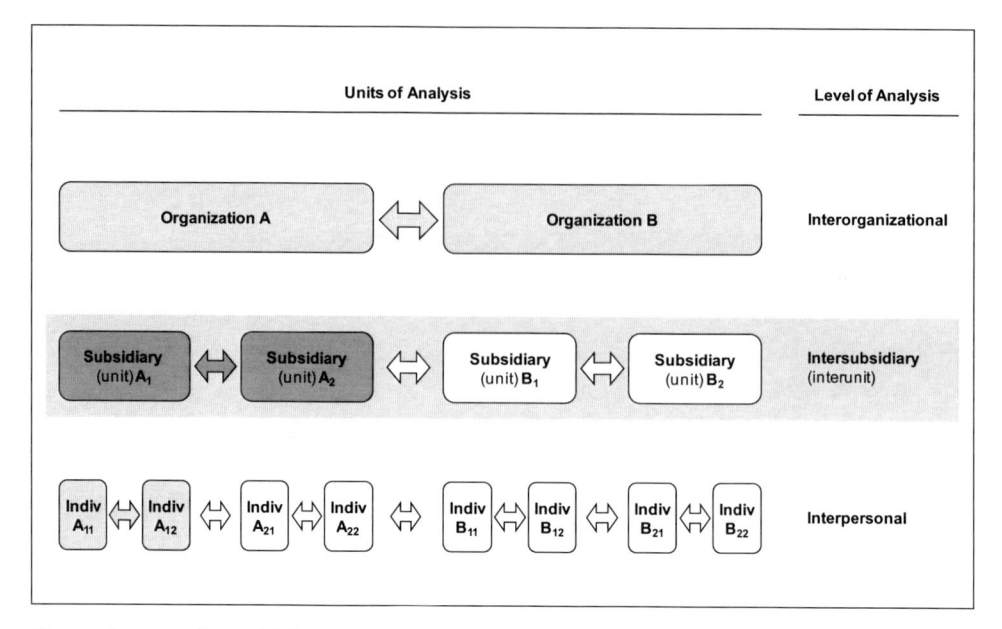

	Units of Analysis	Level of Analysis
	Organization A ⇔ Organization B	Interorganizational
	Subsidiary (unit) A_1 ⇔ Subsidiary (unit) A_2 ⇔ Subsidiary (unit) B_1 ⇔ Subsidiary (unit) B_2	Intersubsidiary (interunit)
	Indiv A_{11} ⇔ Indiv A_{12} ⇔ Indiv A_{21} ⇔ Indiv A_{22} ⇔ Indiv B_{11} ⇔ Indiv B_{12} ⇔ Indiv B_{21} ⇔ Indiv B_{22}	Interpersonal

Figure 1:   Level and Units of Analysis

The above diagram not only delineates the research focus but also suggests that the study of intersubsidiary relationships can borrow elements from both the interorganizational and the interpersonal level. Ghoshal and Bartlett support the first approach when noting that "the relationships between the diverse units of a multidivisional or a multinational corporation have rarely been examined from an interorganizational perspective" (Ghoshal/Bartlett 1990: 608-609). Research on the nature of relationships between individuals is mostly anchored in the field of social psychology. In the course of this research, references to these two fields are made wherever this seems appropriate and insightful. Representing different levels of aggregation, organizations, subsidiaries (units) and individuals can be regarded as the 'subjects' in the formation of (corporate) relationships.

The analytical focus is clearly on the **relationships between foreign subsidiaries** (the 'ties') and not so much on the subsidiaries themselves (the 'nodes') (for a definition of ties and nodes see, for example, Kirsch et al. 1980: 16). Nevertheless, it is important to account for the nodal subsidiaries' characteristics and motivations in order to understand how they interrelate. Subsidiaries can differ substantially in terms of their functional, geographic, product and strategic responsibilities (see, for example, Birkinshaw/Hood 1998b: 782). Suggesting that the type of actor has some impact on the scope of relationships, this research focuses on the relationship between subsidiaries that are located **at the same level of the value chain** – in this case two (or more) foreign subsidiaries engaged in project marketing activities. Such a relationship can be called horizontal to the extent that it comprises two units at the same relative level in the hierarchy (McCann/Ferry 1979: 115) and that it refers to similar functional activities within these subsidiaries.

A **horizontal division of labor** cannot only be achieved through departmentalization (McKenna 1975: 2) but also through international diversification. Vertical relationships tend to be very different in nature (Bengtsson/Kock 2000: 412). On an interorganizational level they are mainly built upon transactions or economic exchange (Ouchi 1980: 130; Ghoshal/Bartlett 1990: 609; Axelsson/Easton 1992: xiv; Easton/Araujo 1992: 63). Interactions typically take place between different functions or value chain activities. Such cross-functional linkages can also be observed in an intraorganizational context (Bartmess/Cerny 1993: 93; Hillebrand/Biemans 2003: 736; Luo et al. 2006: 68-69). They are oftentimes of interest with respect to internal markets and transfer prices (Halal et al. 1993; Halal 1994; Osterloh 1998; Lehmann 2002; Staubach 2005; Cerrato 2006) or the regional configuration of the value chain (see Holtbrügge 2005; Schmid/Grosche 2009 for overviews of related contributions and Frese 2005: 503 for examples). Vertical relationships within firms also touch upon the concepts of authority and power (Ghoshal/Bartlett 1990: 607, 615; Fiske 1991: 14), which appear much less relevant to relationships between peers.

Generally speaking, horizontal relationships have not been analyzed to the same extent as their vertical counterparts. This is true on an interorganizational level (Easton/Araujo 1992: 63; Bengtsson/Kock 1999: 178) as well as an intraorganizational level (Ghoshal/Bartlett 1990: 620; Schmid/Kutschker 2003: 177). Although headquarters-subsidiary relationships and intersubsidiary relationships can have very distinct managerial implications (O'Donnell 2000: 542), a differentiation between the two types of linkages tends to be foregone in both conceptual and empirical work.

Horizontal relationships between actors – organizations, units, groups or individuals – can take a variety of different forms. **'Relationship'** – "used in its original and most comprehensive sense" – refers to "the relative position of two entities on some underlying dimension[s]" (Easton/Araujo 1992: 67). In other words, there exists some kind of linkage, connection or affiliation between two entities of a system or network. A similar conceptualization is used in MNC network models, whose authors – unlike their colleagues in other disciplines – hardly differentiate between 'relations/ relationships', 'flows', 'linkages' and 'interdependencies' (Schmid et al. 2002: 50).

What has been distinguished, however, are the relationship and interaction elements of behavior. While relationships are rather general and long term in nature, interactions – i.e. exchange and adaptation processes – refer to the here and now and "constitute the dynamic aspects of relationships" (Johanson/Mattson 1987: 37). Relationships can thus be regarded as the result of a series of interaction activities (Burt 1983: 35; also see Håkansson/Snehota 1995: 25-26).

Interaction implies that two (or more) entities exchange actions and reactions in an interdependent and not merely sequential manner (Schmid 2005: 239-240). Direct interaction (or even physical presence, as suggested by Schoch 1969: 94), however, is not considered a necessary condition for the existence of a relationship. As such, relationships can also describe interdependencies where actors remain effectively unknown to each other. Prerequisite is that the actions taken by one actor affect the actions or (work) outcomes of another actor (McCann/Ferry 1979: 113-114, Thibaut/Kelley 1959: 10; Thompson 1967: 54-55). In his evaluation of interaction approaches for explaining cooperation, Schmid distinguishes four major content levels that characterize the relationship between cooperating actors: information/communication, transaction/exchange, power/influence and trust/ consensus (Schmid 2005: 241 with reference to Kirsch et al. 1980: 17 and Kutschker/Schmid 1995: 4). In the previous paragraph it has already been argued that the concepts of transaction and power may be less relevant when analyzing the horizontal relationship between subsidiaries. Also, the limitation to cooperation and the focus on interorganizational relationships do not correspond to the goals of this research. The latter sets out to explore a more fundamental aspect of (intersubsidiary) relationships, namely the duality of competition and cooperation.

Similar shortcomings apply when interunit relationships are conceptualized as any kind of interaction, or **flows**, between the nodes of a network (Meier 1997: 151). Although flows of both material and immaterial resources are particularly important to the internal functioning of the MNC (Bartlett/Ghoshal 1998: 196-197; Schmid et al. 2002: 50; Holtbrügge 2005: 565), they do not seem to capture the full scope of intersubsidiary relationships. Products, capital, knowledge or trust do not simply 'flow' among (implicitly cooperating) subsidiaries; their movement will depend on whether these subsidiaries maintain a competitive and/or cooperative relationship with each other. Meier partly accounts for this fact by including influence relationships, such as power, in the characterization of network ties (Meier 1997: 151).

2.2 Types of Intersubsidiary Relationships[8]

Horizontal relationships between actors – organizations, units, groups or individuals – can take a variety of different forms. Representing the two main responses to the scarcity problem, **competition and cooperation** can be considered the most important aspects of interpersonal behavior and social interaction (Weise 1997: 58). Interpreting them more broadly as "interaction phenomena" (Van Lange/De Dreu 2003: 384) allows extending their area of application to an interunit (or interorganizational) level (Bengtsson/Kock 2000: 414). Based on Johanson and Mattson's conceptualization of interactions as the constituting elements of relationships (Johanson/Mattson 1987: 37; see above), competition and cooperation can be regarded as the two fundamental types of (horizontal) relationships.

For the sake of completeness, the dichotomy should be overcome and complemented by both the combination of and the absence of competition and cooperation – relationships that can be termed **coopetition and independence**. On an interorganizational level Bengtsson and Kock take this approach by identifying four types of horizontal relationships between competitors: competition, cooperation, coopetition and co-existence (Bengtsson/Kock 1999: 180-182). Easton and Arujo choose a more ample framework including conflict, competition, co-existence, cooperation and collusion as alternative modes of behavior (Easton/Araujo 1992: 72 with reference to Easton/Araujo 1986). Further parallels can be established to relationships between individuals (Homans 1973: 131-132; Geser 1992: 432; Weise 1997: 58-66). The proposed categorization of relationship types is presented in Figure 2 and its elements subsequently outlined: competition in subsection 2.2.1, cooperation in subsection 2.2.2, coopetition in subsection 2.2.3, and independence in subsection 2.2.4.

---

[8] This section largely corresponds to Schmid/Maurer 2011: 58-62 and Schmid/Maurer 2008: 5-9 (Chapter 3).

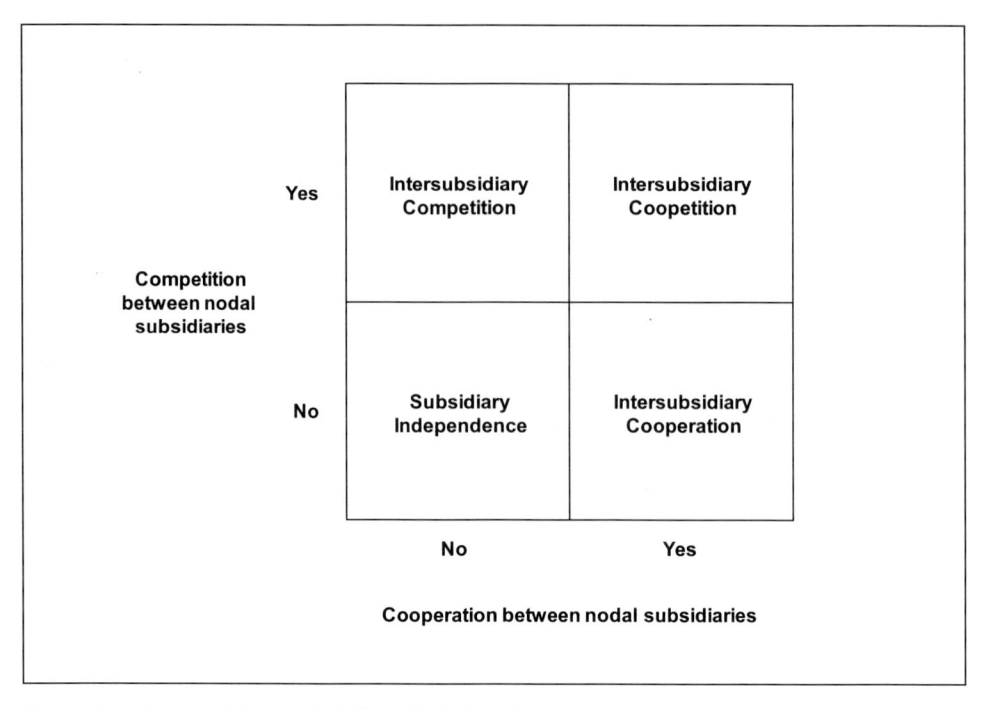

Figure 2: Types of Intersubsidiary Relationships

(2x2 matrix: Competition between nodal subsidiaries [Yes/No] vs. Cooperation between nodal subsidiaries [No/Yes])
- Yes / No: Intersubsidiary Competition
- Yes / Yes: Intersubsidiary Coopetition
- No / No: Subsidiary Independence
- No / Yes: Intersubsidiary Cooperation

2.2.1 Competition

Competition describes a behavior that maximizes the outcome of one actor at the expense of another actor. Therefore, the competition relationship is a zero-sum game (Hirsch 1976: 52; Bengtsson/Kock 1999: 181).[9] The goal is to get the biggest slice of the pie, i.e. achieving a relative advantage over others (Van Lange/De Dreu 2003: 383, 392-393). In competing behavior, individual objectives are more important than common ones (Lewis 1944: 115). Competition need not be bound to direct interaction. Some authors suggest that due to conflicting interests and a lack of rewards the frequency of interaction between competing actors is expected to be low (Homans 1973: 144; Bengtsson/Kock 2000: 414; also see the example cited by Birkinshaw/Lingblad 2005: 681). Others take the opposite stance, arguing that competitors deliberately seek to interact as they are particularly interested in what their opponents think and know (Tsai 2002: 182). For competing firms it may be difficult to completely avoid interaction as they typically come across one another at

---

[9] By stimulating innovation, however, competition may lead to knowledge and growth (Lado et al. 1997: 122).

trade fairs or career fairs, for example, and form part of the same industry association.

It needs to be emphasized, though, that the phenomenon in question refers to competition between the subsidiaries of an MNC, and not to the much more frequently addressed competition between firms (most notably Porter 1980) or individuals (Kohn 1986; Johnson/Johnson 1989; Brown et al. 1998; Pfeffer/Sutton 2000). Just as competition in (industrial) networks is considered a function of the overlap of organizational domains (Thorelli 1986: 39), **intrafirm competition** can be defined as "the extent of overlap between the charters of two or more business units in a single organization" (Birkinshaw/Lingblad 2005: 676).[10] As will be shown, competition for resources and customers complements this view. On an interorganizational level competitors can be regarded as actors that produce and market the same products (Bengtsson/Kock 2000: 415). On an intraorganizational level the same rationale applies: rivalry between subsidiaries or units typically arises when activities and/or objectives overlap (note that according to Mead a fine distinction can be made between competition and rivalry in that competition is behavior oriented towards a goal and rivalry is behavior oriented towards another actor (Mead 1937: 17)). Competition between the foreign subsidiaries of an MNC can be regarded as a special case of interunit competition.

According to Birkinshaw and Lingblad, the extant literature provides little insight as to how intrafirm competition might be managed (Birkinshaw/Lingblad 2005: 674). One of the few exceptions to this is provided by Birkinshaw himself. He develops a set of criteria that allow managers to evaluate the adequacy of internal competition and subsequently decide upon its termination or continuation. In addition, the author provides some very hands-on advice on dealing with internal competition as a dynamic phenomenon (Birkinshaw 2001a: 24). His focus, however, lies on competition between technologies and business units.

2.2.2 Cooperation

Cooperation, on the other hand, maximizes the outcome of a collective or group (Van Lange/De Dreu 2003: 383, 392). Here, the goal is to enlarge the pie, i.e. realize an additional gain, which is then shared among the actors (Weise 1997: 60). Individual rewards can be enhanced by helping or supporting one another or by

---

[10] The concept of a unit's or subsidiary's charter is discussed in subsection 2.4.1.3.

pooling strengths towards a common goal (Homans 1973: 131). In cooperative relationships one actor's activities may represent a satisfactory substitute for another actor's activities (Lewis 1944: 115). Most definitions of cooperation focus on the process of interacting and forming relationships to achieve mutual gain or benefit.

Management literature on cooperation can be divided into two broad streams: cooperation between organizations (external cooperation) and cooperation within organizations (internal cooperation) (Hillebrand/Biemans 2003: 735-736). Cooperation between the subsidiaries of an MNC constitutes a special case of internal or **intrafirm cooperation**. Different types of cooperation can be distinguished depending on whether such cooperation is formal or informal and whether it occurs between vertically or horizontally linked actors (Easton/Araujo 1992: 76-77; Smith et al. 1995: 10). While headquarters-subsidiary relationships form part of an MNC's formal organization structure, intersubsidiary relationships tend not to be specified as explicitly (see Rank 2003 for a differentiated analysis of formal and informal organization structures). Depending on the origin of the relationship, cooperation between subsidiaries may itself contain more formal or informal elements – and touch either the surface or the deep structure of the MNC (Kutschker/Schmid 1995: 18-19).[11] Voluntary cooperation tends to be built upon reciprocal trust and commitment (Lado et al. 1997: 121; Gupta/Becerra 2003: 25; Van Lange/De Dreu 2003: 401; Luo 2004: 35).

Cooperation within firms has occupied a much more prominent position in IB research than its competitive counterpart has. It has been explored from a variety of different angles. The largest body of related literature is dedicated to knowledge exchange within the MNC (e.g., Gupta/Govindarajan 1991; Foss/Pedersen 2000; Gupta/Govindarajan 2000; Buckley/Carter 2002; 2003; Gupta/Becerra 2003; Lagerström/Andersson 2003; Schweiger et al. 2003; Zhao/Luo 2005; Adenfelt/Lagerström 2006). Other scholars take a closer look at resource flows (Gupta/Govindarajan 1986; Randøy/Li 1998), interunit communication (Ghoshal et al. 1994; Marschan 1996; Barner-Rasmussen/Björkman 2005), social interaction (Tsai/Ghoshal 1998; Tsai 2000) or cross-functional cooperation in MNCs (see Hillebrand/Biemans 2003: 736 for an overview). However, very few of these contributions deal explicitly with the interaction between foreign subsidiaries, let alone the cooperation between globally dispersed units involved in project acquisition and execution.

---

[11] For a detailed definition and discussion of deep structure, surface structure and their interplay see Schmid 1996: 115-131.

2.2.3 Coopetition

Traditionally, competition and cooperation have been regarded as opposing behaviors situated at two ends of a continuum. However, there have been a number of attempts to reconcile the two phenomena, several of them taking an interdisciplinary approach (for example, Grunwald/Lilge 1982; Hirshleifer 1982; Thompson et al. 1991; Weise 1997; Jansen/Schleissing 2000). The concept of 'coopetition' has also gained ground in (international) business literature over the past ten years, with most authors adopting an interorganizational perspective (for example, Brandenburger/Nalebuff 1996; Lado et al. 1997; Dowling/Lechner 1998; Dyer/Singh 1998; Khanna et al. 1998; Bengtsson/Kock 2000; Luo 2004; Ullrich 2004; Walley 2007).

Coopetition can be defined as "a mindset, process or phenomenon of combining cooperation and competition" (Luo 2005: 72). Metaphorically speaking, it means cooperating to create a bigger business pie, while competing to divide it up (Luo 2004: 9). It is suggested that the term was first used by Ray Noorda, founder and CEO of Novell in the 1980s (Walley 2007: 14). The simultaneous occurrence of competition and cooperation can be regarded as a third, particularly complex type of relationship (Bengtsson/Kock 2000: 412, 414). For coopetition to exist on an intraorganizational level, relationships need to contain both competitive and cooperative elements.[12] The mere introduction of competitive mechanisms into the organization is regarded as a necessary but not sufficient condition (Jansen/Schleissing 2000: 49). If the relationship between units is primarily competitive, containing basically no cooperative elements, it appears more suitable to speak of intrafirm or interunit competition (rather than coopetition). In general, rivalry and conflict are likely to be less extreme within a firm than across firms (Luo et al. 2006: 69). Compared to the interaction between individuals, however, a lower overall level of cooperation and a higher overall level of competition can be expected. This is due to a lesser degree of trust in intergroup relations, more intragroup support to pursue own interests at the expense of the other group and shared responsibilities (Van Lange/De Dreu 2003: 404-405). So far, the potential of contributing to academic theory by taking the concept of coopetition to the intrafirm level has hardly been tapped (Walley 2007: 12, 25).

---

[12] The two types of interaction are typically divided between activities rather than counterparts (Bengtsson/Kock 2000: 415; also see Walley 2007: 15 with reference to Dowling et al. 1996).

As is the case with both of its components, the concept of coopetition has found far less consideration on an intraorganizational than on an interorganizational level. Few authors have adopted a balanced view of competition and cooperation between subunits. Instead, they have been focusing on either the competitive side (Williamson 1975) or the cooperative side (Gupta/Govindarajan 1986) of interunit relationships. Especially when accounting for the international dimension of an MNC there is a lack of systematic study of various types of coopetition, including that between corporate subunits (Fang 2006: 436).

2.2.4 Independence

In order to draw a complete picture of relationships, one also needs to consider the case that actors belong to the same (internal and/or external) network but remain largely unaffected by each other. One would expect no overlaps in goals or interfaces between activities. In this research this condition is most broadly referred to as **independence**.

Alternative denominations such as 'individualism' or 'co-existence' have misleading connotations: Individualism is a term used in social psychology to describe the tendency of maximizing proper returns while disregarding the returns of others (Van Lange/De Dreu 2003: 393). Co-existence is referred to by some authors as a situation in which the actors' goals and objectives are independent (Easton/Araujo 1992: 75); others perceive it as a relationship where competitors know about each other but do not interact in terms of economic exchange. As long as one actor inherently dominates the other, such a relationship is very well characterized by a state of dependence (Bengtsson/Kock 1999: 180-181). The concept of autonomy does not quite fit in with either competition or cooperation because it is directed towards the locus of decision making (Hennart 1993a: 178). Possessing the ability to make independent choices can be the result of either delegation or initiative (Young/Tavares 2004: 228) or it may be achieved through bargaining between headquarters and subsidiaries (Taggart 1997: 55). It is therefore preferred to speak of subsidiary independence in the most neutral manner.

2.3 Origin of Intersubsidiary Relationships[13]

In an attempt to further understand and classify intersubsidiary relationships one can observe differences in who actually initiates and/or shapes such a relationship, i.e. where the origin of the relationship lies. In a multinational company, headquarters and subsidiaries can be identified as the two driving forces – similar to the parties involved in defining a subsidiary's role or charter (Birkinshaw/Hood 1998b: 775; Phelps/Fuller 2000: 226; Birkinshaw 2001b: 89-93). The resulting relationships are referred to as being either **headquarters-led or subsidiary-led**. Just like individuals, who stay in relations "because they want to or because they have to" (Johnson 1982: 52), competition and cooperation between subsidiaries can contain voluntary and forced elements (Luo 2004: 162; Ullrich 2004: 4; Luo 2005: 73).[14] The chosen terminology should not suggest that intersubsidiary competition and cooperation are the mere result of deliberate headquarters or subsidiary decisions. A variety of different internal and external factors are expected to influence such relationships. For the time being, however, the origin of intersubsidiary relationships constitutes a purely descriptive element of the classification scheme.

It is worth noting that the terminology 'headquarters-led' and 'subsidiary-led' was carefully selected. It is preferred over headquarters- or subsidiary-'driven' or -'initiated' relationships in order to avoid confusion with drivers, determinants, influencing factors. After thorough consideration the terms were also chosen over a number of other word pairs such as formal-informal, managed-unmanaged (or open), mandatory-voluntary, institutionalized-discretionary, planned-emergent (or ad-hoc), or structural-situational, since they seemed to have the least unwanted connotations. As will be shown below, these adjectives may be used to describe certain facets of the respective relationships.

After introducing headquarters-led relationships in subsection 2.3.1 and subsidiary-led relationships in subsection 2.3.2, the rejection of formal and informal relationships as an alternative category merits some discussion in subsection 2.3.3.

---

[13] This section largely corresponds to Schmid/Maurer 2011: 62-65 and Schmid/Maurer 2008: 9-12 (Chapter 4). The considerations in subsection 2.3.3 have been added.

[14] Although intersubsidiary relationships are expected to be either headquarters-led or subsidiary-led, a combination of both origins cannot be ruled out.

2.3.1 Headquarters-Led Relationships

Headquarters can leave the decision to compete or cooperate completely up to the subsidiaries; or it can promote or support a certain relationship by putting in place the corresponding structures, processes and systems. Luo speaks of creating the "organizational infrastructure", critical components of which are intranet system, reward system, knowledge encapsulation system and coordination system (Luo 2005: 84). Design parameters could further comprise subsidiary roles and responsibilities. Headquarters-led relationships imply that it is not left up to the subsidiaries to decide whether to compete or cooperate with their peers. Headquarters plans, defines, implements and manages (or at least monitors) structures, processes and systems that bring about the desired intersubsidiary relationship. Headquarters-led competition and cooperation can be considered as 'structural' in the sense that once the respective processes and incentive schemes are in place, intersubsidiary relationships become somewhat institutionalized. They constitute a key element of the organization and their formation is mandatory to subsidiaries. Why it seems advisable to refrain from equating headquarters-led with formal relationships is addressed in subsection 2.3.3.

Headquarters-led competition can take a variety of forms, involving different levels of aggregation and intensities of competition. Alternative, or complementary, approaches include: setting up profit centers (for example, Fisher/Govindarajan 1992; Hennart 1993b: 542-544; Luo 2005: 87), establishing internal markets (Halal et al. 1993; Halal 1994; Osterloh 1998; Cerrato 2006), issuing internal requests for proposal (RfPs) (Birkinshaw 2001b: 133; Birkinshaw/Hood 2001: 134-135; more generally Porter-Roth 2002) and conducting sales or other employee contests (for example, Murphy/Dacin 1998; Kalra/Shi 2001; Murphy et al. 2004). All of these approaches imply the introduction of a merit- or performance-based reward system as well as the specification of certain rules, responsibilities and procedures. In preparation of an RfP, for example, the processes of calling for, collecting, evaluating and selecting bids need to be defined and the relevant milestones communicated to the units eligible for participation (see Birkinshaw 2001a: 25-26 on management's role in designing processes to manage internal competition). A corporate-level committee is typically established to coordinate and monitor the bidding process. Consequently, such activities can be considered part of what Luo calls the coordination system (Luo 2005: 87). While an intranet system facilitates information availability and process transparency, a knowledge encapsulation system creates a fairer competitive environment by providing units with equal access to resources. A well-designed incentive program allows headquarters to inspire the desired aspects of intersubsidiary competition (Luo 2005: 85-87); it is considered indispensable for making the internal market model work (Birkinshaw 2001b: 116; on the MNC as an internal market system see Cerrato 2006). Generally speaking, top management has multiple means of promoting (or curbing) intrafirm competition: it may make use of direct authority, shape the organizational context to encourage or discourage interunit competition or play an ongoing role in sharing information, facilitating discussions and adjudicating over contested charters (Birkinshaw/Lingblad 2005: 684).

Headquarters-led cooperation requires very similar specifications. Given that the scope for cooperation within an MNC seems even larger than that for competition, subsidiaries need to know who they are expected to cooperate with in which way and how they are rewarded for their collaboration. The incentive system is highlighted as a particularly important component for achieving a collaborative worldwide orientation (Perlmutter 1969a: 14; Hedlund 1986: 30), for promoting technology transfer (Li/Ferreira 2003: 19) and for making the internal market model work (Birkinshaw 2001b: 116; on the MNC as an internal market system see Cerrato 2006). An intranet system serves as an information platform and a basic mechanism for interaction and exchange. Particularly important to knowledge sharing during intersubsidiary cooperation is an encapsulation system that facilitates the encoding, storing and converting of knowledge into a sharable form (Luo 2005: 85-87). Headquarters can achieve cooperation through both formal hierarchical structures and informal lateral relations (Tsai 2002: 180-182). As long as headquarters makes a coordinative effort, the relationship will be considered headquarters-led. Luo notes that informal lateral relations often occur naturally but can be fostered through internal social arrangements that promote interunit communication and interaction (Luo 2005: 87 with reference to Tsai/Ghoshal 1998). The fact that headquarters can facilitate informal relationships provides another argument for adhering to the distinction between headquarters-led and subsidiary-led rather than formal and informal intersubsidiary relationships.

Finally, it should be noted that headquarters may put in place certain structures and processes that impact competition and/or cooperation between subsidiaries without being specifically designed to those ends. One should not overestimate the deliberate planning of intersubsidiary relationships. Managers will not always lay out explicitly how intersubsidiary relationships should be designed. Instead, the latter may become a by-product of certain internal and external influencing factors, which will be discussed in section 3.5. A relationship that is considered headquarters-led should involve direct headquarters initiatives, though. The question when such initiatives can be expected is addressed in Chapter 3.

2.3.2 Subsidiary-Led Relationships

Subsidiary-led relationships are based on subsidiary rather than headquarters initiative. Subsidiaries, like individuals, can be assumed to have a certain disposition or intrinsic motivation to compete and/or cooperate.[15] Depending on the situation (or constellation), competitive or cooperative behavior will appear more promising to them. As long as subsidiaries are fairly autonomous their interaction with peers will be voluntary or freely chosen – although it may be supported by elements of the organizational infrastructure (for a delineation see subsection 2.3.1; also Lagerström/Andersson 2003: 93; Luo 2005: 84; Zhao/Luo 2005: 79). Prerequisite for the existence of a subsidiary-led relationship is that headquarters has not implemented structures or processes aimed at the promotion of intersubsidiary competition and/or cooperation. Without directives from headquarters, subsidiaries, as legally independent entities and players in "the 'game' in the system of relationships", will pursue strategies depending on their own objectives and resources (Doz/Prahalad 1991: 152). In their discretionary decision to compete and/or cooperate with their peers, subsidiaries have to overcome the natural conflict between self-interest and collective interest (Rugman/Verbeke 2003: 133; Van Lange/De Dreu 2003: 382; see also Fehr/Fischbacher 2002 for a discussion of social preferences). Given that these relationships are not necessarily built upon formal structures or processes, subsidiaries can handle them flexibly and allow them to emerge. Referring to subsidiary-led relationships as being ad-hoc, however, would not do them full justice. Subsidiaries may very well have a longer-term vision of how they wish to interrelate with their peers. Since the formation of a relationship takes some time, a certain trend towards competitive and/or cooperative behavior should be observable.

Subsidiary-led competition can be thought of as being 'open' in that competitive tensions are not mediated by headquarters. Subsidiaries can initiate such competition by claiming certain resources, responsibilities or customers (for a discussion of the objects of competition see subsection 2.4.1) that a sister subsidiary currently holds or also has a strong interest in. Eventually it will be settled internally (resource or charter allocation with or without headquarters involvement) or externally (by customer choice). In order to speak of a competitive relationship, competition should not constitute a unique incident but form part of an overall attitude or action

---

[15] Cooperative motivations are activated in individuals when their personal goals and preferences overlap. If, on the other hand, there is little correspondence between their goals and preferences, non-cooperative or competitive motivations are spurred (Van Lange/De Dreu 2003: 11, also with reference to Deutsch 1949).

pattern. Subsidiary-led competition is likely to occur when subsidiaries have some kind of incentive to outperform their peers. Subsidiaries may be compelled to compete even in absence of a formal incentive system. Individual goals lead to competition when situations are structured so that a gain for one side implies a loss for the other side (Doz/Prahalad 1991: 153). The most common example is that of scarce resources – production equipment, finance, technology, marketing skills or management capabilities (Ghoshal/Bartlett 1990: 610). Psychological factors, such as prestige and pride, can also stimulate active competition (Bengtsson/Kock 2000: 413).

Subsidiary-led cooperation is just as open as its competitive counterpart is. Headquarters does not set any limits or standards for intersubsidiary collaboration. The latter can take place most informally through personal conversations or social interaction (for example, Tsai 2002: 181, 183-184), or it can adopt rather formal traits by being confined to a purely professional level. There is no reason why subsidiaries should not be able to introduce similarly effective and adhered-to bilateral structures and processes as headquarters. But what motivates subsidiaries to cooperate? First, subsidiary-led cooperation is mainly expected when subsidiaries realize some kind of gain from teaming up with their peers. While looking to improve their own performance, subsidiaries recognize the opportunities of sharing resources and committing to common task goals. The effort to cooperate is likely to depend on the subsidiary's strategic needs (Zhao/Luo 2005: 76). Proactively, a subsidiary may be interested in enhancing its competitive position; reactively it may try to compensate for strategic vulnerability (Gnyawali et al. 2007: 2). Second, a more altruistic motivation for cooperation is to achieve positive results for others (Van Lange/De Dreu 2003: 392). Such behavior may be based on time-delayed considerations: Cooperation has been found to arise when actors perceive they will be in contact with each other for a long time or recognize they must reciprocate for benefits they have received (Axelrod 1984: 12-13, 20-21). Empirical evidence further suggests that managers are motivated to cooperate by their "long-term allegiance to the corporation" (Birkinshaw/Hood 1998b: 782). On an individual level it is oftentimes the social structure that explains why people act collectively to create a win-win relationship (Axelrod 1984: 23). Some authors refer to the intraorganizational context that facilitates or constrains the formation of relationships as "social capital" (Burt 1992: 8-10; Nahapiet/Ghoshal 1998: 243-245; Tsai 2000: 927). Cooperative behavior is usually built upon a culture of trust (Powell 1990: 305; Smith et al. 1995: 15; Lado et al. 1997: 121; Tsai/Ghoshal 1998: 467; Tsai 2000: 929).

Subsidiaries are able to shape the relationship with their peers within the given organizational context. The greater their scope for decision making, the more flexible they are in forming intersubsidiary relationships. Based on tactical, operational and strategic considerations, subsidiaries are expected to choose between competition and cooperation on a situational basis. Nevertheless, it would be inappropriate to parallel subsidiary-led with situational relationships, since headquarters-led relationships may also vary with situational factors – a logic that will be extended in section 3.4. Picking up the issue of terminology, another word pair that strongly suggests itself for classification purposes is discussed in the following.

2.3.3 A Note on Formal and Informal Relationships

The above delineation of headquarters-led and subsidiary-led relationships may imply that a differentiation between formal and informal relationships would be just as appropriate. McKenna's comprehensive definition of "the formal system" actually reflects a number of characteristics also attributed to headquarters-led relationships: "The **formal** system is the planned pattern of formal relationships and duties (organization chart, job descriptions, position guides), formal rules, operating policies, work and control procedures, compensation arrangements adopted by management to guide employee behavior in certain ways, etc. This represents the deliberate attempt to establish patterned relationships which will meet the objectives effectively and efficiently" (McKenna 1975: 2). Formalization can be seen as the attempt to make the structure of relationships more visible and explicit (Scott 2003: 31). Communication and authority structure are set by hierarchy; and authority provides the legitimization to invoke compliance by subordinates based on formal positions and control over rewards and sanctions.

The formal system is said to be built upon logic, rationality and experience, whereas informal structures are perceived as the result of spontaneous, natural behavior. Nevertheless, the emergent **informal** system "also has structured properties" (McKenna 1975: 3). This aspect corresponds to the nature of subsidiary-led relationships. The fact that they do not result from headquarters' planned organization design does not mean that they are established arbitrarily. Informal relationships between organization members can be defined as not having emerged within the deliberate and authorized process of rule creation (Schreyögg 2003: 14) and thus not being predetermined by any organization charts, process plans or other formal structures and processes (Rosenstiel 1993: 322). Smith et al. stress a different aspect by conceptualizing informal cooperation between actors as adaptable arrangements based on behavioral norms rather than contractual obligations (Smith et al. 1995: 10).

Informal relationships should not be confused with actual or realized relationships. To that end, Rank provides a very useful classification scheme for organizational relationships (Rank 2003: 24). Formal relationships can be divided into fulfilled and unfulfilled relationships. Only the fulfilled formal relationships form part of the actual/realized relationships. The actual/realized relationships further comprise informal relationships, suggesting that formal and informal relationships tend to co-exist (Rank 2003: 22). Over time, formal relationships can evolve into informal ones and vice versa (McKenna 1975: 3; Ring/Van De Ven 1994: 100-101 on organizational change and development processes also see Van de Ven/Poole 1995). Although recognizing that headquarters-led and subsidiary-led relationships may also complement each other, for this research less interrelated concepts are preferred. The dichotomy formal/informal is often used to argue that informal structures or relationships exist alongside formal ones. This does not necessarily have to be the case with headquarters-led and subsidiary-led relationships.

As far as the informal organization is concerned, a parallelization with subsidiary-led relationships is also difficult when conceptualizing it as a deviation from the formal organization plan or a response to deficiencies in the formal system (McKenna 1975: 2-3). It may very well occur that no 'formal plan' has been designed for the specification of intersubsidiary competition and/or cooperation. Finally, when regarded as the set of formal rules on the division of labor and its coordination (Rank 2003: 22, building upon Kieser/Kubicek 1992: 19), formal structures have a strong connotation of representing a company's static infrastructure. The latter typically manifests itself in the organization chart, but does not comprise the competitive and/or cooperative relationships between subsidiaries. While job descriptions determine how individuals are supposed to work together, organizational structures and processes detail how departments and groups must function (Smith et al. 1995: 10). Substituting formal for headquarters-led intersubsidiary relationships, would possibly forego that the latter tend to be built upon flexible and dynamic processes. The classification of intersubsidiary relationships according to their origin rather than the degree of formalization thus seems the most appropriate.

2.4 Contents of Intersubsidiary Relationships[16]

In clarifying the level of analysis, subsidiaries were introduced as one of three 'subjects' in the formation of corporate relationships. Relationships were categorized into being competitive and/or cooperative as well as headquarters- or subsidiary-led. An important question that has not been addressed so far concerns the different contents or 'objects' of the relationship: For what do subsidiaries compete and by what means do they cooperate? Answers allow further classifying intersubsidiary relationships and identifying the types of competition and cooperation that are relevant to a specific research project. They show corporate and local managers the leeway they have to design intersubsidiary relationships and encourage them to reflect upon the respective implications.

For the sake of clarity and coherence, intersubsidiary relationships will be viewed in relation to the interorganizational and interpersonal level. The objects of competition are outlined in subsection 2.4.1, and the objects of cooperation are differentiated in subsection 2.4.2.

2.4.1 Objects of Competition

Competition tends to arise over anything that is scarce but is perceived as valuable (and contestable) by more than one party: resources, responsibilities and business. These objects apply to subsidiaries, organizations and individuals. It seems appropriate to specify the categories according to the level of analysis (and possibly the functional focus). In the case of foreign subsidiaries it is preferred to speak of **competition for resources, charters and customers**. Before taking a closer look at each of these objects, the proposed trichotomy is briefly discussed in relation to other classifications.

---

[16] A condensed version of this section is presented in Schmid/Maurer 2011: 65-73 and Schmid/Maurer 2008: 13-22 (Chapter 5).

2.4.1.1 Choice of Categories

In one of the few contributions to intrafirm competition, Birkinshaw and Lingblad choose a similar distinction when contrasting "internal competition for resources" with competition "at the intraorganizational level" and competition "at the product market level" (Birkinshaw/Lingblad 2005: 675). With specific respect to foreign subsidiaries, Luo distinguishes between competition for parent resources and corporate support, system position, and market expansion (Luo 2005: 75-76). The categories chosen for this research correspond to the two prior conceptualizations in that they cover two objects that are internal and one that is mainly external to the organization (see Luo 2007: 130 for a distinction between competition for inputs and outputs). Other contributions tend to forego one of the three categories. In an earlier contribution Birkinshaw had identified two major types of internal competition between subsidiary units: internal competition for a charter and internal competition for a customer (Birkinshaw 2001b: 113). While including capabilities and practices in his internal market model (Birkinshaw 2001b: 118), the author does not treat competition for parent resources on a par with the other two categories. Although this conceptualization of intersubsidiary competition comes closest to the (albeit external) market-oriented approach of this research, all three objects should initially be considered for the sake of completeness. Modifications and specifications will be necessary depending on the type of subsidiary investigated. The proposed trichotomy differs from existing classifications in that it allows viewing intersubsidiary competition in relation to the interorganizational and interpersonal level. In their broadest sense, the three objects cover the full spectrum of competitive scenarios corporate actors may encounter with their peers.

What follows is a brief description of these objects and an explication of their relevance for subsidiaries engaged in project marketing activities (project acquisition and execution). The link to interpersonal and interorganizational competition is established as appropriate. Figure 3 combines subjects and objects of competition in a matrix, facilitating the reader to follow the discussion. Recall that the *subjects* of competition refer to those elements *between* which competition prevails. The *objects* of competition specify those elements *for* which individuals, units or firms compete. The two resulting categories that are central to this research are shaded in dark grey. Resources are treated more briefly in the following since they are not within the focus of this research.

	Two or more organizations	Interorganizational resource competition	Interorganizational domain competition	Interorganizational customer competition
Subjects of competition	Two or more subsidiaries (units)	Intersubsidiary (interunit) resource competition	**Intersubsidiary (interunit) charter competition**	**Intersubsidiary (interunit) customer competition**
	Two or more (corporate) individuals	Interpersonal resource competition	Interpersonal responsibility competition	Interpersonal business competition
		Resources	Responsibilities (charters)	Business (customers)

Objects of competition

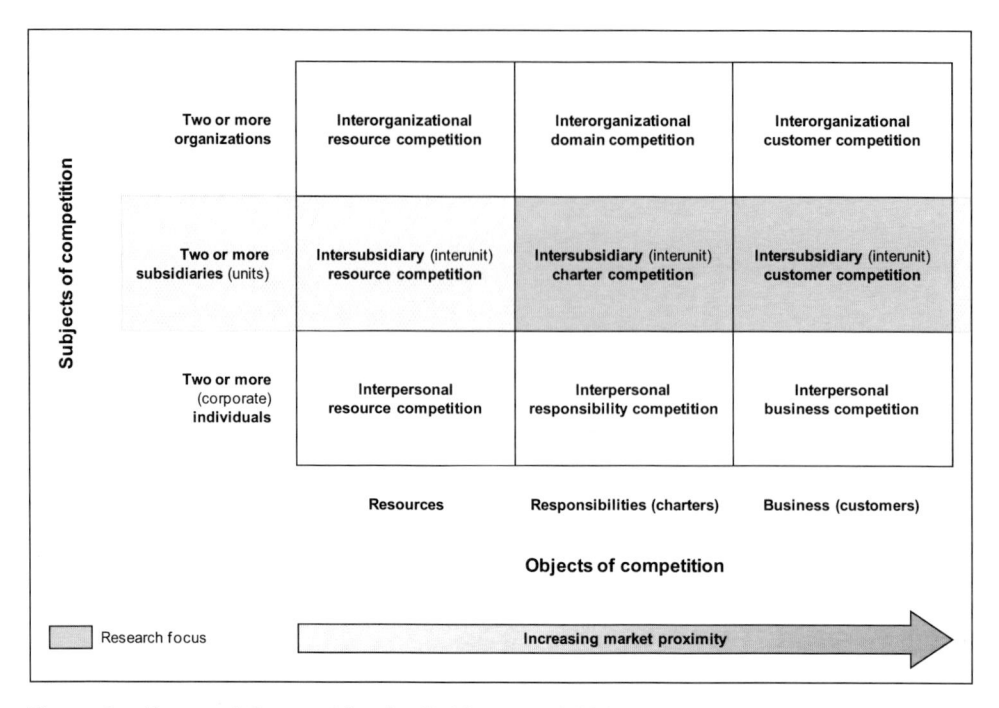

Increasing market proximity

Figure 3: Types of Competition by Subjects and Objects

2.4.1.2 Resources

Competition for scarce resources reflects the traditional, and most intuitive, way of thinking about competition between organizational units (Birkinshaw/Lingblad 2005: 675). Resources can most neutrally be defined as "the stocks of available factors that are owned or controlled by the firm" (Amit/Schoemaker 1993: 35) and typically fall into one of the following categories: financial, human, physical, organizational, technological or intangible resources (see Schiller 2000: 58 for an extensive overview of alternative definitions/delineations of resources in literature).

It should be noted that this brief discussion of resources is intentionally detached from the resource-based view (RBV) as a theoretical perspective.[17] The RBV is introduced in subsection 3.3.2 in an effort to explain, rather than describe, different intersubsidiary relationships.

---

[17] The RBV argues that firms are able to achieve sustained competitive advantage based on heterogeneous and imperfectly mobile resources, which need to be valuable, rare, imperfectly imitable and non-substitutable (Barney 1991: 105-106). Resources that are relevant to intersubsidiary competition and/or cooperation do not necessarily have to create competitive advantage at the corporate level, though (see subsection 3.3.2 for a discussion).

It is management's role to design the organization's structures, processes and systems in favor of an efficient and effective allocation of these resources. Those authors who have accounted for internal competition for resources have mainly done so by adopting an **internal market** perspective (March/Simon 1958; Arrow 1964; Williamson 1975; Hennart 1993b; Halal 1994; Birkinshaw 2001b; Cerrato 2006). Building upon Birkinshaw's (2001b) model of the multinational enterprise as an internal market system, Cerrato is among the few who explicitly consider an international dimension. Applied to the MNC, the idea of an internal (capital) market is one of decentralizing activities and having headquarters act "like a small merchant bank or holding company, investing capital among various enterprises" (Robbins 1990: 322). Managing markets for intermediate goods and services (as well as charters and competencies and practices) across borders can be regarded as a particularly complex task. As Birkinshaw and Cerrato have shown, it is important to differentiate between resource and charter competition, because the mere allocation of resources does not necessarily imply the assumption of some overarching responsibility.[18] Depending on the size and scope of the investment (or endowment), responsibilities may come along with strategic resources such as plants and research centers (Bartlett/Ghoshal 1988: 65). Luo differentiates between intersubsidiary competition for parent resources (and corporate support) and intersubsidiary competition for system position (Luo 2005: 75). His terminology also draws attention to the fact that **internal (or parent) resources** are of primary interest when investigating intersubsidiary competition; resources procured from outside the MNC tend to evoke less competition among subsidiaries.

The same is true for individuals in the corporate context, who mainly compete for resources 'managed' by their superiors. On an interorganizational level, however, external resources constitute the most relevant inputs and objects of competition. They include technology, information, human resources, natural resources, indigenous supplies and favorable government treatment (Luo 2007: 130). Note that Luo includes information as an intangible resource. For the purpose of this research, knowledge (including information) will be treated as a separate category due to its particular relevance for cooperation (see subsections 2.4.2.1 and 0). Although competition for resources is an issue on all three levels of aggregation, differences exist with respect to where these resources are obtained from and who may possibly allocate them. The further one gets down to the individual level, the more important 'soft factors' such as trust and recognition become (for example, Lindskold 1982: 242-243). The latter can be interpreted as resources very broadly in that they

---

[18] See subsection 2.4.1.3 for the definition of a unit's or subsidiary's charter.

represent something of value that one person has to give to another – but typically not in an abundant manner (compare the enumeration of immaterial resources by Schmid et al. 2002: 50).

2.4.1.3 Charters

A **charter** can be defined as "the businesses (i.e., product and market arenas) in which a division actively participates and for which it is responsible within the corporation" (Galunic/Eisenhardt 1996: 256). The notion of a charter can be, and has been, applied to foreign subsidiaries: Birkinshaw and Hood speak of a charter as "[t]he visible manifestation of the subsidiary's role in the MNC", implying a shared understanding between subsidiary and headquarters regarding the subsidiary's market, product, technological or functional responsibilities (Birkinshaw/Hood 1998b: 782). For subsidiaries engaged in project marketing activities, a charter refers to the customers, markets and project phases they are in charge of. The common denominator of these elements is market proximity; they all relate to responsibilities in the acquisition and execution of large, customized projects.

A subsidiary's charter can be distinguished from what Luo calls "system position", i.e. a subsidiary's "strategic role and position in an MNC's entire system or network" (Luo 2005: 75). The latter is about subsidiaries dominating certain primary activities, capitalizing on knowledge, becoming a center of excellence or increasing their authority. The charter concept as used in this research shows some overlap with Luo's value chain and competence excellence positions (Luo 2005: 76), but is geared more towards specific customer and project responsibilities. Another closely related concept is that of a subsidiary **mandate**, which includes single value-adding activities and typically refers to regional or global responsibilities (Birkinshaw 1996: 467, 471; on regional versus global centers of competence see Schmid 2003: 275-276, 283). An example is a subsidiary's world product mandate (Crookell 1986: 106; Rugman/Douglas 1986; Roth/Morrison 1992: 718; Birkinshaw 1996: 469; O'Donnell 2000: 541). The fact that charters may also include activities that subsidiaries perform for the corporation as a whole (Birkinshaw 2001b: 113) shows that the delineation between the two concepts is not clear-cut. For analyzing intersubsidiary competition the term 'charter' is preferred, because it has less connotation of being assigned (or 'mandated') from above and is thus more easily reconcilable with subsidiary-led competition.

As Birkinshaw and Hood's discussion of alternative subsidiary evolution processes shows, charter changes can be driven by headquarters or subsidiary managers (Birkinshaw/Hood 1998b: 784-786). Charters may be gained, lost, extended or diminished, implying that they can comprise short- or long-term responsibilities (for example, Birkinshaw 1996: 472). Whereas headquarters may assign long-term responsibilities for certain customer groups or geographic markets (Luo 2005: 76), subsidiaries could ask for the go-ahead to approach a new customer or secure an individual project.

The more actively subsidiaries participate in shaping their charters the closer the concept is related to that of a subsidiary **initiative**, i.e. "a discrete, proactive undertaking that advances a new way for the corporation to use or expand its resources" (Birkinshaw 1997: 207 with reference to Kanter 1982; Miller 1983). Such initiatives can be externally focused or internally focused. External initiatives arise from the interaction with customers, suppliers or other stakeholders, whereas internal initiatives involve the identification of new business opportunities within the boundaries of the MNC. Internal initiatives tend to be competitive in that one subsidiary challenges others for a new investment or existing activity. Entrepreneurial subsidiaries contribute to "network optimization" by vying for activities that could potentially be performed by some other unit (Birkinshaw/Fry 1998: 53, 56). Particularly internal-global hybrid initiatives, which involve convincing headquarters management to support the pursuit of an opportunity outside the subsidiary's home market (Birkinshaw 2001b: 28, 73), can be conceptualized as top-down projects that are being put up for tender. Regardless of a formalized bidding process, subsidiary managers try to 'sell' their issues to the parent company (Ling et al. 2005). Similarly, charters – representing "issues of competency and power" – tend to be contestable among subsidiaries (Ghoshal/Bartlett 1990: 608). In most corporations there is internal competition for both existing and new charters (Birkinshaw/Hood 1998b: 782). Such competition can be managed in the form of submissions or so-called internal requests for proposal (Jansen/Schleissing 2000: 45; Birkinshaw/Hood 2001: 134). It is up to corporate management to define the rules of the game and decide how openly to handle the competition for charters (Birkinshaw 2001b: 119, 121; Cerrato 2006: 261).

Charter competition is a common phenomenon in upstream activities such as R&D and production and is oftentimes accompanied by internal quasi markets (for an example see Bartlett/Ghoshal 1987b: 48). Competition between technologies or product ideas is a manifestation of charter competition because corporate executives – not external market participants – judge which technology or product to continue and which to close down. Note that in his internal market model Birkinshaw would classify such a scenario as competition for a customer. Rivalry between R&D centers or production sites for new investments (and the associated responsibilities) would be an example for charter competition (Birkinshaw 2001b: 113, 119). In this research, charter competition is distinguished from customer competition in that it involves an **internal decision** about (customer-, market- or project-related) responsibilities.

Going back to the introductory case example, several subsidiaries are interested in participating in the tender. Headquarters can ask them to present how they would go about the acquisition and execution of the project and select the subsidiary with the most convincing proposal. Settled charter competition avoids customer competition because subsidiaries know their turf. Competition can also arise over the contribution to different project phases, such as the provision of basic or detail engineering services. Considering the scope of the projects, a top-down decision on the division of labor can be expected and subsidiaries need to position themselves accordingly. The negotiating power and prospect of a subsidiary will depend on its competitive advantage in terms of resources and competencies (Birkinshaw/Fry 1998: 57; Edwards/Kuruvilla 2005: 14-15). The less stable the business environment, the more charter competition can be expected (Birkinshaw/Lingblad 2005: 676). In the international arena dynamic factors include the emergence of new customers, a shift in local preferences or factor cost differentials and the gradual alignment of subsidiary capabilities. Being confronted with increasingly equivocal environments, many MNCs respond by providing their operating units with higher levels of decision-making autonomy. The challenges related to defining charter boundaries are thus becoming more critical (Birkinshaw/Lingblad 2005: 682). If managers are aware of alternative design options and their implications they will be more successful in identifying when overlapping charters may make sense (Birkinshaw/Lingblad 2005: 684).

To conclude this discussion of charter competition a few words should be given on its relevance for individuals and organizations. On an individual level one would typically not speak of a 'charter' but rather of the responsibilities or tasks an organization member is assigned by his or her superior. Such responsibilities may relate to markets, customers, products, projects, personnel – just to name a few. On an organizational level, the charter concept maintains some of its validity. What charters are for divisions or subsidiaries, 'domains' are for organizations. An **organizational domain** describes the set of activities that determine an organization's boundaries. It comprises the goods and services offered, the markets served, the functions performed and the geographies covered (Thompson 1967: 26-27; Thorelli 1986: 39).

Divisional charters thus form the building blocks of corporate domains (Galunic/Eisenhardt 1996: 256). One can also think of a domain as a set of claims regarding an organization's goals and the actions undertaken for their implementation (Levine/White 1961: 597). Sometimes these claims are very broad, delineating the turf the corporation occupies or the industry it belongs to (Galunic/Eisenhardt 1996: 256). It is important that any such claims are recognized and agreed to by the task environment. There has to be "domain consensus" (Thompson 1967: 29; Zwerling 1980: 352, 356). Domains can be challenged, defended and expanded (Brown 1969: 175; Zwerling 1980: 357). Competition for domains arises when economic or technological trends change the rules of the game or when firms with new business models enter the scene (Brown 1969: 176-177). Domains can also be shifted deliberately in response to other companies' innovations (Arrighi/Drangel 1986: 21). Domain competition shows overlaps with competition for "institutional legitimacy" (DiMaggio/Powell 1983: 150) and competition for "the right to serve the market" (see Mougeot/Naegelen 2005 for examples related to license auctions).

2.4.1.4 Customers

The third object foreign subsidiaries can compete for with one another are customers. One could also use the more general term 'business' to include projects, contracts, orders, etc., but eventually the goal is to serve the customer. To keep this classification applicable to a variety of different subsidiaries one should initially consider both **internal and external** customers. R&D and production units, for example, need to 'sell' their outputs to customers located "in the next stage of the value chain" (Birkinshaw 2001b: 113). Compared to charter competition these units do not contend their areas of responsibility but undertake parallel development or production work. Their technologies, products and services need to convince the internal customer, who decides upon the preferred solution (Birkinshaw 2001b: 113).

For foreign subsidiaries engaged in sales and marketing activities, however, the relevant customer competition manifests itself in an overlapping interest to serve certain external customers. This type of competition resembles what Birkinshaw calls "internal competition between business lines" in that the end customer decides who his preferred provider is (Birkinshaw 2001a: 24-25). Competition is not managed in the sense that headquarters determines who gets to serve which customers; rather, subsidiaries enter into **open competition** for customers in the market place (Phelps/Fuller 2000: 227; Birkinshaw 2001b: 119; Tsai 2002: 184 refers to such competition between units that offer similar products or services in the marketplace as "external market competition"). Subsidiaries may either want to position themselves in terms of a particular customer (or project) or strive to increase their relative market share (i.e. the percentage of the total available market that is serviced by the subsidiary). Such rivalry is mainly bound to downstream activities and may or may not occur with headquarters' knowledge. It is important to consider the international dimension here, since customer responsibilities are likely to be less clear-cut when subsidiaries are dispersed around the globe. One can think of the case that a company maintains two fairly autonomous subsidiaries in China and Japan, when suddenly an interesting business opportunity arises in Korea. Customer competition is the result of both subsidiaries wishing to exploit this opportunity by offering similar products or services to the same customers. In the introductory case example (see section 1.2) one would speak of customer competition if it were the German customer in Korea who took the final decision on which subsidiary he wanted to work with. Especially in a dynamic business environment where customers and subsidiaries are continuously evolving, MNC headquarters should recognize the possibility of intersubsidiary customer competition and decide how to act upon it.

Different practices can be expected in **consumer and industrial markets**. An industrial customer is typically served on an individual basis and could exploit the competitive dynamics by playing subsidiaries off against each other (see Birkinshaw et al. 2001: 236 on the downside potential of a country-by-country sales organization); or he could simply be irritated by being approached from multiple angles and question management's ability to define a clear strategic direction (Birkinshaw 2001a: 21; compare to the drawbacks discussed in section 3.2). Given these dysfunctional effects, headquarters is unlikely to tolerate or even support that multiple subsidiaries interact with a customer in open competition over a longer period of time. In order to ensure that only one face is shown to the customer, many industrial sales organizations have set up an international Key Account Management (KAM) system (for example Millman 1996; Lockau 2000; Arnold et al. 2001; Birkinshaw et al. 2001; Galbraith 2001; Wengler 2006; Belz/Zupancic 2007). Customer competition is thus only expected to appear as a temporary phenomenon, lasting until customer responsibilities are (re)defined.

In consumer markets it is more likely to find headquarters that encourage intersubsidiary customer competition for reasons previously discussed (improved quality and efficiency, etc.) (Luo 2005: 76). **Cannibalization**, or "the extent to which one product's customers are at the expense of other products offered by the same firm" (Mason/Milne 1994: 163), is a manifestation of such competition at the product market level (Rumelt 1974: 10; on cannibalization see, for example, Copulsky 1976;

Nault/Vandenbosch 1996; Sorenson 2000). The international perspective entails some particularities here, which are neglected in most of the existing literature. For example, competition does not only occur between units offering similar products or services but between units offering the *same* products or services in or from different locations (Luo 2005: 79). Frese (2005) speaks of interregional market interdependencies, which arise in the case of substitution competition, i.e. if two or more foreign subsidiaries offer a product that can similarly satisfy customer demand and customers are free to choose which subsidiary they wish to purchase from. Market interdependencies also occur if several foreign subsidiaries are involved in order processing and make agreements with the customer (Frese 2005: 502-503). In this case one would not necessarily speak of intersubsidiary competition, though.

While customer competition is the most obvious form of competition between firms, several conceptualizations of internal competition neglect this external dimension (Birkinshaw 2001b: 113, for example, refers to customers in the internal market; Rugman/Verbeke 2003: 134 speak of internal competition "for intermediate products, charters or capabilities"). Subsidiaries may not always be recognized as the *subjects* of such competition, but rather as the *channels* via which MNCs compete at the international or product market level (Luo 2007: 130). Finally, individuals in the corporate context may also experience customer- and market-related competition. It is most apt to speak of interpersonal competition for *business* (projects, contracts, orders, etc.) since only sales representatives will compete directly for customers. Two fellow engineers, for example, may compete to be awarded the design of a particular project. Compared to charter competition, which is internally oriented, a market interface is necessary for business competition to exist. Individuals are eager to secure business in order to obtain (or maintain) recognition, remuneration, status, etc.

2.4.2 Objects of Cooperation

Cooperation can be conceptualized as all types of collective efforts (Luo 2007: 130). Consequently, there are a variety of different objects through which subsidiaries, organizations and individuals can cooperate. It can be shown, though, that they fall into three broad categories: **resource sharing, knowledge sharing and a split of work**. It is the pursuit of a common goal that distinguishes cooperation from mere transactions, which occur along similar dimensions, namely capital, product and knowledge flows (Gupta/Govindarajan 1991: 770). Again the rationale for the chosen trichotomy is presented before a detailed review of each object is provided.

2.4.2.1 Choice of Categories

Compared to intrafirm competition, for which at least a few authors have offered a classification (Birkinshaw/Lingblad 2005: 675; Luo 2005: 75-76), cooperation has not been broken down as systematically. Instead, authors have illuminated individual aspects, or objects, of such cooperation quite thoroughly. Knowledge sharing has been of particular interest to IB scholars, although especially on an intraorganizational level few of them focus explicitly on horizontal relationships (among the exceptions are Zhao/Luo 2005 and Gnyawali et al. 2007).

A somewhat holistic attempt is made by Luo, according to whom subsidiaries cooperate in four areas: technological, operational, organizational and financial (Luo 2005: 73). The examples the author gives, however, illustrate that he is also primarily concerned with knowledge sharing (Luo 2005: 73-75). He frequently refers to "experience", "capabilities", and "routines" when describing the contents of the four categories and explicitly uses the terms "technological knowledge" and "managerial knowledge" (Luo 2005: 73-75). Resource sharing is most prominently captured in what Luo calls "operational cooperation" (Luo 2005: 74), comprising the shared usage of distribution channels and supply bases. Joint financial optimization is another example of resource sharing. Given its exceptional importance for intersubsidiary relationships, however, knowledge sharing should be treated as a distinct object of cooperation rather than one type of (intangible) resource. What Luo's categorization does not account for is the scenario that subsidiaries collaborate in a pooled or sequential manner to accomplish a certain task – or, more specifically, that subsidiaries split the work related to a specific project. Such cooperation goes beyond the sharing of resources or knowledge. The amount of interaction between subsidiaries that contribute to different phases or elements of a project will depend on the type of coordination. If a particular subsidiary or headquarters takes the lead in coordinating the division of labor, bilateral interaction between subsidiaries may be low. Nevertheless the effort is undoubtedly cooperative.

Cooperation, even more so than competition, ultimately takes place between individuals. When subsidiaries struggle to serve a certain market, their CEO's may or may not feel that they are competing directly with each other. When subsidiaries exchange knowledge about this market in order to beat an external competitor, this process is naturally bound to two (or more) individuals. Similarly, individuals are the users of resources and the providers of labor. The proposed objects of cooperation thus maintain their relevance on this fundamental level. Cooperation between organizations may need more formal arrangements, but also relates to resources, knowledge or the division of labor. Firms can cooperate by pooling resources through strategic alliances, leveraging knowledge through R&D consortia or making their contributions to the improvement of the local industry infrastructure (see Luo 2007: 130 for further examples of interorganizational cooperation). Their goal is to "generate relational rents through relation-specific assets, knowledge-sharing routines, complementary resource endowments, and 'effective governance'" (Dyer/Singh 1998: 676). With respect to the different objects of cooperation both the interpersonal and the interorganizational level will only be touched upon very briefly.

Finally, it should be noted that there are some clear parallels in the defined objects of cooperation and competition. First, resources in both cases are fairly tangible. Although competition for knowledge is not explicitly isolated, the focus is also on tangible resources such as finance, technology and personnel. Second, knowledge and responsibilities (charters) contribute an intangible element. Both have something to do with a (mental) capability or awareness. Third, the split of work and business (customers) constitute market-oriented categories. The question is who does what to satisfy the customer's demands. In analogy to Figure 3, Figure 4 integrates the subjects and objects of cooperation in a matrix. The individual fields and their relevance for the underlying research project are discussed below. Again the two most important categories are shaded in dark grey. Given its prominent position in IB literature as well as its importance for this research, cooperation through knowledge sharing is treated quite extensively.

Subjects of cooperation		Resource sharing	Knowledge sharing	Split of work
Two or more organizations		Interorganizational resource sharing	Interorganizational knowledge sharing	Interorganizational split of work
Two or more subsidiaries (units)		Intersubsidiary (interunit) resource sharing	Intersubsidiary (interunit) knowledge sharing	Intersubsidiary (interunit) split of work
Two or more (corporate) individuals		Interpersonal resource sharing	Interpersonal knowledge sharing	Interpersonal split of work

Objects of cooperation

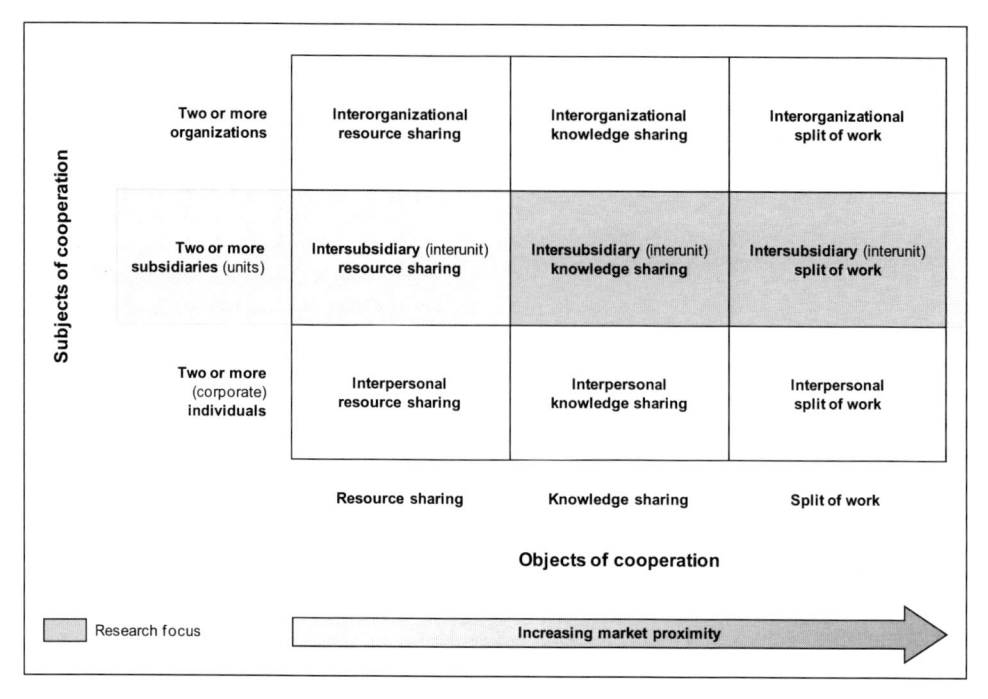

□ Research focus   ⟹ Increasing market proximity

Figure 4:   Types of Cooperation by Subjects and Objects

2.4.2.2 Resource Sharing

As was the case with competition for resources, the following discussion is not explicitly linked to the RBV. Nevertheless, it helps to anticipate some of the ideas addressed in subsection 3.3.2 to describe the scope of intersubsidiary resource sharing. A general definition of resources has already been provided in subsection 2.4.1.2. Proponents of the RBV consider firm resources as strengths that firms can use to conceive of and implement their strategies (for a discussion see Barney 1991: 101-102). These resources are not only heterogeneously distributed across firms but also within firms. In case of an MNC they may be located in different units and also in different countries (Ghoshal/Bartlett 1990: 610). It is this dispersed configuration of resources that constitutes the basis for **intraorganizational resource flows** (Schmid et al. 2002: 52). Exchanging resources between different locations not only validates the value of these resources, it also allows recombining them to create new potential value. Such voluntary and purposive resource deployment is said to be based on three conditions: the existence of an opportunity, the perception of its value-creating potential and the motivation of the parties involved (Moran/Ghoshal 1996: 41-42).

Innovation can be regarded as the connecting link between resource combination and value creation (Tsai/Ghoshal 1998: 468).

Since the focus of this research is on relationships between subsidiaries located at the same level of the value chain, economic exchange of resources is not considered as a content (or object) of cooperation (Easton/Araujo 1992: 63). At the same time, the concept of **exchange**, or sharing, is an important one because resources are not merely transferred from headquarters to subsidiaries but used cooperatively among peers. The **direction of resource flows** within the MNC has been given relatively little attention in IB literature. Although scholars have included resource flows between foreign subsidiaries in their investigations, they do not isolate them to arrive at separate conclusions for vertical and horizontal flows (Randøy/Li 1998: 81-82; Schmid et al. 2002: 67). There is a particular lack of research on intersubsidiary resource flows in German MNCs (Holtbrügge 2005: 565). Also, resource flows are not necessarily related to cooperation but investigated in a more neutral manner. What has been studied are the antecedents and managerial implications of resource sharing among strategic business units (SBUs) (Gupta/Govindarajan 1986). The first result – that synergistic benefits are greater for SBUs pursuing low-cost rather than differentiation strategies – is of little relevance for intersubsidiary relationships. The transferability of the other two results, however, may deserve further exploration: Incentive systems for general managers are most effective when taking into account the level of resource sharing, and resource sharing has a negative effect on managers' job satisfaction due to a loss of autonomy (Gupta/Govindarajan 1986: 696, 708).

Cooperation through resource sharing can either mean that one subsidiary actually shares its resources with another subsidiary or that the two of them exploit resources collectively. Such cooperation creates interdependencies between subsidiaries (Roth/Morrison 1992: 717), but remains largely uncompensated (Luo 2005: 74). The resources that are shared between subsidiaries are similar to those for which they may compete. The focus is on internal (or parent) resources, but cooperation can also extend to external resources such as the joint usage of a market database or a licensed technology. This conceptualization comes closest to what Luo refers to as "operational resources" (Luo 2005: 74). Besides global distribution channels and supply bases he names relationship building expertise, advertising skills and financing policies as examples (for a similar enumeration see Ghoshal/Bartlett 1990: 610).

Important for this research, however, is a clear **distinction between resources and knowledge** (see also Tsai 2000: 925), because the latter is particularly relevant to market-oriented cooperation between subsidiaries. The most frequently used resource categories are physical, financial and human. Organizational, technological and intangible resources represent other common categories. Knowledge is typically included as an intangible or informational resource, particularly in contributions dating from the 1990s onwards (for example, O'Donnell 2000: 528, 543; Schmid et al. 2002: 50; see Schiller 2000: 58 for an overview). Schmid et al. provide an example of this dichotomy by distinguishing between the material and immaterial content of intraorganizational resource flows. They contrast primarily tangible resources such as products, capital and people with primarily intangible resources such as information, trust and knowledge (Schmid et al. 2002: 50-51). Rather than considering knowledge as an economic resource, however, one could also conceive it as a *quality* possessed by people (Buckley/Carter 2000: 56) and treat it as a distinct object of cooperation. As illustrated in the next subsection, this corresponds to the approach followed in this research. It is the aforementioned quality that is essential to the acquisition and execution of large customized projects. Subsidiaries make use of and share a number of resources from the aforementioned categories but few are linked as directly to serving the customer. The boundaries between (mainly tangible) resources and knowledge may be blurred, for example, when certain databases are consulted, human resources pooled or technologies transferred.

This brief review of different types of resources illustrates that their scope is broad enough to include relevant items both for the cooperation between firms and individuals. While on an interorganizational level 'operational resources' will be the most desirable objects of cooperation, individuals may support each other through select physical or organizational resources. Their greatest contribution can be expected to result from the sharing of intangible resources. As noted above, knowledge sharing – which is handled as a distinct category in this research and discussed in the next subsection – is particularly bound to individuals.

2.4.2.3 Knowledge Sharing

Knowledge exchange is certainly the object of intersubsidiary cooperation (and competition) that has found the greatest consideration in IB literature.[19]

---

[19] The following discussion thus goes beyond the selected contents of Schmid/Maurer 2011: 70-72 and Schmid/Maurer 2008: 19-20.

Intersubsidiary knowledge ties have been defined as "direct collaborative relationships between two subsidiaries within a[n] MNC involving [the] creation, transfer, and exchange of valuable knowledge" (Gnyawali et al. 2007: 2). It is this ability to integrate, transfer and exploit knowledge more efficiently and effectively than markets that is often even considered one of the key reasons for MNCs to exist (Gupta/Govindarajan 2000: 473 with reference to several other advocates of internalization theory). The theoretical conceptualization of the **MNC as a "knowledge-sharing network"** (Foss/Pedersen 2000: 341 with reference to Kogut/Zander 1993) emphasizes that linkages exist both between headquarters and subsidiaries and between peer subunits. Whereas the headquarters-subsidiary relationship is typically coined by a unilateral transfer process, intersubsidiary knowledge sharing suggests frequent exchange and joint action (Zhao/Luo 2005: 73).[20] MNCs engage in cross-unit transfer and sharing of knowledge in search of synergy, efficiency and, consequently, competitive advantage (Kogut/Zander 1992: 384; Bartlett/Ghoshal 1998: 14, 137; Buckley/Carter 1999: 80). Knowledge sharing among subunits is expected to create scope economies (Ghoshal/Bartlett 1988: 366; Rugman/Verbeke 2003: 134).

Undoubtedly knowledge sharing is a particularly important dimension of intersubsidiary cooperation. Luo and Zhao underline the closeness of the two constructs by proposing the same determinants for knowledge sharing as Luo identifies for cooperation among peer subsidiaries, namely strategic interdependence, technological linkage, and entry mode (Luo 2005: 77-78; Zhao/Luo 2005: 76-79). But before taking a closer look at existing contributions on intra-MNC knowledge sharing (including antecedents, management processes and effects) and their insights for intersubsidiary cooperation, a brief definition and delineation of knowledge seems appropriate (for general overviews of knowledge classifications in management research see Bendt 2000: 15-16 and also Cerrato 2006: 270). As noted in the previous subsection, knowledge is often considered as a type of **intangible resource** (for example, O'Donnell 2000: 528, 543; Schmid et al. 2002: 50; see Schiller 2000: 58 for an overview). Others deliberately differentiate knowledge (or information) from resources such as goods, services, personnel and capital (for example, Meier 1997: 151; but also inconsistently O'Donnell 2000: 530). Both approaches seem justified and the choice between them should be made based on the specific research objectives. In this research, knowledge sharing is treated as a

---

[20] It should be noted that knowledge transfer from subsidiary to headquarters may also occur (for a discussion see Bendt 2000: 120-122).

separate object of intersubsidiary cooperation because its market-orientation significantly exceeds that of other resources.

Another important yet inconsistently handled distinction is that between information and knowledge. While some see the main difference in information being a *flow* and knowledge being a *stock*, others regard information as a simple form of knowledge (Buckley/Carter 2000: 57-58). For the purpose of this research the categorization of firm knowledge into **information and know-how** seems particularly useful (Kogut/Zander 1992: 386; Zander/Kogut 1995: 77; Gupta/Govindarajan 2000: 474). While information implies knowing *what* something means, know-how refers to knowing *how* to do something (Kogut/Zander 1992: 386). Dividing knowledge into facts and skills is a common approach, and it is mainly the terminology that varies. Some scholars prefer a distinction between **declarative and procedural** types of knowledge (Gupta/Govindarajan 2000: 491; Gupta/Becerra 2003: 24). Declarative knowledge is said to be "of explicit fact", comprising data and factual information. Procedural knowledge is more tacit and captures "how something occurs or is performed" (Zhao/Luo 2005: 74 with reference to Zack 1999: 46). Explicit knowledge can be articulated and put into print, whereas tacit knowledge tends to be context-bound and resides within individuals (Adenfelt/Lagerström 2006: 384). Relevant for this research are the marketing-related examples: declarative knowledge can exist in the form of a customer database, market analysis software or pricing calculation formula; procedural knowledge includes knowing how to reach target customers, increase market share or differentiate products and services (Zhao/Luo 2005: 74).

Other scholars define intracorporate knowledge flow as the transfer of strategically valuable **external market data and expertise** (Gupta/Govindarajan 1991: 773). External market data includes information about key customers, competitors or suppliers. Expertise can refer to input processes (e.g., procurement skills), throughput processes (e.g., engineering capabilities) or output processes (e.g., marketing know-how). It should be noted that intersubsidiary knowledge sharing does not include the transfer of internal administrative information such as financial or benchmarking data (Gupta/Govindarajan 1991: 773).

A more content-oriented approach is the categorization of knowledge by area of application. On a subsidiary level **technological and organizational knowledge** can be identified as the two main categories (Zhao/Luo 2005: 73-74). Sharing technological knowledge on process and product innovation will be particularly relevant for R&D and production units, while market-oriented units will benefit most from developing, sharing and exploiting managerial practices and experience (Luo

2005: 73-74). If organizational knowledge is about how to organize and manage offshore operations (Zhao/Luo 2005: 72), **operational knowledge** deserves separate treatment. Marketing-related examples for operational knowledge include relationship-building (or KAM) expertise and customer (or project) financing skills (Luo 2005: 74 with reference to Govindarajan/Gupta 2001). As far as the relevant knowledge is exchange-related, one could also refer to it as **market knowledge** (Buckley/Carter 2000: 58). At times, technology transfer is interpreted more broadly as know-how transfer. According to Zander and Kogut, "transferred knowledge can reside in design, production, installation, sales and distribution, operation and maintenance, or management" (Zander/Kogut 1995: 77). Similarly, Li and Ferreira distinguish between the transfer of product-, process-, and management-related technologies (Li/Ferreira 2003: 2 with reference to Grosse 1996).

Relevant to subsidiaries is furthermore the distinction between **complementary or substitutive** knowledge, depending on whether the transfer occurs along different stages in the value chain or between units engaged in very similar activities (Gupta/Govindarajan 2000: 491-492). Complementary knowledge can also come from different national markets – its key characteristic is that it provides additional value upon combination (Buckley/Carter 2002: 8, 32). This value-creating potential can be seen as of the reasons why the theory on intrafirm knowledge transfer is considered a particularly useful perspective for studying international interdependence within the MNC (O'Donnell 2000: 543). Knowledge is acquired through a process of learning, meaning either the transfer or **replication of existing knowledge** or the **creation of new knowledge** (Kogut/Zander 1992: 384; Buckley/Carter 2000: 56). Applied to the cooperative relationship between subsidiaries, this means that subsidiaries not only acquire knowledge from each other but also engage in the joint development of knowledge (Gnyawali et al. 2007: 2). The above categorizations help to identify and analyze different manifestations of intersubsidiary knowledge sharing. One could simply refer to knowledge that is important for business as *practical knowledge* (Machlup 1980: 33, 108); but especially when looking at a particular industry and function, it seems useful to have some kind of framework for specifying the type of knowledge that is needed to take informed decisions and actions (Buckley/Carter 2000: 56).

The question that is still open is which insights into intersubsidiary knowledge sharing have been provided in the **existing literature**. The first humbling result of a profound literature search is that the specific investigation of knowledge ties between (foreign) subsidiaries is still a rare find. The majority of both conceptual and empirical contributions on knowledge sharing in MNCs recognize that there are horizontal knowledge flows between subsidiaries, but they treat them in one go with the vertical flows that occur between headquarters and subsidiaries (see, for example, Bendt 2000, who provides a comprehensive analysis of knowledge transfer in MNCs). Given that valuable insights for intersubsidiary knowledge sharing may be embedded in these overarching contributions, some of the more prominent ones are briefly reviewed below. Expected insights relate to determinants, management and effects of intraorganizational knowledge sharing. Note that the selected contributions all include an international dimension and go beyond the mere investigation of the headquarters-subsidiary relationship. Important evaluation criteria are whether the authors explicitly address intersubsidiary knowledge sharing and how informative their findings are for this very phenomenon.

There are still very few empirical investigations on the **determinants (antecedents)** of intra-MNC knowledge transfers. Gupta and Becerra start out with developing a conceptual model that includes three key drivers of interunit knowledge transfer: **strategic context, management systems and policies, and interunit trust** (Gupta/Becerra 2003). The authors mainly speak of *units* but indicate that subsidiaries represent one such type of unit. Of interest for this research project is their proposition that the strategic context of interunit relationships is associated with the amount and type of knowledge that flows between these units. The authors suggest that knowledge transfer between autonomous sales subsidiaries is typically less critical than that between more interdependent production and sales units (Gupta/Becerra 2003: 27). When looking at sales subsidiaries contributing (or wishing to contribute) to a single, large-scale project, however, this statement may need to be put into perspective. In their field study, Gupta and Becerra focus on the role of trust in the relationship among global product centers and geographic marketing areas.

The relevance of the organizational context for knowledge sharing is also revealed in Ghoshal and Bartlett's investigation of the organizational attributes that facilitate the creation, adoption and diffusion of innovations by MNC subsidiaries (Ghoshal/Bartlett 1988). For the purpose of their study the authors define innovation as "any product, manufacturing process, or administrative system that [is] new for the subsidiary" (Ghoshal/Bartlett 1988: 387). Note that, as described above, product and process innovations can be considered to form part of some broader technological knowledge. In their multi-phased, multi-method study, Ghoshal and Bartlett find a positive impact of **normative integration and organizational communication** on a subsidiary's ability to contribute to the different innovation tasks. Relevant for this research is perhaps the notion that socialization and communication play an important role for promoting the exchange of (technological) knowledge between units. This insight is not particularly new to IB scholars (Ghoshal/Bartlett 1988: 384-385). Lagerström and Andersson, for example, have found that socialization of team members is the primary means of fostering the creation and sharing of knowledge in transnational teams (Lagerström/Andersson 2003). Less clear, and more novel, are the influences of local resources and autonomy, which appear to be strongly mediated by the first two variables. However, Ghoshal and Bartlett's study neither explicitly addresses intersubsidiary relationships nor does it include the exchange of knowledge other than technological.

Also related to innovations is Hansen's examination of the role of **strong versus weak ties** for efficient knowledge sharing between subunits (Hansen 1999). Unlike Ghoshal and Bartlett the author is interested in the (bilateral) relationship between subunits rather than their normative integration with headquarters as an influencing factor. His (empirical) findings include that weak interunit ties have benefits in searching for knowledge while strong interunit ties are needed for transferring complex knowledge (Hansen 1999: 82). Again, implications are relevant for product innovation but do not respond to the question of how and why subsidiaries maintain cooperative relationships through knowledge sharing. In search of influencing factors for interunit knowledge sharing, Minbaeva et al. are less interested in the context or foundation of interunit relationships than in the characteristics of the particular subsidiaries. The authors set out to explore the link between MNC subsidiary human resource management practices, absorptive capacity and knowledge transfer (Minbaeva et al. 2003). Their results indicate that both **ability and motivation** (what they conceptualize as absorptive capacity) are needed to facilitate knowledge transfer from other parts of the MNC. Insights into influencing factors that exceed subsidiary characteristics remain outstanding.

While most authors choose to focus on select facets of intra-MNC knowledge transfer, Gupta and Govindarajan provide a fairly **comprehensive approach** to the topic (Gupta/Govindarajan 2000). Building on communication theory they develop the following propositions on the determinants of knowledge transfers within MNCs: (1) Knowledge outflows from a subsidiary are positively associated with: (a) the value of the subsidiary's knowledge stock, (b) its motivational disposition to share knowledge and (c) the richness of transmission channels; (2) Knowledge inflows into a subsidiary are positively associated with (a) the richness of transmission channels, (b) its motivational disposition to acquire knowledge and (c) the capacity to absorb the incoming knowledge. In the empirical part of their study the authors find support for all of the above propositions except (1b). Note that Gupta and Govindarajan focus on individual (nodal) subsidiaries, not on dyadic or systemic relationships which are of interest for this research. They do, however, conduct separate investigations of horizontal knowledge flows among subsidiaries and vertical flows between headquarters and subsidiaries. Strategic orientation or context is not considered as a direct influencing factor; it might, however, impact a subsidiary's motivation to share or acquire knowledge.

Björkman et al. are also dedicated to the impact of organizational mechanisms on interunit knowledge flows in MNCs. Based on agency theory and socialization theory the authors develop a comprehensive model linking knowledge transfer from foreign subsidiaries to other parts of the MNC to a number of influencing factors (Björkman et al. 2004). Their findings show that interunit knowledge transfers can be facilitated through **corporate socialization** mechanisms and a **specification of subsidiary objectives**. Management compensation systems and expatriate managers, on the other hand, do not prove to be relevant to such transfers. The relevance for this research is limited since the receiving unit need not be a subsidiary but can be any part of the parent corporation (Björkman et al. 2004: 451).

There are only two contributions that explicitly focus on the **determinants of intersubsidiary knowledge sharing** in MNCs. Zhao and Luo examine antecedent factors that influence organizational knowledge sharing between emerging market subsidiaries and their peer subsidiaries in other countries (Zhao/Luo 2005). The authors consider knowledge sharing itself as an organizational variable that needs alignment with both strategic properties and infrastructural conditions. They suggest that the frequency with which a nodal subsidiary shares declarative and procedural organizational knowledge with its peers depends on the degree of their **strategic interdependence** and **technological linkage** as well as the chosen **entry mode**. Presumably, organizational knowledge sharing is further enhanced by the subsidiary's degree of **knowledge encapsulation** and the implementation of both an adequate **intranet system** and **incentive system**. In their quantitative empirical study Zhao and Luo find support for the vast majority of propositions. Merely the expected links between entry mode and procedural knowledge sharing as well as between incentive system and declarative knowledge sharing cannot be corroborated. Limitations of Zhao and Luo's work include its relatively narrow focus on organizational knowledge as the dependent variable and subsidiary-level attributes as independent variables. The authors themselves encourage future research on how parent-level characteristics or strategic attributes influence intersubsidiary knowledge sharing (Zhao/Luo 2005: 91). By exploring the link between a company's strategic orientation and intersubsidiary cooperation (of which knowledge sharing is a part), this research is in line with their appeal. It also meets the authors' suggestion to differentiate organizational knowledge based on functions (Zhao/Luo 2005: 92).

Gnyawali et al. offer the second, albeit conceptual, attempt to identify determinants of intersubsidiary knowledge sharing (Gnyawali et al. 2007). In search of factors influencing the formation of knowledge ties among MNC subsidiaries, the authors also focus on subsidiary-level characteristics. They suggest that a subsidiary's motivation to form knowledge ties with peers is driven by its **entrepreneurial orientation** (a proactive force) and its **perceived strategic vulnerability** (a reactive force). These propositions are complemented by a discussion of factors that are expected to influence partner selection and effectiveness of knowledge flow.

Besides exploring the antecedents of intra-MNC knowledge sharing, IB scholars are interested in understanding the mechanisms and processes of **knowledge management.** Since this is not the focus of this research, the related studies are only presented very briefly. Again only contributions with an international dimension are considered – although insights could possibly be derived from studies on topics such as the diffusion of innovations within organizations (Cool et al. 1997) or the barriers to internal knowledge transfer (Szulanski 1996).

Gupta and Govindarajan examine how the nature of **corporate control** varies across subsidiaries that differ in terms of the magnitude and directionality of knowledge flows (Gupta/Govindarajan 1991). The authors develop a framework, or role typology, that allows them to classify subsidiaries according to the extent of knowledge outflow to and knowledge inflow from the rest of the corporation. They do not, however, differentiate between horizontal and vertical flows. Harzing and Noorderhaven pick up on this issue in the concluding remarks to their empirical test and extension of Gupta and Govidarajan's typology. Future researchers are encouraged to look further into intersubsidiary flows and explore the differences to headquarters-subsidiary flows (Harzing/Noorderhaven 2006: 211-212).

Even narrower is a study by Buckley and Carter, in which the authors investigate the **process of knowledge management**, its impact on organizational structure and its spatial aspects (Buckley/Carter 2002). They forgo any insights on intersubsidiary knowledge flows, however, by deliberately limiting their study to the investigation of a single parent and affiliate (Buckley/Carter 2002: 31). The scope of a later study is slightly broader, but even in exploring how knowledge processes are governed in four MNCs no specific attention is given to the intersubsidiary level (Buckley/Carter 2003).

A stronger focus on MNC subsidiaries (or at least subunits) is included in studies on **centers of excellence** and **transnational teams**. Adenfelt and Lagerström have only recently evaluated the impact of these two different organizational mechanisms on knowledge development and knowledge sharing across subsidiaries in MNCs (Adenfelt/Lagerström 2006). The role of centers of excellence for managing firm knowledge has attracted much attention in IB research (for example, Moore/Birkinshaw 1998; Schmid et al. 1999; Holm/Pedersen 2000; Kutschker et al. 2002). Transnational teams, on the other hand, have found much less consideration but seem to be a similarly relevant means of leveraging knowledge and facilitating horizontal cooperation in MNCs (Lagerström/Andersson 2003; Schweiger et al. 2003).

Finally, some investigations into the **effects** of intra-MNC knowledge sharing have been undertaken. The question of how important such knowledge flows are for subsidiary (and thus MNC) **performance** is a particularly challenging one. Mahnke et al. empirically examine the effects of knowledge management tools upon the subsidiary's absorptive capacity, knowledge inflows and business performance (Mahnke et al. 2005). Intra-MNC knowledge flows are further found to enhance subsidiary **bargaining power** both in relations with headquarters and peer subsidiaries (Mudambi/Navarra 2004). A completely different but no-less-interesting question is why some subsidiaries are isolated from the knowledge transfer activities within the MNC (Monteiro et al. 2008).

In search of contributions that provide insights into intersubsidiary knowledge sharing one last topic is worth a brief review: **interunit communication**. Communication among MNC subunits is seen as a necessary condition for sharing complex and often tacit knowledge (Barner-Rasmussen/Björkman 2005: 29 with reference to Ghoshal et al. 1994 and Gupta/Govindarajan 2000). Others describe it as a key source of the MNC's ability to create, adopt and diffuse knowledge (Ghoshal/Bartlett 1988: 365-366). As such it may provide a supporting mechanism for an MNC's move towards a less-hierarchical organization structure (Marschan 1996: 26). Marschan, who has looked into the subject quite intensively, defines interunit communication as "the collective and interactive process of exchanging and interpreting information between units belonging to the same integrated network of the MNC" (Marschan 1996: 5, 25). In the broadest sense the concept comprises both **formal and informal** communication that takes place across national and organizational boundaries. Its scope should be specified according to the respective research questions, though. Marschan distinguishes between different **purposes** of interunit communication, i.e. socialization, coordination and control – acknowledging that the latter tends to be more vertical in nature (Marschan 1996: 28). Sharing knowledge through communication is relevant on different levels within the organization; it concerns top and middle management as well as operating staff (Marschan 1996: 31).

In general it can be stated that the opportunity to communicate enhances cooperative behavior (Van Lange/De Dreu 2003: 399). The **intensity** of interunit communication in MNCs has been linked to subsidiary managers' participation in corporate training programs, their fluency in the language in which the interunit communication takes place and, to some extent, to the use of expatriate managers (Barner-Rasmussen/Björkman 2005). Ghoshal et al. investigate some of the **organizational factors** (formal structure and informal relationships) that influence interunit communication in MNCs (Ghoshal et al. 1994). A key result of their case-study-based research is that interpersonal relationships developed through lateral networking mechanisms have a significant positive effect on the frequency of both headquarters-subsidiary and intersubsidiary communication. Interestingly, subsidiary autonomy is found to have almost no effect on either type of communication. The authors emphasize that they clearly distinguish between vertical and horizontal linkages (Ghoshal et al. 1994: 99). The costs of interunit communication are reduced by a common understanding between the parties (Buckley/Carter 2000: 61).

The above review has shown that intersubsidiary knowledge sharing is indeed a topic of interest to IB scholars, but that studies focusing explicitly on these horizontal linkages are still very limited in number. Buckley and Carter develop some ideas related to big-ticket bidding that allow closing the loop between knowledge sharing and cooperative intersubsidiary relationships in plant engineering. According to the authors, big-ticket bidding is a complex process which draws on the specialized skills of geographically dispersed units (Buckley/Carter 2000: 67-68). The combination of knowledge occurs on a customer-specific basis. When dealing with high-value projects for international customers the ideal organization structure may vary on a case-by-case basis (Buckley/Carter 2000: 68). For the customer it is important that all parts of the "virtual team" work towards the same goal, i.e. meeting his or her requirements (Buckley/Carter 2000: 69). This is ultimately done by communicating and sharing knowledge. For sales and marketing units this knowledge comprises information on market developments, experiences with previous bids or a sense of customer preferences. The challenge is to strike a balance between the increased division of specialized labor and the combination of expertise (Buckley/Carter 2000: 69).

As an object of cooperation, knowledge sharing is equally relevant on an interorganizational level and on an individual level. Both perspectives have found extensive consideration in literature, and discussing them would go far beyond the scope of this research (see, for example, Bartlett et al. 2004: 556-569 and Hamel et al. 1989 on a discussion of competitive collaboration through strategic alliances). It should be noted, though, that ultimately knowledge is carried by individuals. A key question is how these individuals can be motivated to share their knowledge. Foss and Pedersen refer to this issue as the "micro-foundations of knowledge sharing within and between MNC units" (Foss/Pedersen 2000: 343).

2.4.2.4 Split of Work

Finally, subsidiaries can cooperate by carrying out distinct functions or dividing up work packages across countries. It is the division of labor that both results in and derives from knowledge specialization (Buckley/Carter 2000: 58). Bringing together complementary knowledge holds the chance of enhancing profits and growth (Buckley/Carter 2000: 59). There are different ways of bringing together knowledge, though. Subsidiaries can either transfer knowledge back and forth, hence merging and enriching their respective knowledge stocks; or they can contribute knowledge to a venture without actually giving any of it away. A subsidiary's knowledge base can remain unchanged if it merely agrees to assume responsibility for certain tasks. Sharing knowledge and splitting work are thus treated as two distinct objects of cooperation.

The **international division of labor** within an MNC is a topic that has mainly been addressed by the global value chain literature (for example, Porter 1986a; b; Arndt/Kierzkowski 2001; Kaplinsky 2004; Gereffi et al. 2005).[21] The majority of studies, however, take a rather holistic perspective, investigating configurational issues such as concentration (centralization) versus dispersion (decentralization) (see Holtbrügge 2005: 565-566 for a compilation of research on the cross-border configuration of value activities and the related need for coordination; further see Schmid/Grosche 2009 for a comprehensive review of literature addressing the concepts of configuration and coordination in combination). Whereas **configuration** refers to the optimal geographical dispersion of value chain activities, **coordination** describes their synchronization and integration into the company's network (see

---

[21] In this research a 'split of work' between subsidiaries is intentionally referred to in order to dissociate the term (or concept) from the frequently addressed international division of labor between countries or regions.

Schmid/Grosche 2009: 4, 11 for summarized definitions). The demand for coordination results from the chosen split of work and concerns organization members who carry out activities, assume tasks and take the related decisions. A variety of different elements and mechanisms of coordination have been identified (see the tables in Schmid/Grosche 2009: 12, 15 for overviews) and it is important to put them in relation to intersubsidiary relationships. This brief excursus is aimed at explaining why configuration and coordination do not receive more attention in this research.

Intersubsidiary cooperation and competition could possibly be regarded as aspects of structural, person-oriented or, following Martinez/Jarillo 1989, informal coordination mechanisms. The latter explicitly include lateral or cross-divisional relationships but neglect the competitive aspect altogether. Therefore, intersubsidiary relationships are preferably treated as a **distinct phenomenon**. The focus of this research lies on actors (i.e. subsidiaries) and their ties, not on the coordination of dispersed activities or tasks. With respect to configuration and coordination of value chain activities it was exactly this subsidiary perspective which has been criticized for being too narrow, i.e. for not adequately reflecting the company-wide degree of (de)centralization of value chain activities (Schmid/Grosche 2009: 2-3, 40-41). To a certain extent this research corresponds to the call for separate and more detailed investigation of (functional) activities, which resulted from the recognition that an overarching configuration-coordination profile does not exist (Schmid/Grosche 2009: 44, 48-49). However, the goal of this research is to analyze and explain how and why MNC subsidiaries interrelate. The functional focus facilitates access to an underresearched phenomenon but does not constitute an end in itself. Similarly, the configurational (or activity-based) approach reflected in the project marketing models (compare to section 4.3) is merely intended to support the cross-company investigation of intersubsidiary relationships. Relevant to this research is the idea of optimizing not only each subsidiary's contribution to the MNC's objectives but also the interplay between these subsidiaries. Certain interfaces exist between the concepts of configuration/coordination and intersubsidiary relationships, but as argued above there are good reasons for treating them distinctly.

How and why work packages are split among international locations and subsequently joined back together is an issue also dealt with by literature on **offshoring**. A review of this body of literature, however, has shown that the relationships between two or more (captive) offshore facilities have hardly been explored. With respect to the research setting the majority of studies on the "spatial component of intra-firm chains" has been conducted in manufacturing companies (see Edwards/Kuruvilla 2005: 14 for an overview of contributions from various industries). Service offshoring is a topic that has only recently found its way onto the IB research agenda (see Schmid/Daub 2005: 3-4 for a review of related studies). In the marketing- and service-oriented plant engineering industry, subsidiaries may contribute to different phases or components of a project. The choice of international locations is based on a variety of factors, including access to cheap or skilled labor, customers, technology or raw materials (Edwards/Kuruvilla 2005: 14). MNCs stratify their production or service provision process based on these locational factors. One particularity of the project business is that responsibilities can be re-assigned on a case-by-case basis to best respond to customer demands.

In the assessment of intersubsidiary relationships, 'splitting work' does not only mean that subsidiaries carry out different tasks of a project or process, but that they somehow interact or coordinate their activities on a bilateral (or multilateral) basis. The split of work may be managed by headquarters, but as far as intersubsidiary relationships are concerned subsidiaries are only regarded to 'cooperate' if they are aware that they contribute to a common goal. The prevailing (inter)dependence should thus be recognized by the subsidiaries (Luo 2005: 72 with reference to Lado et al. 1997). It should be noted that segmenting the production – or project marketing – process across subsidiaries can "raise issues of power and dependence" (Edwards/Kuruvilla 2005: 14), possibly leading to charter competition as described in subsection 2.4.1.3.

As was the case with knowledge sharing, organizations and individuals can similarly cooperate by splitting work, thus contributing to a successful product, process or project outcome with their particular expertise.

2.5 Classification Scheme for Intersubsidiary Relationships[22]

In the previous subsections the main objects of competition and cooperation between foreign subsidiaries were introduced and discussed. Just like individuals and organizations, subsidiaries may compete for resources, charters and customers, and cooperate through resource sharing, knowledge sharing and a split of work. A comprehensive classification scheme for intersubsidiary relationships results from combining these contents (or objects) of competition and cooperation with their

---

[22] The first paragraph of this section and Figure 5 largely correspond to Schmid/Maurer 2011: 73-74 and Schmid/Maurer 2008: 22-23 (Chapter 6).

potential origin. As described in section 2.3, intersubsidiary relationships can either be led by headquarters or by the nodal subsidiaries. Competition for (external) customers is assumed to constitute the only exception to this dichotomy due to its detrimental effects for the MNC as a whole. The resulting classification scheme for intersubsidiary relationships is depicted in Figure 5. For the sake of clarity, the illustration is limited to cooperation and competition as the two fundamental types of relationship. While independence implies that neither competition nor cooperation between foreign subsidiaries exists, coopetition can be conceptualized as an arbitrary combination of both. It is worth noting that the sequence of the classification scheme (types – origin – contents) is deliberately chosen. For example, it seems more likely that headquarters-led competition involves several different objects than that competition for charters is both headquarters- and subsidiary-led.[23]

Figure 5 reveals that not all objects of competition and cooperation are of equal relevance for this research project. Given that the focus of the research is on customer-related subsidiary activities, rivalry for resources such as parent-company investments, human resources or working capital is of minor interest. Certainly these resources are a necessary operational basis for any subsidiary, but capital intensity decreases when moving from upstream to downstream activities. This may be an explanation for the fact that internal competition between geographically dispersed sales and marketing units has found much less consideration in academic literature than the competitive dynamics between R&D or production locations have. This research is deliberately directed towards the **more market-oriented forms of intersubsidiary competition**, namely competition for charters and customers. If foreign subsidiaries dedicated to winning and executing large-scale industrial projects wanted to gain a competitive advantage over their peers, they would typically try to do so by expanding their customer base and/or project competence.

Similarly, cooperation through the sharing of physical, financial or human resources is of limited relevance for this research. Knowledge is deliberately treated as a separate category because it is information and know-how that is essential when subsidiaries are interested in jointly winning and serving a customer. As mentioned above, there is not always a clear parting line between, say, the exchange of knowledge and the exchange of people carrying this knowledge. Nevertheless, the focus of this research is on foreign subsidiaries seeking competitive advantage by

---

[23] The rationale behind this is that the dominance of headquarters-led versus subsidiary-led relationships is likely to depend on the overall role of each unit, which again is influenced by the strategy and/or management philosophy of the corporation as a whole (see, for example, Perlmutter 1969a; Bartlett/Ghoshal 1998 and the discussion in section 5.1).

sharing customer- and project-related knowledge with their peers or dividing up work packages according to their areas of expertise. Resource flows can be assumed to play a subordinate role in shaping the relationship between foreign subsidiaries engaged in project marketing activities.

To sum up, in the specific research context, competition refers to **overlapping interests in charters and customers**, while cooperation manifests itself in the **exchange of knowledge and the split of work**. Competition for strategic resources as well as the sharing of these is of minor importance to this research project. The developed framework is helpful for structuring the ideas and findings from previous research, for guiding future research and for revealing strategic options for managing intersubsidiary relationships.

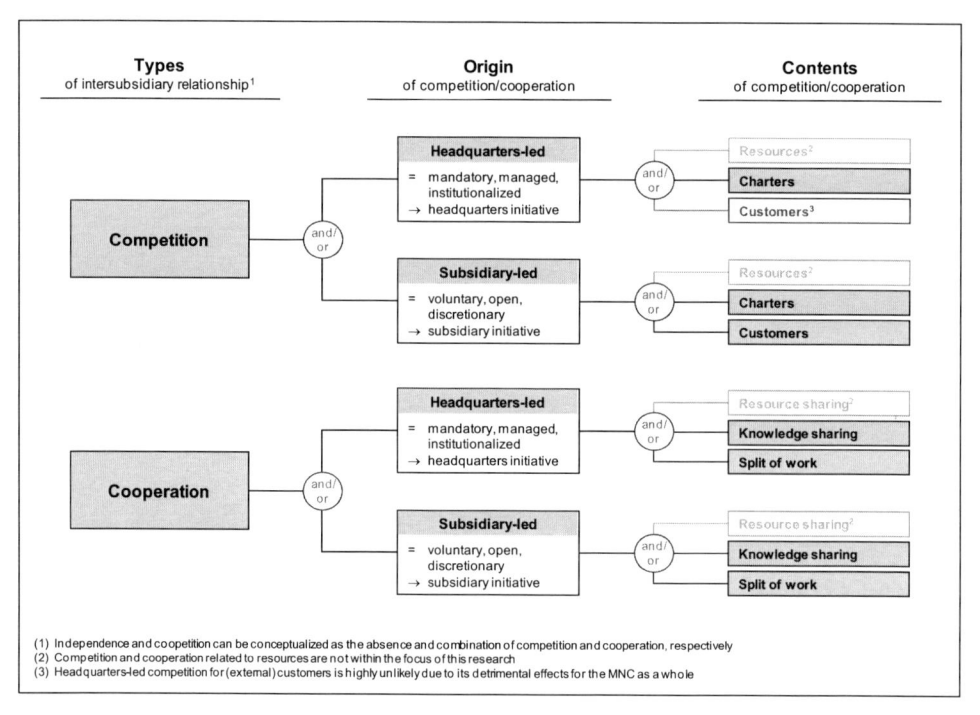

Figure 5: Classification Scheme for Intersubsidiary Relationships[24]

---

[24] The respective figure in Schmid/Maurer 2008: 23 contains a wording mistake with regard to the origin of relationships. Figure 5 should serve as the future point of reference.

3 Explaining Intersubsidiary Relationships

A central goal of this research is to explain why companies operating in the same industry and pursuing very similar business models differ in terms of competition and cooperation between their subsidiaries. The classification scheme developed in the previous chapter allows a profound description of the prevailing intersubsidiary relationship. It does not reveal why, or when, a competitive relationship is preferred over a cooperative one, or vice versa. Since competition and cooperation between subsidiaries imply many opportunities but also some risks, it is essential for managers to understand these tradeoffs. They further need to develop an awareness of the settings in which certain intersubsidiary relationships are likely to evolve. The search for a theory that provides insights into these questions is a difficult one. As stated in subsection 2.2.3, competition and cooperation have long been regarded as two, fairly incompatible, ends of the same continuum. Although a growing body of literature on coopetition has evolved, the phenomenon of internal coopetition has been largely overlooked (Walley 2007: 25). As will be shown, theories that may be insightful for explaining competition and/or cooperation between firms are not easily transferable to an intraorganizational level. Accordingly, the suggestions found in the existing literature are rare. While Luo (2005) currently offers the most comprehensive conceptual approach to intersubsidiary coopetition, he completely refrains from adopting, or even discussing, any substantial theories.

The chapter is structured as follows: Section 3.1 provides the rationale for how relevant theoretical perspectives were selected and how they are subsequently discussed. In section 3.2 the benefits and drawbacks of intersubsidiary competition and cooperation are weighed up against each other. In section 3.3 transaction cost economics, the resource-based view and network approaches are discussed as the main theoretical perspectives. Section 3.4 focuses on the contingency approach as the most promising framework for this research. Following the line of argument, some suggested influencing factors of intersubsidiary relationships are reviewed in section 3.5. Section 3.6 closes the chapter by providing a summary and reflecting upon implications.

3.1 Approach to Theory Selection and Discussion

Given the objective of explaining intersubsidiary relationships, the question is how to identify the most suitable and insightful theoretical perspectives. A good starting point can be found in the **analysis of the benefits and drawbacks** of (intersubsidiary) competition and cooperation. By investigating the perceived positive (and negative) effects of these relationships, conclusions can be drawn regarding the reasons or motivations for which they are entered – thus targeting the core of the interaction phenomena. The goal is not to provide a comprehensive overview of all benefits and drawbacks, but rather to present a sufficient number of arguments to support the relevance – or inherence – of certain theoretical perspectives. These arguments are deliberately kept high level, i.e. differentiating between types of relationship, but not breaking them down further into their origin and contents.

From this analysis, **transaction cost economics and the resource-based view** emerge as the two main lines of reasoning. They build upon efficiency and effectiveness arguments, which are similarly relevant to intersubsidiary competition and cooperation. Although both theoretical approaches can shed some light on the phenomenon of interest, it becomes clear that they are unable to fully explain why companies differ in terms of the prevailing intersubsidiary relationships. Interunit linkages are further anchored in **MNC network approaches**, which combine the objectives of efficient governance and resource sharing. The latter, however, also fall short of taking a differentiated approach to the nature of these linkages. Building upon suggestions in the existing literature, a **contingency approach** is ultimately chosen as the overall research framework.

Before moving on to the review, it should be noted that the indicated theoretical perspectives will be handled somewhat differently. For transaction cost economics and the resource-based view, the goal is to detect and extract their contribution to explaining intersubsidiary relationships. Upon clarification of key terms and concepts, the focus is on evaluating relevant areas of application and the resulting implications for intersubsidiary relationships. The structure for network approaches is identical but shorter, given that (1) they cannot be considered a substantial theory and (2) they allow a focused review of MNC network models (compare to subsection 3.3.3). What follows is a condensed discussion of complementary theoretical perspectives.

The review of the contingency approach takes a slightly different shape. It is chosen as the most promising and justified approach for this research, not least because other scholars have already suggested contingency factors for intersubsidiary competition and/or cooperation. Given this decision, the goal is to demonstrate an awareness of its opportunities and limitations in a more discourse-like manner. The same approach is neither necessary nor desired for transaction cost economics, the resource-based view or network approaches because they are already dismissed based on their content and applicability. The reader is thought to benefit from a brief introduction to the evolution and basic concepts of the contingency approach as well as a critical review of its methods and contents. Given that its potential areas of application are very broad, the contingency approach is specifically evaluated regarding its relevance for the IB field and for this research project. The influencing factors extracted from existing studies in section 3.5 can be considered part of the relevant areas of application. They are intentionally presented more prominently in a separate section as preparation, or basis, for the propositions.

3.2 Benefits and Drawbacks of Intersubsidiary Relationships

Although scholars from various fields have touched upon the benefits and drawbacks of competition and cooperation, a systematic overview of such considerations does not seem to exist. Again, many of the arguments developed in an interorganizational or interpersonal context can be reasonably applied to the intraorganizational level. Taking a differentiated stance on intersubsidiary competition and cooperation is particularly important for corporate managers. From a headquarters perspective the goal is to maximize joint, not individual outcomes and to achieve what is best for the organization as a whole (Van Lange/De Dreu 2003: 411). Headquarters are interested in forging intersubsidiary relationships that are aligned with MNC strategy – just as they look to prevent subsidiary initiatives that diverge from this strategy (Cerrato 2006: 261). Rather than exerting hierarchical control, headquarters can take on the role of governing interdependencies (Cerrato 2006: 261). Subsidiaries will also have their motives for competing and/or cooperating with their peers, but are typically not in the position to define overarching structures and processes. The advantages and disadvantages brought forward are relevant at both levels.

As reflected in Figure 6, the benefits of intersubsidiary competition and cooperation can broadly be grouped into those increasing **efficiency** and those enhancing **effectiveness**. It needs to be acknowledged, though, that the allocation of criteria to these two categories is neither mutually exclusive nor collectively exhaustive. Innovation, for example, can be a means of promoting both efficiency and effectiveness, while gaining prestige may possibly have no effect on either of them. Most arguments, however, are attributable to the dichotomy – oftentimes because the authors have explicitly done so themselves. In the remaining cases the most plausible allocation has been chosen.

Despite the authors' proper references it is striking that the terms efficiency and effectiveness are hardly ever defined. Davis and Pett offer some clarification here. They characterize efficiency and effectiveness as two aspects of firm performance. Whereas efficiency marks "the amount of output obtained from a given input", effectiveness captures "the resource-getting ability of an organization" (Davis/Pett 2002: 87). According to the authors, efficiency is related to the internal functioning of an organization and is typically represented by some input/output ratio (Davis/Pett 2002: 88 with reference to Chamberlain 1968). Effectiveness is represented by the firm's ability to relate to its environment, particularly with regards to the acquisition of scarce resources (Davis/Pett 2002: 88 with reference to Katz 1978). Similarly, Plinke describes efficiency as an *internal* performance measure specifying the relation between output and input, and effectiveness as an *external* performance measure indicating the extent to which a company meets customer expectations (Plinke 2000: 86).

An important modification is necessary when taking this dichotomy to a subsidiary level: On a firm level, resources are procured from the outside. On a subsidiary level, however, resources may also come from other parts of the organization. For the benefits of intersubsidiary competition and cooperation this means that there are some benefits related to the reduction of (relative) costs and others related to a resource utilization that better satisfies customer demands. These benefits may occur both on a subsidiary and on a firm level. From the above argumentation it becomes clear that a mere distinction between cost reduction and revenue enhancement would fall short of capturing the aspired benefits. While efficiency-related arguments dominate for competition, effectiveness-related arguments outweigh for cooperation. Although, as noted above, the attribution of arguments is not always clear-cut, this observation supports the intended identification of relevant theoretical lenses.

Being the most intuitive and straightforward, the **benefits of intersubsidiary cooperation** are discussed first. The central argument is that cooperation grants access to scarce and complementary resources (most prominently Bengtsson/Kock 2000: 424; see Schmid 2005: 243 on reasons for interaction suggested by social exchange theory). Bengtsson and Kock's interorganizational findings can be applied to the relationship between subsidiaries. Cooperation enhances **effectiveness** by allowing subsidiaries to gain market knowledge, reputation and other important resources. Goal achievement is facilitated by pooling competencies (Bengtsson/Kock 2000: 424). Just like cooperating firms, subsidiaries can be expected to achieve progress by jointly developing and utilizing knowledge, increasing product volume and quality, and expanding markets (Lado et al. 1997: 122-123). More specifically, cooperation among subsidiaries is useful to achieve greater transparency on prices, quality and customer support (Ghoshal/Bartlett 1990: 617). Social exchange theory further suggests that cooperating subsidiaries could strive for prestige (Schmid 2005: 243), possibly expressed in parent-company recognition.

On the other hand, cooperation may increase **efficiency**. By working together, subsidiaries – like firms – can gain time and share costs (Bengtsson/Kock 2000: 424). Internal cooperation may reduce risks and transaction costs that result from having to procure resources from the outside (Gupta/Becerra 2003: 25; Zhao/Luo 2005: 74). Additional gains can be realized through specialization and the division of labor (Weise 1997: 60) – provided that specialization does not create subunits with diverging goals that eventually become more important than the goals of the overall organization (Robbins 1990: 315). Overall, cooperation can be said to enhance success. The respective evidence seems to be strong and consistent across a variety of methodologies and markets (Griffin/Hauser 1996: 193).

There are few **drawbacks of intersubsidiary cooperation** since subsidiaries' effort to work together is inherently positive. A longer-term reciprocal commitment may possibly lead to a certain strategic inflexibility and loss of variety (Lado et al. 1997: 122). Conformity or "group think" may prevent fruitful initiatives or innovations (Wimmer/Neuberger 1982: 194). It would be unfavorable if subsidiaries relied too heavily on each other, tried to free-ride their peers' competencies or became inert. More importantly, however, cooperation involves organizing costs, which need to be offset against its benefits (Hennart 1993b: 532; 1993a: 159; 2001: 144).

The potential drawbacks of intersubsidiary cooperation can be converted into **benefits of intersubsidiary competition**. Intraorganizational competition in general is somewhat counterintuitive because hierarchy (or the MNC) as a governance structure is typically chosen to pursue a common purpose and realize economies of scope (Hill et al. 1992: 501; Rugman/Verbeke 2003: 131, 133). The duplication of activities seems to contradict the traditional logic of resource allocation in organizations (Birkinshaw/Lingblad 2005: 674). Nevertheless, the basic advantages of competition can be transferred from an interorganizational to an intraorganizational setting. Lado et al. summarize how competition has been regarded to generate

efficiency in three fundamental ways: by facilitating the optimal allocation of resources, by promoting innovation and entrepreneurship, and by reducing transaction costs (Lado et al. 1997: 110).

Competition between business units (or subsidiaries) similarly implies the quest for efficient internal governance (Hill et al. 1992: 501; Birkinshaw 2001b: 119; Cerrato 2006: 264). Subsidiaries can, however, take on (or be assigned) a variety of different roles and internal competition need not occur. If, for example, one subsidiary is responsible for product development, one for production and three for distinct sales areas, there will be little reason for them to compete. If, however, multiple subsidiaries engage in product development, the dynamics can be quite different. Subsidiaries may then be comparable to individual firms that are forced to develop their products and carry out their activities in the most efficient way (Bengtsson/Kock 2000: 424). In industrial networks competition creates a market-like rationalization pressure (Klaus 2002: 23) and provides an impetus for innovation and flexibility (Staber 2000: 76 with reference to You/Wilkinson 1994). Similarly, subsidiary managers have an incentive to focus on "projects that can pass market-like tests of feasibility, market potential, profitability etc." (Rugman/Verbeke 2003: 134). Within the MNC, flexibility, or "the ability to respond to changes in the competitive environment and re-examine strategic decisions", results from the existence of multiple choices for the production of goods or services (Cerrato 2006: 264 with reference to Aaker/Mascarenhas 1984 and Young-Ybarra/Wiersema 1999). Competition is typically introduced when finding the very best solution is key (Fengler 1996: 114).

But competition does not only enhance efficiency. Internal benchmarking can be used to identify those subsidiaries that are leading in **effectiveness** (Birkinshaw/Hood 1998a: 8). By stimulating innovation, competition can lead to knowledge and growth (Lado et al. 1997: 122) as well as capability enhancement (Birkinshaw 2001b: 87). Competition between units can result in functional or dysfunctional conflict, i.e. "behavior by organization members which is extended in opposition to other members" and brought about by the incompatibility of goals and actions (Thompson 1960: 389; Smith 1966: 511).[25] Functional conflict is said to have a positive impact on organizational effectiveness by stimulating change (Robbins 1990: 414, 425). Competition also drives companies (and units) to improve their business by undertaking measures that are not always demanded by customers

---

[25] For a discussion of the relationship between competition and conflict see Grunwald 1982: 62-71; for structural sources of conflict see Robbins 1990: 418-425, for interdepartmental conflict see Walton/Dutton 1969; Walton et al. 1969.

(Bengtsson/Kock 1999: 188). Such actions, however, require the availability of excess personnel (Fengler 1996: 114) – or, more broadly speaking, a certain level of organizational slack (Bourgeois III 1981: 30).[26]

One of the other **drawbacks of intersubsidiary competition** is certainly that its management can involve significant transaction costs. Internal competition for roles and responsibilities has been described as 'charter competition' (see subsection 2.4.1.3). Birkinshaw refers to a case where headquarters decided against issuing an internal RfP to subsidiaries in order to save time and effort (Birkinshaw 2001b: 133). The costs of reviewing and evaluating bids in such formal processes can be prohibitive (Birkinshaw/Hood 2001: 135). Also, headquarters may need to relocate employees from units that lose charters (Birkinshaw 2001b: 119). Additional costs are incurred by the duplication of effort (Bartlett/Ghoshal 1988: 67; Phelps/Fuller 2000: 227; Birkinshaw/Lingblad 2005: 678) and the resulting waste of resources, destruction of team work and cannibalization (Eisenhardt/Galunic 2000: 96). Maintaining two or more value-adding activities in parallel is expensive, although costs may be compensated by the benefits of shorter lead times and the opportunity to try out different approaches (Birkinshaw 2001b: 118).

Cannibalization costs can be offset by enhanced market coverage and economies of scope (Birkinshaw/Lingblad 2005: 678). However, competing units are prone to not acting in unison when facing the customer, thus running the risk of being played off against each other (see Birkinshaw et al. 2001: 236 on the downside potential of a country-by-country sales organization). Consequently critics associate internal competition with a lack of strategic direction (Birkinshaw 2001a: 21; Birkinshaw/ Lingblad 2005: 682), possibly resulting in a loss of reputation. Finally, the pressure created by competition may entail dysfunctional consequences on an individual level such as lower productivity and achievement, more negative relationships and poorer psychological health (see Kohn 1986 for an extensive "case against competition"). Competition leaves room for subsidiary opportunism, which can jeopardize the parent company's objectives for the MNC as a whole (see Birkinshaw/Fry 1998: 59 for an example).

---

[26] For additional references to the positive sides of intrafirm competition see Nadler/Tushman 1999: 52; Eisenhardt/Galunic 2000: 96; Sorenson 2000: 580; Kalnins 2004: 119.

Finally, it should be noted that headquarters and/or subsidiaries may want to combine the best of both worlds in fostering **coopetition**. Simultaneous cooperation and competition is also referred to as "syncretic rent-seeking behavior", which "emphasizes the positive-sum, efficiency-enhancing effects of competition and cooperation" (Lado et al. 1997: 123). Coopetition can stimulate greater knowledge sharing, technological progress, market expansion and resource utilization than is achieved when each strategy is pursued separately" (Lado et al. 1997: 122; Bengtsson/Kock 2000: 424). Nevertheless, there may also be arguments for maintaining subsidiary independence, especially when the drawbacks of competition and cooperation are overemphasized.

Type of Relationship	Implied Benefits	Possible Drawbacks
Cooperation	**Overall** • Access to scarce or complementary resources (Bengtsson/Kock 2000: 424; Luo 2005: 73-74; Schmid 2005: 243) *** Effectiveness ↑** • Gain competence, market knowledge, reputation and other important resources; pool competencies (Bengtsson/Kock 2000: 424) • Achieve progress by jointly developing and utilizing knowledge, increasing product volume and quality, expanding markets (Lado et al. 1997: 122-123) • Reach greater transparency on prices, quality and customer support (Ghoshal/Bartlett 1990: 617) • Enhance prestige (Schmid 2005: 243) **Efficiency ↑** • Gain time, share costs; use company resources in the most efficient way (Bengtsson/Kock 2000: 424) • Reduce risks and transaction costs that result from external resource procurement (Gupta/Becerra 2003: 25; Zhao/Luo 2005: 74) • Facilitate specialization and division of labor (Weise 1997: 60)	• Loss of strategic flexibility and variety due to longer-term reciprocal commitment (Lado et al. 1997: 122) • Prevention of fruitful initiatives or innovation through conformity or "group think" (Wimmer/Neuberger 1982: 194) • Risk of free-riding and inertia • Organizing costs (Hennart 1993b: 532, 1993a: 159, 2001:144)
Competition	**Overall** • Efficient internal governance (Hill et al. 1992: 501; Birkinshaw 2001a: 119) *** Efficiency ↑** • Facilitate optimal allocation of resources, promote innovation and entrepreneurship, reduce transaction costs (Lado et al. 1997: 122) • Create market-like rationalization pressure (Klaus 2002: 23) • Provide impetus for innovation and flexibility (Staber 2000: 76 with reference to You/Wilkinson 1994; Cerrato 2006: 264) • Find the very best solution (Fengler 1996: 114), also by trying out different approaches (Birkinshaw 2001a: 118) • Shorten lead times through duplication of activities (Birkinshaw 2001a: 118) • Achieve full market coverage, realize economies of scope (Birkinshaw/Lingblad, 2005: 678) **Effectiveness ↑** • Use internal benchmarking to identify units that are most effective (Birkinshaw/Hood 1998a: 8) • Enhance knowledge and growth through innovation (Lado et al. 1997: 122) • Create functional conflict, which stimulates change (Robbins 1990: 414, 425) • Drive units to improve their businesses by undertaking measures not always demanded by customers (Bengtsson/Kock 1999: 188)	• Transaction costs related to the management of competition, e.g., for carrying out RfPs (Birkinshaw/Hood 2001: 135) or organizational slack loss (Birkinshaw 2001a: 119) • Necessity of excess personnel (Fengler 1996: 114) or organizational slack (Bourgeois III 1981: 30) for activities stimulated by competition • Costs related to the duplication of effort (Bartlett/Ghoshal 1988: 67; Phelps/Fuller 2000: 227, Birkinshaw/Lingblad 2005: 678) • Devastation of team work, waste of resources, cannibalization (Eisenhardt/Galunic 2000: 96) • Costs related to units being played off against each other in the market place (Birkinshaw et al. 2001: 236); lack of strategic coherence (Birkinshaw/Lingblad 2005: 682), loss of reputation (Birkinshaw 2001b: 21) • Dysfunctional consequences on an individual level, e.g., lower productivity and achievement, more negative relationships, poorer psychological health (Kohn 1986) • Room for subsidiary opportunism, which may jeopardize parent company objectives (Birkinshaw/Fry 1998: 59 for an example)

* Dominating benefit

Figure 6: Benefits and Drawbacks of Intersubsidiary Competition and Cooperation

3.3 Theoretical Perspectives

The above evaluation of benefits and drawbacks of intersubsidiary competition and cooperation suggests that these relationships can be looked at from (at least) two different, yet compatible angles. The first angle is cost-oriented. Intersubsidiary competition and/or cooperation may reduce costs and increase operational efficiency. At the same time, the implementation and management of such relationships is likely to incur costs. The second angle is rent-oriented. Intersubsidiary relationships may allow developing and/or combining resources to enhance competitiveness – both on a firm and on a subsidiary level. Existing resources provide the basis of such competition and/or cooperation.

Two main theoretical perspectives are supported by these considerations: First, **transaction cost economics (TCE)**, which is directed towards identifying the most efficient governance mode (or organizing method) (Williamson 1981: 548-549; Hennart 1993b: 529-530), and second, the **resource-based view (RBV)**, which is concerned with extracting rents from resources (Peng 2001: 820). Although efficiency arguments outweigh for competition and effectiveness arguments dominate cooperation, the two theories cannot be matched with the two types of relationships. As noted above, cooperation also incurs costs and competition builds upon resources. The combined objectives of efficient governance and resource sharing are captured in **MNC network approaches**. Particularly the cooperative aspect has been emphasized with regard to the existence of intraorganizational relationships in MNCs.

The first two theoretical building blocks – TCE and the RBV – shed some light upon the rationale for each type of relationship; they do not, however, explain why intersubsidiary relationships ultimately differ among companies. The same is true for MNC network approaches, which are more descriptive in nature and at the same time offer little insight into the competitive dimension of intraorganizational relationships. Due to their limited explanatory power, the discussion of the three perspectives is kept fairly brief. Nevertheless, it seems appropriate to provide some reflections and considerations on the topic to support the argument of limited applicability or relevance for the specific research questions. The attempt to transfer core theoretical elements from their original setting to the horizontal relationship between (foreign) subsidiaries inspires some interesting insights. Given that the three perspectives prove insufficient for formulating propositions related to the specific research questions, only key points will be addressed. TCE is discussed in subsection 3.3.1, the RBV is subject to subsection 3.3.2, and network approaches are assessed in subsection 3.3.3. After addressing some complementary theoretical perspectives in subsection 3.3.4, an interim conclusion is drawn in subsection 3.3.5.

3.3.1 Transaction Cost Economics

In search of a theoretical perspective that helps to explain competition and cooperation between (foreign) subsidiaries, TCE is one of the substantial theories that come to the researcher's mind. It is known for framing the general governance problem, i.e. firms having to choose between a market-oriented, hierarchical or hybrid approach. As will be shown, these options are relevant not only to the choice of executing transactions via markets or firms but also to the organization of activities within firms. While intersubsidiary competition is easily recognized as a means of introducing market mechanisms within firms, intersubsidiary cooperation does not necessarily imply a hierarchical management approach. It may rather be the headquarters-led versus subsidiary-led nature of the relationship that determines whether it corresponds to a more hierarchical or market-oriented form of internal governance. These and other issues are reflected upon after a brief clarification of key transaction-cost-related terms and a review of the most relevant ramifications and applications of the theory. The goal is to reveal the contributions of TCE for understanding intersubsidiary relationships and to discuss the difficulties related to a transfer of concepts.

3.3.1.1 Key Terms and Concepts

The main question in TCE is which organization structures (or governance modes) are chosen and implemented to reduce transaction costs and increase efficiency (Fritz 2006: 11). Traditionally, transaction-cost-based thinking has focused on the governance of contractual relations (Williamson/Ouchi 1981: 351). The basic unit of analysis is the transaction (Williamson 1975: xi; 1981: 549; Rindfleisch/Heide 1997: 49). Such a **transaction** can broadly be defined as the **economic exchange** between individuals (Ouchi 1980: 130). A narrower definition refers to the process of clarifying and agreeing on an exchange, which typically precedes the physical exchange of commodities (Picot 1982: 269). This second definition suggests that it may take some effort to work out the details of an exchange and reduce the existing information problems (Picot 1982: 267).

The activities undertaken to give the contracting parties certainty about the exchanged values are called **transaction costs** (Ouchi 1980: 130). However, such costs are not only incurred *ex ante* by initiating and agreeing on an exchange, but also *ex post* for controlling compliance and potentially adjusting the contract (Picot 1982: 270). The goal is to minimize transaction costs by choosing the most efficient governance mode for each transaction (Williamson 1981: 548-549). Williamson defines **governance** as "a means by which to infuse order in a relation where potential conflict threatens to undo or upset opportunities to realize mutual gains" (Williamson 1999: 1090). Bounded rationality and opportunism need to be considered as the two key assumptions of human behavior (Williamson/Ouchi 1981: 351; Rindfleisch/Heide 1997: 31). Characterizing a transaction in terms of uncertainty, frequency and asset specificity helps identify the matching governance mode. In trying to economize on bounded rationality while containing the hazards of opportunism, the choice is typically between markets, internal organization or some intermediate form of bilateral exchange (Williamson/Ouchi 1981: 351-352).

3.3.1.2 Relevant Areas of Application

So far, the transaction cost approach does not seem particularly insightful for explaining and shaping the relationship between two or more units of the same organization that are situated at the same level of the value chain. Such units are not expected to engage in significant economic exchange relationships that would require them to solve a contracting problem. They may compete by performing very similar activities or cooperate to reach a common goal; but they will typically not conduct any transactions. The area of application is broadened, however, if activities and interactions are considered as substitutes for transactions (Michaelis 1985: 75; Hennart 1993a: 159). Recall from section 2.1 that relationships can be regarded as the result of a series of interaction activities (Burt 1983: 35).

Rindfleisch and Heide provide a comprehensive overview of the **contexts** in which transaction cost analysis has been applied (see Rindfleisch/Heide 1997: 32, 39-40). They come to the conclusion that the bulk of empirical studies has focused on the issues of **vertical integration** and **vertical interorganizational** relationships. Typical examples are the analysis of make-or-buy decisions or the development of buyer-supplier-relationships. Also, a growing number of researchers have used transaction cost theory to explore **horizontal interorganizational** relationships, such as the formation of alliances. Based on the above considerations, it is of little surprise that the review does not include any contributions addressing the question of how to design or manage horizontal intraorganizational relationships. However, it can be shown that transaction cost theory does provide valuable insights for structuring the relationship between such units. The following review is limited to contributions that use TCE to explain organizational issues within the firm – or, more specifically, within the MNC.[27]

According to Williamson the transaction cost approach has been applied to the **study of organization** at three levels: (1) the overall structure of the enterprise (i.e. determining the relationship between operating parts), (2) the operating parts themselves (i.e. defining efficient boundaries of the firm) and (3) the organization of human assets (i.e. matching governance with attributes of work groups) (Williamson 1981: 549). The first level bears the greatest significance for the phenomenon of interest, the central question being how operating parts (here: foreign subsidiaries engaged in project marketing activities) of an enterprise (here: an MNC) should be related to one another (here: in terms of competition and cooperation). Williamson not only reflects upon the role of headquarters, he also addresses issues such as the degree of autonomy divisions enjoy in an **M-form** enterprise and the resource competition that prevails between them (for example, Williamson 1975: 137, 143, 147; Williamson/Ouchi 1981: 359-360). By creating **internal market relations** and separating operational from strategic decision making, multidivisional structures are expected to reduce transaction costs as firms grow and become more diversified (Williamson 1975: 137).[28] By referring to competing, i.e. primarily horizontally related, units, Williamson contributes to the understanding of competition between foreign subsidiaries. In the M-form enterprise competition between divisions is introduced 'top-down' as a means of reducing transaction costs. Williamson thus supports the notion of having a headquarters unit, or general management, that determines the extent of intersubsidiary competition – for example, by specifying geographic responsibilities: "Territorialization serves to mitigate interdivisional competition in the product market, but interdivisional 'competition', for performance comparison purposes, in other respects is possible" (Williamson 1975: 140). The competition he refers to is headquarters-led in the sense that it is brought about by certain organizational and managerial arrangements (for the definition of headquarters-led relationships see subsection 2.3.1). Williamson's discussion of the necessary strategic controls, i.e. incentive schemes, internal audits and competitive cash-flow allocation, is certainly insightful for managers of multidivisional firms. Subsidiary-led

---

[27] For a brief, more general discussion of the limited application of TCE to intraorganizational problems see Wengler 2006: 131-132, 158-160.
[28] For a critical discussion and extension of the M-form organization see, for example, Bartlett/Ghoshal 1993; Hoskisson et al. 1993; Pihl 2003.

competition, however, is hardly explicable based on his arguments – as are different forms of intersubsidiary cooperation. Although an international dimension seems to be inherent in Williamson's work (compare his above-cited argument of "territorialization", which may or may not span multiple countries), it is not addressed explicitly.

This international dimension is incorporated by **internalization theory** (Buckley/Casson 1976; Dunning 1980; Rugman 1981), which offers a transaction-cost-based explanation of the existence and functioning of the MNC (for a synthesis and discussion see, for example, Rugman/Verbeke 1992; Rugman 1996; Hennart 2001). The theory – also referred to as the transaction cost theory of international production – argues that firms engage in investments abroad based on ownership- and location-specific advantages as well as intermediate market failure (for a summary see, for example, Birkinshaw 2001b: 99-100). Nearly three decades after the initial publication of Buckley and Casson's seminal work, Rugman and Verbeke emphasize the need to modify their assumptions to account for contemporary MNC organizational structures and their functioning in practice (Rugman/Verbeke 2003: 135). They call for a formulation and operationalization of hypotheses on alternative governance approaches that can be adopted by MNCs. Linking conventional transaction cost thinking with advances in international strategic management, the authors provide an in-depth analysis of the internal functioning of the MNC (Rugman/Verbeke 2001; 2003).

Verbeke and Yuan extend this analysis by exploring **subsidiary autonomous activities** and their **implications for MNC governance** from a transaction cost perspective (Verbeke/Yuan 2005). In doing so they not only take Williamson's issue of divisional autonomy to an international level, they also offer some explanations for headquarters-led and subsidiary-led competition. Building on the bounded rationality construct, they make discrepancies in information selection and judgment responsible for how corporate level managers deal with subsidiary initiatives (Verbeke/Yuan 2005: 44-46). Ideally, managers introduce governance mechanisms that alleviate their bounded rationality constraints and allow them to be more supportive of subsidiary autonomous activities (Verbeke/Yuan 2005: 48). Verbeke and Yuan's work contains some insightful elements for this research. The authors are not interested in how specific transactions should be organized but dedicated to assessing the **organizational consequences of bounded rationality**. Particularly relevant is their proposition that the availability of information and the ability to interpret it correctly influence the level of autonomy corporate management is willing to grant to its subsidiaries. By asking for standardized submissions of project proposals, managers create not only **intersubsidiary competition** but, most notably, a solid basis of information (Verbeke/Yuan 2005: 46). Tolerating or encouraging subsidiary-autonomous activities on a large scale is much easier if management feels capable of taking informed decisions.

Relevant to this research is the notion that (headquarters-led) intersubsidiary competition is promoted to compensate for headquarters' bounded rationality. Subsidiary-led competition could possibly result if vast subsidiary autonomy was granted. In the case of managed competition, the parent company ultimately takes the decision which initiatives to support, or where to allocate responsibilities. One could think of a scenario where corporate management finds subsidiaries to be in a much better position to assess local opportunities and completely withdraws its involvement. Subsidiary-led competition (and/or cooperation) could be the consequence. Verbeke and Yuan do not investigate the effects of varying degrees of autonomy on subsidiary behavior, though.

Hennart has made a significant contribution to the application of transaction cost theory to international business, and, more specifically to the internal functioning of the MNC. His distinction between **organizing methods** (hierarchy and the price system) and **institutions** (firms and markets) serves as an important foundation for this research. Within each institution different methods of organization can be employed, often resulting in a combination of both methods. This includes the implementation of market-like structures within the boundaries of the firm (Hennart 1993a: 158-161; 1993b: 530-531; for a combination of market and hierarchy also see Picot 1982: 275). While hierarchy controls individuals by constraining their behavior, prices do so indirectly by measuring their outputs. Both methods have their benefits and drawbacks. Under hierarchy, individuals are paid a fixed sum to follow orders; they have little incentive to cheat but are likely to minimize effort (to shirk). Under the price system, individuals are rewarded for their output; they will try to maximize effort (minimize shirking) but have an incentive to cheat. Examples for output constraints are bonuses, piecework and stock options (Hennart 2001: 135). Setting up profit centers is another form of introducing price incentives in firms, as illustrated by the M-form structure (Rugman/Verbeke 1992: 769; Hennart 1993b: 541-544). The goal is to minimize the sum of cheating and shirking costs – both via the type of institution and the organizing method.

Hennart calls for a clear distinction between the transaction costs incurred by organizing transactions in markets and the **management costs** related to effecting exchange within the firm (Hennart 1993b: 530). Windsperger supports this view by noting that the optimal (or most efficient) organizational design minimizes the sum of transaction costs and organizational set-up costs (Windsperger 1996: 29, 49; 1997: 193). Similarly Cerrato suggests that an internal market should only be established if its benefits equal (or exceed) the costs involved in managing it (Cerrato 2006: 263). As will be shown in the next subsection, Hennart's conceptualization of price and hierarchy as alternative methods of organizing is helpful for thinking about intersubsidiary relationships. The control modes a company chooses to enforce the desired method are not investigated as part of this research (for details see Hennart 1993a).

3.3.1.3 Implications for Intersubsidiary Relationships

Recall that one of the overarching research questions is how MNCs deal (or can deal) with intersubsidiary competition and cooperation. In transaction cost terms, the situation depicted in the case example can be framed as an organizational problem (Picot 1982: 269): The MNC's overall goal is to sell its products and/or services to customers around the world. In order to cope with the complexity of the global market (e.g., distinct customer demands, such as for a local contact), corporate management needs to set up sales subsidiaries in various geographic locations. It is the bounded rationality of individual organization members and/or units (e.g., limited knowledge of a particular market) that call for a division of labor. In a second step, however, the dispersed units' activities need to be coordinated. Both the aforementioned bounded rationality and the potentially opportunistic behavior of individual units need to be considered when deciding on the most appropriate form of coordination.[29]

Before moving to any details on specific organizational measures, it is advisable to take a look at the 'big picture', i.e. alternative governance modes or – following Hennart – methods of organizing. Although certain parallels between intersubsidiary relationships and methods of organizing can be established, TCE is not able to fully explain the existence of different types of intersubsidiary relationships. First and foremost, the **attribution** of intersubsidiary competition and cooperation **to the continuum** of methods of organizing is **not clear-cut**. It appears to be the headquarters-led versus subsidiary-led nature of the relationships that is decisive for their position on the continuum. Second, TCE provides a rational, **top-down approach** to alternative governance modes or methods of organizing. The goal is to

---

[29] On the concepts of configuration and coordination as well as their rootage in industrial economics see, for example, Schmid/Grosche 2009.

achieve efficiency at firm level (compare, for example, Williamson's aforementioned discussion of the M-form enterprise). The bottom-up articulation of subsidiary motives or initiatives is not included in such considerations. Third, TCE does not include a satisfactory rationale for horizontal intersubsidiary cooperation. It provides a solution to the problem of cooperation in terms of **economic exchange** as well as a starting point for analyzing why **competitive** elements find their way into the firm. These limitations as well as additional difficulties in applying transaction-cost-based reasoning to the analysis of intersubsidiary relationships are substantiated in the following discussion. The focus is on reconciling intersubsidiary relationships with alternative methods of organizing, especially since the remaining two aspects have been touched upon by other authors.

Although Williamson himself notes that the transaction cost approach as such "applies both to the determination of efficient boundaries, as between firms and markets, and to the organization of internal transactions" (Williamson 1981: 548), he has not made an attempt to transfer the traditional trichotomy of **governance modes** – market, hierarchy and hybrid (or network) – to the **intraorganizational context**. Accounting for the core concepts of intersubsidiary competition and cooperation, such a transfer is undertaken in the 'mental exercise' below. It is facilitated by Hennart's distinction of alternative methods of organizing and their delineation against institutional forms. Based on his conceptualization and terminology an attempt is made to attribute intersubsidiary relationships to different methods of internal organization. The options – or, in accordance with Hennart, the continuum – ranges from price (far left) to hierarchy (far right) (Hennart 1993b: 529; see, for example, Picot 1982: 273-274 for a similar continuum between market and hierarchy).

As derived from the introductory case example, the parent company can take a very liberal stance towards its subsidiaries, granting them the autonomy to approach whichever customers they like without prior consultation of either the headquarters or their peer subsidiaries. At least theoretically, this approach can lead to the constellation that two or more subsidiaries of the same MNC participate in a particular tender or set out to develop a project with a particular customer. In this case, it is up to the customer to decide whose offer it finds most attractive. Foreign subsidiaries act in open competition to one another and, being directly rewarded for their output, will have a strong motivation to maximize effort. From a transaction cost perspective such an approach would be expected if the parent company felt that it had a significant informational disadvantage compared to its subsidiaries (compare to subsection 3.3.1.2). Given that the parent company does not interfere with the market mechanism, **subsidiary-led competition** for customers represents a particularly pure form of the **price system** and thus coincides with the far left side of the continuum of organizing methods. Subsidiary-led competition for charters involves a minimal amount of hierarchy in that the final decision on responsibilities is taken by the parent company. In both cases the parent company accepts a certain amount of risk that subsidiaries act opportunistically.

The far right side of the continuum is then occupied by a very centralized, hierarchical method of organizing, in which subsidiaries are given clear rules and responsibilities to which to adhere. The parent company may find the allocation of customer, regional or product-oriented responsibilities most appropriate. If there is no overlap in the assigned product market scope and the parent company can monitor subsidiaries' compliance with the predefined rules, then intersubsidiary competition for customers is suppressed. With top-level decision making being very centralized, the parent company alone settles any uncertainties or disputes that arise over the assigned responsibilities. Based on its informational advantage, the parent company may want to 'force' subsidiaries to cooperate in certain areas. From a top-down perspective sharing knowledge or splitting work among dispersed locations may be perceived as an important competitive advantage. The parent company would then have an interest in constraining subsidiary autonomous behavior and opportunism. It should be noted that operational decision making (such as drawing up contract details or assigning resources to projects) can nevertheless remain highly decentralized, which is typically so for the sales and marketing function of large MNCs (see Turner/Henry 1994: 426; Bartlett/Ghoshal 1998: 111-112). To sum up, the purest form of **hierarchy** implies **no competition** between (foreign) subsidiaries; **headquarters-led cooperation** is an optional feature.

While complete decentralization with open intersubsidiary competition marks one end of the pictured continuum, complete centralization with little discretion on the part of the subsidiaries characterizes the other end. One can now think of numerous constellations between these two extremes, which combine elements of both hierarchy and the price system. In order to extract the 'best of both worlds' the parent company may decide to allow some competition between its subsidiaries (e.g., to avoid inertia) but to settle it internally (e.g., to maintain one face to the customer) (for benefits and drawbacks of intersubsidiary competition see section 3.2). In this constellation, subsidiaries would not face each other as rivals in the (external) market place but within the boundaries of the firm. It is up to the parent company how strongly it becomes involved in the process of managing such competition. The options range from setting up formal requests for proposals (Birkinshaw/Hood 2001:

134-135) and assuming full responsibility in the selection process to leaving it up to the subsidiaries to come to an agreement. Corporate level management can thus act as decision maker, supervisor, facilitator or even mere observer with the power to interfere. Such **headquarters-led competition** for charters forms part of an **intermediate** (or hybrid) method of organizing. Market-oriented or hierarchical elements dominate depending on the degree of management involvement. Hennart reiterates that the simultaneous use of price and hierarchy is compatible with a transaction cost model and does not require any separate theory (Hennart 1993b: 545; 2001: 136). Although cooperation is not – like competition (Cerrato 2006: 260 with reference to Hodgson 2002: 44) – a defining characteristic of markets, voluntary or **subsidiary-led cooperation** (as well as independence or coopetition) also constitutes an intermediate approach. Given the negligible role of the parent company, such a relationship comes closer to a market-oriented than a hierarchical form of internal governance.

At this point it becomes clear that the **boundaries** of the continuum are not so much defined by alternative types of behavior, i.e. competition and cooperation, but by the **origins** of these relationships. Headquarters-led relationships imply that key decisions are centralized; subsidiary-led relationships suggest that certain market forces are at work. In line with this argument, Ehemann sees **centralization and autonomy** as the extreme points of a continuum reflecting how independently (business or) national units take decisions (Ehemann 2007: 8). Centralization, as one key dimension of the organization structure, describes the extent to which decisions are taken at the top (versus the lower) levels of the hierarchy (Ehemann 2007: 7-8 with reference to Pugh et al. 1968: 72 ff., among others). Conversely, decentralization in an MNC refers to "spreading out [...] the authority, responsibility and decision making to and within the foreign subsidiary by the parent company (Ehemann 2007: 11 with reference to Sim 1977). In subsection 2.3.2 on subsidiary-led relationships it was argued that the greater subsidiaries' scope for decision making is, the more flexible they are in forming diverse relationships with their peers (on the proposed relationship between decentralized decision making and charter overlap see Birkinshaw/Lingblad 2005 and the review in subsection 3.5.1). The origin, but also the types of intersubsidiary relationships can thus be thought of as a result, or by-product, of centralization and autonomy. In practice, however, the effects of centralization and autonomy have hardly been examined (for an overview of selected empirical studies on the degree of centralization and autonomy see Ehemann 2007: 22-23). Ehemann herself analyses the effects of subsidiary autonomy in market development on performance and the headquarters-subsidiary relationship (Ehemann 2007: 185-205).

Explanations can be derived from the two key assumptions of human behavior, bounded rationality and opportunism. TCE suggests that headquarters-led relationships are pursued if the parent company has some informational advantage over its subsidiaries and the desire to limit their opportunism (compare to the above discussion of Rugman and Verbeke's analysis of autonomous subsidiary initiatives). In subsidiary-led relationships the parent company is willing to accept some subsidiary opportunism to compensate for its own bounded rationality.

Windsperger makes an interesting remark here, criticizing Williamson (1975) for including opportunism as the only form of egoistic behavior. Egoistic behavior means that an individual tries to maximize his utility (or profit) under consideration of his expectations regarding the actions of transaction partners. It can occur in one of two forms: opportunistic or cooperative behavior (Windsperger 1998: 271). Whether the tendency of opportunistic or cooperative behavior dominates is dependent on subjective and objective (situational) factors. Windsperger's argument is somewhat defeated if opportunism is broadly understood as self-interest-seeking behavior (with or without guile) (Williamson 1975: 26; Williamson/Ouchi 1981: 351; Rugman/ Verbeke 2003: 136). Cooperation with peers could very well be included in this definition.[30] The rationale is that subsidiaries decide to cooperate if they feel that sharing knowledge or splitting work is what is best for them. It should be recognized, however, that this may not be the only reason for cooperation. Subsidiaries may simply want to help their peers – displaying altruistic behavior – or act in the interest of the company as a whole. Such considerations are not sufficiently accounted for by TCE.

The described limitations lead to another key feature of TCE, namely its **top-down approach**.[31] Aware of the tradeoff between cheating and shirking costs, corporate-level management decides upon the predominance of prices or hierarchy within the firm. Similarly, it is up to the parent company to weigh the (primarily cost-related) benefits and drawbacks of intersubsidiary competition and cooperation, and to decide whether or not to enforce the respective relationship.[32] If, however, the subsidiaries are granted enough freedom to establish their own relationships, they may decide about competing and/or cooperating with their peers. As mentioned in the previous paragraph, their decisions may not always be based upon efficiency considerations.

---

[30] For a critical discussion of the concept of opportunism see, for example, Ghoshal/Moran 1996.
[31] Peng 2001: 811 uses the same wording with respect to headquarters' allocation of subsidiary capabilities.
[32] An evaluation and discussion of control costs does not fall within the scope of this research.

Birkinshaw comes to a similar conclusion with respect to parent-driven versus subsidiary-driven investments. He notes that parent-driven investments are reconcilable with the transaction cost theory of international production because they involve an explicit comparison of firm- and country-specific advantages. The parent company evaluates which subsidiary and location is best suited for its undertaking. Lacking such an explicit comparison of benefits and drawbacks, subsidiary-driven investments are difficult to explain in transaction cost terms (Birkinshaw 2001b: 102). According to Birkinshaw the problem with the transaction cost approach in general is that is was developed to explain how firms became international – and is thus difficult to apply to the subsequent development of foreign subsidiaries (Birkinshaw 2001b: 101).

Finally, the discussion has shown that while intersubsidiary **competition** (whether headquarters-led or subsidiary-led) can be considered as a deliberate element (or manifestation) of the price system, intersubsidiary cooperation is much more difficult to explain in transaction cost terms. It is important to note that what is of interest here is horizontal cooperation, not vertical cooperation in terms of economic exchange (as referred to, for example, by Ouchi 1980: 130; Hennart 1993a: 158). Cerrato's reflections on the theoretical underpinnings for Birkinshaw's (2001b) model of the MNC as an **internal market** system support this argument. He suggests that internalization theory provides an efficiency-based framework for assessing the costs related to managing an internal market, but limits its application to the internal market for intermediate goods and services (Cerrato 2006: 263). Both the internal market for charters and the internal market for practices and capabilities, which is inherently cooperative, call for alternative theoretical perspectives. Cerrato's point of view is only partially shared here, since the reconciliation of intersubsidiary relationships with alternative methods of organizing has shown that TCE provides a rationale for introducing headquarters-led (or subsidiary-led) charter competition as well. But efficiency-related arguments are indeed weak when it comes to explaining cooperative ties between subsidiaries operating at the same level of the value chain.

To sum up, in the context of this research TCE represents a top-down approach to organizing activities within firms, which mainly provides an explanation for headquarters-led relationships. Headquarters must weigh costs and benefits of intersubsidiary competition and cooperation. TCE is more suitable to describe and analyze than to serve as a normative theory (Ghoshal/Moran 1996: 40).[33] The theory accounts for intersubsidiary competition as an intraorganizational manifestation of the price system. Other theoretical perspectives are necessary to understand and explain cooperation, as well as certain facets of subsidiary-led relationships.

3.3.2 Resource-Based View

Just as TCE, the resource-based view (RBV) is expected to contribute to an understanding of intersubsidiary competition and/or cooperation – but not necessarily to an explanation of the choice of relationship. The analysis of benefits and drawbacks has revealed that access to scarce or complementary resources is a key reason for firms, and units, to cooperate (Bengtsson/Kock 2000: 424; Luo 2005: 73-74). Whereas TCE asserts that firms focus on minimizing the costs of organizing, the RBV suggests that firms seek to capitalize on and increase their resources and capabilities. The latter is possible by cooperating with external market participants, but also by forging intrafirm cooperation. The RBV is in its essence a **firm-level theory** concerned with how a firm as a whole can achieve and sustain competitive advantage. It may be applied to the subsidiary level, however, if subsidiaries are treated as semi-autonomous units, disposing of distinct resources and capabilities, and taking their own initiatives (Birkinshaw 2001b: 103). Which implications the RBV has for intersubsidiary relationships is evaluated after a clarification of key terms and concepts and an overview of the relevant areas of application. The overall discussion of the RBV is kept fairly brief since resource-related ideas have already been developed with respect to the objects of both competition and cooperation (see subsections 2.4.1.2 and 2.4.2.2).

Before moving to an evaluation of the RBV, it is worth a brief explanation as to why the latter is considered a **valuable perspective** on intersubsidiary relationships in this research despite the **exclusion of resources** as an object of investigation (compare to section 2.5). First, particularly the concept of knowledge sharing is closely linked to that of resources. Although knowledge is deliberately treated as a

---

[33] It should be noted that TCE's descriptive and explicative power may also be questioned. Despite its widespread use, TCE has received manifold criticism (for a comprehensive overview see, for example, Döring 1998: 45-63). Most frequently addressed is the insufficient specification and delineation of the term "transaction costs". Cook and Emerson articulate this concern as follows: "One can hardly imagine a more diffuse and non-discriminating treatment of what is offered as a major concept in an important theory. It is left to us to induce the meaning of the term from situation-specific examples they offer, but examples are never sufficient for theory-building purposes" (Cook/Emerson 1984: 23).

separate object of intersubsidiary cooperation in this research, it is oftentimes considered as a type of (intangible) resource (compare discussion in subsection 2.4.2.3). Second, resources form the basis of competition and cooperation. As illustrated in subsection 3.3.2.3, subsidiaries use their resources and capabilities to compete for charters and/or customers or to cooperate through a split of work.

3.3.2.1 Key Terms and Concepts

The RBV argues that firms are able to achieve sustained competitive advantage based on heterogeneous and imperfectly mobile resources (Barney 1991: 105). Such **resources** can be defined as "all assets, capabilities, organizational processes, firm attributes, information, knowledge, etc. controlled by a firm that enable a firm to conceive of and implement strategies that improve its efficiency and effectiveness" (Barney 1991: 101 with reference to Daft 1983). Simpler and more balanced definitions refer to resources as "anything which could be thought of as a strength or weakness of a given firm" (Wernerfelt 1984: 172) or, even more neutral, "the stocks of available factors that are owned or controlled by the firm" (Amit/Schoemaker 1993: 35). According to Barney, these resources fall into three categories: physical capital resources, human capital resources and organizational capital resources (Barney 1991: 101). Grant suggests six major resource categories: financial, physical, human, technological, reputational and organizational. At the same time he distinguishes between resources as inputs to the production process and **capabilities** as the capacity of resources to perform a certain task or activity. In his understanding capabilities arise from resources and constitute the main source of competitive advantage (Grant 1991: 118-119). Amit and Schoemaker also contrast resources with capabilities, which they regard as "a firm's capacity to deploy resources" (Amit/Schoemaker 1993: 35). The distinction between resources and capabilities has been widely accepted within the RBV literature (for example, Conner/Prahalad 1996: 477; Barney et al. 2001: 630-631; Makadok 2001: 338). The overall idea of conceiving of a firm as a set of resources rather than a portfolio of products goes back to Penrose (1959) (Wernerfelt 1984: 171, 178).

The main **assumptions** of the RBV are "that resources and capabilities can be heterogeneously distributed across competing firms, that these differences can be long lasting, and that they can help explain why some firms consistently outperform other firms" (Barney 2001a: 649). In other words, firm performance is substantially influenced by firm attributes rather than industry characteristics (Barney 2001b: 54). To achieve competitive advantage firms should exploit their differences in resource supply. In order to hold the potential of sustained competitive advantage, firm resources need to be valuable, rare, imperfectly imitable and non-substitutable (Barney 1991: 105-106). According to Barney, sustained **competitive advantage** describes a state in which a firm is implementing a value-creating strategy that is not being implemented by any current or potential competitors and creates benefits they are unable to duplicate (Barney 1991: 102). It should be noted, however, that there are two ways of defining competitive advantage at firm level: with respect to competitors or return expectations (also referred to as economic rents) (Barney 2001b: 48). Amit and Schoemaker define resources and capabilities that are "difficult to trade and imitate, scarce, appropriable and specialized", and which thus bestow a firm's competitive advantage, as "strategic assets" (Amit/Schoemaker 1993: 36). The perceived value of these strategic assets depends on the strategic industry factors, i.e. those resources and capabilities that, at a given time, are the prime determinants of economic rents (Amit/Schoemaker 1993: 36-37). Barney supports this dependency by noting that "the value of a firm's resources and capabilities is determined by the market context within which a firm is operating" (Barney 2001b: 42; 2001a: 645). At the same time, valuable resource positions translate into entry barriers to certain markets (Wernerfelt 1984: 173).

3.3.2.2 Relevant Areas of Application

It has already been noted above that the RBV is actually a firm-level theory. Its main unit of analysis is the firm as a whole (Barney 2001b: 47). The main assumption of this "resource-based view of the firm" (Barney 1996; Barney et al. 2001) – that the heterogeneous distribution of resources and capabilities across firms has performance implications (Barney 2001a: 649) – seems **transferable to subsidiaries**. Although some attempts have been made in this direction (see, for example, Birkinshaw 2001b: 102-108 as well as Birkinshaw 1996; 1997; Birkinshaw/Hood 1998b, and the literature on centers of competence such as Schmid et al. 1999; Kutschker et al. 2002; Schmid 2003), the vast amount of RBV-based IB literature still deals with firm-level issues. This observation is supported by Peng's (2001) comprehensive overview of the key contributions to RBV literature in IB from 1991 to 2000. The author takes a citation-based approach, focusing on articles in leading IB journals that cited Barney (2001b) and/or Wernerfelt (1984) – two of the most influential papers on the RBV – during this decade. He further provides a state-of-the-art review of the identified **RBV literature in IB**. Given their limited relevance for this research, the topics Peng addresses are reviewed only very briefly below, without attempting to replicate any of his analyses and references. The main objective of the exercise is to distill elements that enhance our understanding of intersubsidiary competition and cooperation from a theoretical (resource-based) point of view.

Peng identifies four areas that have been of particular interest to the RBV literature in IB: (1) MNC management, (2) strategic alliances, (3) market entries and (4) international entrepreneurship. He further points to (5) emerging market strategies as an area that has only recently gained ground in the respective literature. According to Peng, the more established areas within IB research, namely MNC management and market entries, were enriched by the RBV, whereas the newer areas, such as strategic alliances, international entrepreneurship and emerging market strategies, were propelled by it (Peng 2001: 819). The following overview shows that the RBV extends or complements several ideas elaborated by internalization theory.

(1) Within Peng's organizing framework, **MNC management** comprises three elements: (1a) global strategies, (1b) subsidiary capability development and (1c) human resource management. Particularly the first two subcategories contain relevant aspects for this research in terms of subsidiary capabilities and contribution.

(1a) TCE and 'eclectic' perspectives – summarized as internalization theory in subsection 3.3.1.2 – argue that MNCs need to equip their foreign subsidiaries with certain firm-specific advantages to overcome the liability of foreignness. The RBV looks to specify the nature of these resources and capabilities (Peng 2001: 810). With respect to **global strategies**, it has been interested in investigating the resources underlying international and product diversification, as well as their impact on firm performance. Inherent to this research is the question of which resources and capabilities are needed to manage a global value chain and satisfy global customers.

(1b) Internalization theory argues that MNCs exist because they are able to exploit and transfer knowledge more efficiently and effectively than external markets. This perspective assumes that subsidiary capabilities are assigned in a top-down manner. The RBV, on the contrary, argues that subsidiaries can contribute significantly to the development of firm-specific advantage (Peng 2001: 811). **Subsidiary capability building** and initiatives facilitate intra-MNC knowledge flows (Barney et al. 2001: 629) and drive subsidiary growth (for example, Birkinshaw 1996; Birkinshaw/Hood 1998b; Birkinshaw et al. 1998). For knowledge outflows to take place subsidiary managers need to be equipped with the adequate incentives, and the receiving units need to be willing to learn (Peng 2001: 811 with reference to Gupta/Govindarajan 2000). The RBV literature on subsidiary capability building enhances our understanding that intra-MNC capability flows often constitute a multilateral process. Since knowledge and capability flows are means (or objects) of intersubsidiary cooperation, this aspect of the RBV is of particular importance to this research.

(1c) In terms of **human resource management** the RBV has generated the insight that top managers and their international experience represent some of the MNC's most valuable, unique, and hard-to-imitate resources (Peng 2001: 812). This argument could be transferred to the subsidiary level, if, for example, subsidiaries would vie for talents or if they were chosen for a particular task based on the qualification of their personnel.

(2) RBV literature on **strategic alliances** is relevant to this research in terms of cooperation between competitors. The RBV focuses mainly on organizational learning, stating that the capability to learn from partners is a key tacit resource – and the main motivation to enter alliances (Peng 2001: 812). While authors have addressed the opportunities of learning from both local partners and the parent company, learning from the experiences of sister subsidiaries does not seem to pose an issue. Just like alliance partners, however, subsidiaries can benefit from sharing similar or, ideally, asymmetric (i.e. complementary) knowledge.

(3) With respect to foreign **market entries**, the RBV raises the level of analysis from the single transaction to the firm. Whereas TCE treats entry modes as a function of intermediate market failure, the RBV sees them as the result of firm-specific capabilities. These capabilities are first developed and then exploited (TCE focuses on their exploitation only). Under the RBV market entries cannot only be 'pushed' by firm capabilities but also 'pulled' by the resources, capabilities and interests of foreign target firms. RBV literature also examines the link between entry modes and performance and has begun to shed light on actual channels of entry (Peng 2001: 813-814). Although subsidiaries are a particular form of market entry, this area of research is only of limited relevance for this research.

(4) The main question the RBV has helped answer in terms of **international entrepreneurship** is why certain small and medium-sized enterprises (SMEs) manage to succeed internationally without passing through different stages of learning and development (suggested by the "stage" model; Johanson/Vahlne 1977). Competitive advantage may be generated by a relative surplus of knowledge on internationalization as well as a more dynamic approach to venturing abroad (Peng 2001: 815). Some of these considerations may be valuable at the subsidiary level,

implying that experienced subsidiaries need not always be more successful in pursuing international business.

(5) Finally, the RBV has significantly contributed to revealing the **emerging market strategies** pursued by MNCs, state-owned enterprises, privatized firms, start-ups and conglomerates (Peng 2001: 815-816). Subsidiary resources and capabilities play only a subordinate role in this field.

Barney et al. (2001) provide an overview of the RBV's areas of application in **strategic management** as well as an agenda for future research.[34] As the five fields of study they identify: Human resource management, economics and finance, entrepreneurship, marketing, and international business. A certain overlap with Peng (2001) is undeniable, although the latter has adopted a purely international perspective. For example, Barney et al. also emphasize the RBV's recognition of people as strategically important to a firm's success or of entrepreneurial processes as the source of heterogeneous outputs. In terms of marketing they add an interesting aspect, which should be kept in mind when returning to the project marketing focus of this research: The RBV can be used to analyze how resources are used and transformed to create value for the customer (Barney et al. 2001: 627-630).

The authors close their article by drawing up an **agenda for further RBV research**. Interestingly the proposed themes all address overarching or firm-level issues, namely (1) the link between resources, dynamic capabilities and knowledge, (2) corporate governance as a source of sustained competitive advantage, (3) valuation issues in management buy-outs and venture capital financing, (4) the impact of the institutional environment on the acquisition and value of resources, and (5) attributes of entrepreneurial resources. In addition, the authors propose to investigate the implications of the RBV for the study of organizational behavior, ethics and corporate social responsibility, and management information systems (Barney et al. 2001: 630-636).

One topic that has not received much attention in the above literature reviews but is of particular importance for this research is the creation of **intraorganizational linkages**. According to Wernerfelt, "looking at economic units in terms of their resource endowments has a long tradition in economics" (Wernerfelt 1984: 171). The investigation of ties rather than nodes seems to represent a much younger area of

---

[34] On the RBV in strategic management also see Bamberger/Wrona 1996a; b.

research, though. In his 1984 article, Wernerfelt still noted that little was known about the extent to which capabilities could be combined across operating divisions (Wernerfelt 1984: 180). By now, researchers have begun to fill this gap. Tsai (2000), for example, analyzes how organizational units create interunit linkages for the exchange of tangible and intangible resources. His focus is on the dynamic process of network formation rather than the analysis of firm-specific resources or their importance for achieving competitive advantage (Tsai 2000: 925). It is the theoretical basis of his work that is most informative for this research. Tsai summarizes that organizational units can establish linkages to exchange resources and learn from each other by sharing knowledge. Such intraorganizational cooperation may be superior to market exchange because units share common values and communication styles. He refers to several studies that have shown interunit linkages to create competitive advantage by facilitating knowledge exchange (for example, Ghoshal/Bartlett 1990; Powell 1990; Nahapiet/Ghoshal 1998; Hansen 1999) or supporting economies of scope (for example, Hill/Hoskisson 1987; Gupta/Govindarajan 1991). Intraorganizational resource and knowledge sharing may have positive performance implications by creating synergies (Rumelt 1974) or it may enhance value creation by facilitating innovation (Tsai/Ghoshal 1998).

Although the RBV is actually a firm-level theory, the above reviews have shown that it has addressed a number of issues that are directly relevant to subsidiary-level research. It is no longer dedicated to the mere explanation of firm performance or competitive advantage based upon heterogeneous resources. Issues such as subsidiary capability development, entrepreneurial processes and interunit linkages have also benefited from a resource-based perspective. The particular insights for intersubsidiary competition and cooperation are discussed in the next subsection.

3.3.2.3 Implications for Intersubsidiary Relationships

Whereas the implications of TCE on intersubsidiary relationships mainly concerned their headquarters-led versus subsidiary-led nature, the RBV emphasizes the **objects of competition and cooperation**. The fact that the RBV is actually a firm-level theory, which can, however, be applied to the subsidiary level has already been addressed in the previous subsections. Under the RBV, headquarters is concerned with achieving sustained competitive advantage for the MNC as a whole. Whether subsidiaries deploy and combine resources out of self interest or collective interest is not an issue addressed by the RBV. Given that resources form the basis of both competition and cooperation between subsidiaries, the RBV has implications for both types of relationship. It does not, however, help to explain why one type of relationship may be preferred over another.

Subsidiaries do not only compete for (parent) resources but also use the resources and capabilities they have to compete for charters and customers. Since competition for resources has already been discussed in subsection 2.4.1.2, the focus here is on the resource-based implications for charter and customer competition.

Cerrato illustrates how the RBV enhances the understanding of **charter competition** by emphasizing that the endorsement of specialized resources is what allows a subsidiary to assume a particular charter (Cerrato 2006: 266-267). Birkinshaw underlines this argument by stating that "the subsidiary's resources, capabilities and local context are the differentiating factors by which it competes for charters" (Birkinshaw 2001b: 119:). Charters are contestable if the resources and capabilities needed to fulfill it are mobile or **non-location-bound** (Cerrato 2006: 267). In other words, foreign subsidiaries can only compete for charters if the necessary resources can be leveraged or developed in multiple locations or countries. There will be some basic resources that are indispensable for fulfilling a charter, and some supplementary resources that are 'nice to have' and may tip the scales towards one or another subsidiary. With respect to large-scale engineering projects, project design and management capabilities would be indispensable, whereas a close relationship with local authorities could constitute a supplementary asset. The functioning of an internal market for charters also depends on how proven and credible subsidiary resources and capabilities are. Subsidiaries that have built a strong track record or **reputation** (which, according to Weigelt/Camerer 1988: 1, is a summary of attributes inferred from past actions) have a better chance of receiving parent support when contesting or bidding for charters (Cerrato 2006: 267; with respect to internal initiatives Birkinshaw/Fry 1998: 55).

Tying up to Rugman and Verbeke's TCE-related statement that bounded rationality constraints push headquarters to allow subsidiary initiatives, Cerrato emphasizes that in many cases market-like mechanisms, based on **decentralized decision making**, are more beneficial to matching subsidiary-specific capabilities with activities performed than a hierarchical approach (Cerrato 2006: 268). Within the RBV literature, however, the price system as a method of organizing hardly seems to play a role. As Birkinshaw notes, it is difficult to reconcile the internal market model with the coordination (or "network management") capabilities that, from a RBV, are needed to achieve competitive advantage at the firm level (see Birkinshaw 2001b:

107-108). There will thus always be a tradeoff between promoting internal competition and building corporate-level capabilities for resource combination.

The influencing factors Cerrato discusses have similar implications for intersubsidiary **customer competition**. Resource mobility and subsidiary autonomy can be regarded as prerequisites for such competition, and customers will consider a subsidiary's reputation in their purchasing decision. With customer competition subsidiaries act even more like two independent firms, which compete based on their individual capability profiles. Just like firms they can be perceived as "a collection of resources and capabilities required for product/market competition" (Amit/ Schoemaker 1993: 34-35). If the goal for subsidiaries is to gain advantage over their peers in terms of efficiency and effectiveness, they actually have a lot in common with competing firms (see, for example, Barney 2001b: 48).

From a resource-based perspective, **cooperation** through resource sharing and cooperation through knowledge sharing can be interpreted as a similar phenomenon. As illustrated in subsection 2.4.2.3 several authors consider knowledge as a particular type of (intangible) resource. Cooperation through a split of work is different in that subsidiaries do not cooperate by directly exchanging resources but by using the resources and capabilities they have to contribute to a common goal.

In his analysis and extension of Birkinshaw's internal market model, Cerrato contrasts the market for competencies and practices against the markets for charters and for intermediate goods and services. Whereas the latter two imply intersubsidiary competition, the former relies on intersubsidiary cooperation. With respect to the intraorganizational exchange of competencies and practices the market concept is thus misleading (Cerrato 2006: 270). In the context of this research the internal market for competencies and practices has much in common with intersubsidiary **cooperation through knowledge sharing**. Cerrato draws on organizational learning and knowledge management literature (rather than the RBV) to explain the extension of the market. He links the internal market for knowledge and competencies to the tacitness of knowledge, the source (or context-specificity) of knowledge, interactions due to flows of products and services, and the degree of interunit communication (Cerrato 2006: 272). As outlined in the previous subsection, knowledge exchange through intraorganizational linkages may just as well be explained by the RBV (see, for example, Tsai 2000). As Conner and Prahalad state, the literature makes clear that "a knowledge-based view is the essence of the resource-based perspective" and knowledge is considered a prime source of competitive advantage (Conner/Prahalad 1996: 477).

When subsidiaries engage in **cooperation through a split of work** they do not necessarily have to interact by exchanging resources. They do need to dispose of certain resources and capabilities to fulfill their part of the task or project, though. Recall Wernerfelt's comment that little was known about the combination of capabilities across operating divisions (Wernerfelt 1984: 180). While intraorganizational knowledge sharing has emerged as an increasingly popular research theme over the past two decades, the question of how foreign subsidiaries contribute or combine their resources and capabilities to master a joint project has received relatively little attention in the existing literature. Both types of cooperation are aimed at pooling or gaining access to dispersed resources. These resources can either be symmetric or complementary, the latter having shown to be more beneficial for creating synergies from business combinations (Harrison et al. 2001). Cooperative capabilities can be interpreted as a resource in themselves, which can be used to achieve sustained competitive advantage (Barney 2001b: 54). The capability to learn from partners may be an example of such a tacit resource (Peng 2001: 812 with reference to Hamel 1991). This relationship shows a different interface between organizational learning – the perspective chosen by Cerrato to explain the internal market for competencies and practices – and the RBV.

This subsection is closed with a few **general remarks** on the relevance of the RBV for this research project. The RBV is a **firm-level** theory which is applicable to subsidiaries if these are considered as semi-autonomous units (Birkinshaw 2001b: 103). A resource-based perspective is helpful for this research given that "geographical location matters" for the development of certain capabilities (Birkinshaw 2001b: 106). Since, in addition, the importance of a resource varies by product or market (Wernerfelt 1984: 175-176), different subsidiaries may be prone to take the lead with respect to certain projects or customers.

As Birkinshaw notes, the criteria the RBV uses to evaluate the potential of resources to create competitive advantage (i.e. resources being valuable, rare, non-imitable and non-substitutable) lose their relevance at the **subsidiary level**. Given that the subsidiary is a part of the whole, it is more important that its resources are complementary to resources located in other parts of the organization; they do not necessarily have to be unique or hard to imitate (Birkinshaw 2001b: 106). Competitive advantage at a corporate level is then gained through the ability to put these building blocks together (Birkinshaw 2001b: 107). The role of management has already been highlighted by Barney a decade earlier, albeit with a slightly different focus. His statement that it is managers who are able to understand and describe the performance potential of a firm's resources (Barney 1991: 117) can have one of two implications for subsidiaries: Either corporate management has the ability to assess subsidiary resources and capabilities, or a solid appraisal is reserved to local management. It should be noted, though, that in the case of open intersubsidiary competition for customers the above evaluation criteria do become important because subsidiaries look to outperform one another (see Gnyawali et al. 2007: 2 for a subsidiary's motivation to enhance its competitive position). In case of cooperation it is indeed the combined value and the resulting synergies that count.

The RBV has been shown to shed some light on a variety of aspects related to intersubsidiary competition and cooperation. Cerrato's analysis has revealed that the RBV cannot only be used to evaluate the effects of resource sharing (i.e. its potential of creating competitive advantage) but also its determinants. It needs to be reemphasized, however, that it is not capable of explaining why MNCs differ in terms of the intersubsidiary relationships they foster.

3.3.3 Network Approaches

Network approaches constitute a third theoretical perspective on intersubsidiary relationships. They can be thought to combine the objectives of efficient governance and resource sharing. The network perspective has become quite influential in recent literature on the MNC – both with respect to external and internal relationships. But despite its focus on the linkages between actors, it falls short of illuminating different types of horizontal relationships within firms. Since this finding is already true for MNC network models – for which an exploration of intersubsidiary relationships would seem most obvious and appropriate – a broader review of the network literature is foregone. The limited relevance of network approaches for this research project is one reason why their discussion will be kept even briefer and more 'compact' than that of the two preceding theories. The other reason is that their advocates cannot claim to have developed a proper theory (Kutschker/Schmid 1995: 10 with reference to Easton/Araujo 1989: 99). Although the term 'network theory' is used in numerous publications, it remains unclear what is actually meant or understood by this term. At least up to now, so-called network theories do not represent a self-contained theoretical concept (Rank 2003: 35).

3.3.3.1 Key Terms and Concepts

Networks are oftentimes regarded as an intermediate form of governance, situated on the continuum between market and hierarchy (for example, Thorelli 1986: 37; Wildemann 1997: 420; also see the discussion and references in Rank 2003: 39-40). Whereas markets are based on spontaneous coordination through market participants and hierarchy is characterized by a super- and subordination of actors, networks imply the existence of long-term **relationships** and **trust** in the validity of values, norms and behavior (Kutschker/Schmid 1995: 25). Other scholars consider networks as an independent form of governance alongside market and hierarchy (for example, Powell 1990: 300-301; also see the discussion and references in Rank 2003: 41-42). The distinction is of little relevance for this research, though. Important reasons for the formation of networks can be found in sharing know-how, coping with the demand for speed, and capitalizing on trust based upon common values (Powell 1990: 324-327).

Depending on their respective scope, (corporate) networks fall into one of two categories: **interorganizational or intraorganizational** networks. Whereas the former refer to relationships with external actors (primarily other firms), the latter focus on the internal relationships between the organizational units of a company (Kutschker/Schmid 1995: 4-5, 7).[35] For the phenomenon of interest, i.e. competition and cooperation between foreign subsidiaries, the intraorganizational perspective is particularly relevant. Intraorganizational network approaches conceptualize organizations as a system of objects (or actors) linked by a variety of relationships (Tichy et al. 1979: 507). On an international level this means that subsidiaries are modeled as semiautonomous units that (are free to) interact not only with headquarters but also with their peer subsidiaries (for example, Ghoshal/Bartlett 1990: 607, 609; Birkinshaw 2001b: 108). Such lateral relationships can be expected to involve a certain amount of competition and cooperation. The existing literature on intraorganizational networks, however, reveals very little about the distinct nature of such horizontal ties.

---

[35] For a further distinction and discussion of inter- and intraorganizational network dimensions see Rank 2003: 43-50, for an overview Struthoff 1999: 59.

3.3.3.2 Relevant Areas of Application

In their flow-related discussion of the four most prominent MNC network models – Bartlett and Ghoshal's TNO, Hedlund's Heterarchy, Prahalad and Doz's DMNC and White and Poynter's Horizontal Organization – Schmid et al. distinguish between headquarters and subsidiaries as the providers and/or receivers of flows (Schmid et al. 2002: 51-52, 58). The authors proactively address it as a limitation of their empirical study, though, that flows to and from headquarters are not analyzed separately from flows to and from sister units (Schmid et al. 2002: 67). As reflected in the brief review below, the same is true for most of the MNC network models. Although their authors recognize both headquarters and subsidiaries as the providers and receivers of flows, very few distinctions are made between the vertical and horizontal direction of these flows.

In characterizing the **transnational organization (TNO)**, Bartlett and Ghoshal refer to strong interdependencies among different units of the MNC, used for integrating dispersed resources and building cooperation (Bartlett/Ghoshal 1987b: 44; 1998: 69, 74). They note that "some companies [...] have developed such relationships, both between headquarters and the subsidiaries, and among the subsidiaries themselves" (Bartlett/Ghoshal 1998: 148), but do not proceed with treating these relationships separately. On the contrary, they remain quite general on the types of units and the "flexible linkages" between them (Bartlett/Ghoshal 1998: 137), noting that of the companies they studied the most successful had forged "interdependent relationships among product, functional, and geographic management groups" (Bartlett/Ghoshal 1998: 106). Then again, the term "unit" is used interchangeably with "subsidiary", recognizing the particular importance of foreign subsidiaries for the functioning of the (network) MNC (Bartlett/Ghoshal 1986: 94). By analyzing and delineating different subsidiary roles and responsibilities, Bartlett and Ghoshal reinforce their focus on the nodes rather than the ties of the integrated network (Bartlett/Ghoshal 1998: 121-128; also see Ghoshal/Bartlett 1990: 620). Their description of the "significant flows" between units, i.e. the sharing of goods, resources and information, remains rather superficial (Bartlett/Ghoshal 1987b: 47, 48; 1998: 70, 196-197). Only in case examples do the authors hint directly at the competitive or cooperative nature of intersubsidiary relationships (for example, Bartlett/Ghoshal 1998: 150-151).

Similarly unspecific are Hedlund's references to interunit relationships within the **Heterarchy**. The author speaks of an increasing "range of types of relationships between units in the company", often implying a "deintegration of relationships" in companies that were traditionally controlled from a single center (Hedlund 1986: 24). Freedom and flexibility are key characteristics of heterarchical MNCs, which are thus "more likely to evolve [...] from contexts with a history of rather autonomous and entrepreneurial subsidiaries" (Hedlund 1986: 32). While Hedlund looks primarily at the composition and integration of the MNC, the ways in which its multiple centers actually interrelate appears of minor interest to him. Although he does suggest that not only relations between one center and units in the periphery should be exploited (as is mostly the case with global product organizations), but also those within the supposed periphery (Hedlund 1986: 22 with reference to Davidson/Haspeslagh 1982).

In Doz and Prahalad's **diversified multinational firm (DMNC)** linkages between subunits take a more prominent position (Doz/Prahalad 1991: 147). The authors refer to this organization as a "network of relationships" and suggest that the more lateral (or diagonal) rather than vertical linkages exist, the greater the organization's adaptability will be (Doz/Prahalad 1991: 152-153). They clearly distinguish the interaction and information flow between subsidiaries and headquarters from that taking place across subsidiaries. The nature of these relationships then reflects the strategic mission assigned to each unit (Doz/Prahalad 1991: 160, with reference to Ghoshal/Nohria 1989). Unique to Doz and Prahalad's conceptualization of the DMNC is that interunit linkages are thought to be latent. Instead of specifying interdependencies in advance they are facilitated as the need for them arises (Doz/Prahalad 1991: 147). At this point it should be noted that network analysis not only allows investigating formulated or planned relationships between nodes but also emergent, informal relationships (Tichy et al. 1979). Despite the relative importance Doz and Prahalad assign to interunit linkages, no further insights are provided on the relationship between foreign subsidiaries. The authors emphasize that one of the MNC's key assets is its opportunity to learn from multiple markets and environments (Doz/Prahalad 1991: 154 with reference to Ghoshal 1987; Ghoshal/Nohria 1989). They do not, however, elaborate on the opportunity for different units (or subsidiaries) of the MNC to learn from one another.

White and Poynter's **Horizontal Organization** can be regarded as the MNC network concept that focuses most on internal relationships. As the name already suggests, the Horizontal Organization gives more importance to lateral processes than to vertical-reporting relationships (White/Poynter 1990: 105). It refers to an MNC which is composed of "discrete units linked by a horizontal network and lateral processes where everyone is responsible" (White/Poynter 1990: 110). Such processes include the flow of products, the development and adjustment of programs as well as the sharing of information and knowledge (White/Poynter 1990: 100-104). White and Poynter look primarily at the proactive collaboration between "geographically dispersed functional units" (White/Poynter 1990: 98). In other words, they are interested in the flexible interaction between different functional activities – R&D, purchasing, manufacturing, sales and marketing – rather than in the relationship between foreign subsidiaries per se (White/Poynter 1990: 105). Nevertheless, they specify the role of the subsidiary manager, who is in charge of seeking and exchanging information with his counterparts in other countries and encouraging his subordinates to do likewise (White/Poynter 1990: 108-109). They give the example of North American general managers who meet with their peers on a regular basis to review their operations (White/Poynter 1989: 59). As is the case with other MNC network models, interunit relationships are mainly considered to be of cooperative nature. White and Poynter do, however, address some competitive elements such as an "internal challenge mechanism" (White/Poynter 1990: 101). While geographically dispersed managers are encouraged to take initiatives, headquarters' involvement in operational decisions is limited (White/Poynter 1989: 56, 57, 59).

Although deliberately not included in the flow-related analysis by Schmid et al., Perlmutter's **Geocentrism** complements this brief review of MNC network models. In geocentric-oriented firms subsidiaries can be regarded as "parts of a whole", collaborating with headquarters and contributing with their specific competence (Perlmutter 1969a: 13). By stating that "communication is encouraged among subsidiaries" Perlmutter suggests the existence of horizontal linkages but does not specify them any further (Perlmutter 1969a: 14). This insight is supported by Schmid and Machulik's (2006) comprehensive review of the original literature on the EPRG concept.[36] The authors provide further evidence of Perlmutter's recognition of lateral communication within the geocentric firm (Schmid/Machulik 2006: 270 with reference to Chakravarthy/Perlmutter 1985). The majority of extracted "relationship characteristics", however, refer to vertical collaboration as well as headquarters' role of coordinating and integrating (subsidiary) activities (Schmid/Machulik 2006: 267 with reference to Perlmutter 1965: 157-161; 1969b: 73; Chakravarthy/Perlmutter 1985: 5). Intersubsidiary relationships are not distinguished as a core element of the geocentric firm.

Finally, the same is true for Forsgren and Johanson's view of the **Multi-Center Firm**. The authors advocate that over time the center-periphery structure of international

---

[36] "EPRG" stands for the four types of firms differentiated by Perlmutter: ethnocentric, polycentric, regiocentric and geocentric.

firms changes to a more complex, reciprocal multi-centered structure (Forsgren/ Johanson 1992: 20). Firm units are linked to each other through exchange relationships in which various functional interdependencies are handled (Forsgren/ Johanson 1992: 24). This view of interunit relationships falls short of capturing the diversity of relationships observable in practice. Taking the authors' conceptualization of the international firm as a political rather than a hierarchically controlled system (Forsgren/Johanson 1992: 23) one step further, it would very much imply competition and cooperation between units. Subsidiaries, however, are merely described as competing for influence with the former center, but not with their peers (Forsgren/Johanson 1992: 21). The authors do recognize that a political perspective on the global firm means that the group is seen as a market for different interests, in which power based on the control of critical resources may not only flow vertically but horizontally (Forsgren/Johanson 1992: 24, 28).

To sum up, the characteristics and contents of relationships between actors is an essential part of network approaches, but so far the relationships between sister units or subsidiaries in intraorganizational networks have not been examined systematically.[37]

3.3.3.3 Implications for Intersubsidiary Relationships

The above review has illustrated that the most prominent MNC network models reveal very little about the actual or potential relationships between (foreign) subsidiaries. While all models somehow imply horizontal linkages between subsidiaries, they are seldom treated separately from vertical headquarters-subsidiary relationships. Vertical relationships have mainly been addressed with respect to coordination and control issues (see Holtbrügge 2005: 565-566 for an overview of research on cross-border coordination; Baliga/Jaeger 1984; Cray 1984; Doz/Prahalad 1984); their horizontal counterparts, however, have received little individual attention in academic literature (Schmid/Kutschker 2003: 177). If network concepts of the MNC already neglect the particularities of horizontal relationships, even fewer insights can be expected from constellations to which intersubsidiary linkages are less inherent. The research gap is all the more notable given that scholars have already laid the groundwork for the analysis of horizontal linkages. Meier, for example, argues that network ties do not only represent certain types of

---

[37] For similar conclusions with respect to the concept of embeddedness see Schmid/Daub 2007: 16-17.

relationships, but that they can also differ in terms of parameters such as strength/intensity, symmetry, reciprocity or multiplexity (Meier 1997: 151). Schmid et al. define a number of flow dimensions in MNCs, including (among others) the content, domain and coordination of flows (Schmid et al. 2002: 50-56).

Another finding from the review of MNC network models is that horizontal (as well as vertical) linkages are thought to be mainly cooperative (see Schmid 2005: 237 for a confirmation of this assumption). Competitive relationships, which need not be limited to network forms of organization, are hardly addressed. Unlike TCE and the RBV, network approaches do not provide the balanced theoretical perspective needed for understanding different types of intersubsidiary cooperation *and* competition.

To sum up, network approaches underline the importance and inherent potential of intersubsidiary relationships, but contribute little to their specification and explanation. Before introducing the contingency approach as a logical consequence of the depicted theoretical insufficiency, some supplementary perspectives deserve a brief discussion.

3.3.4 Complementary Theoretical Perspectives

Above it was argued that network approaches focus mainly on the cooperative dimension of intersubsidiary relationships. The opposite applies to a number of theoretical perspectives discussed by Birkinshaw and Lingblad in an unpublished paper submitted to the Academy of Management Review in 2001 (Birkinshaw/ Lingblad 2001): Literature on internal markets (March/Simon 1958; Williamson 1975; Halal et al. 1993; Halal 1994) organizational slack (Cyert/March 1963; Bourgeois III 1981), intraorganizational evolution (Burgelman 1991; 1994) and redundancy theory (Landau 1969; Felsenthal 1980; Lerner 1987) helps explain the existence of internal competition. Of the four perspectives, Birkinshaw and Lingblad choose **redundancy theory** to develop propositions on the conditions under which internal competition is expected to occur. Given that (a) the authors provide reasonable arguments for their choice and (b) the focus of all four perspectives is even narrower than that of network approaches, only implications from redundancy theory will be discussed here.

Birkinshaw and Lingblad define internal competition as "the existence of duplicate or overlapping activities within the boundaries of the firm that is condoned by senior management as a means of addressing market or technological uncertainty" (Birkinshaw/Lingblad 2001: 6). Lerner had already distinguished between

duplication and overlap as the two primary mechanisms of redundancy (Lerner 1987: 335-336). While duplication emphasizes parallelism (by assigning identical functions to two units, for example), overlap emphasizes ambiguity (by defining roles that include some of the same functions). According to Felsenthal, **redundancy** is a quality that characterizes elements of a system which "make some contribution to the achievement of the system's goal, but this contribution is blurred because some other element(s) make(s) a similar contribution" (Felsenthal 1980: 248). The author illustrates that redundancy can have negative, positive or neutral connotations. Advocates of redundancy theory argue that the objective of introducing redundancy into organizations is to increase **reliability** (Landau 1969: 346; Felsenthal 1980: 247; Lerner 1987: 335). If one part of the system fails, another can take over. Birkinshaw and Lingblad extend this view by arguing that the purpose of duplicate or overlapping activities in internal competition is to enhance the organization's **adaptability** to environmental change (Birkinshaw/Lingblad 2001: 12). Technological or customer-related uncertainty is addressed by pursuing several options simultaneously. This line of argument shows certain parallels with the consequences of bounded rationality, which were discussed as a key feature of TCE (see subsection 3.3.1.2). While redundancy-for-reliability involves two units "pursuing the same ends with the same means", redundancy-for-adaptability involves units "pursuing the same ends with different means" (Birkinshaw/Lingblad 2001: 13). Consequently, units dedicated to ensuring reliability maintain a cooperative relationship. The relationship between units operating independently to allow management to choose the 'best' option will have a competitive element (Birkinshaw/Lingblad 2001: 14).

As far as redundancy-for-adaptability is concerned, the authors propose two design options: duplication and overlap. The type of internal competition that is relevant to this research most closely corresponds to overlap redundancy, which results from ambiguity in the definition of unit roles (Birkinshaw/Lingblad 2001: 16). Intersubsidiary competition for customers and charters can exist only if geographic, customer-oriented or competence-based responsibilities are not rigidly allocated. Duplication redundancy, on the other hand, refers to the existence of two parallel units that compete to try to solve a particular problem. In the context of this research having two subsidiaries working on exactly the same tasks is expected to be observable on a very sporadic basis only – for example, when both develop their project proposals. Compared to redundancy-for-reliability, which is built into organizations on a permanent basis, redundancy-for-adaptability in general tends to be of a more temporary nature (Birkinshaw/Lingblad 2001: 13-14).

Given the preliminary character of their paper, the propositions Birkinshaw and Lingblad develop with respect to the factors that lead organizations to establish and terminate redundancy are not summarized here. A number of determinants actually reappear in their 2005 Organization Science article on intrafirm competition and charter evolution (Birkinshaw/Lingblad 2005) – interestingly detached from redundancy theory (see the review of influencing factors in section 3.5).

To sum up, there are a number of theoretical perspectives which may help shed light on the phenomenon of intersubsidiary competition. Redundancy theory seems particularly useful for understanding different forms of internal competition (or rather redundancy-for-adaptability) and their related organizational mechanisms. But apart from the scenario that units serve as backups for each other, it reveals little about cooperative intersubsidiary relationships. Consequently, redundancy theory does not provide any hints as to why MNCs differ in terms of their intersubsidiary relationships. Before concluding this subsection, two important remarks should be made with respect to two theoretical perspectives, which – contrary to possible expectations – are of little relevance to this research: game theory and the so-called 'theory of competition and cooperation'.

First, it may strike those familiar with literature on (interorganizational) coopetition (for example, Brandenburger/Nalebuff 1996; Ullrich 2004) that **game theory** is not considered as a suitable approach to the research topic. Game theory addresses situations in which the result for a decision maker is not only dependent on his or her own decisions but also on the behavior of others (Ullrich 2004: 10 with reference to Fudenberg/Tirole 1991: 1; Jost 2001: 9, among others). Although peer behavior could be relevant for strategy definition at the subsidiary level, game theory does not seem helpful for answering the specific research questions, i.e. how and why MNCs differ in terms of the prevailing intersubsidiary relationships. Strategic orientation, which is proposed as a key influencing factor, is a firm-level attribute. The focus of this research is on the organizational structures and processes that facilitate intersubsidiary competition and/or cooperation in the acquisition and execution of large-scale projects. Relevant theoretical perspectives need to account for both the headquarters-led and the subsidiary-led origin of relationships. Approaching the topic from a game theory perspective would imply a rather different research focus – such as the study of the competitive game that may unfold when subsidiaries are held in multimarket competition (see Li et al. 2007: 13, 26).

Second, the discussion of different types of internal competition and cooperation in section 2.4 suggested that interunit (or intersubsidiary) relationships may be approached from both an interorganizational and an interpersonal angle. TCE, the RBV and network approaches are all perspectives that were originally developed to explore and explain interorganizational phenomena – although their application to the intraorganizational level has become increasingly common. By conceptualizing the MNC as an interorganizational network (Ghoshal/Bartlett 1990; Forsgren/Johanson 1992) important parallels between the two levels are suggested. Interpersonal approaches tend to have their origins in social psychology. A complete review of related work would exceed the scope of this (managerial) research, but the title of one very early contribution attracts particular attention: "A Theory of Co-operation and Competition" by Morton Deutsch (1949).[38] Beersma et al. provide a compressed yet comprehensive summary of the article: "In his goal interdependence **theory of cooperation and competition**, Deutsch (1949) argued that people's beliefs about how their goals are related determine the way in which they interact, which in turn affects their performance and group cohesiveness. Central to this theory is the categorization of situations that create cooperative or competitive orientations within the people involved" (Beersma et al. 2003: 573-574). Deutsch himself states that the purpose of his article is "to sketch out a theory of the effect of co-operation and competition upon small [...] group functioning" (Deutsch 1949: 129). These statements reveal that Deutsch is more interested in exploring the *effects* of interpersonal (or interunit) competition and cooperation than their determinants – although he does provide a rather rich description of the underlying social situations.[39] Before presenting the basic concepts of his theory and their inherent (psychological) implications, the author reviews the definitions and formulations of cooperation and competition provided by other scholars. May and Doob's work is worth mentioning here. The two scholars develop some basic postulates on the conditions for competition and cooperation. Whether individuals compete or cooperate with one another on a social level depends on (a) the nature of the aspired goal, (b) the rules of the situation, (c) the performance implications of their actions and (d) the number of psychological affiliative contacts they have with one another (Deutsch 1949: 130 with reference to May/Doob 1937: 17). Some of these considerations may be transferable to an interunit or intersubsidiary level. They do not, however, reveal why and when competition is preferred over cooperation and vice versa. Given its limited area of application, Deutsch's framework does not actually constitute a substantial (scientific) theory that helps explain relationships at

---

[38] For an overview of past studies on internal competition in social psychology see Matsuo 2005: 45. The author also reviews competition studies in a management context, but his focus lies on the interpersonal level.
[39] For a summary of positive and negative effects of competition on group performance also see Matsuo 2005: 46-47.

different levels of analysis. Interestingly, in the remaining half of the century there were apparently no attempts to integrate Deutsch's work into such a holistic "theory of cooperation and competition".

3.3.5 Interim Conclusion

The above discussion of theoretical perspectives has illustrated that they all touch upon certain aspects of intersubsidiary relationships but are of limited relevance when it comes to addressing the specific research questions. Consequently, it seems of little value to this research to mingle them into an eclectic approach. Nevertheless, the mere consideration of combining different theoretical angles calls for a brief justification of such practice.

An important foundation is that TCE, the RBV and network approaches can all three be attributed to what Burrell and Morgan define as the **functionalist paradigm** (Burrell/Morgan 1979: 25-28). In 1979 the authors have made an attempt to classify social (or organizational) theories according to their meta-theoretical assumptions on the nature of science and the nature of society. Four different paradigms result from the combination of a subjective or objective approach to science and a sociology of regulation or radical change (for the resulting 2x2 matrix see Burrell/Morgan 1979: 22). The functionalist paradigm represents a perspective that is deeply rooted in the sociology of regulation and adopts an objectivist approach to the analysis of the social world. It is the dominant framework for the study of organizations (Burrell/Morgan 1979: 25). Functional theorists seek to provide rational explanations of social affairs, are pragmatic in orientation and problem-oriented in approach. The functionalist paradigm follows the intellectual tradition of sociological positivism (for an overview of the basic positions and beliefs of positivism and postpositivism see, for example, Guba/Lincoln 2005: 193-196). Relationships are concrete and can be identified, studied and measured via science. Sociological concerns are addressed from a realist, positivist, determinist and nomothetic standpoint (Burrell/Morgan 1979: 26).[40]

So far, IB scholars have made few attempts to approach research topics from an interpretive, radical humanist or radical structuralist point of view (Kutschker/Schmid

---

[40] For a discussion of the assumptions related to ontology, epistemology, human nature and methodology see Burrell/Morgan 1979: 1-7.

2006: 466).[41] It should be noted that when Peng refers to IB's tendency to resist single paradigms (Peng 2001: 822 with reference to Toyne/Nigh 1997), he implies Kuhn's definition of paradigms as "universally recognized scientific achievements that for a time provide model problems and solutions to a community of practitioners" (Kuhn 1962: viii). Burrell and Morgan explicitly state that they are using the term 'paradigm' in a broader sense than that intended by Kuhn (Burrell/Morgan 1979: 36). They regard their four distinct and rival paradigms "as being defined by very basic meta-theoretical assumptions which underwrite the frame of reference, mode of theorizing and *modus operandi* of the social theorists who operate within them" (Burrell/Morgan 1979: 23). A paradigm binds together the work of theorists who have a common perspective on approaching social theory.

Although TCE, the RBV and network approaches provide distinct explanations for certain business phenomena, their proponents share a general understanding of the nature of science and society. The **compatibility of theories** located in one and the same paradigm will consequently be much higher than that of theories belonging to different paradigms. Particularly the compatibility of TCE and the RBV has frequently been addressed in IB literature. Citing the founding father of TCE, Peng argues that "while the relation between TCE and the RBV is both rival and complementary, it is probably 'more the latter than the former'" (Peng 2001: 820 with reference to Williamson 1999: 1106). Having evaluated the similarities and distinctions between the two theories, Mahoney comes to the same conclusion: TCE and the RBV can be viewed as complementary – the former being a theory of firm rents, the latter a theory of the existence of the firm (Mahoney 2001: 655). Windsperger chooses a similar line of argument for such complementarity, pointing out that TCE aims at explaining the coordination function of the firm, while the RBV investigates the development of specific resources and organizational capabilities (Windsperger 1998: 267 with reference to Chandler 1990: 594). In terms of this particular research, one could also think of TCE as taking a top-down approach to the decision between market and hierarchy, while the RBV adds a bottom-up perspective by investigating the basis of competition and cooperation.[42] Argyres and Zenger go yet another step further by encouraging scholars to abandon the idea that a meaningful distinction existed between TCE and the RBV and instead recognize that the two theories are not only complementary but "inextricably intertwined" (Argyres/Zenger 2007: 5). They call on

---

[41] Denzin and Lincoln consider all research to be "interpretive" and differentiate between four major paradigms that structure qualitative research: (1) positivist and postpositivist, (2) constructivist-interpretive, (3) critical and (4) feminist-poststructural (Denzin/Lincoln 2005: 22).

[42] For a discussion of the implications of TCE and the RBV for intersubsidiary relationships see subsections 3.3.1.3 and 3.3.2.3, respectively.

their peers to seek to analyze aspects of this complex interaction – a request Barney had launched nearly a decade earlier by urging managers to consider the cost of creating or acquiring capabilities in determining a firm's boundaries (Barney 1999: 140, 143-144).

There are several practical examples of IB scholars choosing an **eclectic approach**, i.e. employing more than a single theory to arrive at an explanation for or an exemplification of certain phenomena. Birkinshaw, for example, sets out to reconcile the phenomenon of subsidiary initiative with the exact three theoretical perspectives on the MNC presented above: TCE, the RBV and network approaches (Birkinshaw 2001b: 98-109).[43] He evaluates the extent to which his ideas on subsidiary entrepreneurship are consistent with or relevant to these theories and proposes necessary modifications or extensions. As Cerrato criticizes, Birkinshaw does not apply the same theoretical rigor to his analysis of the three different types of internal market that form part of his model (Birkinshaw 2001b: 117-120; Cerrato 2006: 262). Cerrato himself tries to fill this gap by linking the configuration of each type of market to a particular research stream: Internalization theory addresses the questions related to the establishment of the market for intermediate products or services, the RBV provides useful explanations for the market for charters, and organizational learning and knowledge management literature sheds light on the market for capabilities or practices (see Cerrato 2006: 262 for an overview). By following Birkinshaw in "disentangling the internal market model" (Cerrato 2006: 261) the author does not take on the challenge of identifying an all-encompassing theory or framework, either. He further forgoes the identification of alternative theoretical approaches to each sub-market. As reiterated in subsection 3.3.2.3, intraorganizational cooperation through the exchange of knowledge and competencies, for example, may also be explained by the RBV. Finally, Cerrato himself admits that the distinction between three markets does not take into account the connections and commonalities among them. Despite their drawbacks, both Birkinshaw's and Cerrato's contributions are highly relevant to this research. The two examples should suffice to illustrate how multiple theoretical perspectives are combined for explanatory purposes when a single theory seems to fall short of elucidating a particular phenomenon.

As revealed in the previous subsections, there is no substantial theory that can comprehensively explain the horizontal relationships between multiple units (here:

---

[43] The author himself recognizes that what he calls "the network theory of the MNC" is more adequately referred to as a paradigm or framework.

subsidiaries) within an MNC. A pluralistic approach helps understand different facets of the phenomenon, which can then be joined together to form a comprehensive whole.[44] But even in combination the theories do not prove useful for explaining why differences in intersubsidiary relationships exist across firms. Consequently, a contingency approach suggests itself for finding an answer to this question. Explaining interunit (not necessarily intersubsidiary) relationships through the existence of certain influencing factors corresponds to the (few) attempts that have been made by other scholars. Their propositions will be summarized following a (critical) discussion of the contents and characteristics of the contingency approach. The identification of relevant influencing factors for competition and cooperation between MNC subsidiaries has certainly been inspired by this previous work.

3.4 Contingency Approach

Since the evaluated theories are not able to provide an answer to the question of why MNCs differ in terms of their intersubsidiary relationships, an alternative path needs to be followed. Ideally this approach leaves room for the identification of plausible, managerially relevant determinants of the observed differences. This overall logic is best captured by contingency theory, which traces differences in the structure of an organization and the behavior of its members back to situational factors (see, for example, Ebers 1992; Schmid 1994; Kieser 2002). How to explain formal organization structures and specifications becomes particularly relevant if one implies that these structures have a strong influence on organizational efficiency. However, since it can be assumed that there is no such thing as universally efficient organization structures, organizations need to adapt their structures to the respective situation. In other words, the situation an organization finds itself in to a certain degree determines its structures.

Applying this logic to the underlying research question means that intersubsidiary relationships (which form part of the formal and/or informal organization structure) can be traced back to certain internal and/or external influencing factors. Previous work in the field inspires the identification of relevant influencing factors, but ultimately comparative empirical research is needed to examine the proposed relationship. Before addressing the specific research question, however, a general overview of the contingency approach is provided. It should be noted that this

---

[44] See, for example, the reference to Sydow's demand for an eclectic approach/perspective in Petry 2006: 31.

contingency approach actually comprises a number of approaches which differ in terms of the particular contingency they stress as being most influential (which is why the term 'contingency theory' seems misleading). Based upon a brief introduction to its historical roots (subsection 3.4.1), the basic concepts and methods of the contingency approach are outlined (subsection 3.4.2) and critically evaluated (subsection 3.4.3). Examples from IB research illustrate some important particularities (subsection 3.4.4) and lead up to the review of key research implications (subsection 3.4.5).

3.4.1 Historical Development

Contingency theory has its philosophic roots in **critical rationalism**, which was advanced by Karl Popper in the early 20th century (see, for example, Popper 1934; 1972). Schmid demonstrates how critical rationalism unites the basic concept of classical rationalism with select methods of classical empiricism (Schmid 1994: 5-11). Achieving scientific knowledge is still based upon the interaction of intuition and deduction but is complemented by the demand for empirical investigation of the derived hypotheses, theories and principles (Kern 1979: 11-16). This focus on empirical investigation – accompanied by the recognition that such investigation will never be able to fully support the developed theories – is particularly relevant to the underlying research.[45] In the 1960s and 1970s, Popper's scientific understanding coined the social sciences in general and organization research in particular. Large-scale quantitative empirical investigations were considered the best solution to an objective and exact science. It is against this background that the development of the contingency approach needs to be understood.

The contingency approach has evolved from a number of theories or scientific programs. The question as to whether different manifestations of the organization structure can be ascribed to distinct situations first arose in the attempt to verify Max Weber's bureaucracy concept. A central finding was that organizations by no means corresponded to an ideal type of bureaucracy (Kieser 2002: 169). In the 1950s management scholars increasingly shared the notion that there could not be any general organization principles which at the same time provided specific design recommendations. Instead they vowed for considering the **respective problem definitions** (Kieser 2002: 170). Joan Woodward was among the first to claim that when formulating design recommendations for global organization structures, each

---

[45] For a discussion of the key components of critical rationalism see Schmid 1994: 8-10.

organization's initial situation needed to be considered. In empirical analyses she established a relationship between structural characteristics such as spans of control and hierarchical levels and the manufacturing technique an organization employed (Woodward 1958; 1965). The confinement to a single influencing factor is characteristic of the early days of the contingency approach (see, for example, Child 1970). Burns and Stalker, for example, mainly analyzed the impact of the environment on organizational structure (Burns/Stalker 1961). Empirical investigations supported their hypothesis that organic structures were more efficient in dynamic environments, mechanistic structures in static environments.

The contingency approach was significantly shaped by scholars from the Anglo-Saxon world. A group of researchers from the United States mainly dealt with the methodological aspects of the approach and carried out numerous empirical investigations. Later a group of researchers from Great Britain, the so-called 'Aston Group' around Derek Pugh, dedicated themselves to the improvement of measuring techniques, the simultaneous consideration of multiple variables and the attempt to develop an integrated concept (see, for example, Pugh/Hickson 1971; Pugh 1981). Their work is considered as having given important direction to quantitative empirical organization research. As will be shown, however, the contingency approach may just as well form the basis of qualitative research.

3.4.2 Concepts and Methods

The contingency approach assumes that the **structure** of an organization and the **behavior** of its members can be attributed to differences in the **situation**. Depending on the situation, structure and behavior will be of varying **efficiency** (Ebers 1992: 1818; Schmid 1994: 12). Linked to these propositions are the questions of which situational factors lead to which structures and behaviors, and which consequences alternative structure-behavior constellations have for organizational efficiency (Ebers 1992). The corresponding framework is depicted in Figure 7.

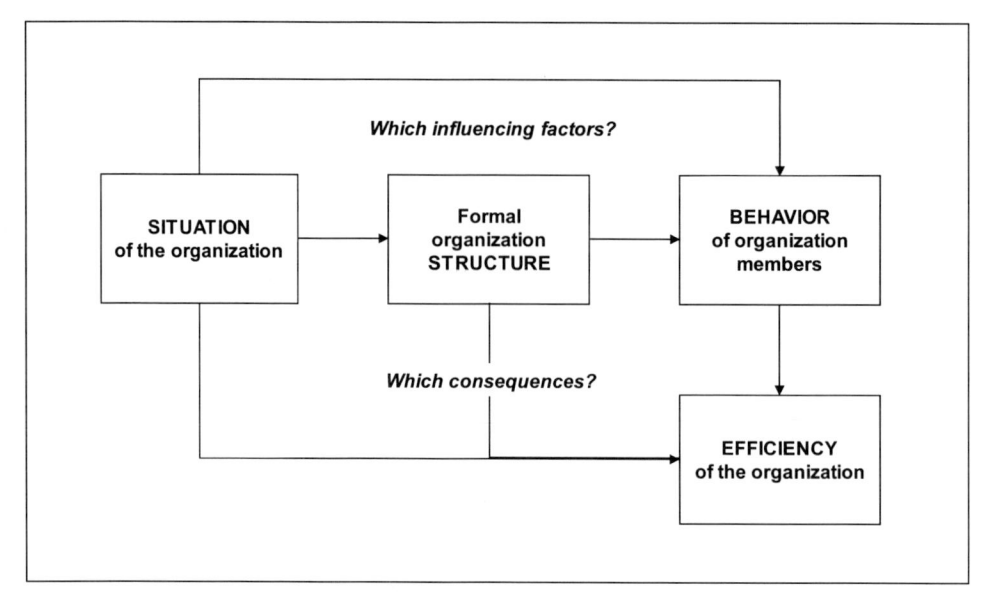

Figure 7: The Contingency Approach as a Scientific Program
Source: Kieser/Kubicek 1992: 57.

One would expect the contingency approach to be built upon some kind of theory that yielded testable hypotheses concerning the above relationships; but as Kieser notes this has not been the case (Kieser 2002: 176). Instead, scholars have geared their activities towards identifying empirical patterns, which they try to explain retrospectively by means of so-called ad-hoc assumptions (on ad-hoc theory adjustment within situational analysis see Caldwell 1991: 15-16). In any case, the disclosure of causal relationships between situation, structure, behavior and efficiency requires the **operationalization** of these concepts.

Dimensions for operationalizing the concept of organization **structure** can be derived from Weber's bureaucracy concept (see Pugh/Hickson 1971) as well as classical organization theory (Woodward 1958; 1965). In accordance with Weber, Pugh and Hickson define the following five variables: specialization, standardization, centralization, formalization and configuration. In more recent conceptualizations of the contingency approach additional coordination variables are introduced. The importance of coordination mechanisms increases with a rising degree of specialization (Ebers 1992: 1822; Kieser 2002: 173). All of the above variables have in common that they characterize the formal structure of an organization, i.e. that they are independent of the personal attributes of its members. This objectivity claim persists in the analysis phase. Structural parameters are preferably captured through issues that are objectively observable or communicated by top management rather than revealed by interrogating organization members. Initially nominal scales were used for measurement purposes; interval scales followed. Data is and has been evaluated by means of correlation and factor analysis (see Pugh/Hickson 1971: 77 on measuring the centralization of decision making).

The concept of the **situation** is typically operationalized through variables such as environment, size and manufacturing technique (Daft 1983: 15; for selected empirical results see Kieser 2002: 176-182). Additional, or alternative, dimensions of the internal and external situation can be taken from an overview provided by Kieser (Kieser 2002: 175). Similarly Ebers attributes the situational factors to three levels of analysis: global environment, task environment and internal situation (Ebers 1992: 1823). All situational factors have in common that they are not based upon a specific theory but rather on plausibility assumptions (Kieser 2002: 175). In empirical investigations both perception measures – in terms of interviews – and hard data are used. Kieser, however, emphasizes that the goal of situational analyses is to identify organizational rules and regulations under the objective conditions of the situation.

The effects the organization structure has on the **behavior** of its members, and indirectly on the **efficiency** of the organization, are particularly difficult to grasp empirically. So far scholars have not convincingly succeeded in isolating the effects of the organization structure from the numerous other influencing factors (Kieser 2002: 176). Although a specification of the efficiency term constitutes an important precondition for establishing such a contingency, Kieser himself refrains from providing a definition that goes beyond 'a company's target achievement' (Kieser 2002: 171). In the context of the contingency approach, the conceptualization of efficiency as an internal performance measure specifying the relation between output and input seems valid (Plinke 2000: 86; compare to the discussion in section 3.2).

Given their deductive-nomological stance, the advocates of the contingency approach tend to favor large-scale, oftentimes written surveys as well as document analysis (Ebers 1992: 1825). Qualitative methods have mostly been used on a supplementary basis only, as they oppose the purely objective development of knowledge (compare, for example, the overview of contingency studies on performance evaluation of foreign subsidiaries in Schmid/Kretschmer 2010: 236-258; Schmid/ Kretschmer 2006: 20-29). In more recent approaches this constraint tends to be loosened in favor of finding answers to very distinct organizational problems (see section 3.5 for relevant examples).

3.4.3 Critical Assessment of the Contingency Approach

Although – or exactly because – the contingency approach has found such broad implementation in organization research, it is important to highlight some critical points with respect to methods and contents. Several scholars have addressed these issues (see, for example, Child 1972: 191; Türk 1989: 1-10; Frese 1992: 190-197). The following argumentation reflects the assessment by Kieser, who has succeeded in providing a particularly concise summary (Kieser 2002: 183-191). One goal of the review is to avoid the replication of certain mistakes or misconceptions in this research – which is why key takeaways are summarized for each subsection. Exactly these practical implications are the reason for not having included such a systematic assessment for the previously challenged theoretical perspectives (particularly TCE, the RBV and network approaches). In section 3.3, the latter were evaluated in terms of their contribution to explaining differences in intersubsidiary relationships. Given that the explanatory power of the alternative theories turned out to be limited, enhancing awareness of their methodological and content-related pitfalls was not necessary – it is however, for the chosen contingency approach.

3.4.3.1 Methodological Criticism

Kieser formulates five critical points regarding the methodology of the contingency approach (Kieser 2002: 183-191; similarly see Schmid 1994: 16-18): (1) Important situational and structural **characteristics** are not considered. Conceptions of the organization structure and the situational influencing factors have constantly been – and continue to be – extended. (2) The **measures** used are not valid, not reliable and not comparable across different studies. Measures do not correspond to the standards of empirical social research and differ even if the same structural dimensions are at issue. (3) The statistical **methods** used are not appropriate. In the aggregation of correlating indices or measures it is not considered whether the underlying organizational issues are actually substitutable; non-linear relationships between variables are not investigated sufficiently. (4) **Samples** are not representative and not comparable. On the one hand, the population of relevant organizations is unknown; on the other hand, results are oftentimes biased due to the focus on organizations that are willing to participate. In international management the results of situational research may also be distorted because values and interests, as well as the comprehension of terms, concepts and scales may differ across cultures (Schmid 1994: 17-18). (5) The informational **content** of the empirically supported results of the contingency approach is low. Although causal relationships are revealed, important factual or practical consequences are neglected. Practical design recommendations are oftentimes sacrificed for generalizability achieved through abstraction.

Schmid's criticism begins at the epistemological basis of the contingency approach. He criticizes that by concentrating on the method, the reflection on the actual research goals and objects is overshadowed. Oftentimes empirical studies are not directed towards the investigation of an underlying theory but the collection and analysis of objectively identifiable and measurable data. In general, the transfer of methods from the natural to the social sciences is problematic – universal laws oftentimes have limited explanatory power in management studies (Schmid 1994: 16-17). Due to the deficits described above, organization design has received little support from the contingency approach. Kieser, however, notes that the informational content of the results can be substantially increased through industry-specific analyses. Such an approach allows a more precise identification of structures and situational factors and makes problem solutions more comparable or transferable (Kieser 2002: 184). The intercultural problematic however persists.

Key takeaways for this research are to (1) be very clear on the research goals and objectives, (2) try to identify the most important and relevant influencing factors, (3) provide a solid justification for the chosen samples, (4) enhance informational content and managerial implications through industry-specific analyses, (5) give priority to the profound investigation of a particular theory rather than mere data collection and (6) possibly address intercultural differences.

3.4.3.2 Content-Related Criticism

Regarding content Kieser criticizes the contingency approach in the following six points (Kieser 2002: 185-191 and similarly Schmid 1994: 14-15): (1) The situation does not determine the organization structure but at best sets certain design ranges. In response to specific situational factors there is not just one correct structural form. Instead there are **multiple options** to choose from, since valid algorithms for the identification of ideal structural alternatives do not exist. Possibly two (or more) structures could turn out to provide similarly satisfying solutions. The example of innovative manufacturing techniques has shown that situational factors can also open completely new organizational horizons. The situational factors are not to be regarded as given. Managers can actively change a situation rather than passively adapting to it. Their philosophies and motives exert a strong influence on organization design. Also, organizations do not always have to be (maximally) efficient to survive. Markets are imperfect, so that deficits in one area can very well be compensated by above-average performance in another area. (2) The contingency approach does not contain a concept that explains the **adaptation** of the organization structure to the situation. In terms of a functional explanation it is argued that the organization structure needs to adapt to specific situational requirements. This statement, however, is neither based on a plausible causal mechanism nor does it reveal through which processes such adaptation exactly occurs. (3) The contingency approach neglects the execution of **power** in organizations. The functional interpretation of organization structures masks which influence the behavior of organization members, particularly management's quest for authority, has on their design. (4) The contingency approach propagates a conservative organization design. Finding solutions is limited to **historical experiences** with organization structures but does not encourage the search for currently undiscovered alternatives. If practice adhered to the results this would lead to a self-reinforcing cycle. (5) Organization structures cannot be conceptualized and captured in an objective manner, i.e. independent of the perceptions, intentions and actions of the organization members. Interpretative or constructivist approaches hold the view that the activities of organization members are less determined by formal rules and regulations but rather reflect the result of **negotiation** processes. Explanations for such action are therefore more likely to be found in the analysis of value systems, symbols, etc. than in the organization structure. (6) Regularities in the relationships between situation and organization structure differ from **culture** to culture. A more detailed analysis of organization design in different cultures reveals that the differences are hard to explain by means of situational factors. Instead they seem closely linked to the cultural development of the respective country.

Against the background of this criticism, Ebers addresses four demands to organization research: It should (1) consider the construction of social reality, (2) include the flexibility of decision makers, (3) account for social and historical conditions and (4) attach a higher importance to processes (Ebers 1992: 1832; on the active role of decision makers in organization design also see Kieser 2002: 191). Schmid further calls for an examination of not only managers' but other **actors' perspectives** (Schmid 1994: 25). The above claims have led to several advancements of the contingency approach, of which Child's concept of strategic choice (Child 1972) and Mintzberg's structural types (Mintzberg 1979) are particularly noteworthy. Most of these advancements arrive at the conclusion that an organization is successful if it manages to realize a fit between structure and situation. In addition, they reflect the claim that strategies and structures are coherent among themselves. It becomes apparent that the organization structure is not solely determined by the situation. But even the advancements of the contingency approach are not able to explain why and how a certain structure evolves.

Again, **key takeaways** for this research are to (1) account for design ranges or two (or more) similarly adequate structural responses, (2) reflect upon change and adaptation processes, (3) consider power and negotiation issues in organizations, (4) allow for innovative organizational options, cultural implications and economic trends and (5) try to explain the fit between structure and situation without assuming that the situation is the only possible influencing factor.

Although the contingency approach has been severely criticized, its achievements should not be diminished. Content-wise the contingency approach broadened the perspective of organization research by drawing attention to the structural differences among organizations and highlighting the importance of situational influences. At the same time the broad range of formal organization structures became evident. Empirical results show that due to a variety of influencing factors there is no such thing as the best organizational form in general (Ebers 1992: 1817). In terms of methodology, the contingency approach not only led to an abundance of empirical data on organizations but also contributed to an important refinement of the methods used in organization research (Ebers 1992: 1829).

3.4.4 The Contingency Approach in IB Research

IB scholars are also very interested in what the choice of an organization structure depends on (Kutschker/Schmid 2006: 542). The empirical work undertaken to answer this question can be divided into two groups: comparative analyses of MNCs and comparative analyses of independent organizations in different cultures (Kieser 1989: 1574). Both streams have some important implications for this research.

A large number of studies exist which examine MNCs, their organization structures, headquarters-subsidiary relationships as well as coordination and control mechanisms in the tradition of the contingency approach.[46] Kutschker and Schmid present three classical empirical studies that investigate the development of international organization structures (Kutschker/Schmid 2006: 542-550). The authors

---

[46] Welge (1980), for example, analyzes what influences the efficiency of subsidiaries of German MNCs. For an overview of studies on performance evaluation of foreign subsidiaries see Schmid/Kretschmer 2010: 236-258; Schmid/Kretschmer 2006: 20-29.

of these studies try to establish a link between the choice and sequence of organization structures and progressive international expansion. The latter is operationalized by the percentage of foreign to total sales and the level of foreign product diversity (Stopford/Wells 1972; Franko 1976), complemented by the level of foreign manufacturing (Egelhoff 1982).

What the three aforementioned studies have in common is that they are led by a **structure-follows-strategy** perspective: an MNC's international organization structure is determined by its internationalization strategy (or the related situational factors). This perspective goes back to the seminal work by Alfred Chandler, who in his historical studies of U.S. corporations found that managerial organization developed in response to the corporation's business strategy (Chandler 1962). In the meantime this assumption has been discussed quite controversially (see, for example, Hall/Saias 1980; Schewe 1998; Harris/Ruefli 2000). Not only may organizational decisions be influenced by a variety of other factors (such as company history, personal experience, management philosophy); the reverse perspective also needs to be considered: the development of an appropriate organization structure may constitute an important condition for the successful implementation of a strategy (see, for example, Ortmann/Sydow 2001: 428). The structure of an organization should allow (and encourage) its members to best fulfill the respective strategic requirements. A balanced view that advocates a fit between strategy and structure seems most reasonable and will be readdressed in the course of this research.[47]

Another important aspect is that the presented studies are suggestive of supporting the **culture-free thesis**. Although differences between U.S. and European corporations were addressed (compare Franko 1976 and Egelhoff 1982), the reasons for such differences were not investigated. Particularly cultural influences were neglected. Given firms' increasing global market presence, intercultural comparisons of organization structures have gained both theoretical and practical relevance. Several scholars have set out to investigate whether culture had an influence on the organization structure or not. Harbison and Myers were among the early proponents of the culture-free thesis, postulating that the organization structure is not determined by cultural factors but rather follows the logic of industrialization (Harbison/Myers 1959; Kieser 1989: 1576). Other scholars share the belief that the relationship between organizational dimensions (split of work, formalization, (de)centralization, etc.) and contextual factors (size of the organization, environmental changes,

---

[47] On the standard logic of contingency theory that a fit between environmental and structural characteristics enhances performance see, for example, Lawrence/Lorsch 1967; Galbraith 1973.

technology, etc.) is relatively stable across cultures (see, for example, Donaldson 1985). The proclaimed stability in grand relationships, however, does not exclude differences in details (for examples see Kieser 1989: 1576-1577). Empirical studies have revealed that MNCs choose different strategies for the design of headquarters-subsidiary relationships depending on the cultural affiliation of their home country. Similarly, organization structures of foreign subsidiaries are to a certain extent influenced by the culture of the host country (Kieser 1989: 1582). Depending on the method of investigation, organization structures are more likely to be regarded as culture-free or culture-bound. The more precise the concepts and methods employed and the narrower the area of investigation, the more likely differences are to appear. Qualitative analyses leave more room for the emergence of differences than quantitative ones (Kieser 1989: 1576). As will be argued later, the relative strength of corporate culture and the focus on factual issues (e.g., by interrogating experts) are also important for assessing the influence of national culture on organizational parameters.

3.4.5 Research Implications

The main conclusion from the above discussion is that the contingency approach can provide a very useful and problem-oriented approach to organizational analysis if it is applied with the necessary diligence. In this research, a strong effort is made to act upon the key takeaways derived from the critical assessment of the contingency approach, as well as the particularities inherent in respective IB research.

More specifically, this research sets out to identify and investigate contingency factors that account for cross-company differences in intersubsidiary relationships. The operationalization of organization structure is extended from a vertical perspective – focusing on centralization, configuration and coordination (see, for example, the conceptualization in Ehemann 2007: 7-8)[48] – to horizontal interaction patterns. Interunit, or intersubsidiary, relationships are considered as an important characteristic of the formal and/or informal organization structure.[49] The list of potential influencing factors is long, but – as demonstrated in the next section – can be reduced to a few, particularly convincing parameters. Explicitly referring to

---

[48] Oftentimes centralization (concentration) and decentralization (dispersion) are considered as the two extreme alternatives of configuration (see, for example, Schmid/Grosche 2009: 4-5).
[49] Compare to Birkinshaw/Lingblad 2005: 684, who not only suggest to treat intrafirm competition as a legitimate attribute of an organization but regard the characteristics of a unit's charter as "relatively new facets of organization design".

cooperative and competitive behavior, Wimmer and Neuberger emphasize that one should always ask how strong the effect of the respective situational factors is (Wimmer/Neuberger 1982: 198).

As the discussion of alternative theoretical perspectives has revealed, none of them is able to provide a set of contingency factors that is likely to explain why MNCs differ in terms of their intersubsidiary relationships. Consequently, contingencies between situational factors and intersubsidiary relationships are predicted fairly independently of the discussed theories – although it should be recognized that some aspects do help in the development of propositions. Reviewing the existing literature for proposed influencing factors is a logical first step, which is undertaken in the next section. This review underlines that it is common practice not to develop or define contingency factors based on substantial theories but rather by applying sound business logic.

Finally, it is worth noting that the contingency approach lacks the theoretical basis for assessing the value or performance of a particular organization structure (Windsperger 1997: 192 with reference to Ouchi/Van de Ven 1980; Ebers 1992; Frese 1992). The objective of this research is to explain how and why MNCs differ in terms of their intersubsidiary relationships and to possibly trace how and why the respective relationships have evolved. A performance-related assessment of each scenario is feasible only on a most general and company-centric level.[50] The derived contingency framework of intersubsidiary relationships is presented in Figure 15 (section 5.2) upon introduction of its dependent and independent variables.

3.5 Influencing Factors

As indicated in the previous section, a review of contingency studies on interunit competition and/or cooperation is an important starting point for identifying those factors that are expected to have the greatest effect on why MNCs differ in terms of their intersubsidiary relationships. In other words, the goal is not to integrate all potential influencing factors into a contingency framework of intersubsidiary relationships but rather to focus the investigation on the most convincing one(s). At the same time, it is crucial to find **factors that are valid for both** competition and cooperation or, better even, explain the choice between the two. The number of

---

[50] On the difficulties of linking intrafirm competition to organization performance see Birkinshaw/Lingblad 2005: 682-683.

relevant studies is limited since up to now it has been a common approach in literature to focus on either the competitive or the cooperative aspect of interunit relationships (Tsai 2002: 180). Another limitation is that the developed propositions should be broad enough to comprise interunit (or intersubsidiary) competition and cooperation in general and not just select subcategories, i.e. certain origins or objects (for an overview see sections 2.3 and 2.4).

In order to get a good grasp of suggested influencing factors despite the limited number of contributions fulfilling all of the above criteria, the following studies are reviewed: (1) studies referring to interunit (or intersubsidiary) competition *or* cooperation in a very broad sense, i.e. without restrictions regarding origin or content and (2) studies taking a balanced contingency approach to interunit (or intersubsidiary) competition and cooperation, even if they neglect some possible manifestations.

The following three subsections are dedicated to a discussion of the determinants of interunit competition (subsection 3.5.1), cooperation (subsection 3.5.2), and coopetition (subsection 3.5.3), respectively.

3.5.1 Determinants of Interunit Competition

Birkinshaw and Lingblad are among the few authors to develop propositions regarding the environmental and organizational determinants of intrafirm competition (Birkinshaw/Lingblad 2005: 684). Just as Birkinshaw (2001a), however, the authors focus on competition between technologies and business units rather than subsidiaries, and neglect international particularities. This becomes evident when they state that in a stable business environment charters evoke little discussion, whereas in a turbulent environment with rapidly evolving growth opportunities they become highly contentious (Birkinshaw/Lingblad 2005: 676). In MNCs, however, responsibilities may not be as clearly assigned across international operations even if the business environment presents itself as relatively stable. The authors do, however, mention the example of Volkswagen, whose national sales subsidiaries are actively discouraged from selling products to neighboring countries (Birkinshaw/ Lingblad 2005: 677). As implied by the previous argument, Birkinshaw and Lingblad define intrafirm competition as "the extent of overlap between the charters of two or more business units in a single organization" (Birkinshaw/Lingblad 2005: 676), thus adhering to the concept of charter competition (for a discussion and application to foreign subsidiaries see subsection 2.4.1.3). A unit's charter is conceptualized as comprising three elements: the product markets served, the capabilities held and the intended charter as communicated to the rest of the organization (Birkinshaw/ Lingblad 2005: 676).

According to Birkinshaw and Lingblad two key variables define the relationship between units: charter overlap (high versus low, reflecting the percentage of one unit's product market space for which other units are competing) and charter boundary state (solid versus fluid, depending on the level of alignment between two charters and the degrees of freedom managers have to move beyond their charters). The authors combine these two variables in a matrix yielding four different generic forms of interunit relationships, but – given their interest in intrafirm competition – focus the rest of the paper on the two forms involving high charter overlap (Birkinshaw/Lingblad 2005: 677-678). Based on their stylized model, Birkinshaw and Lingblad develop a set of propositions regarding the environmental and firm-level factors that cause the two types of intrafirm competition to emerge. The anticipated effects are summarized in Table 1.

	Determinants of competition	Explanation / comment	Effect on level of „charter overlap"	Effect on fluidity of „charter boundary"
Environment	Environmental equivocality ↑ (p. 679)	No organization can reasonably expect to understand all environmental changes underway; individual units thus need a high degree of freedom to seize opportunities	↑ Temporary overlap explicitly allowed to achieve "best answer" to prevailing market conditions	↑ Units should be free to adapt their activities to the prevailing market conditions
	Industry maturity ↑ (p. 680)	Industries go through a process of evolution (life cycle) with two dimensions • Technological (product and process innovation) • Institutional (convergence through learning)	↓ As the industry matures, a dominant technology and specific business model emerge and the pressure for cost reduction leads to the elimination of duplication	↓ The charter definition is specified once dominant technologies and institutional norms become established
	Market heterogeneity ↑ (p. 680)	Extent to which customer preferences of product attributes differ; the number of addressable market segments increases with the demand for high product variety	↑ Multiple units engaged in ensuring product variety and closeness to market in order to best meet customer needs	– No effect expected
Organization	Decentralization of decision making ↑ (pp. 680-681)	Extent to which decision-making authority lies in the hands of the managers of the organizational unit	↑ Managers will steer their units' charters towards what they perceive as the most attractive market opportunities; overlaps may be the result	No net effect expected • Unit managers defend their perceived territory (↓) • Self-interest drives search for new opportunities (↑)
	Normative integration ↑ (p. 681)	Extent to which individual compliance with organizational goals is achieved through shared values; complements decentralization	– No effect expected	↑ Normative integration facilitates charter realignment according to overall firm interests
	Fungibility of unit capabilities ↑ (pp. 681-682)	Capacity to apply capabilities to areas and opportunities outside the current charter	– No (direct) effect expected	↑ Fungibility of capabilities enables unit to move beyond the focus of its current product market areas

Table 1: Determinants of Intrafirm Competition according to Birkinshaw/Lingblad (2005)

The determinants suggested by Birkinshaw and Lingblad refer to **intrafirm competition only**. What may influence cooperative behavior between units is not an issue. Therefore, their work merely sheds light on one aspect of intersubsidiary relationships and contributes little to the identification of factors that tip the scale towards more or less competition and cooperation. Their proposed environmental factors also lose some of their relevance when comparing firms operating in the same industry. Organization-specific factors then become more interesting. The most relevant proposition for this research is that decentralized decision making enhances charter overlap (Birkinshaw/Lingblad 2005: 680-681; for a brief discussion of the link between centralization/autonomy and intersubsidiary relationships see subsection 3.3.1.3). This logic could be applied to the project acquisition and execution of plant engineering companies as follows: the more autonomous foreign subsidiaries are, the more they will try to cover a large part of the value chain themselves; from a corporate perspective, this leads to overlapping activities. Neither normative integration nor the fungibility of capabilities is expected to have an effect on charter overlap – a concept that is of greater relevance to this research than a change in charter boundary state. By stating that "[d]ecentralization is an appropriate response to equivocality" Birkinshaw and Lingblad indirectly suggest that the proposed influencing factors may be somewhat interrelated (Birkinshaw/Lingblad 2005: 681).

Finally, the authors establish the working hypothesis that intrafirm competition is most prevalent in related diversified companies (Birkinshaw/Lingblad 2005: 683 with reference to Rumelt 1974). This statement can be taken as a hint that the company's overall **strategy** has an impact on the level of intrafirm competition. Birkinshaw and Lingblad are not the only scholars to suggest such a relationship. Phelps and Fuller add an international dimension when proposing that "competitive processes, through which affiliates win or lose responsibilities, are related to **organizational form** within multinationals." They expect competition between affiliates to be stronger in multidomestic firms than in vertically integrated firms (Phelps/Fuller 2000: 228; for a brief discussion on the directionality of the strategy-structure relationship see subsection 3.4.4). But before drawing too much attention to a specific contingency, other proposed sets of influencing factors shall be reviewed.

3.5.2 Determinants of Interunit Cooperation

Interestingly, the determinants of cooperation in its entirety have hardly been examined (an exception are Li/Ferreira 2003; Li et al. 2007, which are discussed in the context of coopetition). What has been investigated are the factors affecting **knowledge transfer**, as a particular facet – or object – of interunit cooperation (see Cerrato 2006: 270 for a brief overview of the respective studies). According to Cerrato's review, the feasibility and effectiveness of the transfer (Szulanski 1996) is determined by the type and richness of the transmission channels, the absorptive capacity of the receiver unit (Cohen/Levinthal 1990; Lane/Lubatkin 1998) and the quality of the relationship between sender and receiver (Schlegelmilch/Chini 2003). Further reference is made to Gupta and Govindarajan's (2000) exploration of factors acting as barriers or facilitators to knowledge transfer. These factors, which influence knowledge inflows and outflows to a different extent, include: (1) the value of the source unit's knowledge stock, (2) the motivational disposition of the source unit to share knowledge, (3) the existence and richness of transmission channels, (4) the motivational disposition of the target unit to acquire knowledge and (5) the absorptive capacity of the target unit (for an overview of the theoretical framework see Gupta/Govindarajan 2000: 477). The studies reviewed by Cerrato have in common that they focus on characteristics of the sender unit, the receiver unit and/or the transmission channels. The same is true for Gnyawali et al., who address three questions: (1) What factors motivate a focal subsidiary to form knowledge ties with peer subsidiaries? (2) Once this motivation is established, what factors influence the decision to select a particular partner? (3) Once the tie is formed, what are the contextual factors that will likely influence the effectiveness of knowledge flow between the partners? (Gnyawali et al. 2007). The authors examine the conditions under which intersubsidiary collaborative or knowledge ties are formed but focus on what can be defined as subsidiary-led cooperation (see subsection 2.3.2). Entrepreneurial orientation and strategic vulnerability are regarded as key motivational factors.

Zhao and Luo, on the other hand, list a number of studies that address how intracorporate knowledge sharing is shaped by **external environment conditions** (Zhao/Luo 2005: 72). The authors themselves set out to explore what internal factors account for the sharing of organizational knowledge between emerging market subsidiaries and their peer subsidiaries in other countries. They define organizational knowledge as "knowledge about how to organize and manage offshore operations and investments" (Zhao/Luo 2005: 72) and divide it into a declarative and a procedural component (for a distinction see subsection 2.4.2.3). As can be taken from Table 2, their propositions suggest positive relationships between the frequency of organizational knowledge sharing and features of both the strategic and infrastructural context. It should be noted that infrastructural characteristics seem to represent requirements for – rather than determinants of – intersubsidiary knowledge sharing. The authors themselves speak of the infrastructural context "as conditions of organizational infrastructure in which knowledge sharing is proceeded" (Zhao/Luo 2005: 76).

	Antecedents of organizational knowledge sharing	Explanation / comment	Effect on the frequency of sharing declarative knowledge	Effect on the frequency of sharing procedural knowledge
Strategic Context	Strategic interdependence (pp. 76-77)	Extent to which work processes that have strategic implications are interrelated Shaped by MNE subsidiaries' distinct strategic roles	↑	↑
	Entry strategy (pp. 77-78)	Two primary equity-based entry modes: (a) wholly owned subsidiaries (b) joint ventures	(a) ↑ due to integration and centralization	(b) ↑ due to complementarity and learning
	Technological linkage (pp. 78-79)	Extent to which a subsidiary's innovation and production is reliant upon the technological knowledge/assistance of other subsidiaries Shaped by nodal subsidiary's operational needs	–	↑
Infrastructural Context	Knowledge encapsulation (pp. 79-81)	Routinized process of encoding, storing and converting knowledge into a retrievable and sharable form	↑	↑
	Intranet system (p. 81)	Information platform that connects intracorporate users across nations and facilitates interactive learning	↑	↑
	Incentive system (p. 82)	Provides recognition and rewards for sharing ideas and expertise within the organization; reflects corporate commitment to these goals	↑	↑

Table 2: Antecedents of Organizational Knowledge Sharing according to Zhao/Luo (2005)

Although Zhao and Luo examine only a small aspect of intersubsidiary cooperation – namely the sharing of organizational knowledge – their work seems worth reviewing given that they are among the very few scholars who empirically test the respective hypotheses.[51] Also, the contingency they establish between knowledge sharing and the strategic context that links a nodal subsidiary with the MNE network will prove particularly relevant in the context of this research. Nevertheless, evaluating the determinants of (organizational) knowledge sharing can only be an incomplete substitute for understanding the factors influencing intersubsidiary cooperation as a whole. Although both the strategic and the infrastructural context are likely to have a similar effect on cooperation through a split of work, contingencies do not necessarily have to be the same. Even more knowledge-specific aspects such as those included in Cerrato's review may not offer any explanation for the intersubsidiary division of labor. The goal, however, is not to identify similarly specific determinants for each object of cooperation but to find influencing factors that are broad enough to explain different manifestations of cooperative relationships between subsidiaries. This also includes different origins of cooperation.

Factors explaining interunit (or intersubsidiary) cooperation more broadly are included in studies on coopetition, which are reviewed in the next subsection.

3.5.3 Determinants of Interunit Coopetition

Ever since the concept of coopetition was first introduced to popular science by Brandenburger and Nalebuff (Brandenburger/Nalebuff 1996), scholars have addressed a variety of its facets. The intrafirm manifestation of coopetition, however, has only recently become of academic interest. Adopting a social-network perspective, Tsai examines how different **coordination mechanisms**, namely centralization and social interaction, affect knowledge sharing in a large, multiunit corporation and how interunit competition moderates this relationship (Tsai 2002: 179). Particularly striking is his empirical finding that centralization has a significant negative effect, and lateral relations have a significant positive effect on knowledge sharing among units that compete with each other for market share (rather than for internal resources) (Tsai 2002: 185-186). This result underlines the relevance of examining units with sales activities in more detail. Tsai, however, focuses his study

---

[51] Merely two sub-hypotheses were not supported by the findings: (1) the sharing of *procedural* organizational knowledge is not influenced by the entry-mode choice; (2) the sharing of *declarative* organizational knowledge is not associated with the development of an incentive system (Zhao/Luo 2005: 87, 89).

on business units rather than subsidiaries, and his work does not explicitly comprise an international dimension (Tsai 2002: 182). Most importantly, the author does not offer a set of propositions that help to explain interunit cooperation and competition in a balanced manner. Competition is regarded as a moderating factor only.

Li and Ferreira come much closer to the focus of this research by investigating intersubsidiary competition and cooperation within multinational enterprises (MNEs) and their impact on technology transfer. Drawing on organizational design and strategy implementation literature, the authors suggest that subsidiaries' competitive and cooperative relationships, which in turn determine intersubsidiary technology transfer, are influenced by an MNE's **international strategy** as well as certain **structural characteristics** – the role of the headquarters, intersubsidiary social communication and the reward system (Li/Ferreira 2003: 2-3). The respective influencing factors are summarized in Table 3.

It should be noted that the type of competition the authors refer to is not clear-cut. On the one hand, they speak rather generally of "multimarket competition"; on the other hand they distinguish three "reasons" for the existence of intersubsidiary competition: rivalry for parent resources, market commonality and undefined responsibilities (Li/Ferreira 2003: 4-7). Cooperation is conceptualized only indirectly via technology transfer (Li/Ferreira 2003: 1-3).

	Influencing factors	Explanation / comment	Effect on cooperation among MNE subsidiaries	Effect on competition among MNE subsidiaries
Strategy	**MNE strategy** • International • Multinational • Global • Transnational (pp. 10-12)	• Subsidiaries that are autonomous from each other replicate domestic strategy • Fairly autonomous subsidiaries have own aspirations for growth • Subsidiaries rely on the same value chain to offer standardized products • Global efficiency and local responsiveness creates high subsidiary interdependence	– – (↑)[1] ↑	– ↑ ↓ ↓
Structure	**Role of MNE headquarters** → Centralization (pp. 13-15)	Headquarters can influence subsidiary behavior based on ownership relations, informational advantages and resource support	↑	↓
	Inter-subsidiary social communication (pp. 15-17)	Informal information exchange between subsidiaries enhances mutual awareness and promotes integration and socialization	↑	↓
	Reward system • Subjective • Objective (pp. 17-19)	• Goal is to maximize the overall performance of the MNE network • Goal is to maximize the performance of the individual subsidiary	↑ (↓)[2]	↓ ↑

(1) The authors speak of "tightly coupled subsidiaries" without explicitly referring to cooperation
(2) The willingness to cooperate may be driven by self-interest

Table 3:   Influencing Factors for Cooperation and Competition among Foreign Subsidiaries according to Li/Ferreira (2003)

Despite some overlap with the factors identified by Tsai, Li and Ferreira come to fundamentally different conclusions. In their opinion, headquarters that have strong control over intersubsidiary relationships have the ability to convert competitive pressures into cooperative ties (Li/Ferreira 2003: 14-15). Unlike Tsai they present multimarket competition between subsidiaries as an obstacle – rather than a potential virtue – for technology transfer (Li/Ferreira 2003: 4). Such contradictions motivate further investigation of influencing factors and their corresponding causalities. General agreement seems to exist on the fact that the role of the headquarters has an impact on the relationship between subsidiaries.

Li and Ferreira, together with a third co-author, advanced and refined their ideas in a 2007 working paper with the same title (Li et al. 2007). Since the basic line of argument as well as the essence of the propositions has remained unchanged, Table 3 includes only the output of their original work. In their later paper, the authors choose to elaborate on select topics, use slightly modified concepts (for example, decentralization versus subsidiary autonomy, systemic/individual versus subjective/ objective reward system) and add a third category (MNE as a network) to their classification of proposed influencing factors. Given that intersubsidiary social communication and its implications correspond strongly to the concept of normative integration, subsuming it under structural characteristics seems perfectly reasonable (see, for example, Hedlund/Rolander 1990: 16, 25-26). Normative integration and centralization are both organizational characteristics that take on different shapes depending on the type of MNC in question. The explicit reference to the MNE as a network, however, suggests strong overlaps with the transnational model.

The influencing factors Li and Ferreira propose for intersubsidiary competition and cooperation are all very relevant to this research. As noted above, the selected characteristics of an MNC's organization structure are closely related to its strategic orientation. This linkage becomes even more evident when explicitly considering Bartlett and Ghoshal's typology of multinational companies rather than the integration-responsiveness (I-R) framework in general (as done by Li/Ferreira 2003: 10 with reference to Prahalad 1975; Doz 1980; Doz et al. 1981; Prahalad/Doz 1987). The features of Bartlett and Ghoshal's typology are outlined in subsection 5.1.2. Most appropriately one would consider the reward system as a means or mechanism of strategy implementation rather than a structural characteristic per se (compare to Zhao/Luo 2005: 76, 82).

Finally, it is Luo who provides the most comprehensive framework for the understanding and analysis of **coopetition between foreign subsidiaries**. As will be demonstrated below, he, too, suggests a link between a company's strategy and its intersubsidiary relationships. Coopetition to him is "a mindset, process, or phenomenon of combining cooperation and competition" (Luo 2005: 72). Before integrating these two pillars into a single typology, the author systematically examines the contents and determinants of cooperation and competition, respectively (Luo 2005: 73-80). Subsidiaries cooperate by sharing technological know-how, operational resources, organizational capabilities or financial management tools (Luo 2005: 73-75). While realizing economies of scope through cooperation, firms achieve internal efficiency through interunit competition (Luo 2005: 75 with reference to Hill et al. 1992: 501). Subsidiaries compete for parent resources, corporate support, system position and market expansion (Luo 2005: 75-76). The indirect distinction between internal and external competition is analogous to Tsai. According to Luo, the levels of cooperation and competition between subsidiaries depend on a series of contingent factors. As can be taken from Table 4 and Table 5 the author focuses on those factors that relate to an internal configuration perspective. He himself calls them "critical variables" and notes that they are by no means exclusive (Luo 2005: 88).

	Determinants of cooperation	Explanation / comment	Effect on cooperation among foreign subsidiaries
Strategy	Strategic interdependence	"Percentage of strategic resources and/or main outputs that inflow or outflow between a focal subsidiary and its peer subsidiaries, in this subsidiary's total resource flow and/or output flow" (p. 77) Subsidiary roles and relationships vary with the international strategy of the MNE; frequent resource exchange creates interdependencies and calls for a high level of coordination and cooperation (p. 77)	↑
Structure	Wholly-owned subunit form	Business processes in wholly-owned subsidiaries tend to be tightly integrated and synchronized, their organizational structure relatively centralized (p. 77) Superiority to joint venture form with respect to coordination efficiency, internalization effectiveness, knowledge safeguards and resource-sharing productivity (p. 78)	↑
Structure	Technological linkage	"Extent to which a nodal subsidiary's innovation and production is reliant upon technological knowledge or assistance offered by other subsidiaries" (p. 78) Such reliance requires organizational guidance and practice for exploiting the technology; cooperation is oftentimes directed towards productivity improvements (p. 78)	↑

Table 4: Determinants of Cooperation among Foreign Subsidiaries according to Luo (2005)

	Determinants of competition	Explanation / comment	Effect on competition among foreign subsidiaries
Strategy	Local responsiveness	Fierce competition in local markets increases subsidiaries' dependency on (scarce) parent resources (such as capital investments, technological support) (p. 78) The more difficult the host countries' environmental conditions, the stronger intrafirm competition for parent resources is expected to be (p. 79)	↑
Structure	Market overlap	Percentage of a focal subsidiary's sales in or revenue from the market(s) in which peer subunit(s) have a major presence, in this subsidiary's total sales or revenue" (p. 79) Competition is oftentimes geared towards sales growth and/or profit in some common (international) markets; should be encouraged if market potential is high and subsidiaries have abundant and adequate resources and capabilities (p. 79)	↑
Resources	Capability retrogression	The demand for parent resources and support will increase as subsidiaries face a decline in capabilities and a weakening of their competitive position; the responsibility for such retrogression may lie with the subsidiaries or the parent company (p. 79) In addition to tapping parent resources, some subunits may seek to cooperate with peers to strengthen their capabilities (p. 79)	↑

Table 5: Determinants of Competition among Foreign Subsidiaries according to Luo (2005)

Most relevant to this research – which focuses on the relationship between MNC subsidiaries in the plant engineering industry – are Luo's propositions that cooperation is intensified by an increase in **strategic interdependence** and **technological linkage** (Luo 2005: 77-78), and that competition is enhanced by an increase in **local responsiveness** and **market overlap** (Luo 2005: 78-80). The wholly owned subsidiary form is already implied and capability retrogression represents an influencing factor with relatively narrow implications. It needs to be re-emphasized that the focus of this research is not on cooperation and competition related to internal resources. Whereas the other determinants can be interpreted to have implications for the remaining objects of cooperation and competition, capability retrogression seems solely relevant to competition for parent resources.

With his propositions, Luo gives important impulses for the identification of both **strategic and structural influencing factors**. He suggests that global integration versus local autonomy has an impact on intersubsidiary relationships as does the extent to which technologies and responsibilities are distributed across the organization. Market overlap can be considered as a structural dimension because from an internal perspective it implies that responsibilities are not clearly assigned. One statement that needs to be critically evaluated in this context is that "[t]he choice of international strategy largely depends on the degree of interrelationship among subsidiaries" (Luo 2005: 77). In accordance with Luo's own propositions the logic may very well be the other way around, i.e. that the degree (or type) of interrelationship among subsidiaries is determined by the choice of international strategy. The ambiguity of the argument underlines that a clear **strategy-structure relationship** is difficult to establish (compare to subsection 3.4.4).

Some of the above aspects re-appear in the two-dimensional **typology** Luo proposes based on his findings – and which could prove helpful when developing or evaluating alternative models of project acquisition and execution. According to the subsidiaries' relative level of competition and cooperation with their peers, the author distinguishes between (1) *aggressive demander* (high competition – low cooperation), (2) *silent implementer* (low competition – low cooperation), (3) *ardent contributor* (low competition – high cooperation), and (4) *network captain* (high competition – high cooperation) (Luo 2005: 80-84). For each type, the characteristics and implications are analyzed from both a subsidiary and a headquarters perspective. According to Luo, "each type [of subunit] has unique normative environments or conditions that justify the level of cooperation and competition consistent with its identity" (Luo 2005: 88). The author also tries to specify some of the circumstances under which the different types are beneficial to the welfare of the overall organization. It should be noted that – on an interorganizational level – the basic idea had already been captured by Lado and Boyd, who in their taxonomy distinguish between competitive, monopolistic, cooperative and syncretic rent-seeking behavior, respectively (Lado et al. 1997: 118). Similarly, Bengtsson and Kock identify different types of coopetitive relationships between competitors, ranging from cooperation-dominated over equal to competition-dominated relationships (Bengtsson/Kock 2000: 416).

Interestingly, there are certain parallels between the four types of situations or identities and Bartlett and Ghoshal's typology of multinational companies (for an overview see, for example, Bartlett et al. 2007: 203-206 as well as subsection 5.1.2), again suggesting a link between MNC strategy and intersubsidiary relationships. The aggressive demander depends on corporate support to develop its country-specific capabilities – taking advantage of localization advantages just like a multinational company does. The silent implementer produces and sells standardized products in his host market – implementing headquarters' strategy the way a global company does. The ardent contributor is equipped with distinctive resources and knowledge –

which it could use for adaptation purposes like an international company does.[52] Finally, the network captain, being considerably autonomous yet interrelated with its peers, has both local responsiveness and global integration duties – reflecting the exact complexity of a transnational company (Bartlett/Ghoshal 1998: 68-70; Luo 2005: 82-84).

In the context of coordination Luo himself makes explicit reference to the effect of a company's strategic orientation on intersubsidiary relationships (Luo 2005: 87). When proposing that "[c]ooperation will increase, and competition will decrease, if an MNE adopts global strategy (i.e., relative standardization across national markets, allowing strategic and operational control by the headquarters)" he is not fully consistent with his previous arguments, though. In the discussion of his typology he claims that the silent implementer, producing and selling standardized products, is characterized by both low cooperation and low competition. And, indeed, intersubsidiary cooperation does not seem necessary if subsidiaries are simply to execute headquarters' strategy. It would be helpful if Luo distinguished between global and international strategies to better capture the degree of freedom subsidiaries actually have. The author's subsequent statements are more easily reconcilable with his previous arguments: "Contrarily, competition will increase, and cooperation will decrease, if an MNE employs multidomestic strategy. The duality of cooperation and competition is more salient under transnational strategy than under global or multidomestic strategy" (Luo 2005: 87). It is worth mentioning that the second part of this statement contrasts with Li and Ferreira's proposition of competition between highly interdependent subsidiaries being relatively weak (Li/Ferreira 2003: 12). The authors of the two papers do agree, however, that competition is expected to be high under multinational strategy and low under global strategy.

One last piece of work that is worth being included in this brief review is Cerrato's (2006) analysis of the **MNC as an internal market system**. Although the author does not explicitly refer to intersubsidiary competition and cooperation as his dependent variables, he does adopt a balanced view on the two phenomena. Cerrato advances Birkinshaw's (2001b) work by analyzing the factors that affect the creation and working of **three different types** of internal market: (1) for intermediate products

---

[52] The parallels here are the least clear-cut because the ardent contributor is regarded more as a center of excellence, which assumes responsibility for the whole company in a certain area. On the concept of centers of excellence see, for example, Moore/Birkinshaw 1998; Schmid et al. 1999; Holm/Pedersen 2000; Kutschker et al. 2002.

or services, (2) for charters and (3) for capabilities or practices.[53] In doing so, he builds upon internalization theory, the RBV and organizational learning literature, respectively (compare to subsection 3.3.5). Due to its limited relevance for subsidiaries involved in project acquisition and execution activities, the market for intermediate products or services is neglected here; competition for delivery of products or services to the next stage of the value chain is not an issue – although it could, for classification purposes, be considered as competition for internal customers. Competition for external customers, however, is not accounted for by the internal market concept. Nor does it include cooperation through a split of work. Nevertheless, competition for new and existing charters is highly relevant for this research, as is cooperation through capability (or knowledge) transfer (compare to section 2.4 and the classification scheme in section 2.5). The proposed influencing factors for these two types of intersubsidiary relationship are summarized in Table 6 and Table 7.

Particularly for the first set of influencing factors it needs to be emphasized that they do not necessarily have to promote intersubsidiary competition but rather provide a **platform** for subsidiaries to compete for charters. This is a fine distinction, but open communication between headquarters and subsidiaries, for example, cannot per se be regarded as a trigger for intersubsidiary competition. At the same time such communication may more adequately be considered a manifestation rather than an influencing factor of cooperation.

Also not ideal is the fact that some of the proposed influencing factors are **interrelated**. Cerrato himself points to the overlap between decentralization of decision making and subsidiary reputation/performance: Subsidiary track record reduces uncertainty perceived by the parent company, providing less reason for formal control and allowing for higher autonomy (Cerrato 2006: 268). Similarly, he establishes a link between tacitness and the concept of context-specificity (Cerrato 2006: 270).

---

[53] Cerrato himself admits that the concept of a market is misleading and not appropriate here, given that in the transfer of competencies and practices (and thus interunit cooperation) the nonmarket (and noncompetitive) character of the MNE is what matters (Cerrato 2006: 270).

	Determinants	Explanation / comment	Effect on the implementation of an internal market for charters
Resources	Resource mobility	"The contestability of a charter is related to the degree of mobility of its underlying resources and capabilities and, consequently, the type of competitive advantage they allow to achieve (location-bound vs. nonlocation-bound" (p. 267) "As far as resources and capabilities needed to fulfill a charter are nonlocation-bound (i.e. can be transferred across the MNE), charters are contestable" (p. 267)	↑
Subsidiary	Strong track record	"The effectiveness of an internal market depends on the subsidiary's reputation or credibility in the eyes of the parent company" (p. 267) "Prior international responsibilities [...] increase a subsidiary's credibility and enhance support by the parent company in the evaluation of the possibility that a subsidiary can challenge an existing charter or bid for a new one" (p. 267)	↑
Headquarters	Decentralized decision making	"A greater decentralization of decision-making processes is a necessary condition for the working of an internal market as it would provide subsidiaries with the degrees of freedom needed to pursue the strategic initiatives that better can exploit existing subsidiary-specific capabilities and build new ones" (p. 268) Citing Rugman & Verbeke, 2003: 134: "bounded rationality constraints force MNE headquarters to allow autonomous initiatives of subsidiaries to flourish" (p. 268)	↑
HQ-subs. relationship	Frequent and open communication	"Communication speeds the process by which the parent company acquires confidence about the subsidiary's capability to perform activities successfully" (p. 269) "A relationship based on frequent and open communication would allow the subsidiary to explain the value of their projects and give headquarters the opportunity to have as much as possible information to evaluate subsidiary initiatives" (p. 269)	↑

Table 6: Factors Affecting the Establishment of an Internal Market for Charters according to Cerrato (2006)

Finally, the author accounts for the possibility that the propositions developed might change depending on the **stage of internationalization** of the firm (Cerrato 2006: 273). This remark closes the loop to the previous studies, which suggest that an MNC's international strategy has an important influence on its intersubsidiary relationships. Given that Cerrato's model does not cover the entire spectrum of intersubsidiary competition and cooperation, no further discussion is presented. Instead, the most striking findings from the reviewed contingency approaches are summarized and their implications evaluated in the next section.

	Determinants	Explanation / comment	Effect on the implementation of an internal market for knowledge and competencies
Knowledge	Tacitness of knowledge	"Tacitness is a quality of knowledge that makes the transfer more complicated. [...] The transfer of tacit knowledge is a costly process because it requires investments from the parties involved in order to make the knowledge understandable for the received unit" (p. 270)	↓
Knowledge	Context-specificity	Citing Foss & Pedersen, 2002: 64: "[...] the more context specific the knowledge is, the smaller the absorptive capacity of the received and and the less it can be used in other MNC units" (p. 271)	↓
Sender-receiver relationship	Interactions due to exchanges of products/services	"Greater interdependence [between the MNE's units] in terms of flows of product/services enhances the tranfer of knowledge. In fact, any exchange of products and services implies a flow of knowledge as knowledge is always somewhat embodied in products and services" (p. 271)	↑
Sender-receiver relationship	Frequent and open communication	"Communication [among the MNE's units] builds trust and facilitates the sharing of tacits knowledge" (p. 272)	↑

Table 7: Factors Affecting the Establishment of an Internal Market for Knowledge and Competencies according to Cerrato (2006)

3.6 Summary and Implications

Since the review of substantial theories such as TCE and the RBV has not provided any satisfactory explanations for cross-company differences in intersubsidiary relationships, the **contingency approach** was identified as having the most potential in this respect. As the preceding literature review has shown, several other scholars seem to have come to the same conclusion (albeit with varying degrees of theoretical depth and rigor), developing **propositions** on the link between certain influencing factors and the manifestations of interunit (or intersubsidiary) competition and/or cooperation. Although the international dimension or subsidiary form is not always addressed explicitly, their studies provide guidance and inspiration to this research. On the one hand, they reveal that the determinants of intersubsidiary relationships are manifold. On the other hand, they allow identifying the supposedly **most relevant factor(s)** by means of aggregation and comparison. It is this latter aspect that is emphasized below given its importance for the elaboration of propositions within the context of this research.

Most broadly speaking, the identified (internal) determinants have in common that they relate to either a company's strategy or structure. **Strategic orientation** strikes as a particularly relevant concept, given that it can be interpreted to include strategic as well as structural dimensions. For example, the influencing factors suggested by Li and Ferreira – i.e. international strategy, role of MNE headquarters, intersubsidiary social communication and the reward system (Li/Ferreira 2003: 10-19) – can be aggregated to represent a company's strategic orientation in Bartlett and Ghoshal's sense (for an overview of Bartlett and Ghoshal's concept see subsection 5.1.2). Similar lines of argument are followed by other scholars: Zhao and Luo establish a contingency between knowledge sharing and a subsidiary's strategic context (Zhao/Luo 2005: 76-77) and Birkinshaw and Lingblad suggest that decentralized decision making enhances charter overlap (Birkinshaw/Lingblad 2005: 680-681). Most interestingly for this research, Luo argues that cooperation is intensified by an increase in strategic interdependence and technological linkage and that competition is enhanced by an increase in local responsiveness and market overlap (Luo 2005: 77-80). Consequently, he expects multidomestic strategy to be accompanied by high competition and low cooperation, and transnational strategy to promote both cooperation and competition (Luo 2005: 87). The fact that Li and Ferreira come to a diverging conclusion here – assuming that competition between highly interdependent subsidiaries will be relatively weak (Li/Ferreira 2003: 12) – prompts the desire for empirical exploration. With Zhao and Luo constituting the only exception, none of the propositions has been examined in practice – although such an undertaking was only recently recognized as being "a fruitful avenue for additional research" (Li et al. 2007: 28).

Inspired by the above review, the resulting **goal of this research** is twofold: (1) to develop proper propositions on the relationship between an MNC's strategic orientation and its intersubsidiary relationships and (2) to investigate these propositions empirically. In doing so, this research tries to act on another suggestion for (future) research, i.e. to consider managerial implications by applying the relevant theoretical lenses to the analysis of case studies (Cerrato 2006: 273).

Before proceeding along this path, it is necessary to grasp the chosen research setting. The next chapter is thus dedicated to an overview of the plant engineering sector, the project marketing function and the related models of intersubsidiary relationships.

4 Intersubsidiary Relationships in Project Marketing of Plant Engineering Companies

The goal of this chapter is to make the intersubsidiary relationships described and referred to in the previous chapters more tangible and to ultimately answer the first research question (compare to section 1.4): Which alternative models exist for the acquisition and execution of large industrial projects with particular respect to competition and cooperation between foreign subsidiaries? By understanding the unique industry and functional characteristics, research findings are also more easily transferable to other settings.

First, the characteristics and trends of the plant engineering sector are introduced (section 4.1). Second, the project marketing function is delineated and its process defined (section 4.2). Third, combining industry and functional focus with the relationships outlined in Chapter 2, conceptual models of intersubsidiary relationships are developed (section 4.3).

4.1 Plant Engineering

Definitions and delineations of the plant engineering sector can mainly be found in German-speaking publications. This can be explained by the fact that the industry has historically constituted an important component of the German economy (see, for example, Bretschneider 1980: 1; Schwanfelder 1989: 16-17; Gleich et al. 2005: 4; Stroh 2006: 13-14; VDMA 2007: 8-9). The VDMA (Verband Deutscher Maschinen- und Anlagenbau – German Engineering Federation), which offers the largest engineering industry network in Europe, defines **large industrial plant manufacturers** as companies capable of processing one or more factory or power generation plant projects a year with a volume of at least €25 million each. They must have the comprehensive technical and process expertise necessary to handle all aspects of the entire project, including the planning, designing and engineering of the plant and the production or international procurement of the facilities and equipment, along with delivery, installation, commissioning and provision of the financing. In terms of order volume, the most important segments in 2005 were: air and gas liquefaction, chemical plants, construction and construction materials, electrical engineering, paper and cellulose, power stations, raw materials production and processing, steelworks and rolling mills, and textiles (VDMA 2008; see also for technology portfolio, product and service range).

In academic literature, large-scale plant engineering is described as the individual, project-based and often turnkey construction of complex, technologically demanding industrial manufacturing plants. Large plants, such as power plants, refineries, steel mills, chemical plants and cement plants, have in common that – although uniting known and proven technologies – their composition and manifestation follows individual customer needs (Allers 2002: 361). The desired solution tends to be realized by one or more suppliers in a multi-year process. It comprises complex products and services, which are ultimately put together into an operational unit at the plant location. Given their complex structure, these solutions can be regarded as unique (Schiller 2000: 14). Suppliers typically fall into one of three groups: (1) pure technology companies which own and sell (i.e. license) proprietary technology, (2) large contractors who perform engineering, procurement and construction (EPC) work based on third party technologies and (3) technology-driven plant manufacturers who design and construct plants based on their own (and/or third party) technologies.[54] The focus of this research is on the third, most comprehensive category. Nevertheless, the term 'contractor' is used interchangeably, given that engineering companies with proprietary technology also engage in EPC contracts.

A prime characteristic of the plant engineering industry is its **international scope**. Key reasons for this international orientation of supply and demand are seen in different development stages and countries' specialization on certain branches of production (Günter 1979: 63). Maintaining worldwide operations is a prerequisite for almost any player, given that companies need to respond to project requests from various continents (Schwanfelder 1989: 15-16; Rapp 2004: 20; Gleich et al. 2005: 183). The internationalization process is reinforced as customers increasingly demand the employment of local resources and competitive pressures induce companies to transfer larger project elements abroad (Bretschneider 1980: 2, 23; VDMA 2006: 16, 28). While companies strive for localization on the one hand, they need to achieve a maximum of global efficiency, on the other hand. This is true not only for project execution but also for project acquisition, since engineering companies have to carry proposal costs in advance (Bretschneider 1980: 2). Unlike consumer products, industrial plants need to be built on-site and cannot be shipped to where they are needed. More upstream value chain activities, such as project acquisition and engineering, however, can very well be carried out from dispersed

---

[54] The distinction between these three types of companies was reiterated in the interviews (P7, P10). Whereas large contractors pursue a high-volume – low-margin business, pure technology companies are prone to the highest margin but need to maintain significant R&D investments. Technology-driven plant manufacturers range between the two in terms of both revenues and margin.

locations. These activities then need to be integrated and coordinated (VDMA 2006: 28). Lastly, the fact that companies are dealing with extremely complex projects and technologies creates a third strategic need, namely the worldwide leveraging of innovations and learning (Bartlett/Ghoshal 1998: 33). Such a demand is best met through intersubsidiary cooperation – whereas intersubsidiary competition may be used as a means of achieving efficiency (Hill et al. 1992: 501). Businesses in the plant engineering industry are thus driven by the simultaneous demands for global efficiency, national responsiveness and worldwide learning. An exemplary two-dimensional visualization is included in Figure 8.[55]

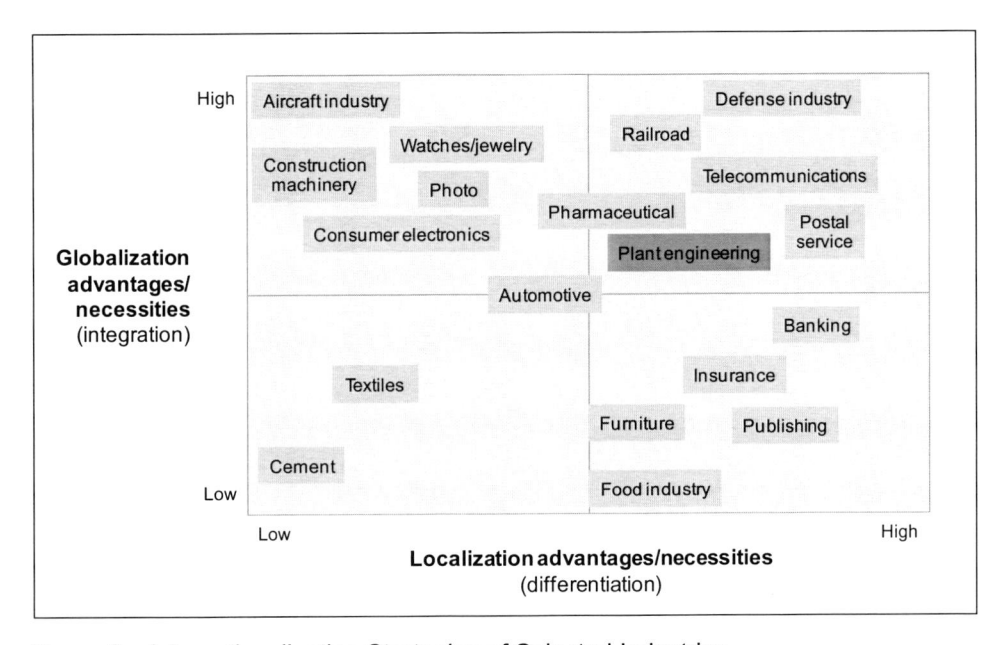

Figure 8: Internationalization Strategies of Selected Industries
Source: Meffert 1986: 694; 1990: 98.

Given that the research is embedded in the IB context, the technological dimension of plant engineering is largely neglected here. Another relevant characteristic of the plant engineering industry, however, is the **large contract value**. Projects can reach a contract value of up to several hundred million Euro (Gleich et al. 2005: 183; VDMA 2006: 15). At the same time, project marketing is a long-term venture – several years

---

[55] It needs to be recognized that the industry classification presented in Figure 8 has neither been explicitly discussed nor substantiated empirically. Also, it may be questioned whether the assessment made 25 years ago is still valid today. Figure 8 should therefore be considered as a suggestion for thinking about the driving forces behind plant engineering relative to other industries.

may lie between the first inquiry and the final contract (Königshausen/Spannagel 2004: 1127). Against this background it is understandable that subsidiaries may want to compete for participation in such projects. On the other hand, it may be exactly this project size that could let them recognize that a lot can be gained from cooperation. The sheer project dimensions also account for the fact that the sales and marketing function plays such an important role in the industry (Königshausen/Spannagel 2004: 1126; Backhaus/Voeth 2007: 305). Plant engineering companies tend to manufacture only few (if any) components themselves but source them from external suppliers (Gleich et al. 2005: 183; VDMA 2006: 29; Backhaus/Voeth 2007: 309). While plant engineering used to be a buyer's market (N.N. 1978: 38), the interviews with industry experts have revealed that it has changed into a seller's market – meaning that demand exceeds supply, which enhances the negotiating power of the supplier.

4.2 Project Marketing

This research is dedicated to exploring intersubsidiary relationships in the functional context of project marketing. Given the existing variations in both terminology and conceptualization (which become particularly apparent when comparing German and Anglo-Saxon literature) a precise definition and delineation of the concept is needed (subsection 4.2.1). Building upon this definition, the related scope of activities is outlined (subsection 4.2.2). The traditional focus on external relationships and transactions (subsection 4.2.3) is contrasted with the need for understanding internal relationships and structures (subsection 4.2.4). Drawing on the concept of process-oriented marketing (subsection 4.2.5), the project marketing process is outlined (subsection 4.2.6), giving particular attention to project acquisition and execution.

4.2.1 Definition and Delineation

Project marketing is an important **subcategory** of business-to-business (B-to-B) and **industrial marketing**. Industrial marketing, as opposed to B-to-B marketing, excludes the marketing to wholesale and retail agents (Backhaus/Voeth 2004: 7). A key element of German industrial marketing literature is the differentiation of four business types: goods, systems, plants and supplies (Backhaus/Voeth 2007: 200-203; Büschken et al. 2007: 14). In Anglo-Saxon literature the differentiation of industrial goods according to product or service characteristics is still predominant. Based on the insight that "today most 'products' of international companies increasingly exhibit project-like features" (Skaates/Tikkanen 2000: 1), project marketing is considered an important, and distinct, mode of B-to-B marketing. The INPM has established itself as an issue-based research group (see subsection 4.2.3 for details).

In its broadest sense a **project** describes "a temporary endeavor undertaken to create a unique product or service" (Pinto 2001: 35). Such a project can be found in any single firm – a conceptualization that is coherent with project management literature. In project marketing literature, however, projects always involve a buying and a supplying organization (Skaates/Tikkanen 2000). Cova et al. capture this feature by referring to a project as "a complex transaction covering a package of products, services and work, specifically designed to create capital assets that create benefits for a buyer over an extended period of time" (Cova et al. 2002: 3).

In an attempt to bridge the gap between project management and project marketing (see below for a delineation), Cova and Salle extract four common **project characteristics** from the vast amount of literature on project management: (1) finite budget and schedule constraints, (2) complex and interrelated activities, (3) clearly defined objectives and (4) uniqueness. They compare these characteristics to the main characteristics of project transactions as included in the DUC model in project marketing: discontinuity, uniqueness and complexity (Cova/Salle 2005: 355 with reference to Mandják/Veres 1998). Project operations can be subdivided into partial projects, turnkey projects and turnkey plus projects (Skaates/Tikkanen 2003: 504). Examples of projects are buildings, factories, power stations, and defense systems, but also a limited series of landing gears or the setting up of a complex management service for electrical distribution (Cova/Salle 2007: 138). The focus of this research is on **large industrial plants**, which typically represent turnkey projects in that a complete system (or better: a ready-to-use facility) is delivered to the buyer (Siebel 2001: 56, 288; Königshausen/Spannagel 2004: 1135; Backhaus/Voeth 2007: 330).

While German literature treats plants and systems as distinct business types, the line is not drawn as clearly in Anglo-Saxon literature. **'Systems selling'** has in fact established itself as the closest translation for what is called 'industrielles Anlagengeschäft' in German-speaking countries (Günter/Bonaccorsi 1996: 532). It had first been dealt with from a marketing perspective in the early 1970s (Mattson 1973; Günter 1979). Although systems selling – or "the sale of a complex combination of products and services offered by a company in an industrial market" (Skaates/Tikkanen 2000: 2) – is often used synonymously with the delivery of projects, fine differences exist between the two concepts. While most projects can be considered systems, systems do not necessarily have to be supplied as projects, i.e. in a sequential or procedural manner. An example for a (partial) project that would not be considered a system is the provision of design, planning and/or engineering services. Since plant engineering companies typically accomplish their tasks on a progressive basis and may indeed provide services only, **project marketing**, not systems selling, is the preferred concept for this research. Note that Backhaus et al. explicitly consider industrial plants as part of project business, while treating systems as a subcategory of relational business ("Verbundgeschäft") (Backhaus et al. 1994: 66-68; see Backhaus/Mühlfeld 2005: 41, 44-46 for the English wording).

Project marketing also appears more suitable than project management because it comprises the management of business (and, as will be shown, internal) relationships before, during and after the delivery process (Skaates/Tikkanen 2003: 504). Project marketing thereby takes a longer-term perspective than project management, which focuses on the temporary endeavor that takes place after the signing of the contract (Cova/Salle 2005: 355). One can think of project marketing to include project management but not vice versa (Skaates/Tikkanen 2003: 504). This research follows a broad definition of **marketing** as the orientation of all decisions and activities towards customer needs (Meffert 2000: 4). A more narrow functional understanding of marketing including all activities related to the preparation and execution of market transactions (Frese/Lehmann 2002: 508) seems less appropriate.

Given that project marketing is a relatively established concept at least in Anglo-Saxon literature, two clarifications (or extensions) are important for its use in this research: First, the relevant scope of project marketing activities needs to be extended to comprise not only project acquisition but execution. Second, the traditional transaction-oriented perspective needs to be complemented by an internal organization focus. Based on these two points the project marketing process can be outlined on a step-by-step basis.

4.2.2 Scope of Activities

The term 'project marketing' should not conceal that for a majority of tasks the responsible organizational function is sales. The **sales function** in mechanical and plant engineering comprises all activities related to the acquisition of new customers and the servicing of existing customers. VDMA benchmarking data reveals that among the companies surveyed, project development and offer preparation as well as acquisition are the most widespread sales functions. They are followed by order processing, marketing services and research, calculation, shipping, customer services, call center, field service, and design-to-order services (in order of descending frequency) (Banki et al. 2006: 11, 13). In large plant engineering, **sales and marketing** are oftentimes used interchangeably, referring to the same or a similar bundle of activities (see, for example, N.N. 1978: 36). From a process perspective, the sales function is typically in charge until the contract has been signed.

Less consensus exists on the scope of project marketing activities, which may or may not include project execution. Mirroring the Anglo-Saxon understanding of the concept, Cova et al. outline a project marketing process that comprises three major time frames: independent of any project, pre-tender and tender preparation. Project marketing thus ends with the signing of the contract (Cova et al. 2002: 53). In their approach the subsequent phase, "during project completion", is not considered part of project marketing. There have been suggestions to model the project marketing cycle into six phases, though: search, preparation, bidding, negotiation, implementation and transition (Cova/Salle 2005: 356). The latter are more compatible with German literature, where the marketing process for industrial plants is consistently described to comprise both **project acquisition and execution**. As outlined above, project marketing is the English term that comes closest to what German-speaking scholars refer to as "Anlagenvermarktung" (Königshausen/Spannagel 2004: 1128), "Vermarktungsprozess im Anlagengeschäft" (Heger 2000: 14), "Marketing komplexer Anlagen" (Günter 1979: 19), or simply "Anlagen-Marketing" (Engelhardt 1977: 9). The option of using a literal translation and speaking of "plant marketing" is discarded because the term has a different, if any, connotation in English-speaking countries.

This research builds upon the **extended conceptualization** of project marketing, which has established itself in German literature and captures some recent reflections by leading Anglo-Saxon scholars. In their "Introduction to the IMM Special Issue on Project Marketing and the Marketing of Solutions" Cova and Salle emphasize that even if winning the contract is the prime objective of the project marketing process, the approach continues during the project realization and follow-up phases (Cova/Salle 2007: 140).

4.2.3 Traditional Focus: External Relationships and Transactions

Knowledge advances in the field of project marketing can mainly be attributed to researchers of the International Network on Project Marketing and Systems Selling (INPM) (Günter/Bonaccorsi 1996; Skaates/Tikkanen 2003). The INPM is loosely affiliated with the **Industrial Marketing and Purchasing (IMP) Group**, a community of researchers emphasizing "the interactive and relational nature of exchange on business-to-business markets" (Skaates/Tikkanen 2003: 503). IMP researchers have developed a dynamic model of buyer-supplier relationships in industrial markets – the interaction model – and demonstrated its applicability through comparative studies across a number of European countries. The results of their studies were published in two seminal books (Håkansson 1982; Håkansson/Snehota 1995; for a self-presentation see IMP Group 2007).

Given the focus of this research it is important to briefly outline some elements of the conceptual framework Håkansson and Snehota have developed for the description and analysis of **business relationships** (Håkansson/Snehota 1995: 5). Such relationships between industrial companies, organizations and institutions have received growing attention in the 1980s and 1990s. Based on a comprehensive (albeit not elaborated) review of respective studies from Europe, the U.S. and Japan, the authors find that intercompany relationships tend to have certain "structural" and "process" characteristics (Håkansson/Snehota 1995: 6). **Structural** characteristics, which are "readily evident even to outside observers", comprise continuity, complexity, symmetry and informality (Håkansson/Snehota 1995: 7-8). From a structural point of view companies seem to be tied together by long-lasting, broad, relatively balanced and informal relationships. The initial impression of stability is changed when taking a closer look at interaction processes (Håkansson/Snehota 1995: 10). **Process** characteristics, which are "less evident to an outside observer", refer to mutual adaptations, cooperation and conflict, social interaction and routinization (Håkansson/Snehota 1995: 9-10).

While all of these characteristics could also be applied to and investigated at the intraorganizational level, they are not considered the most appropriate to grasp the essentials of **intersubsidiary relationships**. Between a buying and a selling organization a relationship exists by definition – any exchange requires a certain degree of mutual orientation and commitment by the providing and receiving party. Correspondingly, Håkansson and Snehota speak of a relationship as "mutually oriented interaction between two reciprocally committed parties" (Håkansson/Snehota 1995: 25). The authors point to the high degree of interdependence between business organizations, whose existence depends on the exchange with other economic subjects. As discussed in section 2.1, intraorganizational relationships are to a far lesser extent built on such transactions. Therefore it seems more appropriate to begin with the basic nature (or type) of relationship as suggested in section 2.2. Unlike two companies involved in a vertical, mainly cooperative exchange relationship, horizontally related units may also experience states of competition, coopetition or independence. The manifestations of these four basic types of relationship between subsidiaries are of primary interest to this research. Structural issues of continuity, complexity, symmetry and informality are subordinate to such investigation.[56] The same is true for process characteristics. At first glance the subcategory "cooperation and conflict" may seem to capture the research focus, but it is critical to note that it does include any references to competition. Buying and selling organizations (or rather their exchange-related units) simply do not tend to enter into competition – a phenomenon that is all the more interesting to observe between the units (or subsidiaries) of a particular company.

Håkansson and Snehota further propose two dimensions that capture the **effects** produced by business relationships, and which can thus be used to categorize them (Håkansson/Snehota 1995: 25-26): the substance (what is affected?) and the function (who is affected?) of a relationship. Three layers of substance add up to a relationship and create its distinct profile: activity links, resource ties and actor bonds (Håkansson/Snehota 1995: 26-27). The relationship then has an effect (or function) on different actors: the dyad itself, each of the two companies and third parties (Håkansson/Snehota 1995: 27-28). It is worth noting that the **substance** dimension shows important parallels to the objects of cooperation: Activity links are closely related to a split of work, resource ties have much in common with resource sharing and actor bonds are the prerequisite for knowledge exchange. The **functions** of a relationship, however, are not explicitly studied in this research, which is concerned with the determinants rather than the effects of the delineated relationships.

Against this background it should be noted that Håkansson and Snehota also discuss **contextual elements** or interdependencies within which any company operates and which affect its development. These include technology, knowledge, social relations, administrative routines and systems, as well as legal ties (Håkansson/Snehota 1995: 13-16). In this research a more comprehensive concept is chosen as a main influencing factor: a company's strategic orientation (see section 5.1). Finally, Håkansson and Snehota's observation that major supplier-customer relationships are

---

[56] For a discussion of formal versus informal relationships see subsection 2.3.3.

subject to continuous **change** (Håkansson/Snehota 1995: 10) inspires the investigation of how intersubsidiary relationships develop over time.

In accordance with Håkansson and Snehota's work a review of the most influential developments in project marketing literature over the past decade (see Cova/Salle 2007: 139-141) shows that the **INPM** is primarily dedicated to **external marketing issues** (Skaates/Tikkanen 2003: 503). Much of the INPM's work has originated from the IMP Group's marketing management perspective, which sees the firm as a nexus of exchange relationships (Skaates/Tikkanen 2003: 508-509 with reference to Möller/Wilson 1995). While INPM researchers emphasize the importance and complexity of the project marketing milieu, they neglect the configuration of internal relationships. Skaates and Tikkanen suggest that an enhanced understanding of project-marketing-related structures and processes can be reached by examining these issues within their environmental context (Skaates/Tikkanen 2003: 509). While the authors encourage the investigation of how project-selling firms manage their market-oriented competence development, they do not consider the question of how internal organizational structures may enhance or impede such a development.

From the above reviews it becomes clear that both the INPM and the IMP Group focus on **external business relationships and transactions** rather than the internal functioning of the organizations involved. Although project marketing researchers frequently speak of 'suppliers', 'selling firms' or 'organizations that sell projects' they hardly specify any internal processes, configurations or responsibilities. Their focus lies on the interaction between buyer and supplier. Kirsch et al., who provide a review of personal and organizational interaction approaches (Kirsch et al. 1980: 76-91), acknowledge that a differentiated design of the marketing function is necessary depending on the complexity of the buying situation (Kirsch et al. 1980: 87). If the exchange concerns a highly complicated product, a flexible marketing organization is necessary, in which multiple departments interact and communicate with each other (Kirsch et al. 1980: 87-88 with reference to Håkansson/Östberg 1975: 120). Kirsch et al. criticize that Håkanssson and Östberg's interaction approach abstracts from the intraorganizational aspects of the problem (Kirsch et al. 1980: 89), but hardly contribute to such a perspective themselves. **Interaction approaches** are multi-organizational in that they involve two or more elements of a marketing system that participate in the transaction of industrial goods (Kirsch et al. 1980: 93-94). This external perspective also dominates much of the international marketing literature. Respective monographs reflect that internal structures and processes are given relatively little attention compared to aspects such as business dynamics, market entry strategies, international marketing policy, strategic planning, etc. (see, for example, Backhaus et al. 2003; Berndt et al. 2003; Ghauri/Cateora 2005; Zentes et al. 2006). Although the authors address issues such as the formal organization structure and coordination requirements, they provide few insights on the allocation of responsibilities and the relationship between globally dispersed units.

4.2.4 Research Gap: Internal Relationships and Structures

Although marketing seems to be moving away from a transactional focus to a relationship focus (Filiatrault/Lapierre 1997: 220), the reference point for these relationships is mainly external, not internal. As indicated in the previous subsection, organizational aspects of project marketing have hardly been addressed. A few attempts have been made to create a **link between the customer interface and internal structures**. Galbraight, for example, argues that the increasing importance of the customer has organizational implications for the supplier: the latter needs to respond to customer demands by coordinating activities across countries, businesses and functions. Lateral networking capability is key for creating multiproduct solutions for global customers (Galbraith 2001: 18, 21). Drawing upon information processing and resource dependency theory, Birkinshaw et al. look at global account management from an **organizational perspective** – and not as most of their peers in terms of the vendor-customer relationship (Birkinshaw et al. 2001: 233). They see global account management as "a set of systems and procedures that increase the information processing capacity of the MNC in response to the heightened information processing needs resulting from global customers" (Birkinshaw et al. 2001: 234).

While information processing theory focuses on the internal organization of the firm, resource dependency theory helps the authors explain the **dynamics of interorganizational bargaining power** (Birkinshaw et al. 2001: 235-236). Moving from a country-by-country customer relationship to a global one most likely results in a shift of bargaining power that could either favor the customer (because all sales are controlled through a central channel) or the vendor (because typically the customer reduces the number of suppliers) (Birkinshaw et al. 2001: 236). Dysfunctional effects are expected from an **organizational mismatch**, which would occur if the vendor was organized on a country-by-country basis while the customer had a global purchasing operation. The customer could then realize price concessions by trading local sales managers off against each other (Birkinshaw et al. 2001: 236). This last aspect is particularly relevant to this research because it bears parallels with intersubsidiary competition for customers. Fifteen years earlier Frese had already pointed to the necessity of considering the structure of the customer's procurement organization when evaluating what is perceived as acting with "one face to the customer" (Frese 1985: 275). Birkinshaw et al. further suggest that global account management need not only be instituted in response to external customer-centered stimuli but also consider the organization's ability to coordinate activities among corporate and national units (Birkinshaw et al. 2001: 246).

Despite these attempts to reconcile external marketing objectives with internal networking and coordination capabilities, little is known about their practical implications. This is particularly true for project marketing literature, where a mono-organizational approach to structures and processes is missing almost entirely. With respect to systems selling, Helm outlines the tasks of subsidiaries, which are typically in charge of distinct marketing areas or customers, and illustrates the conflict potential between headquarters and subsidiaries (Helm 2004: 83-84). He does not, however, discuss how subsidiaries interrelate in serving the customer based on alternative configurations of responsibilities.

4.2.5 Starting Point: Process-Oriented Industrial Marketing

In search of a concept that supports an internal perspective on project marketing activities, process-oriented marketing (POM) marks a starting point. POM strikes as an **innovative research approach** (Diller/Ivens 2006: 20; Diller/Ivens 2007: 480) that aims at achieving both high marketing efficiency and high marketing effectiveness. Key issue is the optimal organization of marketing processes with respect to customer satisfaction. While market orientation as the guiding principle is maintained (Diller/Ivens 2007: 480-482), the **organizational component** plays a much greater role in POM than in traditional marketing concepts (Diller/Ivens 2007: 483-484). From the existing conceptual literature it can be inferred that market orientation consists of three elements: customer orientation, competitor orientation and interfunctional coordination (Narver/Slater 1990: 21-22). Coordination and integration of geographically dispersed (marketing) activities seems just as important, though (Diller/Ivens 2006: 15).

Although the focus of this research is not on the design, implementation, improvement or measurement of marketing processes (Diller/Ivens 2006: 18), a **process-oriented approach to intersubsidiary relationships** seems particularly useful. Different process steps (or project phases) may be characterized by different types of relations. While subsidiaries may compete for the charter to serve a particular customer, they may cooperate through knowledge sharing once responsibilities have been assigned. The overall relationship would then be a coopetitive one. A process perspective allows identifying the decisions and milestones that shape or trigger a certain relationship. By tracing its development along the project lifecycle, the content of the relationship becomes more tangible. Specifying process responsibilities forms part of the implementation of a process-oriented management concept (Diller/Ivens 2006: 19). The latter is in line with a general trend in business administration that goes from thinking in structures to thinking in processes (Kutschker/Schmid 1995: 13 and, more comprehensively, Kutschker/Schmid 2006: 641-649).

The process perspective per se is not new to the project marketing community. Looking beyond the transactional situations of competitive bidding to include all the strategic and commercial processes of the supplying company poses a key challenge for project marketing researchers. In this respect the development of a processual model of project marketing has been considered a major achievement in the field (Cova/Salle 2007: 138-139). Again, the focus of the model is on decisions, behavior and interactions that characterize the buyer-supplier relationship; interunit relationships are not included.

In this research, the process perspective helps define the relevant scope of project marketing activities and trace the (dynamic) nature of intersubsidiary relationships. Once the project marketing process has been outlined, subsidiaries' (and headquarters') involvement in each core activity and/or decision can be mapped.

4.2.6 The Project Marketing Process

The purpose of this subsection, which takes a processual or project lifecycle perspective (see Cova/Salle 2005: 356), is twofold: First, project acquisition and execution are presented as the constituting elements of what has previously been defined as the project marketing process. Second, the foundation for analyzing intersubsidiary relationships is laid by outlining and describing the activities characterizing the individual phases of this process.

4.2.6.1 Basis and Contribution

German industrial marketing literature has a long-standing tradition of taking a **'phase-differentiated' approach** to the marketing of large industrial projects (subsequently referred to as 'project marketing' as specified above). Early attempts to outline the marketing process for large industrial plants date back to the late 1970s and early 1980s (Backhaus/Günther 1976: 257-264; Engelhardt 1977: 25-26; Bretschneider 1980: 61; Blessberger 1981: 63-75), while the most recent publications show that both the approach and the results are still highly relevant (Heger 2000: 14; Königshausen/Spannagel 2004: 1128-1141; Backhaus/Voeth 2007: 309-311). Comparable contributions in Anglo-Saxon literature are difficult to find. This may also be explained by the fact that plant engineering has always represented an important pillar of the German economy (again see Bretschneider 1980: 1; Schwanfelder 1989: 16-17; Gleich et al. 2005: 4; Stroh 2006: 13-14; VDMA 2007: 8-9). Given that plant engineering has evolved into a global industry, however, the lack of contributions in English no longer seems justified. At the same time there is a need to integrate the existing contributions into a comprehensive yet concise 'state-of-the-art' project marketing process, including all relevant phases, milestones, decisions and activities.

The following represents an attempt to fill this gap and to lay the foundation for the analysis of intersubsidiary relationships. Although successful project marketing takes into account the particularities of each assignment and may thus involve significant variations in terms of content, it usually follows a typical sequence.[57] The phase breakdown presented in this chapter builds significantly upon the work by Königshausen and Spannagel (2004) but also incorporates relevant elements of the earlier sources cited above. Additional insights were gained from (mainly confidential) company documents and firm websites. Individual references are omitted in the description of the process since there are significant overlaps in the phases chosen by various authors, and differences are mainly attributable to wording or grouping. The goal is to present a **typical, holistic, yet practice-oriented project marketing process**, not a review of academic contributions on the topic. The description should be precise and suffice for understanding the plant engineering company's key activities in each phase. It does not aim at going into the same detail as contributions that are entirely dedicated to such a process outline or individual facets of it (such as the bidding process, project organization, contract negotiation, risk management,

---

[57] A sequential approach is chosen for illustrative purposes. It is important to note that phases frequently overlap in practice, which was emphasized by several interviewees (most explicitly P4, P5; for an introduction of the abbreviated interview transcripts see section 6.4).

etc.). The English terms were cross-checked with company information provided on the internet, and the entire process was reconciled with industry experts.

For complexity reasons the project marketing process is divided into **two major phases**: project acquisition and project execution. In practice, these two phases follow each other seamlessly.[58] As illustrated in Figure 9, the project acquisition phase comprises pre-acquisition, concept/study, and project planning and structuring. Engineering and procurement, construction, and close-out/operations form part of the project execution phase. Once each of the phases has been outlined, they will be joined back together into a top-level process that provides the basis of the development of alternative project marketing models. The sub-phases that are particularly relevant to these models are shaded in black. While pre-acquisition will be included as the ongoing element of project marketing, locally bound operations will be neglected. Given the focus of the research, the description of each project phase is oriented towards the activities performed by the supplier rather than his interaction with the buyer.

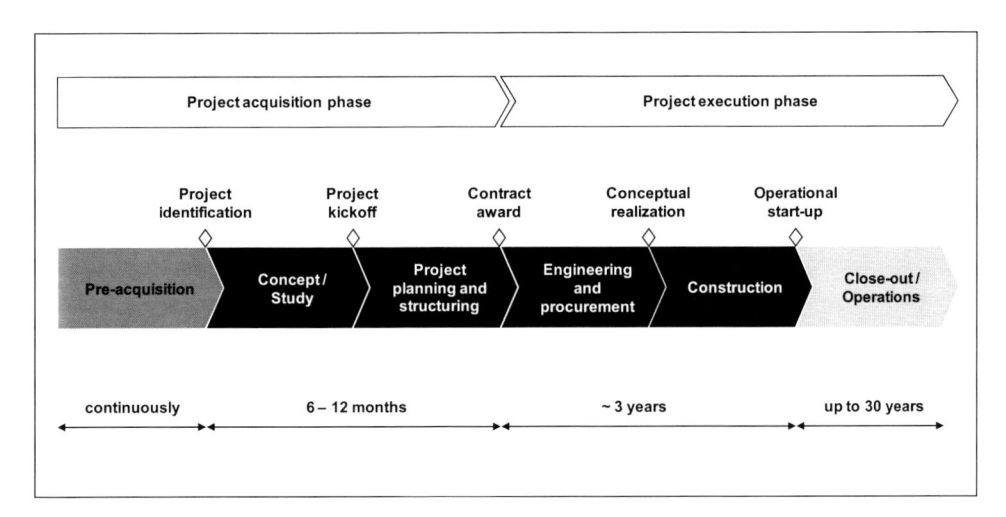

Figure 9: Simplified Overview of the Project Marketing Process

---

[58] As noted earlier, the two phases may even overlap.

4.2.6.2 Project Acquisition

Project acquisition begins with a plant engineering company's decision to approach a customer and, if successful, ends with the mutual decision to conclude a contract. The overview in Figure 10 serves as a guideline for describing and discussing the elements of the project acquisition phase.

Pre-acquisition is an ongoing process that begins with the development of a customer- (or customer segment-) specific sales strategy and usually ends with the identification of a certain project. Since the latter does not yet exist, the phase can also be labeled as "independent of any project" (Cova et al. 2002: 53, 142; Cova/Salle 2007: 140). In practice it is oftentimes referred to as 'business development'. Defining **strategic objectives** and setting sales targets are essential prerequi-sites for successful project marketing. Suppliers further need to specify the scope and contents of what they are able (and willing) to offer to their customers. Some authors prefer to combine these decisions in a separate strategic marketing phase (Cova et al. 2002: 52-53). Once the sales strategy has been approved, the respective marketing and communication activities can be implemented. Such activities include the participation in trade fairs, the hosting of expert conferences, the organization of roadshows, and the selective placement of advertisement and specialist articles. These instruments can be used to establish new and maintain existing customer relationships. The supplier's goal is to identify potential customers and projects.

Like in most industrial markets, ongoing **relationship management** in plant engineering is usually performed by a global Key Account Management (KAM) organization (see, for example, Millman 1996; Lockau 2000; Arnold et al. 2001; Birkinshaw et al. 2001; Galbraith 2001; Wengler 2006; Belz/Zupancic 2007). Key account managers coordinate and maintain the relationship with strategically important customers (or other network partners) on a technical, commercial and personal/social level. They represent the customer interface in that they are responsible for acting upon or diffusing any relevant customer information. Customers who do not have a key account manager assigned to them are typically served through representatives of a regional sales organization located at headquarters, foreign subsidiaries or local sales offices.

Already in the pre-acquisition phase it is important to distinguish between **a proactive and a reactive acquisition mode** (see also Bansard et al. 1993: 126; Backhaus/Voeth 2007: 311-313; alternatively labeled active versus passive approach). While some plant engineering companies prefer to engage in project development together with the customer, others almost exclusively participate in calls for tendher. Suppliers pursuing a proactive acquisition strategy aim at creating new customer demand; those pursuing a reactive acquisition strategy take action only once the customer has articulated his existing demands. In order to increase revenues and reduce risks, companies are likely to strive for a combination of both channels. Although the supplier eventually establishes contact with the customer regardless of the acquisition strategy, the type of (external) relationship that prevails in this initial phase differs significantly.

Project development means that supplier and customer collaborate closely to identify and define promising business opportunities. The initiative for such collaboration can be taken by the supplier or the customer. Most plant engineering companies offer consulting services, which allow them to better understand their customers' problems and desires, to maintain a close customer relationship and to take early notice of planned projects. Ideally, the supplier is involved in the definition of project specifications or the preparation of tender documents. In case of a new customer, the supplier will already have conducted market research and prepared a proposal before approaching the customer. Project development itself can be more or less proactive depending on whether the plant engineering company is treated as a single-source contractor, a co-developer or an equity partner in the development of new technologies.

Relationship management in preparation of a **tender offer** is different in that such a process of organized competition tends to be fairly anonymous (see Barrmeyer 1982: 8-11 for an outline of the tender process). The plant engineering company needs to make sure the customer is aware of its qualifications if it wishes to be selected for participation in a restricted (private) tender. In case of an open (or public) tender such acquaintance is of minor importance – unless price is not the only selection criterion. Typically any vendor or contractor who can guarantee performance is admitted to the process. Plant engineering companies pursuing a reactive acquisition strategy need to stay informed about upcoming tenders and evaluate opportunities up front. When a particular project takes shape, situational analysis – or the preliminary evaluation of a project – is just as important as it is in the context of project development. Interestingly, most Anglo-Saxon literature on project marketing (in the narrow sense) implies that industrial projects are primarily acquired in response to tenders (for example, Cova et al. 2002: 53, 142; Skaates/Tikkanen 2003: 505-506). Cova and Salle describe the invitation to bid as part of the overall process and as a trigger for action on the part of the supplier (Cova/Salle 2005: 356).

Project development is not adequately reflected in the related conceptualizations of the project marketing process. German scholars (and practitioners), on the other hand, strongly emphasize the importance of supplier involvement in project development (Heger 2000: 15; Königshausen/Spannagel 2004: 1130; Backhaus/ Voeth 2007: 312). Besides having a higher success rate, project development also has the advantage that the supplier is compensated for his initial effort and does not have to advance offer-preparation costs amounting to 3-5% of the total project value (Schwanfelder 1989: 23; Heger 2000: 18; Königshausen/ Spannagel 2004: 1131).

The identification of a project or the acceptance of an inquiry (invitation to bid) initiates the actual project acquisition and planning phase. In the **conceptual or study phase** the supplier reviews the project in question by performing a high-level analysis of the customer's requests and/or needs and by revealing the project's key risks and opportunities. At the same time, the plant engineering company needs to assess how its own resources and capabilities match the customer's requirements. Such an initial evaluation of the project's supply and demand side is sometimes referred to as a **pre-feasibility study**. Provided that there are no major concerns with the envisaged project, the go-ahead for detailed analysis can be given.

A **feasibility study** is part of every project marketing process. The goal is to evaluate the technical and commercial feasibility of the project in greater detail. Setting up a conceptual business plan is imperative for modeling project parameters and running scenarios. Usually an expert team composed of engineers, merchants and business unit managers is responsible for **project selection** based upon such criteria as strategic importance of the project, commercial and financial risks, competitive positioning, probability of success, project costs and volume, prior experiences with the customer, etc. Whether the supplier is interested in a particular project based on a call for tender or an opportunity identified in collaboration with the customer, the conceptual or study phase is a central element of any acquisition process.

Once the project is selected the offer phase or **project planning and structuring phase** begins.[59] This is where the actual project kickoff occurs, since the project's scope and management responsibilities are determined.[60] The central element of **project development** (in the narrow sense, as opposed to the aforementioned acquisition strategy) is to work out a detailed business plan – ideally together with the customer. Such collaboration will be less likely in case of a competitive tender. Both

---

[59] If the conceptual or study phase had come to a negative result, the customer would have had to receive a rejection.
[60] Official kickoff may be after the project/contract has been awarded.

supplier and customer contributions to the project need to be spelled out explicitly. Usually a Memorandum of Understanding (MoU) is signed as a basis for further cooperation.

Upon approval of this agreement, the **project design** phase takes the project to the next level. Front-end engineering and design (FEED) is initiated to set the technical basis of the project, and the overall project structure is elaborated to incorporate all relevant parties.[61] Large industrial projects usually require a complex organization structure, which will vary depending on whether the supplier acts as a general contractor or as part of an open or silent consortium. Additional stakeholders include customers, banks, export credit agencies (ECAs) and government agencies. Work packages are allocated to the respective parties based on the previously compiled list of supplies and services. Externally, the plant engineering company may pass on certain tasks to subcontractors; internally, it needs to define its division of labor since the customer has a right to know who he will be dealing with upon execution of the contract. Setting up an adequate project organization (such as staff, matrix or pure project, see, for example, Frese 2005: 516-523) is one aspect, dividing responsibilities among headquarters and (foreign) subsidiaries is another.

An important element of the project design phase is the **preparation of the technical, commercial and financial offer**. This document specifies the customer's expectations regarding the technical solution as well as a detailed list of each project partner's agreed scope of supplies and services. It further outlines the project's commercial parameters, including price-setting factors such as terms of payment and delivery, imputed interests, tax burdens and risk management costs. The plant engineering company has a strong interest in protecting itself against technical and manufacturing risks, credit and payment risks, country and exchange-rate risks. It is of utmost importance to disclose these risks and weigh them against the respective opportunities. Project responsibilities and execution strategy are also part of the proposal. Finally, the supplier can structure and arrange financing together with banks, ECAs and, possibly, with commodity traders. Advising and supporting customers on financial and tax issues has become an increasingly important feature of project marketing.

---

[61] In some firms Basic Engineering (as supplier-independent design) is completed before the contract is signed; FEED packages (or project design packages) can also come from the client or third parties. Whether or not a FEED is completed also varies with the type of industry or technology.

The result of the project design phase is a **preliminary offer**, which is released to the customer once the project-related risks have been assessed and accepted. The degree to which the customer was involved in the elaboration of the offer depends on whether he developed the project together with the supplier or placed an invitation to bid. The subsequent **offer negotiation phase** allows the two parties to refine and revise any contract details, to consider a re-evaluation of project risks and to make adjustments in price. Ideally, the engineering company defines its negotiation strategy before engaging in discussions with its counterpart. In case of a tender most bidders will be dismissed prior to the negotiation phase. Once all discrepancies and open issues have been resolved, the contracting parties sign a Letter of Intent (LoI; also called NoA or Notice of Award), which documents the results of the negotiations and the conditions under which the parties are willing to conclude the contract. If these conditions are met to mutual satisfaction, the **final contract** is signed. The project is now ready for execution. What follows on the part of the plant engineering company is the **internal handover** from the sales team to the execution team.

Milestones	◇ Project identification	◇ Accept inquiry or identify project	◇ Give go-ahead for detailed evaluation	▼ Project kickoff[1]	◇ Approve cooperation agreement	◇ Assess risks and approve offer release	◇ Contract award	▼ Reassess risks and approve contract	
Phases	Pre-acquisition	Concept / Study			Project planning and structuring			Execution	
Decisions	Approve sales strategy	Accept inquiry or identify project	Give go-ahead for detailed evaluation	Select project and define responsibilities	Approve cooperation agreement	Assess risks and approve offer release		Reassess risks and approve contract	Internal handover
Activities	Strategy development	Relationship management	Project review	Feasibility study	Project development	Project design		Offer negotiation	
	Define sales strategy and objectives for target market segments and customers	Carry out marketing and communication activities	Perform high-level analysis of customer requests/needs	Evaluate technical and commercial feasibility in greater detail	Work out detailed business plan (together with customer)	Initiate FEED (set design basis)[2]		Define negotiation strategy	Hand project over to execution team
	Define scope and contents of a potential offer	Pursue proactive and/or reactive project acquisition (project devt. versus tender participation)	Identify key risks and opportunities	Develop conceptual business plan	Specify supplier and customer contributions	Define project structure and allocate work packages		Refine and revise contract details	Objective: Fulfill commitments regarding schedule, quality/scope and profit expectations
	Decide upon active versus passive project acquisition	Conduct situational analysis and explore opportunities	Assess proper resources and capabilities	Facilitate project selection	Detail scope of supplies and services	Prepare technical, commercial and possibly financial offer		Consider re-evaluation of project risks	
			(Pre-feasibility study)		Draft MoU	Disclose all project risks/ opportunities		Sign LoI/NoA	

(1) Official kickoff may be after the project/contract has been awarded
(2) In some firms Basic Engineering (as supplier-independent design) is completed before the contract is signed; FEED packages (or process design packages) can also come from the client or third parties

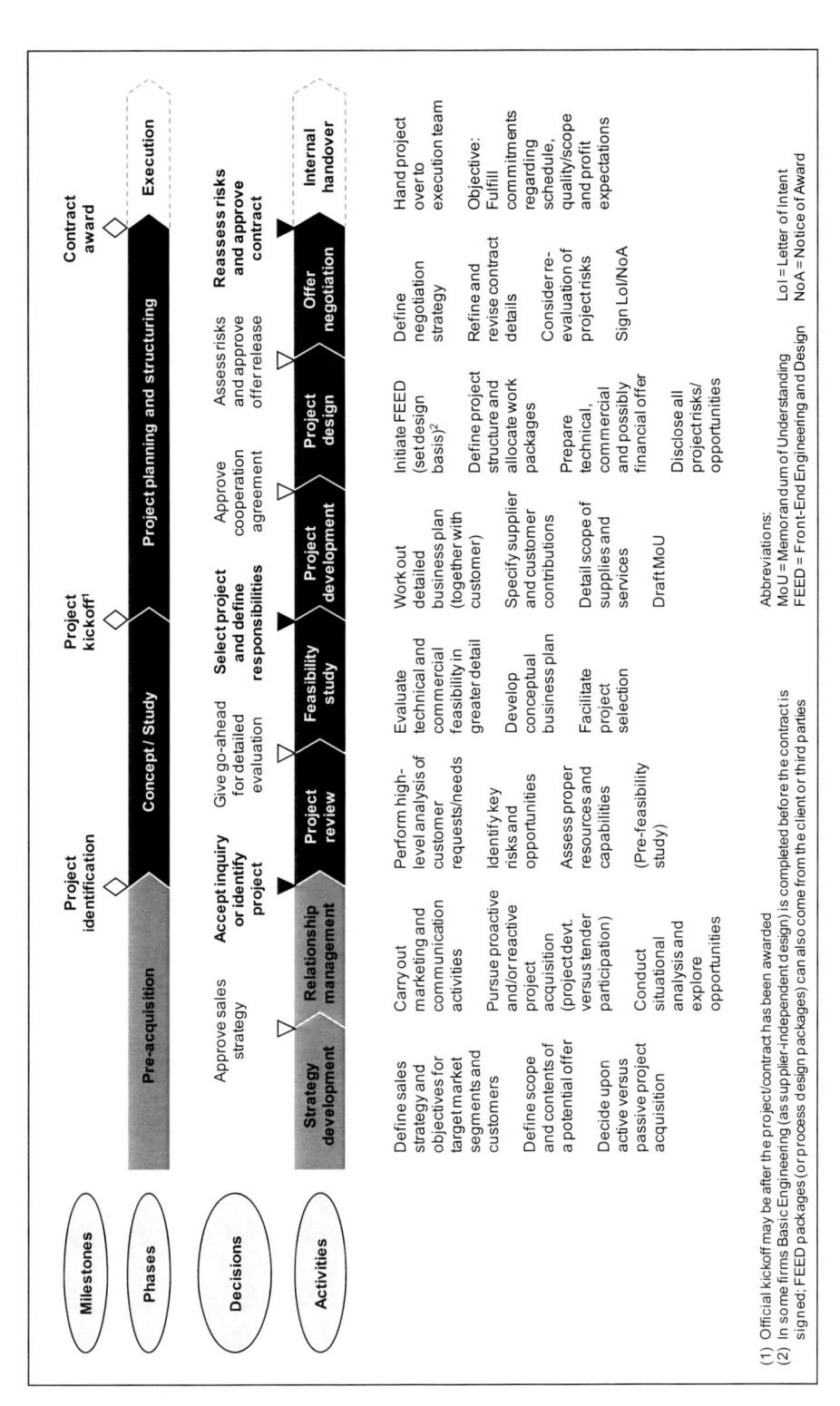

Abbreviations:
MoU = Memorandum of Understanding
FEED = Front-End Engineering and Design
LoI = Letter of Intent
NoA = Notice of Award

Figure 10: Overview of Project Acquisition Phase

4.2.6.3 Project Execution

The objective of the execution phase is to fulfill the contractual commitments regarding project schedule, scope, quality, and profit expectations to the customer's satisfaction. As depicted in Figure 11, project execution begins with the **engineering and procurement phase.** Engineering can be divided into a basic engineering and a detail engineering phase. The goal of both is to design processes, plant and piping, civil/structural/architectural items, mechanical/electrical equipment, instrumentation and automation. Part of **basic engineering** is to lay out the overall plant design and dimensions, and to plan buildings, layout and assembly. It further comprises the preparation of general arrangement drawings and process flow diagrams as well as the definition of operating concepts. Once this groundwork is laid, **detail engineering** continues with specifying materials, components and systems. The responsible engineers conduct design qualification and installation planning in 2D/3D and perform detailed risk analyses. As the name reveals, engineering constitutes one of the core activities of plant engineering companies and an important source of competitive advantage.

Procurement of key materials and components is closely linked to the engineering work. In fact, the phases may very well overlap, since engineers need to take into account what can be procured at what price within a given time. Early procurement is particularly important in times when there are bottlenecks in the supplier market. It is the contractor's responsibility to define a project-specific sourcing strategy, to negotiate the terms and conditions for materials, equipment and subcontracts, and to expedite the process of delivery. For cost and flexibility reasons most plant engineering companies have completely sacrificed in-house production. Some companies prefer to manufacture knowledge-intensive equipment and components themselves, but even there the level of vertical integration remains low. At least 50% of the total production volume is normally outsourced. Sometimes the customer even determines which subcontractors to use, leaving the plant engineering company in charge of quality management. Nowadays supplies and components tend to be procured in those countries that offer the best quality at the best price, reflecting that not only sales but also procurement in the plant engineering industry is inherently international. Another trend in this direction is the increasing demand for local content, which means that a certain amount of supplies and services needs to be provided by local companies. Procurement further involves planning and managing the supply chain and other logistics processes, including pre-assembly, shipping, transportation, etc. Last but not least, the contractor needs to inspect and ensure the quality of goods and services.

The end of the engineering phase marks the conceptual realization of the project. The plant engineering company should be able to certify that the project has been designed to contractual specifications and then lead over to the **construction phase**. Here the plant engineering company is in charge of supervising the ongoing assembly and construction activities and managing its subcontractors. Besides ensuring safety and solving technical problems, an important task is to monitor how the project advances and to perform regular quality audits. Upon confirmation of the mechanical completion of the plant, test runs are initiated as part of **commissioning**. The objective is to guarantee the plant's performance and to demonstrate its functional capability to the customer. Functional (or pre-commissioning) tests are followed by operational (or commissioning) tests before a trial operation is launched. It is only after the successful completion of all these test runs that the acceptance (or performance) tests are carried out. Successful performance tests conclude the commissioning phase and – upon signing the preliminary acceptance agreement – trigger the operational start-up of the plant.

Commissioning could also be considered part of operations because the customer already starts earning money with the new plant. More intuitively, however, the **operations phase** begins with the **completion** of the plant/project. Although the operational (or technical) start-up has occurred, the project has not yet been concluded from a legal point of view. During completion it is up to the contractual parties to close any remaining "punch items" and to negotiate claims if necessary. At this point it should be noted that **claims management** is an important ongoing task of the plant engineering company's project execution team (see, for example, Backhaus/Köhl 1999; Köhl 2000; Gleich et al. 2005: 183-184; Müller/Stroh 2007). Claims management implies the negotiation and settlement of demands resulting from any flaws in or deviations from the contract. The goal of this management approach is to prevent the emergence and/or escalation of claims. The plant engineering company will want to demonstrate that it fulfilled its contractual obligations, whereupon it can demand full payment and return of securities from the client. Both sides have an interest in monitoring guarantees and warranties when signing the acceptance protocol.

The acceptance is only preliminary to the extent that the customer is entitled to an agreed-upon **warranty** period. During this time (usually twelve months from acceptance) the plant engineering company remains in close contact with the customer. It has committed itself to coordinating relevant units or suppliers when technical support is needed. Depending on the contract, the supplier may actually assume plant management responsibilities. Upon expiration of the warranty period, the final acceptance is signed. At that point the contractor has no more contractual obligations and the full responsibility is transferred to the operator.

In **Build-Operate-Transfer (BOT) models** the plant engineering company itself may be in charge of operations for a limited or unlimited period of time. In such an arrangement, the customer – oftentimes a public entity – cedes the overall project responsibility to the supplier. The latter is not only in charge of construction and operations but also for financing the project, which is why in most cases a legally independent project company or special-purpose vehicle (SPV) is set up.[62] Even if the plant engineering company does not operate the facility after the warranty period, additional **services** may be specified in the contract. The supplier may be engaged to assess damages and perform maintenance work, undertake plant improvement, revamp and retrofit measures, or facilitate spare and wear parts supply. It may also provide training to operating personnel. All of these activities help the plant engineering company to foster the client relationship and drive follow-up projects.

---

[62] On BOT models see extensively Levy 1996 and Hintze 1998, but also Corsten/Corsten 2000: 95-96; Siebel 2001: 3-4; Kutschker/Schmid 2006: 902-903; Backhaus/Voeth 2007: 309.

Milestones		Hand over to detail engineering	Certify design to specifications	Give go-ahead for construction	Confirm mechanical completion	Sign preliminary acceptance agreement	Confirm completion of punch items	Final acceptance
Phases	Engineering and procurement				Construction		Close-out / Operations	
	Basic Engineering	Detail Engineering	Procurement	Construction	Commissioning	Completion	Warranty	Service
Decisions				Give go-ahead for construction		Sign preliminary acceptance agreement		Cede responsibility to operator
Activities	Design process, plant and piping, civil/structural/architectural items, mechanical/electrical equipment, instrumentation and automation	Specify all materials, components and systems	Define project-specific sourcing strategy	Supervise assembly and construction activities	Conduct test runs and demonstrate the plant's functional capability to the customer	Close any remaining punch items	Maintain close client contact during warranty period (usually 12 months from acceptance)	Perform maintenance work
	Lay out overall plant design and dimensions	Perform detailed risk analyses	Negotiate terms and conditions for materials, equipment, and subcontracts (+ expediting)	Manage subcontractors	• Functional/pre-commissioning tests	Negotiate claims and demonstrate contract fulfillment	Coordinate relevant units/suppliers when support is needed	Undertake plant improvement, revamp and retrofit measures
	Prepare general arrangement drawings and process flow diagrams	Conduct design qualification and installation planning in 2D/3D	Plan and manage supply chain/logistics processes (incl. pre-assembly, shipping, transportation etc.)	Monitor progress and perform quality audits	• Operational/commissioning tests	Demand full payment and return of securities from the client	Assume plant management responsibilities (optional)	Facilitate spare and wear parts supply
	Plan buildings, layout and assembly		Ensure/inspect quality of goods and services	Ensure safety	• Trial operation	Monitor guarantees and warranties		Train replaced operating personnel
	Define operating concepts			Solve technical problems	• Acceptance/performance tests			Maintain client relationship and drive follow-ups

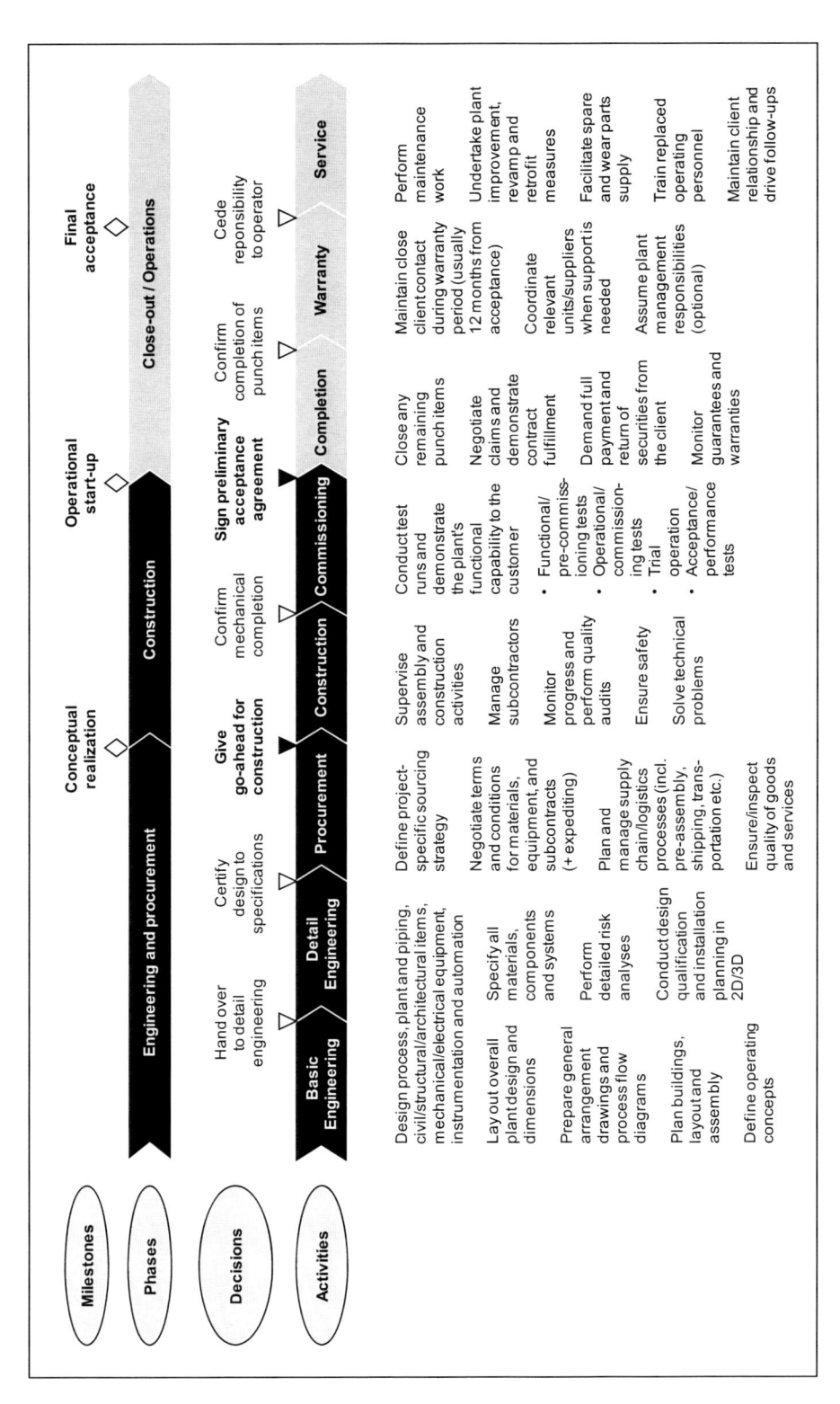

Figure 11: Overview of Project Execution Phase

4.3 Models of Intersubsidiary Relationships in Project Marketing

The previous chapters and sections have laid the conceptual foundation for the analysis of intersubsidiary relationships in a specific research setting, namely project marketing of plant engineering companies. It is now possible and necessary to bring the different elements together and to explicitly address the first research question (recall from section 1.4):

Research Question 1: Which alternative models exist for the acquisition and execution of large industrial projects with particular respect to competition and cooperation between foreign subsidiaries?

The models are developed by combining the role subsidiaries play in the project marketing process with the type of relationship they maintain with their peers. Prior to introducing the models, the methodology for mapping responsibilities and relationships is outlined (subsection 4.3.1). The eight models representing headquarters-led and subsidiary-led independence, cooperation, competition and coopetition, respectively, are presented in subsections 4.3.2 to 4.3.9.

4.3.1 Mapping Responsibilities and Relationships

As noted in section 1.4, the existing literature on plant engineering and industrial marketing provides quite an informative basis for defining a typical project marketing process (see from above Backhaus/Günther 1976: 257-264; Engelhardt 1977: 25-26; Bretschneider 1980: 61; Blessberger 1981: 63-75; Schwanfelder 1989: 18-25; Heger 2000: 14; Königshausen/Spannagel 2004: 1128-1141; Backhaus/Voeth 2007: 309-311), but few references are made to where responsibilities are allocated. The objective of this research is to identify and analyze different types of **intersubsidiary relationships** that may characterize such a process. While most project marketing literature is dedicated to the customer interface, the question here is how the supplier is – or can be – set up internally. Their international scope gives MNCs many different possibilities of which units to involve in which phases of the project marketing process. The focus here is on foreign subsidiaries, i.e. geographic rather than product or functional units, and headquarters. The complexity of the project marketing process suggests that it will be difficult for these units to operate independently of one another. While there is plenty of scope for intersubsidiary cooperation – through knowledge sharing or a split of work – there is also the possibility of intersubsidiary competition – for charters or customers. Why MNCs choose or – implying a less proactive behavior – display certain setups will be addressed in the second research question.

First, the task is to outline **alternative project marketing models**, which differ in terms of the relationships between foreign subsidiaries. Given that headquarters can have a significant impact on intersubsidiary relationships (see subsection 2.3.1), its role in the process needs to be considered as well. The models are derived by mapping subsidiaries' and headquarters' involvement in each process step. This is done in **matrix form**, showing headquarters and subsidiaries as actors on the vertical axis and the relevant process steps on the horizontal axis. In order to reduce complexity, an MNC's subsidiaries are not listed individually. For conceptual purposes a lead subsidiary is chosen ('subsidiary 1', if applicable) and the remaining subsidiaries are treated collectively ('subsidiaries 2-n'). This approach is justified by examples of international projects, which show that there tends to be one subsidiary that sets itself apart by holding a larger stake in the project than the other subsidiaries involved. Although more than one subsidiary can assume a 'leading' role with regard to a specific process step, the 'lead subsidiary' carries some overarching responsibility from both an internal (e.g., headquarters) and external (e.g., customer) perspective. A more fine-grained analysis may be necessary in the empirical part of the research but is counterproductive to the development of expressive models. A similar simplification is necessary in terms of the project marketing process. Relationship management, feasibility study, project design, engineering and construction are extracted as the main **activities**. Concentrating on these activities seems sufficient for illustrating distinct types of intersubsidiary relationships. Nevertheless, one should keep the remaining upstream and/or downstream activities that belong to the same project phase at the back of one's mind (for example, project design could be complemented by elements of project development and offer negotiation).

When thinking about how units may interrelate along the project marketing process, not only activities are important but also **decisions**. Where key decisions are taken often reveals which unit is guiding the process (see subsection 2.4.2.4 and, in particular, Schmid/Grosche 2009 on the implied importance of both elements for the configuration and coordination of value chain activities). Key decisions that mark the transition from one process step to another include project identification, project selection, contract approval, construction go-ahead and preliminary acceptance. For each process step and decision one can now ask which unit is a) responsible/leading and b) involved/participating. A more common distinction is that between responsible and supporting units, which is discarded since it does not allow for the incorporation of a competitive element. If, for example, a particular subsidiary has an interest in performing activities that are currently in the hands of another subsidiary, it plays a role in this process step, i.e. is involved, but is not supporting it. The distinction between **leading and participating units** refers to exactly this role – it does not yet say anything about the nature of their relationship. In principle, both leading and participating units may act independently, compete and/or cooperate. This is also true for two leading subsidiaries that contribute equally to a certain activity. The only restriction to the statement is that the constellation of having one leading and one participating subsidiary makes independence between the two unlikely. While headquarters' role is considered in the models, the relational focus is limited to subsidiaries.[63]

In order to facilitate comprehension of the project marketing models and their graphical illustration, the corresponding legend is introduced and explicated below (Figure 12).

●	Responsible / leading unit	◆	Cooperation through knowledge sharing
○	Involved / participating unit	◇	Cooperation through a split of work
——	Primary flow of information or feedback	⚡	Competition for (internal) charters
······	Optional flow of information or feedback	⚡	Competition for (external) customers

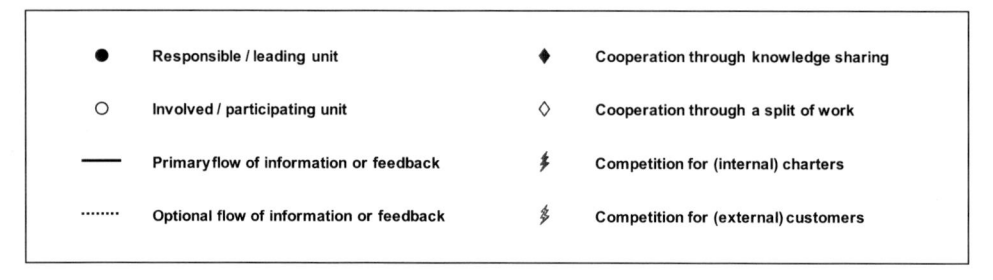

Figure 12: Legend to Project Marketing Models

Solid and empty circles are used to indicate the actors' leading or participating role in each process step – resulting in a so-called 'spaghetti chart'. Connecting lines between these circles illustrate the sequential **flow of information or feedback** between actors. In other words, these lines reflect the interaction that is necessary to advance from one process step to the next. A solid line depicts the primary flow; a dotted line an optional flow. Returning from flows to stocks, the relationship between subsidiaries is mapped as it presents itself for each process step. For an **intersubsidiary relationship** to exist, at least two subsidiaries need to have a (potential) stake in a single process step or decision. Where this is the case, the

---

[63] It should be noted that in the empirical investigation the depicted relationships may also be established between subsidiaries and headquarters if the two contribute to the process as quasi-peers.

prevailing relationship will be one of independence, competition or cooperation. In the models, cooperation through knowledge sharing and a split of work is indicated through solid and empty diamonds; competition for charters and customers is represented by solid and empty flashes.

How subsidiaries interrelate within different process steps adds up to their overall relationship, which will be mainly **independent, cooperative, competitive or coopetitive**. Coopetition is not expected to occur within a single process step but is considered as the result of subsidiaries competing in one process step and cooperating in another one. It is this overall relationship that is categorized as being **headquarters-led or subsidiary-led** – although it is recognized that headquarters and subsidiaries may also drive single activities.

Finally, it seems necessary to differentiate between **tenders and project development** at the beginning of the process, since the acquisition strategy has an impact on the locus of project identification and the intensity and direction of information flows.

Altogether, **eight distinct models** of intersubsidiary relationships are derived in a logical manner based on a profound understanding of the project marketing process and the business dynamics of the plant engineering industry. The objective is to combine the relationship parameters discussed in Chapter 2, i.e. types, contents and origin, with the specific research setting. In accordance with the research question, the focus is on the horizontal relationship between subsidiaries. Obviously, these eight models are not exhaustive but rather 'modular'; one can think of an infinite number of variations and combinations. The models represent **exemplary constellations** of intersubsidiary relationships, making the latter more tangible and facilitating the creation of a link between these relationships and certain influencing factors. As such, the models serve as a **foundation for the empirical part of the study**, where a company's intersubsidiary relationships are classified according to how the project marketing process is set up. Decisive for this classification is the overall relationship between subsidiaries, which consists of cooperative and/or competitive actions that may be mainly headquarters- or mainly subsidiary-led.

How exactly and how frequently subsidiaries exhibit a certain behavior is not directly relevant for a **classification of the relationship**. What matters is whether they act independently, only compete, only cooperate, or compete and cooperate simultaneously (i.e. within the same process chain). Interviews with industry experts confirm that the models reflect key issues with regard to intersubsidiary relationships during project acquisition and execution. Nevertheless, it needs to be recognized that the models constitute a starting point for rather than the result of empirical analysis. Consequently, some models are likely to prove more relevant in practice than others. A two-part overview of the eight models is presented in Figure 13 and Figure 14, followed by a brief discussion of each one.

169

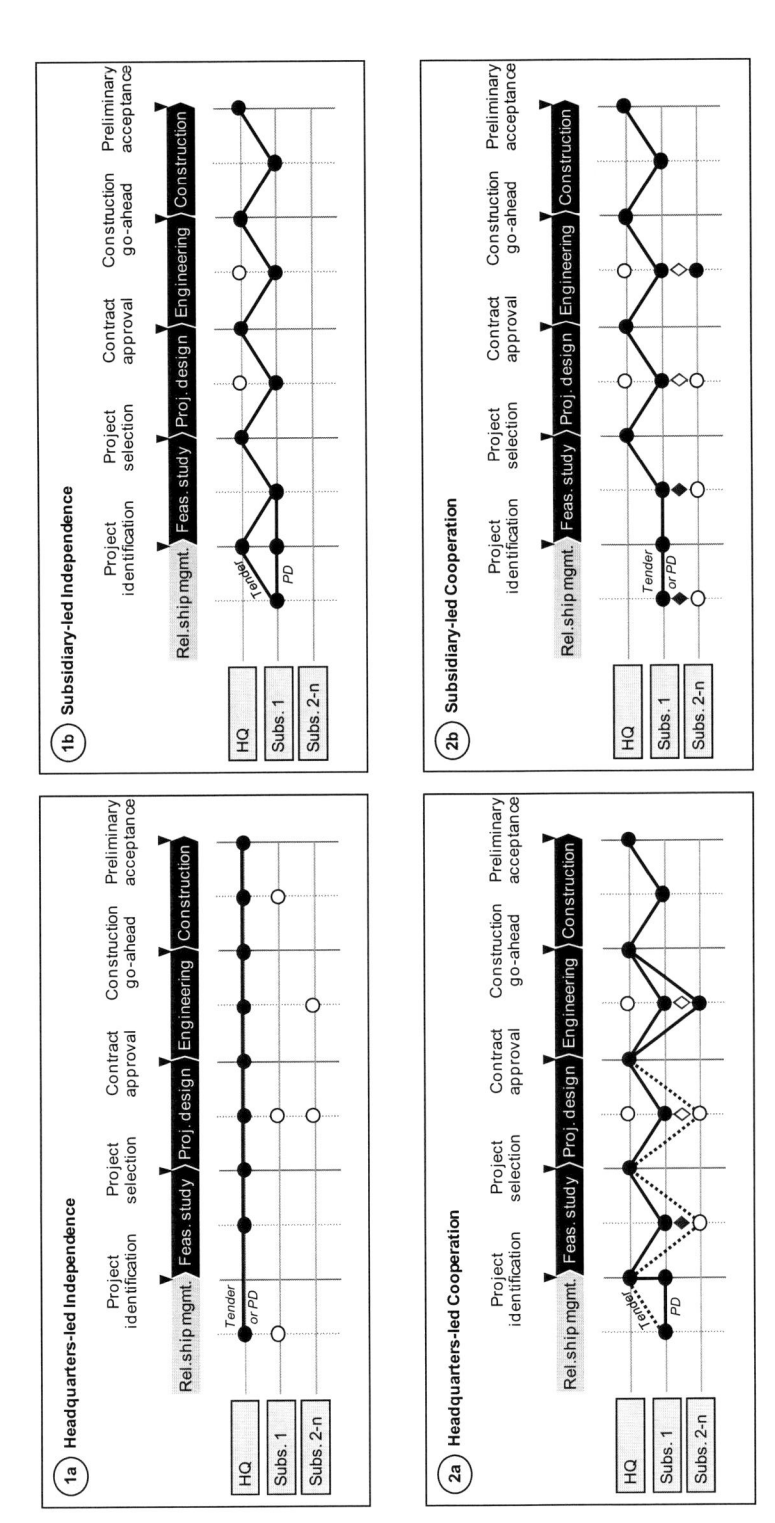

Figure 13: Project Marketing Models – Part I: Independence and Intersubsidiary Cooperation

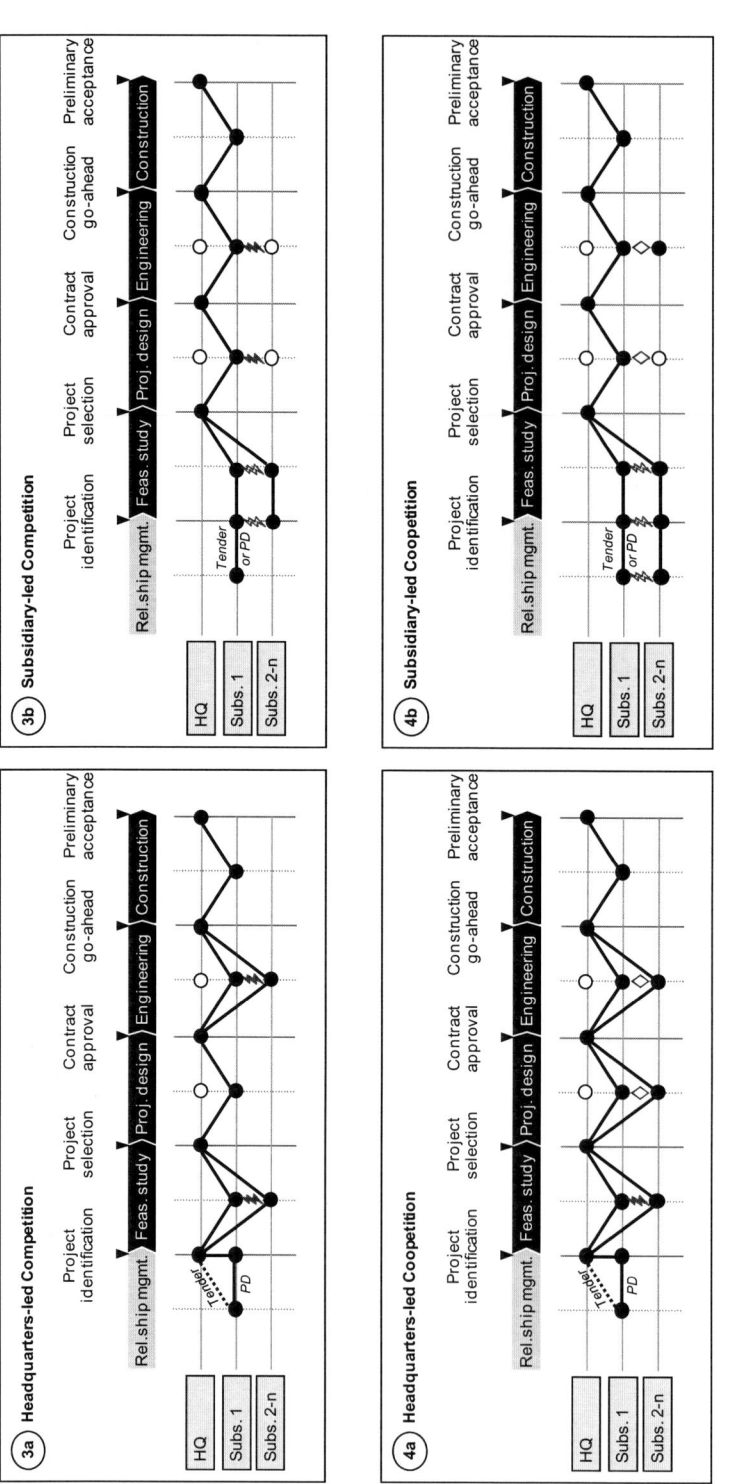

Figure 14: Project Marketing Models – Part II: Intersubsidiary Competition and Coopetition

4.3.2 Headquarters-Led Independence

In the first scenario, headquarters is responsible for the entire project marketing process. Virtually all process steps and decisions are centralized with the parent company: customer relationships are managed from a central location, the project is evaluated and designed by headquarters, and engineering and construction are also carried out by headquarters personnel. In the plant engineering industry such centralization seems realistic only if the customer is located in the same region or country as the parent company. Otherwise some subsidiary support in relationship management and location-bound downstream activities would be assumed. While customer proximity is certainly beneficial to relationship management, the review, design and engineering of a project could possibly be accomplished from a distance. Construction activities, however, are bound to the location of the plant. Unless headquarters provided complete execution teams, subsidiary involvement would thus be necessary.

Headquarters-led independence represents a scenario in which the overall process is managed by headquarters. Whether the project is identified, evaluated and won in a tender process or through project development (abbreviated as 'PD' in Figure 13 and Figure 14) together with the customer is irrelevant in this case. Given the strong role of the parent company, subsidiaries do not interrelate in a cooperative or competitive manner. It is worth noting that an alternative manifestation of headquarters-led independence would be that headquarters explicitly assigns customer/project responsibility to a specific subsidiary, advising the latter to complete the job on its own.

4.3.3 Subsidiary-Led Independence

Unlike in the previous scenario, a lead subsidiary is now responsible for large parts of the project marketing process. Even if key decisions are taken or need to be approved by headquarters, a particular subsidiary – typically located in the same region or country as the customer – is in charge of relationship management and project-related activities. A call for tender may formally be addressed to headquarters and not to the relationship-managing subsidiary, but the latter is expected to be well aware of the process. Project development, on the other hand, implies the interaction between the customer and a local relationship manager and is thus managed directly by the subsidiary. The parent company may contribute its expertise to certain process steps such as project design or engineering but otherwise takes a less operational stance. However, given the scope of the projects and their related risks, it is assumed that all major decisions – such as the selection, approval, certification and acceptance of a project – need some form of central authorization. Otherwise subsidiary-led independence involves only a single subsidiary. Disregarding the possibility of an MNC having only this one subsidiary, the lead subsidiary chooses not to turn to any of its peers in support of certain process steps. Such a scenario seems most likely if responsibilities are clearly assigned and no value added is expected from intersubsidiary cooperation.

4.3.4 Headquarters-Led Cooperation

One can think of a scenario in which the parent company wishes to encourage intersubsidiary cooperation in project marketing. In such a case headquarters is likely to reduce its operational engagement to a minimum, remaining in charge of key decisions but leaving project-related activities to its subsidiaries. Headquarters-led cooperation may seem more likely when the company takes notice of a project via a call for tender, because project development usually implies that one subsidiary has already taken the lead. Since project responsibilities are not assigned to a single subsidiary, the initial information flow between headquarters and the relationship-managing subsidiary is expected to be less intense than in the previous case of subsidiary-led independence.

But headquarters-led cooperation may also occur in the context of project development. The relationship-managing subsidiary may be required to inform headquarters of any prospective projects so that the decision of which units to involve in subsequent activities can be taken centrally. Irrespective of the acquisition mode, headquarters will entrust the lead subsidiary with the preparation of the feasibility study, urging it to cooperate with its peers. Depending on the extent to which the lead subsidiary is in charge of coordination, information and feedback may also flow between headquarters and the cooperating subsidiaries. The latter may have a certain knowledge or expertise that headquarters regards as valuable to the compilation of the feasibility study. Once the project has been selected for further pursuit, headquarters may expect similar benefits from cooperation in project design. Here, the lead subsidiary may be asked to have certain subtasks – such as preliminary engineering work – accomplished by one of its peers. Taking the demand for cooperation one step further, headquarters cannot only require one subsidiary to be assisted by its peers but assign equal responsibilities to two or more subsidiaries. At least temporarily the lead subsidiary then has to sacrifice – or rather share – its role. Upon approval of the project, headquarters could, for example, split basic and detail engineering tasks among two subsidiaries. While basic engineering could be conducted in the customer's home country, labor-intensive detail engineering could be accomplished in a transition economy such as India or China. Construction of the facility, then again, would be incumbent on the local subsidiary.

4.3.5 Subsidiary-Led Cooperation

While in the previous scenario, cooperation was imposed by the parent company, there is also the possibility that a lead subsidiary, i.e. one that has been assigned extensive customer and project responsibilities, actively pursues the input of its peers. This may already begin with relationship management, if, for example, the subsidiary expected its peers to be able to contribute valuable customer insights from previous projects or knowledge on CRM tools. Suggesting a dominant position of the lead subsidiary, even in case of a tender the identification of a project occurs at the local level. In subsequent activities it is the lead subsidiary that decides whether or not to encourage the contribution of its peers. One should be aware, though, that cooperation requires reciprocal consent. Instead of having peers merely contribute to a certain activity, the lead subsidiary may be willing to share extensive responsibilities. In project design or engineering it could not only cede partial but entire work packages to sister subsidiaries, possibly making sure that subsequently it is in full control of construction activities. In subsidiary-led cooperation, information flows to the decision-making parent company are likely to be channeled via the lead subsidiary – even in case of a fairly equal split of work. Besides being responsible for key decisions, headquarters may again participate in select process steps – without impacting intersubsidiary relationships, however.

4.3.6 Headquarters-Led Competition

The parent company may not only encourage subsidiaries to cooperate in the project marketing process; it may also spur competition between them. Whether it takes notice of a potential project through a call for tender or through the relationship-managing subsidiary (see subsection 4.3.4), it may launch an internal request for proposal (RfP) to determine which subsidiary gets to take the lead in the project marketing process. With an RfP headquarters promotes a rather formal type of charter competition. Adhering to a structured process, the interested subsidiaries get to prepare and submit proposals on how they would go about designing and executing the respective project. In order to do so they need to undertake parallel feasibility studies. They are all treated equally in terms of the information they receive from headquarters and the feedback they may provide. Upon appraisal of the proposals headquarters selects the most promising solution and gives the respective subsidiary the go-ahead for project design. Depending on the terms of the RfP further competition could be promoted in the allocation of engineering responsibilities, for example.

Charter competition does not necessarily have to imply a formal RfP; the parent company could also ask subsidiaries to articulate their interest in assuming certain engineering responsibilities. One should note that charter competition can either arise for current or for subsequent activities. In case of the RfP, subsidiaries need to undertake parallel feasibility studies in order to prepare their proposals and possibly win the project. In the engineering example, competition would typically be settled before the work is done. In most cases, however, some duplication is inevitable, because subsidiaries dedicate their effort to the same ends. At the same time they are incited to develop their best offers, which may eventually compensate the costs of duplication. Headquarters-led competition for customers is unlikely due to its detrimental effects (refer to section 3.2 for details).

4.3.7 Subsidiary-Led Competition

If intersubsidiary competition is not initiated by the parent company but results from subsidiary activities, rivalry for customers (as opposed to charters) may very well arise. Whether the relationship-managing subsidiary identifies a project via a call for tender or project development, another subsidiary may possibly take notice of the same opportunity. As long as responsibilities are not clearly assigned, this subsidiary may claim that it is equally – or even better – able to serve the customer and may suggest proving this ability in the preparation of a feasibility study. The two subsidiaries face customer competition in the identification of the project and, if they do not manage to settle their conflicting interests bilaterally, during the subsequent project review phase. Ultimately it should be the customer who decides which project proposal he is in favor of. Assuming a certain degree of central coordination, the parent company may need to approve of the chosen subsidiary proceeding with the project.

Subsidiary-led competition may also occur for charters, though. Even if the parent company does not actively encourage or manage such competition, subsidiaries may feel that responsibilities are contestable. A particular subsidiary may try to challenge its leading peer by demonstrating its abilities in project design or engineering, for example (activities in which the parent company may also participate). The less interested and involved headquarters is in the allocation of responsibilities the more likely it is that subsidiaries have to come to terms themselves. The lead subsidiary typically remains in charge of any necessary communication and coordination with headquarters.

4.3.8 Headquarters-Led Coopetition

As specified in subsection 2.2.3 coopetition refers to a relationship characterized by simultaneous competition and cooperation. Headquarters-led coopetition can therefore be conceptualized by a combination of headquarters-led competition and headquarters-led cooperation. As specified above, the parent company could launch an internal RfP after having been informed of a project opportunity by the customer or the relationship-managing subsidiary. Based on the subsidiaries' proposals headquarters may come to the conclusion that two (or more) subsidiaries should cooperate by splitting work in subsequent process steps. Instead of determining one lead subsidiary, responsibilities are distributed evenly according to the subsidiaries' capabilities. While one subsidiary may be in charge of structuring customer needs, setting up the business plan and drafting the commercial offer, another subsidiary may be entrusted to develop an innovative technical solution, assess related risks and prepare the technical offer. A similar distinction could apply to engineering, where the parent company could, for example, assign process design and layout planning to one subsidiary and mechanical and electrical fine-tuning to another subsidiary. The overall intersubsidiary relationship is coopetitive, since subsidiaries compete in one process step and cooperate in another.

4.3.9 Subsidiary-Led Coopetition

Subsidiary-led coopetition also represents a combination of competition and cooperation but significantly constrains the role of the parent company. A variation to subsidiary-led competition is presented here, suggesting that even relationship management responsibilities are not determined in advance. This could be the case with a completely new customer, located in a country that is currently not covered by any subsidiary. Subsidiaries could already compete for customers in this early phase, but also, as suggested above, in project identification or the preparation of the feasibility study. If they do not manage to reach a bilateral agreement on who may take the lead, it will be up to the customer to signal his preference for a certain subsidiary.

Once headquarters has granted its approval (if necessary), the lead subsidiary may realize the benefits of cooperation with its peers. Intersubsidiary competition may have revealed some previously unknown capabilities that would enhance the lead subsidiary's performance or directly add value to the customer. The sister subsidiaries could agree on splitting work packages in project design and engineering, with the lead subsidiary maintaining the information flow with headquarters. The model suggests that it depends on the lead subsidiary how much responsibility it is willing to share with its peers. A subsidiary may participate in project design but assume full responsibility for certain engineering-related tasks. Instead of, or in addition to, splitting work, subsidiaries could also share knowledge on selected issues. A similar variation applies to the competitive side: If relationship management competencies were eventually assigned by headquarters, charter competition, not customer competition would prevail. For the relationship to be considered subsidiary-led, however, such competition may not be actively promoted by the parent company. Again, important for the existence of coopetition is that competition in one process step is complemented by cooperation in another process step.

5 Link between Strategic Orientation and Intersubsidiary Relationships

Now that the range of alternative project marketing models has been outlined, it is possible – and necessary – to look into the reasons for different constellations of intersubsidiary relationships. As suggested in sections 3.4 and 3.5, a contingency framework linking the models to a particular influencing factor best meets these objectives. The second research question reveals that it is the MNC's strategic orientation, which is expected to have a significant impact on intersubsidiary competition and cooperation (compare to section 1.4).

This chapter begins with an explanation for choosing strategic orientation as a key influencing factor and an introduction to Bartlett and Ghoshal's typology of multinational companies (section 5.1). Explicit propositions are then developed on the link between this influencing factor and alternative intersubsidiary relationships (section 5.2). Characteristics and results of the empirical study are presented in subsequent chapters.

5.1 MNC Strategic Orientation as a Key Influencing Factor

As concluded in section 3.6, the concept of strategic orientation unites both strategic and structural elements and thus covers many of the ideas IB scholars have included in their contingency studies on interunit (or intersubsidiary) relationships. In the context of this research, strategic orientation is conceptualized according to Bartlett and Ghoshal's typology of multinational companies and – constituting a comprehensive approach to international business – is broader in scope than the conventional definition of strategy as "the determination of the long-term goals and objectives of an enterprise, and the adoption of courses of action and allocation of resources necessary for carrying out these goals" (Chandler 1962: 13). The fundamental choice between a local and a global strategic orientation (or a combination of both) can be thought of as "the amalgam of many decisions" (White/Poynter 1989: 55).

Bartlett and Ghoshal's typology builds upon the Integration-Responsiveness (I-R) framework, whose advocates initially used the relative importance of the integration and responsiveness pressures to map industry characteristics (Doz/Prahalad 1991: 159). Its dimensions being more refined and more concrete, Bartlett and Ghoshal's typology is preferred over the I-R framework for analytical purposes. Nevertheless, a brief introduction is given to "the popular integration-responsiveness framework of international strategic orientation" (Devinney et al. 2000: 674) to reveal where the core concepts and ideas have originated from (subsection 5.1.1). Based on these results, Bartlett and Ghoshal's typology of multinational companies is discussed (subsection 5.1.2).

5.1.1 The Integration-Responsiveness Framework

Extending the differentiation and integration dimensions introduced by Lawrence and Lorsch (1967), Prahalad (1975) and Doz (1976) provided one of the first conceptualizations for examining international strategy. Based upon their initial ideas, a highly influential framework was developed, "which shifted the analysis of organization design from formal structure to managerial processes" (Li/Ferreira 2003: 10). The most comprehensive description of the features of the so-called **Integration-Responsiveness (I-R) grid** comes from Prahalad and Doz (1987). The authors themselves speak of having defined "a methodology for capturing, in a managerially meaningful scheme, the characteristics of a wide range of businesses" (Prahalad/Doz 1987: 13; also see Doz/Prahalad 1991: 158).[64] Each business imposes specific demands on senior management. These demands refer to the relationships between MNC units and fall into three categories: the need for global integration, the need for global coordination and the need for local responsiveness (Prahalad/Doz 1987: 14-15). Global integration, or the centralized management of geographically dispersed activities on an ongoing basis, can be understood as a response to cost-reduction pressures. Global strategic coordination, or the central management of resource commitments in pursuit of a strategy, is geared towards gaining and maintaining competitive advantage. Local responsiveness, or subsidiaries' autonomous decision-making ability with respect to local market demands, allows for national differentiation and adaptation. Given that the needs for integration and strategic coordination are often related, Prahalad and Doz reduce their framework to two main demands: **global integration and local responsiveness** (Prahalad/Doz 1987: 16).

In summary, the I-R framework allows mapping and evaluating the pressures on a given business (Prahalad/Doz 1987: 18). Integration pressures include the

---

[64] When Prahalad and Doz speak of "business" they refer to a set of related product markets and tasks, not a company. In this sense a "business" covers more than a product line but typically less than a whole industry (Prahalad/Doz 1987: 13). One may think of it as a specific industry sector.

importance of multinational customers, the presence of multinational competitors, investment intensity, technology intensity, pressure for cost reduction, universal needs and access to raw materials and energy (Prahalad/Doz 1987: 18-20). These parameters may lead to an increase in intrafirm flows of goods, capital, information, knowledge, technology, etc. (Ghoshal 1987: 437; Kobrin 1991: 426). Local-responsiveness pressures comprise differences in customer needs, differences in distribution channels, availability of substitutes and the need to adapt, market structure and host government demands (Prahalad/Doz 1987: 20-21). By affecting not only entire businesses but also individual activities, tasks and functions, these pressures have important implications for how MNCs organize themselves.

The I-R framework is most evidently rooted in contingency theory. It further assumes that competitors within a single industry will perceive the pressures differently (Johnson 1995: 622; also see Ghoshal 1987: 429). Johnson finds empirical support for his corresponding proposition that the three basic strategies – globally integrated, locally responsive and multifocal – exist within a single global industry context (Johnson 1995: 621, 631). The author provides one of a limited number of empirical examinations of the I-R framework (also see, for example, Roth/Morrison 1990; Venaik et al. 2002). He proposes that "[i]n the future, the framework might be extended to the analysis of other strategic issues such as structural configuration" (Johnson 1995: 633). In fact, this structural component is what Bartlett and Ghoshal address in their typology of multinational companies. As called for in subsection 3.3.4, their typology accounts for a certain degree of reciprocity between strategy and structure.

5.1.2 Bartlett and Ghoshal's Typology of Multinational Companies

The concept of strategic orientation is most prominently captured in Bartlett and Ghoshal's typology of multinational companies (for a similar assessment see Harzing 2000: 102). The authors advocate that a company's strategic orientation influences the configuration and coordination of its international activities (see Bartlett/Ghoshal 1998: 24-33 for examples from different industries). This logic can be extended to propose a link between strategic orientation and intersubsidiary relationships. Developing the respective line of argument is a main goal of this research – and understanding the basic features of Bartlett and Ghoshal's typology an essential prerequisite.

5.1.2.1 Conceptual Typology

Based on their strategic capabilities, companies are defined as being either **international, multinational, global or transnational** (Bartlett/Ghoshal 1998: 15-20; Harzing 2004: 45-48; Bartlett et al. 2007: 203-206). Ideally these capabilities match the prevailing industry forces, i.e. the demand for internationalization, localization, globalization or combined globalization and localization (Bartlett/Ghoshal 1998: 23; Kutschker/Schmid 2006: 291). Companies advocating the opportunities of worldwide learning focus on transferring innovations and knowledge to local units, giving them at least some say in which products or strategies to adopt. Companies dedicated to enhancing local responsiveness tend to keep assets, resources and responsibilities decentralized, granting subsidiaries substantial decision-making autonomy in their respective markets. And companies wishing to achieve global efficiency typically pursue a more centralized approach, using subsidiaries mainly as distribution channels for domestic products. Finally, the attempt to respond to all three strategic challenges – local responsiveness, worldwide learning and global efficiency – simultaneously results in a network-like organization structure, with subsidiaries taking on differentiated roles (Bartlett/Ghoshal 1998: 55-63, 101-102).

Given that a company's strategic orientation constitutes a response to diverse industry requirements for global integration and national responsiveness, more than four types of MNCs can be expected in practice. Scholars are divided about whether to think of integration and responsiveness as the two ends of a continuum (Harzing 2000: 103) or the independent elements of a spectrum (Welge/Holtbrügge 2006: 138-139). With global integration, national responsiveness and worldwide learning constituting the respective axes, Bartlett and Ghoshal span a **three-dimensional space** in which companies can benchmark themselves against their competitors (Bartlett/Ghoshal 1998: 315-316). In any case hybrid forms are likely and plausible – just as the transnational company combines characteristics of both global and multinational companies (Harzing 2000: 115).[65] The conclusion that companies can combine elements of different archetypes is important for the empirical part of this research – and so is the insight that strategic orientations can change over time. The "evolution of corporate structure" (Leong/Tan 1992: 450) can take a variety of different forms. As Kutschker and Schmid highlight, for Bartlett and Ghoshal there is no specific internationalization pattern or deterministic sequence of strategic alternatives (Kutschker/Schmid 2006: 296). The only development path addressed in

---

[65] Harzing excludes the international model from her analysis, arguing that it is difficult to fit within the scheme and was not included in Bartlett and Ghoshal's original classification (Harzing 2000: 103).

Bartlett and Ghoshal's own work is that towards the TNO (for example, Bartlett 1986: 377; Bartlett/Ghoshal 1998: 19, 66).[66]

Bartlett and Ghoshal's research was based on case studies in nine MNCs from three different industries – consumer electronics, branded packaged goods and telecommunications switching (Bartlett/Ghoshal 1998: 16). While one-dimensional strategies proved to be sufficient throughout most of the 1980s, environmental demands have become increasingly complex since then. Consequently, most industries now call for such a simultaneous optimization of strategic demands (Bartlett/Ghoshal 1987a: 7-8). In the logic of the **environment-strategy-structure** paradigm, a **fit** is furthermore required between a company's strategy and its organizational characteristics (Bartlett/Ghoshal 1998: 60; Harzing 2004: 45). Interunit ties can be regarded as such a structural characteristic. Interestingly, Bartlett and Ghoshal's models focus almost entirely on the headquarters-subsidiary relationship. Only the transnational model implies the existence of – mainly cooperative – horizontal relationships between subsidiaries (Bartlett/Ghoshal 1998: 55-60, 70, 102). This becomes evident by looking at Bartlett and Ghoshal's diagrammatic representation of the four organization models as included in Table 8. The models are characterized by distinct structural configurations, administrative processes and management mentalities (Bartlett/Ghoshal 1998: 55).

---

[66] Similarly Perlmutter does not see any pre-determined development path with respect to the EPRG profile (Schmid/Machulik 2006: 256 with reference to Heenan/Perlmutter 1979: 21-22). How and why firms evolve from one orientation to another in practice remains to be investigated, though (Schmid/Machulik 2006: 257).

Company characteristics	Multinational	Global	International	Transnational
Key strategic capabilities	Building strong local presence through sensitivity and responsiveness to national differences	Building cost advantages through centralized global-scale operations	Exploiting parent company knowledge and capabilities through worldwide diffusion and adaptation	Multinational flexibility, global competitiveness and worldwide learning
Development and diffusion of knowledge	Knowledge developed and retained within each unit	Knowledge developed and retained at the center	Knowledge developed at the center and transferred to overseas units	Knowledge developed jointly and shared worldwide
Role of overseas operations	Sensing and exploiting local opportunities	Implementing headquarters' strategies	Adapting and leveraging headquarters' competencies	Making differentiated contributions by national units to integrated worldwide operations
Configuration of assets and capabilities	Decentralized and nationally self-sufficient	Centralized and globally scaled	Sources of core competencies centralized, others decentralized	Dispersed, interdependent and specialized
Structural configuration and coordination	Decentralized federation	Centralized hub	Coordinated federation	Integrated network

Table 8: Bartlett and Ghoshal's Typology of Multinational Companies
Source: Bartlett/Ghoshal 1998: 18, 57-60, 75, 102.

As far as **interunit ties** are concerned, the first three models focus entirely on the vertical relationship between headquarters and subsidiaries (Bartlett/Ghoshal 1998: 70). It can be assumed, though, that in practice the foreign subsidiaries of international, multinational and global companies also interrelate to a certain extent – especially since Bartlett and Ghoshal themselves refer to the transnational as an "idealized organization" (Bartlett/Ghoshal 1998: 66). Although there has been a trend towards more strategic and organizational flexibility, it remains difficult to find a company that actually succeeded in implementing a transnational organization model (Schmid/Bäurle 1994: 993; Bartlett/Ghoshal 1998: 259). Administrative heritage poses a severe constraint to rapid organizational change (Bartlett/Ghoshal 1987a: 14).

The proposed link between a company's strategic orientation and the nature of interunit relationships is supported by the authors' own – albeit few – references to occurrences of **interunit competition and cooperation** (Bartlett/Ghoshal 1987b: 47-48; 1988: 59, 70; 1998: 13, 61, 69, 74, 102, 105-107, 141, 148). These references provide an initial justification for the link between a company's strategy and organization model and the nature of intersubsidiary relationships. Whereas the authors address internal competition mainly in the context of empirical examples, they position internal cooperation as a key attribute of the transnational organization model. For example, they describe how NEC and Matsushita established internal competition for research projects (Bartlett/Ghoshal 1987b: 48; 1988: 59; 1998: 23,

61, 105, 141) and how Procter & Gamble and Ericsson created headquarters-subsidiary competition in product development (Bartlett/Ghoshal 1987b: 48; 1998: 107, 171). Interunit collaboration, on the other hand, is introduced as an important feature of the integrated network (Bartlett/Ghoshal 1987b: 47; 1998: 102). Distributed and specialized capabilities create interdependencies that naturally lead to cooperation (Bartlett/Ghoshal 1998: 69, 74, 105-106, 148). The idea is that dispersed resources should benefit the entire corporation (Bartlett/Ghoshal 1998: 71). A systematic analysis of intersubsidiary relationships, which goes beyond these sporadic references, has not occurred.

5.1.2.2 Empirical Investigation

Although Bartlett and Ghoshal's typology may have its critics, it is thought to provide an appropriate and insightful framework for analyzing intersubsidiary relationships in MNCs. Giving it such a prominent position in this research has the positive side effect that it is subjected to further **empirical investigation**. So far, only a few scholars have set out to test the typology – the most prominent being Leong/Tan (1992) and Harzing (2000). As illustrated below, both studies are dedicated to augmenting the empirical basis for the typology by collecting data from a large number of companies from diverse regions and industries. Intersubsidiary relationships only play a subordinate role in these contributions.

Based on a brief literature review, Leong and Tan develop hypotheses to examine the extent to which (1) the four organizational structures proposed by Bartlett and Ghoshal are adopted among companies and (2) their various characteristics actually correspond to the respective organizational type. The prevalence of the transnational company in relation to the other three types of organization is given particular attention (Leong/Tan 1992: 450-451, 453). In a **large-scale survey** the authors ask MNC managers to categorize the structure of their organization into one of the four types defined by Bartlett and Ghoshal and to indicate their level of agreement with statements regarding the three dimensions "configuration of assets and capabilities", "role of overseas operations" and "development and diffusion of knowledge" (Leong/Tan 1992: 454).

The results provide only **partial support of the typology**. In sum, the demarcations between multinational and especially global companies relative to other organizational types were more evident than those for international and transnational companies (Leong/Tan 1992: 456-457). Managerial responses need to be seen against a number of methodological limitations, however. There is some uncertainty as to whether managers may have misclassified their organizations. Also, perceiving one's organization to be of a certain type does not mean that it actually reveals all the characteristics normatively prescribed to it (Leong/Tan 1992: 462). Unlike personal interviews, surveys do not leave any room to immediately corroborate or clarify statements. Other recognized drawbacks of Leong and Tan's approach include that the survey is completed by only one respondent per organization and that his or her assessment is not validated externally. Managers may also report the intended rather than the actual structure of their organization (Leong/Tan 1992: 455).

Since Leong and Tan adhere closely to Bartlett and Ghoshal's original typology, their references to **intersubsidiary relationships** are few. One statement explicitly addresses cooperation and dependence of overseas units, triggered by the dispersed location of specialized skills and resources. Two other statements need to be interpreted to include headquarters: one refers to the autonomy of overseas units and their non-reliance on expertise from other units; the other one to interunit knowledge transfer (Leong/Tan 1992: 458-459). Only for the last one does the difference in agreement among the respective organization types prove statistically significant. As such, Leong and Tan's study contributes to the empirical investigation of Bartlett and Ghoshal's typology, but does not offer any further insights into intersubsidiary competition and/or cooperation.

In her **quantitative study** Harzing takes Bartlett and Ghoshal's study as a starting point but ultimately sets out to test typologies that she constructed based on a larger number of characteristics (Harzing 2000: 102).[67] Drawbacks of her approach include that she deliberately neglects the international type of MNC (Harzing 2000: 103), draws her conclusions based on subsidiary responses only (Harzing 2000: 111) and needs to recognize that her survey may have included some ambiguous questions (Harzing 2000: 115). Nevertheless, the results of her empirical analysis provide a high level of support for the hypothesized typologies (Harzing 2000: 114). Harzing is able to clearly distinguish three types of MNCs – global, multidomestic and transnational – that differ systematically on a number of characteristics (Harzing 2000: 115). She thus contributes to a large-scale empirical confirmation of Bartlett and Ghoshal's typology (Harzing 2000: 116).

---

[67] For an overview of the hypothesized configurations of MNC and subsidiary strategy and structure see Harzing 2000: 110; for an operationalization of the respective variables refer to the Appendix to the article (Harzing 2000: 120).

In Harzing's set of propositions there is only a single one that explicitly refers to **intersubsidiary relationships**: Intersubsidiary flows of products, people and information are expected to be low in multidomestic and global companies, and high in transnational companies. This contingency captures some elements of intersubsidiary cooperation, but makes no assumptions on competition. The same line of argument is applied to the level of interdependence, i.e. the percentage of intra-company sales and purchases in relation to total sales and purchases; under this construct, however, headquarters and subsidiaries are collectively treated as relevant units (Harzing 2000: 108-110).

5.1.2.3 Research Implications

Harzing encourages future researchers to "choose carefully variables to be included in the configurations" and to "devise objective performance measures" (Harzing 2000: 116). This research refrains from assessing performance in a systematic manner, but its focus on intersubsidiary relationships does contribute to an amplification of Bartlett and Ghoshal's typology. By choosing a **qualitative research approach**, managers' identification with one of the four structural types can be investigated more thoroughly. At this point it is necessary to reemphasize that the focus lies on the plant engineering companies' project marketing activities. By using Unilever as an example, Bartlett and Ghoshal recognize that the needs for integration and differentiation can vary significantly across functions (as well as businesses and tasks) (Bartlett/Ghoshal 1987b: 46; 1998: 111). Meffert specifically addresses internationalization strategies in marketing and distinguishes global marketing from a global company (Meffert 1986: 689-692, 700). As outlined in Chapter 4, **project marketing** is a very comprehensive concept in plant engineering and strong overlaps can be expected between a company's overall strategic orientation and project-marketing-specific requirements. But even then sales, for example, may have more localization advantages than marketing (Meffert 1990: 100 with reference to Ghoshal 1987: 429). The goal can thus only be to identify tendencies. Nevertheless, an awareness of functional particularities is essential when empirically investigating Bartlett and Ghoshal's typology. Both Leong and Tan and Harzing neglect this aspect of strategic orientation and adopt a purely aggregated view.

Before concluding this section on strategic orientation, a brief note is necessary on why the **intercultural dimension** is deliberately neglected in this research.[68] For two reasons the international location of headquarters or subsidiaries is not assumed to have a decisive impact on structural characteristics: (1) in large MNCs corporate culture is expected to be relatively stronger than national culture and to provide a binding element, (2) the research focus is on factual rather than social or psychological issues, where cultural imprint may be of greater relevance. Interviewees are interrogated in their role as functional or topic experts rather than as individuals with personal preferences. Also, in their research Bartlett and Ghoshal – as well as Leong and Tan and Harzing – have shown that the different structural types can be found in multiple geographic areas. Nevertheless, cultural sensitivity may be needed in the interview situation. Before addressing the applied research methods any further, however, the propositions they are meant to investigate are developed in the next section.

5.2 Propositions on Intersubsidiary Relationships

Having outlined Bartlett and Ghoshal's typology as well as some prominent attempts to analyze it empirically, an explicit link can be established between a company's strategic orientation and alternative intersubsidiary relationships. This objective is captured in the second research question (recall from section 1.4):

Research Question 2: How does a company's strategic orientation influence the relationship between its foreign subsidiaries, as reflected in alternative project acquisition/execution models?

This research question is addressed in two consecutive steps: First, theoretically grounded propositions on the contingency between strategic orientation and intersubsidiary relationships are developed and second, these propositions are tested in practice. The focus of this section is the conceptual **development of the propositions**. Following an introduction to the applied contingency framework in subsection 5.2.1, the propositions for multinational, international, global and transnational companies are derived in subsections 5.2.2, 0, 5.2.4 and 5.2.5, respectively. Table 9 in subsection 5.2.6 provides a summary of the propositions on competition and cooperation by type of company.

---

[68] For a discussion of the culture-free thesis refer to subsection 3.4.4.

5.2.1 Scope and Contents of the Contingency Framework

The overarching proposition is that each of the four types of MNCs delineated by Bartlett and Ghoshal is characterized by a distinct pattern of intersubsidiary independence, cooperation, competition or coopetition – the elements of which are captured in the alternative project marketing models developed in section 4.3. Given that these models represent exemplary and somewhat 'modular' rather than exhaustive constellations, it is unlikely that all eight of them can unambiguously be assigned to a particular type of strategic orientation. They were primarily meant to make the scope of intersubsidiary relationships more comprehensible and tangible – not to portray the exact scenario related to each type of company. If the latter had been the intention, four comprehensive models would have had to have been developed. Combining headquarters-led and subsidiary-led occurrences of cooperation and/or competition in one model, for example, would have added unnecessary complexity, although in reality, such combinations may very well occur. Following the development of each proposition, a note will be made as to which project marketing model(s) incorporate(s) the relevant features. More importantly, however, the modeling approach will be used to establish common ground in the empirical part of the research.

The adequacy of differentiating between headquarters-led and subsidiary-led relationships, i.e. their **origin**, is also reflected in the propositions – the reason being that an MNC's strategic orientation comes along with different roles of its units. The **objects** of these relationships, on the other hand, are not further differentiated in the propositions because an MNC's strategic orientation is not expected to influence how exactly subsidiaries shape their relationships. Nevertheless, it should be recognized that competition is limited to charters and customers, whereas cooperation refers to knowledge sharing and a split of work. Headquarters-led competition for (external) customers is not considered an option due to its dysfunctional effects (compare to subsection 2.4.1.4). If there happen to be indications for more specific object-related propositions this will be noted.

Finally, the propositions are intended to adopt a **balanced view** of the cause-and-effect relationship between strategy and structure (see subsection 3.4.4): Strategic orientation has an impact on intersubsidiary relationships but it cannot be ruled out that MNCs design these relationships to support the implementation of a particular strategy. In terms of theoretical underpinning the propositions mainly build upon Bartlett and Ghoshal's original sources; they are further inspired by previous work on antecedents of intersubsidiary competition and cooperation (see section 3.5). Before advancing to the formulation of the propositions, the contingency framework reflected in the second research question is visualized in Figure 15.

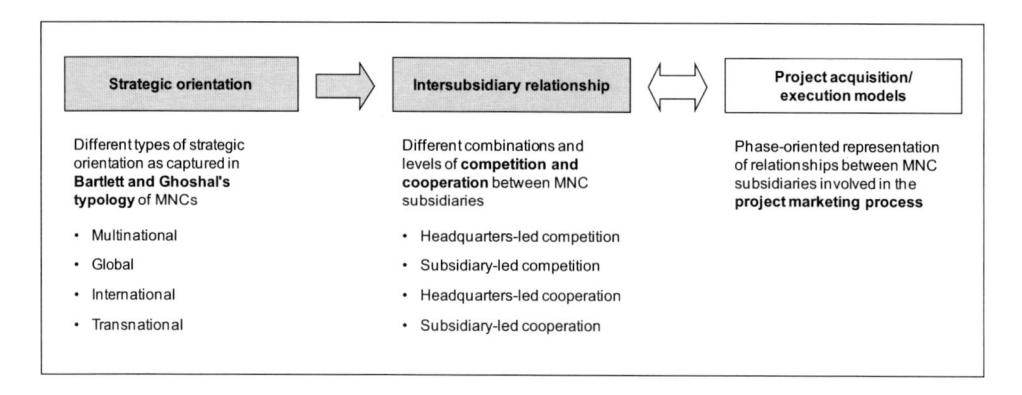

```
┌─────────────────────────────────────────────────────────────────────────────┐
│                                                                             │
│   ┌─────────────────────┐      ┌─────────────────────────┐      ┌─────────────────────┐
│   │ Strategic orientation│  ⇒   │Intersubsidiary relationship│  ⇔   │ Project acquisition/│
│   └─────────────────────┘      └─────────────────────────┘      │  execution models   │
│                                                                 └─────────────────────┘
│                                                                             │
│   Different types of strategic   Different combinations and    Phase-oriented representation
│   orientation as captured in     levels of competition and     of relationships between MNC
│   Bartlett and Ghoshal's         cooperation between MNC       subsidiaries involved in the
│   typology of MNCs               subsidiaries                  project marketing process
│
│   • Multinational                • Headquarters-led competition
│   • Global                       • Subsidiary-led competition
│   • International                • Headquarters-led cooperation
│   • Transnational                • Subsidiary-led cooperation
│
└─────────────────────────────────────────────────────────────────────────────┘
```

Figure 15: Contingency Framework of Intersubsidiary Relationships

5.2.2 Intersubsidiary Relationships in Multinational Companies

In a multinational company many key assets, responsibilities and decisions are decentralized. Foreign subsidiaries are managed as a "portfolio of independent businesses" (Bartlett/Ghoshal 1998: 56-57), thus enjoying a considerable amount of local autonomy (Bartlett et al. 2007: 204). Headquarters does not impose subsidiary behavior and relies mainly on personal control mechanisms. Given its passive role in coordinating local activities, headquarters may tolerate competition between subsidiaries but is not expected to actively foster or manage it. Its 'laissez-faire' attitude reflects its belief that subsidiaries know best how to optimize their situation in the local environment (Bartlett/Ghoshal 1998: 56). Therefore, **headquarters-led competition** between subsidiaries is **not expected** in a multinational company.

A high degree of subsidiary independence is likely to foster subsidiary-led competition, though, if subsidiaries are interested in developing the same markets or serving the same customers (Galunic/Eisenhardt 1996: 264; Luo 2005: 79). An example would be two fairly autonomous subsidiaries in China and Japan that are vying for a new business opportunity in Korea. If a project is attractive, subsidiaries are likely to face competition from other units (Birkinshaw/Fry 1998: 52). The less headquarters chooses to be involved in (and informed of) local operations – i.e. the more independently subsidiaries can act – the more likely competition will be for customers and market share rather than for charters. If headquarters is interested in maintaining one face to the customer and avoiding market overlaps, the two subsidiaries may experience internal competition for responsibilities. In a multinational company such competition is not expected to be institutionalized, but to occur on a case-by-case basis. Whether or not market interdependencies are coordinated is indeed a question of organizational design (Frese 1985: 272; Frese/Lehmann 2002: 519).

In multinational companies **subsidiary-led competition** between subsidiaries is **expected to be high** because local entities follow their own strategic objectives (Bartlett/Ghoshal 1998: 56) and typically refrain from coordinating activities amongst each other. Subsidiaries are driven by self-interest and look to protect their own turf and autonomy (Bartlett/Ghoshal 1998: 67, 106). Headquarters does not decide what exactly subsidiaries have to do but – as the example of ITT as a multinational company shows – lets them fight out responsibilities among themselves: "[the European system houses] began disagreeing about who should take what role in this vital project"; "as a result duplication of effort and divergence of specifications began to emerge" (Bartlett/Ghoshal 1988: 67). With national responsiveness being perceived as the key strategic challenge, subsidiaries compete based on local differences and competencies. In addition, subsidiary-led competition is facilitated because key activities and capabilities are duplicated. Rigid internal structures that would eliminate competitive tensions do not match the idea of giving subsidiaries the flexibility necessary to adapt to host-country conditions. The result of merging these two arguments is that decentralized decision making enhances charter overlap (Birkinshaw/Lingblad 2005: 680-681). Phelps and Fuller, too, are convinced that "competitive processes, through which affiliates win or lose responsibilities, are related to organizational form within multinationals". They underline the proposition that there is greater scope for open competition between affiliates in multidomestic firms than in firms with more complex forms of integration (Phelps/Fuller 2000: 228). Similarly, Li et al. suggest that under multinational strategy intersubsidiary competition is likely to be intense when compared to the competitive intensity among subsidiaries of international firms. Local subsidiaries' desire to grow motivates them to compete with their peers at other geographic locations (Li et al. 2007: 16). The idea of duplication in polycentrism has already been addressed by Perlmutter nearly forty years ago (see, for example, Perlmutter 1969a: 12, 15 and the related discussion by Hedlund 1986: 14-17; further references are provided by Schmid/Machulik 2006: 280-281).

Since subsidiaries' role in a multinational company is to respond to local market demands, there is relatively little need for them to cooperate with their peers (see, for example, Li et al. 2007: 16). Headquarters is not expected to foster cross-border cooperation because it is mainly interested in having subsidiaries design tailor-made solutions for national markets. Neither knowledge exchange nor a split of work seems particularly supportive to this end. With headquarters' involvement in subsidiary activities being very limited in multinational companies, **headquarters-led cooperation** between subsidiaries is **not expected**.

Subsidiary-led cooperation would be an option only if subsidiaries took the initiative due to self-interest (see subsection 2.3.2 for potential motives for cooperation). For example, a subsidiary in Argentina could be eager to learn claim management techniques from its Spanish counterpart. The relative independence of local units, however, makes it difficult to exploit their knowledge and competencies (Bartlett et al. 2007: 204). **Subsidiary-led cooperation** between subsidiaries is **expected to be low** in a multinational company because proprietary knowledge is needed for local markets and subsidiaries are fairly self-sufficient (Bartlett/Ghoshal 1998: 67, 75; Zhao/Luo 2005: 77). Bartlett and Ghoshal themselves state that "knowledge does not flow among the various parts of the company" (Bartlett/Ghoshal 1998: 67). Instead, each subsidiary develops and retains a proper knowledge base. With activities and capabilities duplicated around the globe, subsidiaries do not depend on each other's support and have few reasons to split work. If subsidiaries are held responsible for performance in their own market(s), they have little incentive to cooperate (Bartlett/Ghoshal 1998: 106-107). On the contrary, they may even make a great effort to protect their autonomy. This may be particularly important if subsidiaries need proper development capacities to convince headquarters of their ability to pursue certain external initiatives (Birkinshaw/Fry 1998: 53). Subsidiaries could, however, be interested in acquiring more broadly applicable managerial know-how.

Proposition 1: In a *multinational* company the relationship between (foreign) subsidiaries is characterized by (a) no headquarters-led competition, (b) high subsidiary-led competition, (c) no headquarters-led cooperation, and (d) low subsidiary-led cooperation. The main feature of subsidiary-led competition is best reflected in project acquisition model 3b.[69]

---

[69] Model 1b, subsidiary-led independence, could possibly be a feature of the multinational company, if subsidiaries deliberately chose to refrain from competing with their peers. Assuming a certain degree of self-interest, however, such deliberate independence becomes increasingly unlikely.

5.2.3 Intersubsidiary Relationships in Global Companies

In a global company most strategic assets, resources, responsibilities, and decisions are centralized (Bartlett/Ghoshal 1998: 60). Subsidiaries' role is to implement plans, policies and strategies developed by the parent company (Bartlett/Ghoshal 1998: 58, 67). **Headquarters-led competition** between subsidiaries is **expected to be low** because headquarters takes all major decisions (Bartlett/Ghoshal 1998: 59) – including an assignment of subsidiary responsibilities. In order to serve the world market efficiently, headquarters needs to be in control of each subsidiary's contribution. Subsidiaries are regarded as delivery pipelines that have clear tasks (mainly sales and service) assigned to them (Bartlett/Ghoshal 1998: 58, 60). Headquarters could possibly introduce headquarters-led competition for charters if it increased worldwide efficiency. For example, subsidiaries could be invited to submit their candidature for operating a regional distribution center.

Subsidiary-led competition between subsidiaries is **not expected** in a global company because local entities have very limited freedom to take initiative (Bartlett/Ghoshal 1998: 59). Any expansion into new markets or the acquisition of new projects is controlled by headquarters. Overlaps in subsidiary activities would be contradictory to the exploitation of global efficiencies (Harzing 2000: 109). Birkinshaw and Lingblad support this argument by stating that "in those organizations where top management judge it inappropriate to allow unit charters to overlap, the primary mechanism by which they enforce their judgment is likely to be a centralization of decision making around the product market scope of organizational units" (Birkinshaw/Lingblad 2005: 681). A clear delineation of responsibilities suppresses competition for both customers and charters. Subsidiaries' high reliance on the same value chain is another reason why intersubsidiary competition is unlikely to occur in companies pursuing a global strategy (Li et al. 2007: 16).

In a global company there is little need for cooperation between subsidiaries since essential know-how is provided by headquarters, and subsidiaries are usually not assigned interrelated value chain activities. Instead they serve as extended workbenches of their parent companies (Forsgren/Johanson 1992: 21). Regarding itself as the organization's hub, headquarters is unlikely to support direct linkages between subsidiaries. Horizontal knowledge exchange may very well be regarded as a distraction from the mere execution of headquarters' strategy. The specialization of national entities could lead to a split of work if so desired by the parent company. In practice, however, this will hardly be the case since upstream activities like manufacturing and R&D tend to be centralized for efficiency reasons (Bartlett et al.

2007: 204). Overall, in a global company **headquarters-led cooperation** between subsidiaries is **expected to be low**.

Bundling activities in specific locations also suppresses subsidiary-led cooperation because subsidiaries see little value in exchanging knowledge on value chain activities they are not in charge of. And even if they were to benefit from sharing knowledge – on best sales practices, for example – they are typically not encouraged to take such independent action. Likewise, workflow planning is considered a central task; subsidiaries will barely be entitled to divide work packages amongst each other. Therefore, **subsidiary-led cooperation** between subsidiaries is **not expected** in a global company.

Proposition 2: In a *global* company the relationship between (foreign) subsidiaries is characterized by (a) low headquarters-led competition, (b) no subsidiary-led competition, (c) low headquarters-led cooperation, and (d) no subsidiary-led cooperation. The main feature of headquarters-led independence is best reflected in project acquisition model 1a.[70]

5.2.4 Intersubsidiary Relationships in International Companies

In an international company many assets, resources, responsibilities and decisions are decentralized but controlled from headquarters (Bartlett/Ghoshal 1998: 58). Subsidiaries depend on headquarters for new products or processes, but are considerably free in implementing and adapting strategies on a local level (Bartlett/Ghoshal 1998: 56). **Headquarters-led competition** between subsidiaries is **expected to be low** because headquarters holds the managerial reins and is in charge of determining subsidiary responsibilities. Ericsson, as an example of the international company, illustrates these characteristics: "headquarters have given some of these units responsibility for handling certain export markets" (Bartlett/Ghoshal 1988: 69). Despite their operational independence, subsidiaries are regarded as appendages to a central domestic operation and are managed quite formally (Bartlett/Ghoshal 1998: 57). A key objective of the international company is to leverage learning and exploit technologies on a worldwide basis (Bartlett/Ghoshal

---

[70] Model 1b does not apply since subsidiary-led independence implies that subsidiaries are free to choose whether or not they incorporate their peers in the execution of a project. In a global company such decisions are expected to be taken centrally. Subsidiary-led independence should not be confused with an alternative manifestation of headquarters-led independence, i.e. headquarters assigning responsibility to a particular subsidiary but requiring it to complete the job on its own.

1998: 27). Knowledge and information tend to be developed at the center and transferred to subsidiaries (Bartlett/Ghoshal 1998: 57-58, 67). Headquarters could possibly introduce headquarters-led competition between subsidiaries to enhance the creation and exploitation of innovations. Bartlett and Ghoshal themselves state that international companies would use "all the different means to achieve this end" (Bartlett et al. 2007: 204). For example, subsidiaries could compete for projects based on their suggestions for innovative product applications abroad.

Similarly, **subsidiary-led competition** between subsidiaries is **expected to be low** in international companies. Limited subsidiary autonomy and defined responsibilities restrict open competition for both customers and charters. Although headquarters is willing to delegate responsibility, subsidiaries' primary role is to leverage capabilities and resources developed in the home market (Bartlett/Ghoshal 1998: 57).

As described above, vertical knowledge transfer from the parent company to subsidiaries is an essential characteristic of the international company. However, the promotion of horizontal cooperation also seems beneficial considering that sources of non-core competencies are decentralized (Bartlett/Ghoshal 1998: 67). The overall corporation could benefit from subsidiaries sharing their experience with local product adaptations or project lifecycle extensions. With headquarters realizing this potential, **headquarters-led cooperation** between subsidiaries is **expected to be moderate**. Due to subsidiaries' focus on their local markets the promoted cooperation will comprise knowledge exchange rather than a split of work.

From a subsidiary perspective this very focus on the local market may reduce the need for cooperation. Decentralized competencies and relative autonomy, on the other hand, may encourage it. Overall, **subsidiary-led cooperation** between subsidiaries is **expected to be moderate** in an international company.

Proposition 3: In an *international* company the relationship between (foreign) subsidiaries is characterized by (a) low headquarters-led competition, (b) low subsidiary-led competition, (c) moderate headquarters-led cooperation, and (d) moderate subsidiary-led cooperation. The main features of headquarters-led and subsidiary-led cooperation are best reflected in project acquisition models 2a and 2b.[71]

---

[71] Competitive elements may tip the scale towards coopetitive models 4a and 4b. The reference to two (or more) project acquisition and execution models underlines that these are not mutually exclusive (compare to subsection 4.3.1). The same is true for proposition 4.

5.2.5 Intersubsidiary Relationships in Transnational Companies

A transnational company aims at achieving competitive advantage by combining global efficiency, local responsiveness and worldwide learning (Bartlett/Ghoshal 1998: 68). Although it represents a somewhat ideal state, companies can be observed making an effort in developing the respective capabilities (Bartlett/Ghoshal 1998: 66). Only in companies with significant transnational features (to be referred to as a 'transnational company'), headquarters-led competition for charters seems to be a real option. Headquarters could decide to introduce such competition as part of a flexible coordination process (Bartlett/Ghoshal 1998: 76). Where appropriate, subsidiaries can be requested to submit internal proposals, for example, for the pursuit of a particular project. Such internal contests add value when competencies are dispersed but transparency about their location is not fully given (see Birkinshaw/Hood 2001: 134-135 for benefits and drawbacks of formal requests for proposals). This is the case in a transnational company, where assets, resources and capabilities are distributed and specialized (Bartlett/Ghoshal 1998: 69). Headquarters and subsidiaries can find the best solution for the customer collectively by revealing – and possibly pooling – individual subsidiaries' strengths. Maintaining specialized operations does not mean that duplication needs to be completely eliminated. Bartlett and Ghoshal themselves give examples of companies that deliberately promote a healthy level of internal competition (Bartlett/Ghoshal 1998: 105, 141). Taking the above considerations together, **headquarters-led competition** between subsidiaries is **expected to be moderate** in a transnational company.

Phelps and Fuller argue that in closely integrated companies such as the type which are transnational "parent company-managed competition is likely to be apparent, since open competition might be counterproductive to the synchronization of a group of vertically related plants" (Phelps/Fuller 2000: 228). When interpreting headquarters-led competition as an alternative (or even a reaction) to subsidiary-led competition between subsidiaries, the latter needs to be considered as an option as well. Although subsidiaries are given a broader mandate within the transnational organization, the overall structure remains dispersed (Bartlett/Ghoshal 1998: 103). Depending on their respective capabilities, subsidiaries can be fairly autonomous and define their own development paths. Based on such ambitions, subsidiaries can enter into competition with their peers – for local, regional or global responsibilities. **Subsidiary-led competition** between subsidiaries is thus **expected to be moderate** as well.

Since the overall company functions as an integrated network, where units coordinate their activities to achieve some common goal (Bartlett/Ghoshal 1998: 101), charter competition is more likely to occur than customer competition. Harzing, however, notes that "since Transnational companies also have to respond to the demand for cost efficiency by focusing on economies of scale, they are not so prone as Multidomestic companies to duplicate value chain activities" (Harzing 2000: 109). Network transparency should further prevent subsidiaries from approaching the same customers independently of one another. Some ideas developed by Hedlund with respect to Perlmutter's geocentrism can be transferred to the transnational company: "The actions of a subsidiary in Country A influence prospects for the subsidiary in Country B, perhaps because they face the same competitor, who has to divide his resources between the two markets. Thus competition is not confined within each national market but system-wide" (Hedlund 1986: 15). Although Hedlund speaks of external competition here, the prevailing interdependencies may similarly promote internal competition – for customers and particularly for charters. Charters do not necessarily have to be assigned or formally approved by headquarters; they can also be contested and defined among multiple organizational units. In a transnational company competition for charters is most likely resolved bilaterally or together with headquarters.

Unlike the issue of competition, Bartlett and Ghoshal touch upon a variety of aspects of cooperation between foreign subsidiaries in a transnational company. Multilateral cooperation is a central element of the integrated network. Specialized subsidiaries contribute their expertise to a common goal both in terms of knowledge and individual work packages. In a transnational company relationships are said to be built on interdependence, suggesting "collaborative information sharing and problem solving, cooperative resource sharing, and collective implementation" (Bartlett/Ghoshal 1998: 106). Being an integral part of the network itself, headquarters encourages the development of resources that benefit the entire corporation (Bartlett/Ghoshal 1998: 73). It contributes to the formation of an infrastructure that allows components, products, resources, people and information to flow freely among interdependent units (Bartlett/Ghoshal 1998: 102). **Headquarters-led cooperation** between subsidiaries is **expected to be high**. Complex communication linkages facilitate headquarters-led cooperation through knowledge exchange, and work interdependencies reflect headquarters-led cooperation through a split of work (Bartlett/Ghoshal 1998: 70). Flexible centralization allows realizing economies of scale while capitalizing on factor cost differentials (Bartlett/Ghoshal 1998: 69, 102). While some interdependencies are natural outcomes of the configuration of assets and resources, others are "specifically designed to build self-enforcing cooperation among interdependent units" (Bartlett/Ghoshal 1998: 69). In a transnational company, headquarters' role in achieving cooperation between subsidiaries can be seen in encouraging such interdependent relationships rather than creating new units or administrative processes (Bartlett/Ghoshal 1998: 106).

Subsidiary-led cooperation between subsidiaries is **expected to be high** as well. It is sparked by subsidiaries' realization that cooperating with their peers helps them achieve their own interests (Bartlett/Ghoshal 1998: 106, 148). Lacking a dominant headquarters position, the transnational company encourages subsidiaries to drive knowledge exchange and a split of work among differentiated but specialized units (Bartlett/Ghoshal 1998: 75). A high degree of interdependence requires a high level of cooperation and coordination. In other words, "subsidiaries with a higher degree of strategic interdependence will more actively share organizational knowledge with peer subsidiaries" (Zhao/Luo 2005: 77). Individual subsidiaries' autonomy, however, may be limited depending on their roles and responsibilities in the overall organization (Bartlett/Ghoshal 1998: 71-72, 121-130).

Proposition 4: In a *transnational* company the relationship between (foreign) subsidiaries is characterized by (a) moderate headquarters-led competition, (b) moderate subsidiary-led competition, (c) high headquarters-led cooperation, and (d) high subsidiary-led cooperation. The main features of headquarters-led and subsidiary-led coopetition are best reflected in project acquisition models 4a and 4b.[72]

5.2.6 Summary of the Propositions

The propositions are summarized in Table 9. How they are investigated in practice is described in the next chapter.

---

[72] Model 3a, i.e. headquarters-led competition, is unlikely to occur without simultaneous headquarters-led encouragement of cooperation. It should thus be regarded as a building block rather than the prominent feature of a particular type of company.

Types of intersubsidiary relationship		Multinational		Global		International		Transnational	
Competition	Headquarters-led	HQ plays subordinate role only; does not impose subsidiary behavior; could tolerate (subsidiary-led) competition but is not expected to manage it	–	Subsidiaries execute HQ strategy; HQ takes major decisions, including subsidiary responsibilities; (charter) competition may be an option if it increases worldwide efficiency	(–)	Subsidiaries are to adapt and apply HQ competencies to local markets; responsibilities are determined by HQ, (charter) competition may be an option if it increases innovation	(–)	Competition for charters is a valid option – especially when core competencies are dispersed but not fully given; HQ and subsidiaries find the best solution together	(✓)
	Subsidiary-led	Autonomous subsidiaries may be interested in the same markets/customers; subsidiaries compete on the basis of local differences; competition is facilitated by the duplication of activities	✓	Subsidiaries are told by HQ exactly what their responsibilities are; very limited freedom to take initiative, e.g., to expand into new markets or compete for projects	–	Limited subsidiary autonomy and defined charters restrict subsidiary-led competition (recall that competition for parent resources is not considered)	(–)	Competition as a result of subsidiary autonomy; to be resolved collectively; network transparency implies charter rather than customer competition; demand for cost efficiency limits duplication	(✓)
Cooperation	Headquarters-led	Subsidiaries' role is to focus on the local market; cooperation with peers is not regarded as necessary and thus not accounted for by HQ	–	No need for cooperation since essential know-how comes from HQ and activities tend to be bundled in one location for efficiency reasons; specialization could lead to split of work	(–)	Vertical knowledge transfer is obligational; the promotion of horizontal cooperation seems beneficial considering that non-core competencies are decentralized; national focus limits split of work	(✓)	Multilateral cooperation as a central element of the "integrated network"; specialized subsidiaries contribute their expertise to a common goal (knowledge exchange and split of work)	✓
	Subsidiary-led	Cooperation only if subsidiaries take initiative due to self-interest; unlikely since proprietary knowledge for local market is needed and activities tend to be duplicated	(–)	Subsidiaries are to follow orders/execute HQ strategy and not to take initiative in cooperating with their peers; workflow planning as a central task	–	With (semi-autonomous) subsidiaries focusing primarily on their local markets, the perceived need for cooperation may be low; decentralized competencies may encourage it, though	(✓)	Autonomous subsidiaries can take initiative (and have an incentive) to cooperate with their peers (through knowledge exchange and split of work)	✓

Expected level: – None   (–) Low   (✓) Moderate   ✓ High

Table 9:   Summary of Propositions – Competition and Cooperation by Type of Company

6 Empirical Study and Findings

In this chapter the results of the four case studies are presented. By focusing on the evaluation of the propositions developed in section 5.2 – i.e. the link between an MNC's strategic orientation and its intersubsidiary relationships – the investigation of the **second research question** is completed. The case studies are further used to extract additional influencing factors and to address the third research question (recall from section 1.4):

Research Question 3: Which managerial implications can be derived from any developments in the concerned companies' strategic orientation and/or intersubsidiary relationships?

The goal is to not only describe and explain intersubsidiary relationships but to identify managerially relevant implications by considering the evolution of strategy and structure. Although this third research question is not addressed with the same depth and rigor as the previous two questions, complementing the descriptive and explanatory goals with a partially normative one enhances practical relevance. The answers to this question take the shape of a brief discussion and summary, arriving at some conclusions on the suitability and success of individual strategies or intersubsidiary relationships in a given business environment.´

Before moving to the empirical findings of this research project, however, it is necessary to provide an overview of the methodology and methods employed. In section 6.1 case studies are first presented and discussed as the overarching research methodology. Section 6.2 then introduces interviews and thematic coding as the chosen methods for data collection and analysis, respectively. Following an appraisal of the research approach based on a number of acknowledged quality criteria in section 6.3, section 6.4 provides some preliminary remarks on the scope and comparability of the case studies. Finally, the cases of Companies A, B, C and D are presented in sections 6.5, 6.6, 6.7 and 0, respectively.

6.1 Research Methodology: Case Studies

Important for the choice of methodology is the overall research paradigm. Recall from subsection 3.3.5 that paradigms constitute "universally recognized scientific achievements that for a time provide model problems and solutions to a community of practitioners" (Kuhn 1962: viii). As such they reflect researchers' philosophies and assumptions about the world and the nature of knowledge (Hussey/Hussey 1997: 47; on philosophical foundations of the research also see McGaughey 2004: 530-531; Denzin/Lincoln 2005: 22). Scholars have differentiated between a variety of different paradigms (see, for example, Burrell/Morgan 1979: 22; Denzin/Lincoln 2005: 22), which are not easily equated. On a most basic level, one can distinguish between two extreme paradigms or philosophies: positivist and phenomenological – also referred to as quantitative and qualitative, respectively (Hussey/Hussey 1997: 47-48 with reference to Creswell 1994; for corresponding dichotomies see, for example, Chapman et al. 2004: 288). Under such simplification this research is situated in the **phenomenological paradigm**, which is concerned with understanding human behavior from the participant's own frame of reference (Hussey/Hussey 1997: 52).[73] Intersubsidiary relationships, representing the relevant phenomenon or "occurrence [...] of which the cause is in question" (Allen 1990: 893), cannot be detached from the individuals and units forming them. The positivistic paradigm, in contrast, assumes that the study of human behavior should be conducted in the same distant and logical way as studies undertaken in the natural sciences (Hussey/Hussey 1997: 52). The phenomenological paradigm focuses on the meaning rather than the measurement of social phenomena. It tends to produce qualitative data, uses small samples and is concerned with generating theories (for a full contrasting overview of the two paradigms see Hussey/Hussey 1997: 54). All of these aspects apply to the underlying research project.

Of the phenomenological methodologies, **case studies** prove the most suitable for the empirical part of this research (for an overview of alternative methodologies see, for example, Hussey/Hussey 1997: 59). To Yin a case study is a comprehensive research strategy, "an empirical inquiry that investigates a contemporary phenomenon within its real-life context, especially when the boundaries between phenomenon and context are not clearly evident" (Yin 2003: 13-14). A case study is both the process of learning about a particular case and the outcome, or product, of such learning (Ghauri 2004: 109). Bonoma notes that it is oftentimes a management situation that is being analyzed – with the context in which management behavior takes place being of particular importance (Bonoma 1985: 203-204). In this research the phenomenon of interest refers to intersubsidiary relationships formed within different types of MNCs; the extent to which these relationships are influenced by the

---

[73] The phenomenological paradigm thus concerns a different conceptual level than the functionalist paradigm addressed when classifying theories in subsection 3.3.5. To help clarify uncertainties regarding different uses of the term 'paradigm', Hussey and Hussey refer to Morgan (1979), who suggests that the term can be used at three different levels: philosophical, social and technical.

strategic context remains to be explained.[74] The relevant behaviors cannot be manipulated by the investigator (Yin 2003: 6). Case studies help understand the dynamics present within a single setting and are "particularly well suited to new research areas or research areas for which existing theory seems inadequate" (Eisenhardt 1989: 534, 548-549).

Previous chapters have illustrated that intersubsidiary relationships still lack distinct recognition in IB research and existing theories contribute little to their understanding. Although case studies are often associated with descriptive or exploratory research, they can also be used for situations where "the researcher is [...] confronted with 'cause-and-effect' problems" (Ghauri/Grønhaug 2005: 59, 114). They are particularly useful when concepts or variables are difficult to quantify. As illustrated above, this research comprises **exploratory, descriptive and explanatory elements** (Yin 2003: 3). It wishes to accomplish an in-depth investigation into the manifestations and determinants of intersubsidiary relationships. This goal is also reflected in the research questions. Yin recommends case-study research when 'how' or 'why' questions are being asked (Yin 2003: 9). The second and central research question is a 'how' question, but also the first and third questions – both introduced by 'which' – call for insights that go beyond what could be retrieved from surveys.[75] The research questions ultimately determine the choice and the design of the cases. Further benefits are derived from developing theoretical propositions, which guide data collection and analysis (Yin 2003: 14, 22).

Although the little existing research on intersubsidiary relationships calls for an inductive approach, the developed propositions add a deductive element. While **inductive** research refers to a study in which theory is developed from the observation of empirical reality, **deductive** research describes a study in which a conceptual and theoretical structure is developed and tested by empirical observation (Hussey/Hussey 1997: 13). Given that the research was triggered by the observation of a very particular phenomenon in the plant engineering industry and ultimately aims at "building theory from case studies" (Eisenhardt 1989: 539; also Ghauri 2004: 112), its overall logic is inductive. The developed propositions focus attention on core relations, guide the selection of relevant cases and help structure the data collection and analysis process. Although they suggest general patterns of intersubsidiary

---

[74] Although contingencies play an important role in this research, it needs to be differentiated from situational analysis. The goal is to portray how contextual elements condition an action, but the situation itself is not a key unit of analysis per se (compare to Clarke/Friese 2007: 364).

[75] A survey is a positivistic methodology in which an unbiased sample of subjects is analyzed to make inferences about the population it was drawn from (Hussey/Hussey 1997: 63-64).

competition and cooperation, they do not build upon a substantial theory that has yielded comparable results before. Instead they follow a somewhat pragmatic contingency logic, which limits their deductive character. The overall research approach can thus be regarded as moving from the specific to the general rather than the other way around (Hussey/Hussey 1997: 13). Recognizing that case studies are useful for both theory development and testing, Ghauri and Grønhaug emphasize the need for "integrative interpretation" (Ghauri/Grønhaug 2005: 115 with reference to Selltiz et al. 1976).

Integrative interpretation is particularly important when using comparative case studies, i.e. asking or studying the same questions in a number of organizations and comparing them with each other to draw conclusions (Ghauri/Grønhaug 2005: 116). Whether single- or multiple-case designs should be used is determined by the research problem and objectives (Ghauri/Grønhaug 2005: 119). Since a central goal of this research is to establish a link between an MNC's strategic orientation and its intersubsidiary relationships, **multiple cases** need to be analyzed for comparative purposes. Explanations rely on assumptions on general causal relationships that cannot be validated through the study of a single case (Hammersley et al. 2000: 238). Although there is no upper or lower limit with regard to the number of cases to be included in a study (Miles/Huberman 1994: 30; Yin 2003: 51; Ghauri/Grønhaug 2005: 119), it is important that every case serves a particular purpose (Yin 2003: 47; Ghauri/Grønhaug 2005: 120). In this research, the rationale for multiple, i.e. four cases derives from the prior hypothesizing of different types of conditions and the desire to have subgroups covering each type (Yin 2003: 52). Ideally, one would find four companies, each of which represents a different type of MNC according to Bartlett and Ghoshal's typology.

Such concept-directed data gathering and analysis, which is often applied in qualitative research, is called **theoretical sampling** (Corbin/Strauss 2008: 145, 150). Purposeful, non-probability samples are chosen for theoretical reasons (Ghauri/Grønhaug 2005: 156). Yin prefers to speak of literal or theoretical "replication" and explicitly contrasts this method against (statistical) sampling procedures (Yin 2003: 47-48). In this research, cases are mainly selected for theoretical replication, i.e. predicting contrasting rather than similar results. Since the differentiating factors are only revealed when studying the particular case, there is no upfront guarantee that the four cases will actually cover the four types of MNC. Objective indicators are used as far as possible, but ultimately the research relies upon self-typing by the organization's managers (Snow/Hambrick 1980: 533; see discussion below). It should also be considered that so far the empirical analyses of

Bartlett and Ghoshal's typology have not yielded consistent evidence for the existence of all four types of MNC (recall from subsection 5.1.2). Subjecting the typology to another empirical test is thus an additional contribution of this research. It should be noted that theoretical sampling need not occur on an iterative basis but may be completed prior to the analysis (Corbin/Strauss 2008: 150).

The cases for this research were selected by first delineating the target population, i.e. all multinational large-scale plant engineering companies, and then assessing the accessible population (Ghauri/Grønhaug 2005: 118). It seemed more promising to gain (broad) access to firms with either headquarters and/or significant operations in Western Europe, and in some instances existing contacts could be used. Corbin and Strauss refer to this as the "practical way" of doing theoretical sampling (Corbin/Strauss 2008: 153). The study indeed includes four large-scale plant engineering companies with headquarters in Western Europe – the decisive factor being the headquarters of the plant engineering activities. In all four firms these activities are bundled in a separate division; in two instances they take the form of a limited liability company. As noted above, assessing the respective company's strategic orientation is a central part of the empirical study. Nevertheless, the cases were chosen with the expectation that they would represent different types of multinational companies. With explorative interviews and document analysis supporting this notion, the specific sampling decisions evolved during the research process (Corbin/Strauss 2008: 157).

Within each case (or company), intersubsidiary relationships constitute the main units of analysis (Yin 2003: 22). Closely related subunits are the subsidiaries engaged in these relationships. Multiple cases combined with multiple units of analysis result in a **multiple-case embedded design** (Yin 2003: 40, 42, 52). One needs to be aware of a common pitfall of this design: focusing only on the subunit level and failing to return to the larger unit of analysis (Yin 2003: 45). Thorough analysis of each (sub-)unit should be followed by an aggregation of findings and conclusions should clearly stem from the case data (Ghauri 2004: 120).

Yin discusses – and refutes – a number of traditional **prejudices** against the case-study strategy (Yin 2003: 10-11). First, case-study research is often associated with a lack of rigor. The researcher thus needs to make a strong effort to avoid bias and follow some systematic procedures, including a fair report of all evidence. Second, case studies are said to provide little basis for scientific generalization. It needs to be recognized, however, that although cases may not be generalizable to populations or universes, they are generalizable to theoretical propositions. The goal of doing case studies is to expand and generalize theories (analytic generalization) rather than enumerating frequencies (statistical generalization). A previously developed theory is used as a vehicle for comparing and generalizing the results of the study (Yin 2003: 32-33). Third, case studies are often thought to take too long and result in massive, unreadable documents. This complaint needs to be confronted by a focused approach, the choice of appropriate methods as well as precise analysis and documentation. Which methods of data collection and analysis were chosen for the underlying research is outlined in the next section.

6.2 Research Methods

Research methods comprise the various means by which data can be collected and/or analyzed (Hussey/Hussey 1997: 54). Given that relatively little is known about the manifestations and influencing factors of intersubsidiary relationships, **qualitative** research methods appear most suitable (Ghauri/Grønhaug 2005: 110). Compared to their quantitative counterpart, qualitative methods put emphasis on understanding rather than testing and verification, advocate a rational rather than critical approach, prefer measurement in natural rather than controlled settings, have an explorative rather than a hypothetical-deductive orientation, focus on processes rather than results and adopt a holistic rather than a particularistic perspective (for a full list of differentiating elements see Ghauri/Grønhaug 2005: 110 with reference to Reichardt/Cook 1979). Qualitative methods are flexible and – employing only a limited number of observations – try to explain different aspects of a problem area. Low numbers are justified because the objective is to do in-depth studies rather than gaining proof by numbers (Ghauri/Grønhaug 2005: 112). In this research, methods are chosen with the objective of investigating the developed propositions and shedding light on different facets of the phenomenon. Interviews are presented as the primary method for data collection in subsection 6.2.1, followed by an introduction to thematic coding as the appropriate method for data analysis in subsection 6.2.2.

6.2.1 Data Collection: Interviews

The appropriate methods for data collection depend on the research problem and its purpose. In order to build insightful case studies the researcher needs to have sufficient information to characterize and explain the unique features of the case. This data is typically collected through multiple sources such as documents, reports, interviews and observation (Yin 2003: 8; Ghauri/Grønhaug 2005: 114-115). Allowing the researcher to gain a broad yet accurate picture of the situation, in-depth **interviews** are often considered the best data collection methods for inductive studies. Interviewees can respond freely to open-ended questions without being restricted to a few alternatives, and the researcher can ask for elaboration of aspects that seem unclear or incomplete. The opportunity to ask follow-up questions and enter into a dialogue with the interviewee is particularly valuable in cases of sensitive or complex issues (Hussey/Hussey 1997: 158; Ghauri/Grønhaug 2005: 132-133). Corporate strategy, a central theme in this research, certainly qualifies as such an issue. Interviews are particularly well suited for exploratory and theory-building studies (Daniels/Cannice 2004: 186). Standardized questionnaires may be useful for testing hypotheses but leave little room for flexible exploration.[76]

In the early stages of this research project, **explorative interviews** with key informants in the plant engineering industry helped to confirm the relevance of the topic, identify scenarios and delineate the research problem. Interviewees were mostly board members and senior employees of plant engineering companies, who have a broad overview and profound knowledge of their company, its strategy, organization and evolution. Valuable industry information further came from representatives of the German Engineering Federation (VDMA). These interviews were mainly personal; some were conducted by telephone. In the explorative phase of this research interviews were well prepared but questions were deliberately kept very open. Orientation and learning were the main objective of this phase.

The 'formal' interviews, which were intended to expand knowledge on the defined topic and investigate the propositions, were more systematic in their approach. One preferably speaks of **semi-structured interviews**, which differ from unstructured interviews in the sense that topics, sample sizes, interview partners and questions are determined before entering into the interview process. Through the preparation of and flexible adherence to an interview guideline the researcher wishes to minimize bias arising from the sequence or scope of questions (Ghauri/Grønhaug 2005: 132). The researcher also needs to make sure that questions posed and constructs used are understood in the same way. Nevertheless, the "process of open discovery" is (or has been) set forth in the formal round of interviews. Issues and questions may vary slightly from one interview to the next as different aspects of the topic are revealed and different experts are interviewed (Hussey/Hussey 1997: 156-157). Compared to structured interviews, semi-structured interviews demand greater sensitivity on the

---

[76] On questionnaires as a data collection method see, for example, Hussey/Hussey 1997: 161-164.

part of the interviewer since oftentimes personal or value-laden matters arise. A researcher conducting semi-structured interviews must control the situation, ask the right questions, adapt to unexpected situations and – particularly when dealing with sensitive or confidential issues – develop trust (Ghauri/Grønhaug 2005: 118). The reward is a collection of in-depth information for each case, which subsequently requires objective analysis. **Expert interviews** can be regarded as a specific form of applying semi-structured interviews (Flick 2006: 165 with reference to Meuser/Nagel 2002). Interviewees are of less interest as a (private) person than in their roles as (representative) experts in a specific field.

In preparation for the interviews an **interview guideline** was drafted in English and German. It was checked for comprehensiveness and completeness with academic staff and selected (senior) professionals. Flick notes that in expert interviews the interview guideline "has a much stronger directive function with regard to excluding unproductive topics" (Flick 2006: 165). It supports the researcher's diligent preparation and focused execution of the interview. The final guideline, which can be viewed in Appendix II, is structured in six parts: (0) Opening, (1) General Information, (2) Intersubsidiary Relationships, (3) Strategic Orientation, (4) Influencing Factors, (5) Closing. The focus and approach of core parts (2) to (4) are addressed following some general remarks on the interview setting.

The planning phase further included the determination of the most suitable and accessible companies for the case studies as well as the identification of the right **persons to interview** (Ghauri/Grønhaug 2005: 119). For confidentiality reasons the names of the four companies cannot be disclosed – they shall be referred to as Companies A, B, C and D. In most cases the potential interview partners were contacted by means of a formal cover letter, which outlined the background of the dissertation, explained the purpose of the empirical study, kindly requested their participation in the interviews, ensured confidentiality and announced a follow-up call to their office (Ghauri/Grønhaug 2005: 134). If prior contact had existed with the recipient, the standard letter was accompanied by a personalized note. All first-round addressees were willing to contribute to the interviews and simultaneously acted as 'door openers', recommending further contact persons within their organization either before or after the interview had taken place. Given that in each case the most knowledgeable persons for emerging topics were identified, one could speak of 'within-case theoretical sampling' (refer to section 6.1 for the introduction of theoretical sampling). Based on the references and contact information provided, these interview partners were mainly addressed via email. Finally, in each company interviews could be conducted with at least one board member at headquarters level, one director of a key subsidiary and either a senior Sales or Project Management professional as functional representative. There was only one exception to this rule, where the initial contact was established with the head of the German subsidiary, which has historically been very independent and constitutes a key pillar of an organization that has just changed ownership. In one of the other three companies the positions 'board member at headquarters level' and 'director of a key subsidiary' were united in a single respondent; here, two heads of corporate functions provided valuable insights as additional interview partners. A complete list of the interview partners is included in Appendix I.

Given that intersubsidiary relationships are the main topic of interest, a brief explanation may be necessary as to why more subsidiary managers were not included in the empirical study. The explorative interviews had revealed that usually only one or two subsidiaries are involved in a specific project. To make the relevant issues more tangible, in each organization such a project was taken as the basis for discussion. Given that each project has its particularities, interviewees were asked to think of a typical, i.e. representative, large-scale project in their organization. Intersubsidiary relationships were then traced by going through the project acquisition and execution process step-by-step. This approach proved very valuable for maintaining and regaining focus in the conversation and for making results comparable across cases. At the same time such a project focus requires interviewing those who have the best overview of the overall project constellation, i.e. managers involved in – or, better yet, responsible for – project acquisition and execution. Given their level of responsibility for the overall success of the project, their bias towards individual subsidiaries is limited. The same is true for headquarters, which is typically involved in such large-scale projects and often assumes a coordinating role. Dissolving the hierarchical status, it may also act as (equal) partner to other subsidiaries, though. The interviews have shown that functional and headquarters input complements the individual subsidiary's perspective, which may or may not be more partial. Although perception gaps between subsidiaries regarding their relationships may exist, they are not the topic of this research (for a discussion of perception gaps between headquarters and subsidiaries see, for example, Schmid/Daniel 2007). It is assumed that triangulation between headquarters, subsidiary and functional perspective – so-called "unit triangulation" (Marschan-Piekkari et al. 2004: 254) – provides a sufficiently differentiated yet coherent picture of intersubsidiary relationships in project acquisition and execution. And indeed, the empirical research provided no indications that results would shift by including more subsidiaries in the interviews – it can be said to have reached the level of saturation (Corbin/Strauss 2008: 149).

The interviews were conducted in March/April 2008. They were all one-to-one and face-to-face – with one exception, respectively – and varied in length between 50 minutes and 1 hour 45 minutes, with an average **duration** of approximately 1 hour 15 minutes (in accordance with the recommendation by Ghauri/Grønhaug 2005: 134). Although the interviews were deliberately kept brief due to managers' time constraints, good preparation and a structured approach permitted collecting the relevant information. The total meeting time was often longer as interviews were preceded by informal conversation and/or followed by a lunch. How much time the interviewee had to spare was clarified in advance, as was his consent to tape-recording the interview. Assuring them absolute **confidentiality** and anonymous use for academic purposes only, all interviewees granted their permission that the information they provided be recorded, transcribed and archived. As appropriate, interviewees received a preparatory email a few days ahead of the meeting, recalling key questions and the objective of discussing intersubsidiary relationships based on a specific project. Given that managers have so many different and important topics on their agenda, such a brief reminder acted very much in favor of a focused approach.

With one exception the interviews were all conducted in German, given that this was the common mother tongue for both the interviewer and the vast majority of respondents. A careful translation process is required when the **interview language** differs from the reporting language (Marschan-Piekkari/Reis 2004: 237).

Particularly part (2) of the interview guideline benefited from the aforementioned preparation – both by the interviewee and the interviewer. The goal was to document the prevailing intersubsidiary relationships in the style of the project acquisition and execution models introduced in Figure 13 and Figure 14. In order to **make the topic more tangible** for the interview partner, the initial focus was on the objects, not the origin of intersubsidiary competition and cooperation. Whether the relationship was headquarters-led or subsidiary-led usually became clear in the course of the conversation – and was explicitly addressed otherwise. A spaghetti-chart template with key activities and decisions as vertical strings and participating units (headquarters, lead subsidiary and other subsidiaries) as horizontal strings served to support and guide the discussion. The classification scheme for intersubsidiary relationships presented in Figure 5 was used selectively for illustrative purposes – with the positive side effect of proving its practical value.

In part (3) the interviewee was asked to self-type his company's strategic orientation according to Bartlett and Ghoshal's typology. The latter was visualized in accordance with Table 8 and outlined verbally. The depth of explanation provided depended on how quickly respondents grasped the concept. A common understanding was assured by adhering as closely as possible to Bartlett and Ghoshal's own criteria – an approach that further contributed to an empirical investigation of their typology. Overall, managers seemed to find the differentiation rather intuitive and had little difficulty positioning their company (or division) among the four alternatives. Snow and Hambrick speak of such **self-typing** as an explicit option for identifying and measuring an organization's strategy (Snow/Hambrick 1980: 532-533). An advantage of this approach is that (top) managers' perceptions and opinions largely determine the organization's (intended) strategy (for a discussion or intended versus realized strategies see Snow/Hambrick 1980: 530-531). It is also ideal to capture current developments as managers are most up-to-date on the organization's directions and involved in particular action steps (Snow/Hambrick 1980: 534-535). A frequently addressed concern is that managers resist attempts to classify their own organization because they believe it is unique (Snow/Hambrick 1980: 533). This phenomenon, however, could not be observed with any of the company representatives included in the empirical study. Other shortcomings such as variations in different managers' perspectives within a single organization and the tendency to report intended rather than emergent or realized strategies did not prove true, either. Merely a lack of external or objective confirmation of the responses needs to be recognized, with interviews being the single most important source of information. As suggested by Snow and Hambrick, instructions to the respondent for classifying strategy are vital for achieving coherent results (Snow/Hambrick 1980: 533).[77] The above shortcomings were successfully counteracted by (a) highlighting the academic and practical value of classification, (b) asking more than one manager for his opinion and interpreting information provided by those interviewees not directly confronted with the question, (c) explicitly asking managers to reflect upon the actual, currently pursued strategy rather than an ideal state (and treating the latter as a separate issue) and (d) collecting and analyzing complementary company information such as reports and presentations. Relying on multiple sources of information enhances the validity of the strategy measure (Snow/Hambrick 1980: 537); nevertheless, it would have exceeded the scope of this research to obtain ratings of individuals external to the focal organization. It can be assumed that managerial assessments are based on a combination of intuition and analysis (Werder 1999: 673-674; for further thoughts on the rationality of management see, for example, Putnam/Mumby 1993).

---

[77] Snow and Hambrick suggest to use industry competitors as a frame of reference, to consider the organization as a whole (or the relevant division) and to think of the organization's typical pattern of behavior over time (Snow/Hambrick 1980: 533).

Finally, in part (4) of the interview guideline, managers were asked to reflect upon what impacted the intersubsidiary relationships they had previously outlined. They were explicitly asked to assess the influence their company's (or division's) strategic orientation had on these relationships. Addressing this proposed relationship so proactively helps to understand whether managers actually see such a link or whether it is only an indirect result or 'construct' of the research. In any case it was important not to lead the interviewee in a certain direction but to be very open in terms of relevant influencing factors.

To sum up, the interviews fulfilled their objective of collecting data that contributes to the exploration, description and explanation of the phenomenon of intersubsidiary relationships. Theories were generated, or refined, in the process of trying to establish causal links between variables, as captured in the propositions. Consequently interviews were conducted in an iterative manner, each building upon or including insights generated in the previous ones. Before the results are presented an overview is given of how the collected data has been analyzed.

6.2.2 Data Analysis: Thematic Coding

In qualitative research data collection and analysis are often undertaken simultaneously (Ghauri/Grønhaug 2005: 202). Analysis, conducted through conceptualization rather than using statistics (Ghauri/Grønhaug 2005: 206), is "the act of giving meaning to data" (Corbin/Strauss 2008: 64). It involves taking data apart, conceptualizing it and developing those concepts into a comprehensive whole. Structure and order are introduced to the mass of collected data (Marshall/Rossman 2006: 154). Data analysis varies with the aim of the research, which can be description, conceptual ordering or theory building. The ultimate goal of this research is to arrive at an explanation of intersubsidiary relationships by systematically integrating concepts and establishing links between them. Although concepts can be regarded as the actual basis of analysis (Corbin/Strauss 2008: 64), their development is reliant upon the **transcription** of recorded data, i.e. the written documentation of the conducted interviews (compare Hopf/Schmidt 1993: 57). As Charmaz highlights, all qualitative research entails analyzing texts (Charmaz 2006: 35). The interviews were transcribed following the general rule of transcribing only as much and as exactly as required by the research question (Flick 2006: 290 with reference to Strauss 1987). In expert interviews the factual content is more important than the way things are said, making it unnecessary to establish rules for transcribing pauses, extended sounds, emphases, etc. Content-wise the interviews were transcribed literally, merely omitting fillers and repetitions that would make it more difficult to understand a particular sentence. Interpreting the resulting texts forms the core of the empirical study.

The interpretative approach to this research is best described as **thematic coding**. Other methodological approaches to text analysis include theoretical coding (grounded theory), qualitative content analysis, typing and typological analysis as well as global evaluation (Kuckartz 2007: 4; see Flick 2007: 476-478 for a contrasting overview). Thematic coding – frequently applied in qualitative projects as a common-sense technique (Kuckartz 2007: 83) – is particularly suitable for studies in which theoretically based group comparisons are to be conducted in relation to a specific issue (Flick 2006: 312). The groups under study are derived from the research question and are thus defined a priori (Flick 2006: 307). Sampling is oriented to the groups whose insights on the issue seem most instructive. When assuming that the chosen cases shed light on different aspects and manifestations of intersubsidiary relationships, the research issue can most broadly be interpreted as "the social distribution of perspectives on a phenomenon or process" (Flick 2006: 307).

In contrast to grounded theory, thematic coding involves previous (theoretical) knowledge. Rather than refining and unifying categories around a core category in later stages of the research, the central phenomenon of the study is specified in advance. In section 6.1 it was argued that the overall logic of the research was inductive, given that the goal is to build theory departing from the observation of a particular phenomenon. This theory need not be completely novel, though; it is perfectly legitimate to set out to scrutinize and advance predefined theoretical considerations (compare Kuckartz 2007: 84). Although the developed propositions may not be tested for their general validity, they may very well be investigated for individual cases. As suggested above, thematic coding – implicitly used in many qualitative studies – is not as precisely defined as grounded theory or qualitative content analysis. Nevertheless, the method has been found to comprise four consecutive steps (Hopf/Schmidt 1993: 57-63; Flick 1996: 160-163; Kuckartz 2007: 83-91), which may be adapted for and applied to this empirical study: (1) development of a coding system, i.e. category scheme, (2) coding of the material, (3) individual case analysis, (4) comparative case analysis.

(1) Flick – who views thematic coding as a modified version of Strauss' (1991) theoretical coding approach – suggests that categories and thematic domains be developed based on the first case and then assessed for all further cases (Flick 2006: 309). However, given that the empirical part of this research is preceded by a

conceptual approach to the topic, several core concepts and categories are delineated in advance. Rather than being developed during continuous data analysis, statements of possible relationships (Corbin/Strauss 2008: 203) are part of the propositions, i.e. hypothesized prior to – or in preparation of – the empirical study. So-called free codes are created to capture the central, pre-defined themes of the research.[78] The resulting **category scheme** is largely congruent with the classification scheme for intersubsidiary relationships that was introduced in section 2.5. As reflected in Figure 16, it further captures the proposed contingency between an MNC's strategic orientation and the prevailing intersubsidiary relationships (compare to Figure 15).

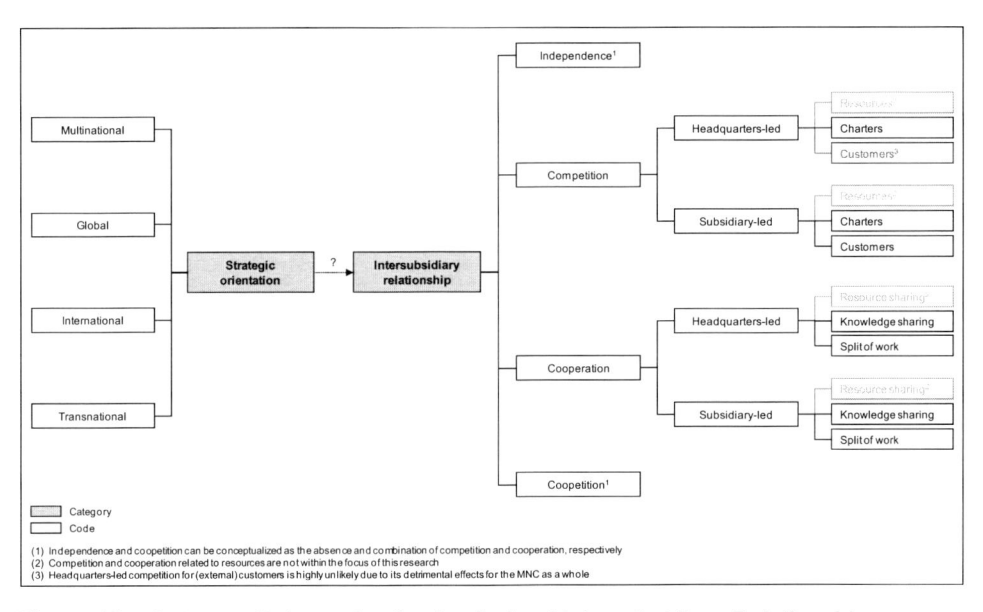

Figure 16: Category Scheme for the Analysis of Intersubsidiary Relationships

The chosen thematic structure shows overlaps with several components of the coding paradigm originally suggested by Strauss (1987: 27-28), i.e. conditions, (inter)actions, strategies and tactics, and consequences.[79] These four aspects can indeed be seen as the relevant ones for this research on intersubsidiary relationships. An MNC's strategic orientation not only summarizes its core strategy, in

---

[78] This approach is in line with Hopf and Schmidt (1993), who provide a detailed overview of how they elaborated the coding manual for the analysis of their material.
[79] The coding paradigm is supposed to help structure data and clarify relations between categories (see, for example, Corbin/Strauss 1990: 13-14; Flick 2006: 308; Kelle 2007: 201-202; Corbin/Strauss 2008: 89).

the context of this research it is also regarded as an essential condition for the prevailing intersubsidiary relationships. In this particular case, the phenomenon of interest is the (inter)action of subsidiaries per se. Consequences may relate to both the MNC's strategic orientation as well as its intersubsidiary relationships.

It is important to emphasize that this approach is not meant to reduce openness to novel findings but rather to give structure to the investigation of an empirically observable yet under-researched phenomenon. Given the large amounts of interview data, an initial category scheme helps to systematically extract relevant statements, concepts and relationships. Miles and Huberman similarly suggest to create "a start list of codes" but to remain flexible enough to adjust them during fieldwork (Miles/Huberman 1994: 65).

(2) **Coding** is "the fundamental analytic process used by the researcher" (Corbin/Strauss 1990: 12) – and thus the core process not only in classic grounded theory methodology (Holton 2007: 265). By attaching concepts (or codes) to the empirical material, coding leads to the development (or investigation) of theories through a process of abstraction (Flick 2006: 296). Concepts are words that stand for ideas contained in data; they reflect interpretations of the researcher (Corbin/Strauss 2008: 159). A text can be coded with varying degrees of detail – line by line, sentence by sentence, or paragraph by paragraph (Flick 2006: 300; also see Ghauri/Grønhaug 2005: 207; Charmaz 2006: 50-53). As indicated above, it is also quite common for initial categories and codes to be modified during the research process (Ghauri/Grønhaug 2005: 208). The interpretation of data as well as the integration of additional material end when theoretical saturation has been reached, i.e. further coding, refinement of categories, etc. no longer provide or promise new knowledge (Flick 2006: 303; also see Holton 2007: 281).

In this research, the interview transcripts were coded according to the category scheme presented above. Selected text elements or passages were assigned single or multiple codes as appropriate (Weber 1990: 32-36). Additional codes and quotations were created in order to capture ideas that are not directly related to the propositions but illuminate additional facets of the research questions. They are not included in the category scheme but enrich the compilation of the case studies. For example, data was implicitly analyzed for context and process – as suggested by Corbin and Strauss in their most recent publication. The authors define **context** as the set of conditions, within which the case is situated and which gives rise to problems or circumstances (Corbin/Strauss 2008: 229-230). Moving from a macro to a micro perspective, in this research the context comprises the overall economic environment, trends in the plant engineering industry, company-specific events (such as international expansion or a recent merger) and the personal situation of the interviewee. The researcher is further asked to bring process into the analysis by looking at patterns of ongoing strategic action or interaction (emotion is less relevant to this factual research). **Process** reflects responses to problems and circumstances arising out of the (changing) context (Corbin/Strauss 2008: 87, 229, 247). These responses lead to certain outcomes or consequences. The question is how the main issues of the research – in this case intersubsidiary relationships – are handled or managed over time (Corbin/Strauss 2008: 261-262). This dynamic aspect has been considered in the interview guideline by asking how strategic orientation and intersubsidiary relationships have evolved.

The initial category scheme was left unchanged for the sake of clarity and commensurability. Although recognizing that a further subdivision of codes could enhance their concreteness and empirical anchoring (see, for example, Kelle/Kluge 1999: 67-68), certain codes were deliberately left top level. In particular, no subcategories were defined for the four types of strategic orientation (i.e. multinational, global, international and transnational), because their characteristics were not discussed individually in each interview. In order to keep interviews with top managers in an acceptable timeframe, interviewees were asked to self-type their company according to an annotated overview chart (see subsection 6.2.1 for details).

To conclude this subsection on coding, it is worth noting that nowadays computer programs facilitate the consequent breakdown of texts. In this research **ATLAS.ti** is used, which is software based on the approach of grounded theory and theoretical coding according to Strauss (1987) and his subsequent work with Corbin. The program is typically filed in the category of "conceptual network builders" (Flick 2006: 350 with reference to Weitzman 2000: 809), and there in the group of "code-based theory builders". ATLAS.ti is equally applicable to thematic coding and the related comparison of groups.[80]

(3) For each of the four MNCs, **individual case studies** were compiled based on the coded interviews. They are presented in Chapter 6. The primary goal was to extract the information relevant for investigating the propositions developed in section 5.2, i.e. the characteristics of the MNC's strategic orientation and its intersubsidiary relationships. Each case indicates how and why the respective proposition is (or is

---

[80] For further details on the computer-based analysis of qualitative data see, for example, Kelle 2000; Kuckartz 2007; Kuckartz et al. 2007.

not) demonstrated (compare to Yin 2003: 50), yields additional influencing factors and allows drawing conclusions from developments in the company's strategic orientation and/or intersubsidiary relationships. Additional insights on the company's internal and/or external situation complement the case analysis as appropriate. In qualitative research it is important to ensure that events and meanings can be assessed based on the background information provided (Corbin/Strauss 2008: 306). Also, the opportunity to speak with so many high-caliber representatives of multinational plant engineering companies should be seized to develop an awareness of issues that may be explored further in future research.

(4) A **comparison** of the four MNCs, their strategic orientation and intersubsidiary relationships completes the case analysis. The findings are mirrored against the propositions, although it needs to be emphasized that possible contingencies do not allow for statistical generalization (Yin 2003: 32). The problem with generalization in qualitative research is that most statements are made with respect to a specific context and its inherent relations, conditions and processes (Flick 2006: 391). The goal is to gradually transfer findings from case studies and their contexts to more general and abstract relations, such as a typology (Flick 2006: 393). Flick proposes three steps that can help achieve at least a certain level of generalization when moving from the case to the theory: First, clarify which degree of generalization is (realistically) aimed at. Second, cautiously integrate different cases and contexts (consider variations deliberately included through theoretical sampling). Third, systematically and constantly compare the collected material (Flick 2006: 392).

With regard to the first step, the modest goal of this research is to establish an initial basis for linking manifestations of intersubsidiary relationships to an MNC's strategic orientation. The proposed link is used to systematically explore an under-researched phenomenon, while remaining open to arrive at different conclusions. As described in section 6.1, cases are selected for theoretical replication – their analysis may (or may not) enhance confidence in the respective findings. The empirical results of the case study are compared based on a previously developed theory, which is what Yin refers to as "analytic generalization" (Yin 2003: 32-33). This theory specifies conditions under which a phenomenon has been discovered and which are linked to certain consequences through actions/interactions (compare to Corbin/Strauss 1990: 15).

6.3 Review of the Research Approach

When performing qualitative research in general and qualitative case-study research in particular, it is necessary to fulfill a number of quality criteria. Although most scholars agree on this necessity, there is little consensus on why and how the quality of research should be evaluated.[81] Broadly speaking, there are two distinct positions (Flick 2006: 368): one group of researchers is trying to apply the 'classical' quantitative criteria of validity, reliability and objectivity to qualitative research (for example, Kirk/Miller 1986; Brühl/Buch 2006), the other prefers devising proper, 'method-appropriate' criteria for qualitative research (for example, Guba/Lincoln 1989; Steinke 1999; 2004). Giving a full overview of the two positions, including descriptions of each criterion and ways of ensuring and evaluating it would exceed the scope of this research. The goal is to develop an awareness of key criteria in order to critically assess the process (and eventually the outcomes) of the empirical study. To this end, Miles and Huberman's standards for the quality of conclusions in qualitative research are adopted and applied to this study (Miles/Huberman 1994: 278-280). The authors try to align qualitative criteria with the established scheme used for the evaluation of quantitative research.[82] Pairing traditional with new terms, they distinguish between (1) objectivity/confirmability, (2) reliability/dependability/ auditability, (3) internal validity/credibility/authenticity, (4) external validity/ transferability/fittingness, and (5) utilization/application/action orientation. In the following each criterion is briefly outlined and assessed for this study:

(1) In terms of **objectivity/confirmability** the basic issue is to achieve relative neutrality and reasonable freedom from unacknowledged researcher biases. Conclusions should depend on the subjects and conditions of the inquiry rather than on the inquirer (Miles/Huberman 1994: 278 with reference to Guba/Lincoln 1981). Objectivity is best achieved by describing the study's general methods and procedures and by making the process of data collection and analysis transparent. The latter has been done in this research by dedicating an individual chapter to the empirical study. Case studies are presented in a way that reveals how conclusions were derived from the collected and evaluated data. If so desired, the complete (coded) interview transcripts could be reviewed by an external auditor. All study data are retained and handed over to the supervisor upon completion of this research.

---

[81] Corbin and Strauss not only point to this dilemma, they also review some literature on the issue (Corbin/Strauss 2008: 297-301). With particular respect to grounded theory research, the authors have developed several lists of criteria for evaluating the research process and the empirical grounding of findings (Corbin/Strauss 1990: 17-20; 2008: 305-309).
[82] A similar approach is followed by Yin (2003).

(2) The issue with **reliability/dependability/auditability** is whether the process of the study is consistent, reasonably stable over time and across researchers and methods. Reliability is given by formulating clear research questions and making sure that the study design is congruent with them. Qualitative research tends to be reliable if findings show parallels across data sources and analytic constructs are clearly specified. In this study the research questions were formulated very early in the process and explicitly guided the course of the investigation. The underlying concepts were explained profoundly and systematically, establishing links to theoretical contributions or practical examples as appropriate. Multiple data sources were consulted (mainly interview transcripts but also some additional documents)[83] and data were collected over the full range of settings and respondents suggested by the research questions. Merely multiple observers and peer reviews were difficult to achieve given the researcher's profound involvement with the research object and her bilateral dialogue with top management representatives at the respective firms.

(3) The criteria **internal validity/credibility/authenticity** are about truth value. The central question is whether the findings of the study make sense and are credible to participants and readers. Ideally the researcher has an authentic portrait of what she is looking at. Internally valid research includes context-rich and meaningful descriptions and ensures that the account makes sense. Conclusions are plausible, comprehensive and confirmed through triangulation. In this research rich description is the essence of the case studies presented in the remainder of this chapter. Contextual elements are explicitly considered – not least to allow for potential rival explanations for the manifestation of intersubsidiary relationships. The account is most definitely a plausible one. It has been demonstrated at the outset of the research that the topic of intersubsidiary relationships is of relevance to both IB scholars and MNC managers (see section 1.1) – and this statement could only be confirmed in the interviews. Triangulation has primarily occurred between interviews conducted at headquarters and subsidiary level. Certain limitations to the completeness of data collection and analysis exist, however, given that most interview partners could not be asked for follow-up meetings. Finally, the chosen measures (and/or specifications) reflect the constructs in play. Alternative intersubsidiary relationships were derived and delineated in Chapter 2. The resulting classification scheme (see Figure 5) allows a systematic assessment for each investigated MNC. Similarly, an overview of alternative strategic orientations ensured that managers self-type their MNC based on the same, clearly defined

---

[83] Given their confidentiality (internal presentations) or size (annual reports), these additional documents are not included in the Appendix. All relevant information was discussed in the interviews and is therefore included in the transcripts.

characteristics. The four types of strategic orientation were operationalized based on Bartlett and Ghoshal's proper characteristics (see Table 8).

(4) With respect to **external validity/transferability/fittingness** the goal is to make sure that conclusions of the study have larger import, are transferable to other contexts and can be generalized to a certain extent. In externally valid studies, characteristics of the original sample are fully described to allow adequate comparisons with other samples. Possible threats or limits to generalizability are examined and the scope or boundaries of reasonable generalizability are defined. "Thick description" allows readers to assess the potential transferability. Settings for further investigation are suggested. For this research, the issue of generalizability has already been addressed in subsection 6.2.2. Although the four chosen MNCs – by definition – belong to the same industry, the sample is sufficiently diverse in terms of strategic orientation and intersubsidiary relationships. The transparency resulting from a profound description of MNC characteristics permits drawing both intra-industry and inter-industry comparisons. Correspondingly, replication in other settings or industries is encouraged to elaborate the aspired cross-case theory.

(5) The criterion **utilization/application/action orientation** captures the question of pragmatic validity. Utilization is given if the findings of the study are accessible to potential users and stimulate "working hypotheses" as guidance for future action. Results offer usable knowledge in terms of raising awareness and developing insight and self-understanding. Promoting an enhanced understanding of intersubsidiary relationships and their managerial implications is an explicit goal of this research (see section 1.4). Field work has shown that academic research on the topic inspires managers to reflect upon alternative manifestations of intersubsidiary relationships. Interviewees have frequently articulated their interest in the results of the study, which will certainly be made accessible to them. The specificity of the research setting provides a significant amount of "usable knowledge" for managers in the plant engineering industry, but ultimately research findings can be shown to transcend industry borders.

Having illustrated that the approach to this research fulfills important quality criteria, the following sections are dedicated to the presentation of the empirical findings.

6.4 Scope and Comparability of the Case Studies

The **extent of the case studies** varies with the number and diversity of conducted interviews (the transcripts of which will be referred to as P1-P13). Despite the individuality of each case study, the same analytical procedure is applied to all of them. They begin with a qualified classification of the company's strategic orientation (first subsection) and continue with an exploration of its intersubsidiary relationships (second subsection). Finally, the link between these two variables is established and discussed; additional influencing factors are compiled and developments and their managerial implications evaluated (third subsection). Before moving to the presentation of the results, a few overarching comments and explanations need to be made for each of these topics. The structure of this section follows the just outlined structure of the case studies; a repeated introduction of subsections is foregone.

6.4.1 Strategic Orientation

Given the diverse empirical constellations of industry requirements and firm capabilities, finding **hybrid forms** of strategic orientation is expected to constitute the rule rather than the exception (compare to subsection 5.1.2.1). For the investigation of the propositions this insight has the implication that results may need to be compared to the expectations regarding different types of strategic orientation. Since the latter are preferably conceptualized as a spectrum, not a continuum, speaking of a 'combination' of elements seems more appropriate than of results lying 'in between' what is expected for two archetypes. Such an approach seems justified by the fact that Bartlett and Ghoshal's four archetypes are all based upon the same dimensions or 'company characteristics' (compare to Table 8).

6.4.2 Intersubsidiary Relationships

As will become evident, each interview and each series of interviews has its particular focus. Rather than reflecting only those results that are comparable across the four companies, the case studies deliberately include these particularities in order to reveal the complexity of the topic. As set out in the introduction to this research project, rich description contributes to the exploration of an under-researched phenomenon. It further needs to be recognized that competition and cooperation between subsidiaries may not have the same prevalence and significance in each of the four companies. An **example project** is reviewed for all of them, seizing the opportunity of gaining insight into diverse project constellations whilst enhancing **comparability**. Respondents were asked to outline a large-scale project that in its entire constellation – and particularly in terms of intersubsidiary competition and cooperation – is typical of their company and business model (the objective of discussing an exemplary project was communicated in advance; see interview guideline in Appendix II). For each company competition and cooperation are evaluated as the main types of intersubsidiary relationships and in all four cases the discussion of the reference project appears to fit best in the subsection on cooperation.

Given that large-scale engineering companies' business consists of a portfolio of **different projects** (and possibly project types, compare to subsection 4.2.1), the analysis of a representative project is the closest one can get to generating comparable results. In order to avoid that the perceived variations are mainly attributable to project particularities, impressions related to other project constellations and general circumstances are captured as well. If the chosen project admittedly does not fully reflect typical constellations, alternative manifestations are pointed out in the case studies (compare, for example, Figure 19 and the discussion of Company C's exemplary technology project in subsection 6.7.2). Where appropriate, more than one project type is discussed. Company B, for example, distinguishes between local and global projects, Company C between technology and EPC business.

6.4.3 Discussion of Intersubsidiary Relationships

The discussion of intersubsidiary relationships in the context of the case studies is extended to three topics: (1) Review of the propositions, (2) additional influencing factors, (3) developments and their managerial implications. The following subsections provide some overarching comments on each of these issues.

6.4.3.1 Review of the Propositions

Since the extent of intersubsidiary competition and cooperation is reflected on a scale ranging from none via low and moderate to high, intermediate values would be thinkable. The question is what exactly lies between 'moderate' and 'high'. In order to refrain from too-fine-grained analysis that would offer very little additional insight, in this research a **discrete rather than continuous** treatment of the dependent variable is preferred. This approach corresponds to the previously described conceptualization of the independent variable: Hybrid forms of strategic orientation are likely, but typically represent a mix of characteristics rather than a linear transition from one archetype to another.

A **cross-case discussion** of the values the independent variable is found to take on is included in section 6.9.2.1.

6.4.3.2 Additional Influencing Factors

The additional influencing factors extracted from the interviews can be considered a by-product of the qualitative study, the main objective of which was to investigate the propositions. During the conversation interviewees articulated **other determinants of intersubsidiary competition and/or cooperation** that illustrate the complexity of the topic and should be preserved as a basis for future research. If interviewees did not proactively mention such additional influencing factors, they were asked if they see any in an open-ended question. The examples included in the interview guideline (see Appendix II) were for reference purposes only. The fact that strategic orientation was identified as the single most important and comprehensive influencing factor for intersubsidiary relationships does not mean that all other determinants can be dismissed. Despite this recognition, there was not a single interviewee who questioned the importance of strategic orientation and called for the investigation of an alternative contingency. Nevertheless, it would be a waste of insight not to conserve the findings – even if a discussion, let alone investigation, of the compiled influencing factors, exceeds the scope of this research. The categories they were assigned to were developed by common sense and in case of ambiguities the allocation was explained in the respective section. An initial link between the influencing factors compiled in the course of this research and those previously suggested by other scholars is established in section 7.3.1. A systematic evaluation of overlaps and discrepancies remains subject to future research.

6.4.3.3 Developments and Their Managerial Implications

An even more dynamic aspect than possibly facing intermediate manifestations of the independent and dependent variables is that of strategic orientation developing and changing over time. Recall from section 5.1 that strategy concerns a company's long-term goals, which is why significant change is hardly expected to occur from one day to the next. Nevertheless, companies need to continuously challenge their strategies and adjust them according to evolving internal and external parameters. Consequently, the classification of an MNC's strategic orientation represents a snapshot that requires frequent review by the researcher. As suggested by the third research question, empirical evidence of historical and/or planned **strategic developments** are given particular attention within this part of the research. Whether the case study has a stronger focus on the past, present or future reflects each company's managerial concerns and challenges. Such diversity is thus deliberately accepted.

6.5 Empirical Findings on Company A

As the newly acquired business unit of a U.S.-based combined technology and EPC company, Company A offers project management and EPC services for upstream and downstream projects in the oil and gas, and petrochemical industries. With headquarters in Western Europe and six further office locations (or subsidiaries) across Europe, the Middle East and Asia, it represents the original "concert" of execution centers (P2). Its acquisition was complementary given that the goal had been to achieve significant synergies between the technology and engineering businesses (P1). Overall, the engineering unit now has a much larger relative revenue share in the combined company and forms part of the company's core business (P2).

6.5.1 Strategic Orientation

When assessing Company A's strategic orientation it is important to consider that due to the acquisition it is currently in a transition phase (P2). Whereas the acquirer (and new parent company) has a centralized decision-making function and appears to correspond most closely to the global model, Company A shows many characteristics of the multinational type (P1). Subsidiaries act very independently – even being entitled to align the local sales organization according to their own benefit (P2) – and potential conflicts are resolved on a project basis rather than being subjected to some general rule (P3). Lately, however, there has been a trend towards more formalization and central coordination (e.g., capacity management) via unit headquarters in order to cope with the drawbacks of far-reaching national independence (P1). Headquarters enjoys a "primus inter pares" status and officially leads the EPC activities (P2). By requesting bi-weekly sales reports from the subsidiaries, headquarters promotes a degree of centralization that is higher than in purely multinational companies. Subsidiaries benefit from finding a mode of interacting or arranging themselves, but eventually sales activities need to be subjected to some central regulation (P2). Central approval of large-scale projects, however, still needs to be established upon integration (P2). The fact that the engineering know-how is mainly developed and retained in two locations – headquarters and the German subsidiary (P1) – constitutes another deviation from the multinational model. Altogether, Company A's strategic orientation is best summarized as **multinational with global tendencies**. It is shown that strategic orientation may well change with top management (P1).

For the combined entity the ultimate goal is to arrive at the transnational model. An integrated network is thought to promise the most success for large engineering companies that are engaged in a multitude of different activities. Given that key informants perceive the overall strategic orientation to be adjusted approximately every two to three years, it may be a bit early to draw conclusions regarding the expanded company. However, it is not believed that the new parent company wishes to increase the dependency of the engineering unit; strings simply need to be pulled more centrally when taking on new talent via multiple acquisitions (P1).

6.5.2 Intersubsidiary Relationships

6.5.2.1 Competition

In Company A, competition between subsidiaries is most prevalent – or can even be said to occur only – in the project acquisition phase (relationship management and feasibility study) (P1, P2). Once the project is selected, time is crucial; whoever is in charge of execution has access to all resources (P1). It is worth noting that relationship management (prior to the feasibility study) is considered the most important phase of a project – or rather for winning a project. Interacting with the customer very early and understanding his concerns and preferences is the key to success (P1). Oftentimes once a project is publicly known it is too late for a new provider to enter into negotiations.

Competition between relationship managers may broadly be interpreted as intersubsidiary competition because in MNCs sales activities are typically performed via multiple geographic locations. In Company A the scenario that two relationship managers (actively) approach the same customer belongs to the past – although they sometimes do get in each other's way. The goal is to have one contact person who channels the customer's desires and delivers the right response (P1). In reality some competition continues to exist between relationship managers, who – as key account managers – are typically located in the country or region of the respective customer's headquarters.[84] Despite assigned responsibilities relationship managers are naturally hesitant to give away a multi-million project they managed to secure (including the related senior attention) just because it is not their official account (P1). The goal is then to try and create a win-win situation by recognizing everyone's effort rather than spurring an open conflict.

An example of such intersubsidiary competition is that of a German key account having acquired a significant stake in a Central European company, which the Czech subsidiary rightly claims to be in their territory (P2). The two subsidiaries entered into (internal) competition for who may cover the customer and secure a substantial project. In this case one can speak of **subsidiary-led competition for charters**, since both parties recognized that it was against everyone's interest if they approached the customer from two sides – proposing different concepts and, in the worst case, not even knowing of each others' activities. Headquarters was called in to resolve the conflict and eventually the two subsidiaries turned competition into cooperation by preparing a joint presentation. Although the customer would have liked to receive German engineering competence at Czech prices, he ended up accepting the offer (P2). Now technological workings are conducted in Germany while the Czech subsidiary performs FEED for utilities and oversees a number of local contractors.[85]

It is worth noting that prior to the acquisition the so-called inquiry-review committee decided which subsidiary was responsible for which project. Potential projects were presented and discussed via telephone conference every two to three weeks, with "buddies" between Sales and Operations being pre-defined at this stage (P2). Although the process had features of an internal tender, the committee should not be misinterpreted as a competitive bidding platform. The following example of a project

---

[84] Company A's sales organization is set up according to three criteria: regional, i.e. country-specific, customer-specific and technology-specific. Key accounts are defined by where the customer's headquarters, its key decision makers and planning competency are located. A subsidiary's previous experience with a customer may also be a reason for the latter being treated as a local key account (P2). 'Normal' inquiries are handled by an additional, lower-level sales organization (P1).
[85] As introduced in subsection 4.2.6.2, FEED stands for 'front-end engineering and design'.

in Poland illustrates that the committee mainly served to settle conflicts of interest between subsidiaries (P2): While the German subsidiary, which was historically managing the key account, deemed the project uneconomical, the Czech sister company, which maintained a relationship with the customer's new parent company, had a strong interest in pursuing it. The Czech subsidiary itself, however, neither had the experience nor the resources to extend the offer. Eventually the inquiry-review committee took the decision not to bid. Without such a committee it is necessary (or rather effective) to have one person, i.e. the chairman, to take an informed decision (P2). The example also illustrates that intersubsidiary competition is constantly fueled by market distortions such as changing ownership structures. It is difficult to realign the sales organization at the same pace.

Changing ownership structures do not only affect the customer organization but also the focal company itself: the realignments necessary upon the acquisition enhance intersubsidiary competition for charters, particularly customer responsibilities (P2). In order to ensure an equal degree of capacity utilization, there is now a central allocation of projects to subsidiaries (P1). Since the relative stake of the engineering unit has increased, the new parent company wishes to have a stronger say in which projects they pursue (P2).

Overall, intersubsidiary coordination is preferred over competition, which has been found to be counterproductive – as illustrated by the following example (P1): Despite their clear preference for German project execution, customers asked for quotes from both the Czech and the German subsidiary. Having successfully driven prices down, they eventually awarded the contract to the German provider. In order to prevent such a double loss (the German subsidiary needs to accept a discount while the Czech subsidiary goes away empty-handed), Company A's management now tries to determine the most suitable provider, i.e. subsidiary, in advance. Ample telephone conferences and discussions are summoned to this end. Nevertheless, a certain sense of competition between subsidiaries is triggered by customers having clear preferences for the providing national unit. Reasons for such preferences may be found in cultural sensitivity or technology leadership (P1). There used to be some customers who were willing to pay a premium to choose which subsidiary executes their project. Subsidiaries respond to the perceived competition by positioning themselves (and promoting their capabilities) accordingly.

In the past – under different management – competitive activities have been more prevalent. Far-reaching national independence had led to subsidiaries pursuing their own interests, e.g., designing their sales organizations to their own benefit (P1, P2).

Intersubsidiary competition is now increasingly being curtailed – a development that accompanies Company A's evolution from a rather decentralized multinational company to a more centralized global one.

Another form of competition exists between Company A's technology and engineering units for securing projects. The technology unit may also choose an external engineering company to build the plant (P1). Such competition between business units, however, is not the focus of this research.

The above illustrations show that in Company A **headquarters-led competition is low** and **subsidiary-led competition is moderate**. Although headquarters does not actively encourage intersubsidiary competition, the set-up of the sales organization and certain decision-making processes allow for it to occur. Subsidiaries have recently lost some of their independence but continue to be driven by self-interest, which is reflected in a competitive stance towards their peers.

6.5.2.2 Cooperation

In Company A intersubsidiary cooperation tends to be initiated by the subsidiaries themselves. The subsidiary in which the key account manager is located typically decides on which other subsidiaries to involve in subsequent project phases (P1).[86] The more sophisticated the customer is, the more formal this coordination process tends to be (P1). By splitting work among international locations, Company A can account for local particularities. The lead subsidiary may decide that buildings be laid out in the country where the plant is ultimately built. Local colleagues know best whether air conditioning is needed, what kind of foundation needs to be built or what wall thickness is required (P1). Besides splitting work, subsidiaries perform communication and (knowledge) exchange for mutual control purposes, i.e. to avoid mistakes being made (or persisting) until the construction phase begins (P1).

In the early phases of a project, Sales and Operations – which are oftentimes located in different subsidiaries – compete for the stake each unit takes in the project (P2). Once work packages have been defined and allocated, however, cooperation takes over. Competition during execution is non-existent (P2). Similarly, salesmen, who

---

[86] Even if it is up to the sales representative to decide whom to involve in a project, ideally there is a matrix (customer – region – technology) for orientation purposes (P2).

may be inclined to compete due to their personality or temper, eventually need to cooperate in front of the customer (P2).

Different facets of intersubsidiary cooperation are illustrated by an exemplary project for a German specialty chemicals company in Singapore (P1, P2). At the time of the interviews the detail engineering phase had not begun yet, but later EPC realization with Singapore as lead office (and contractual partner) was aspired. The project is visualized in Figure 17 and subsequently described. The form of illustration corresponds to the project marketing models developed in section 4.3, and consequently the legend introduced in Figure 12 applies.

Initially, Germany as the lead subsidiary was responsible for maintaining the relationship with the key account. In this particular example it was the technology unit which identified and secured the project. The German engineering subsidiary committed to pursuing it and supported the customer with a rough cost estimate. **Subsidiary-led cooperation through knowledge sharing** occurred as the German subsidiary solicited local price information from its sister company in Singapore. Given that the latter was accompanying a similar project for another customer at the time, they were able to provide valuable insights and recent market data (P2). The example shows that coordination with the local subsidiary – here Singapore – is already necessary during the acquisition phase in order to take into account local norms and standards (P2). Involving the local subsidiary in early phases of the project further increases the likelihood of it being chosen for EPC execution, which is to the benefit of the company as a whole (P2). In this particular example the size of the involvement did not require approval by headquarters; the decision to go ahead with the project was taken by the German subsidiary itself (P3).[87]

---

[87] The necessity to have a project approved depends on the scope of the project (approval internally in subsidiary, by engineering headquarters, by corporate headquarters). Regular coordination with Operations has not been institutionalized yet (after acquisition) (P2).

227

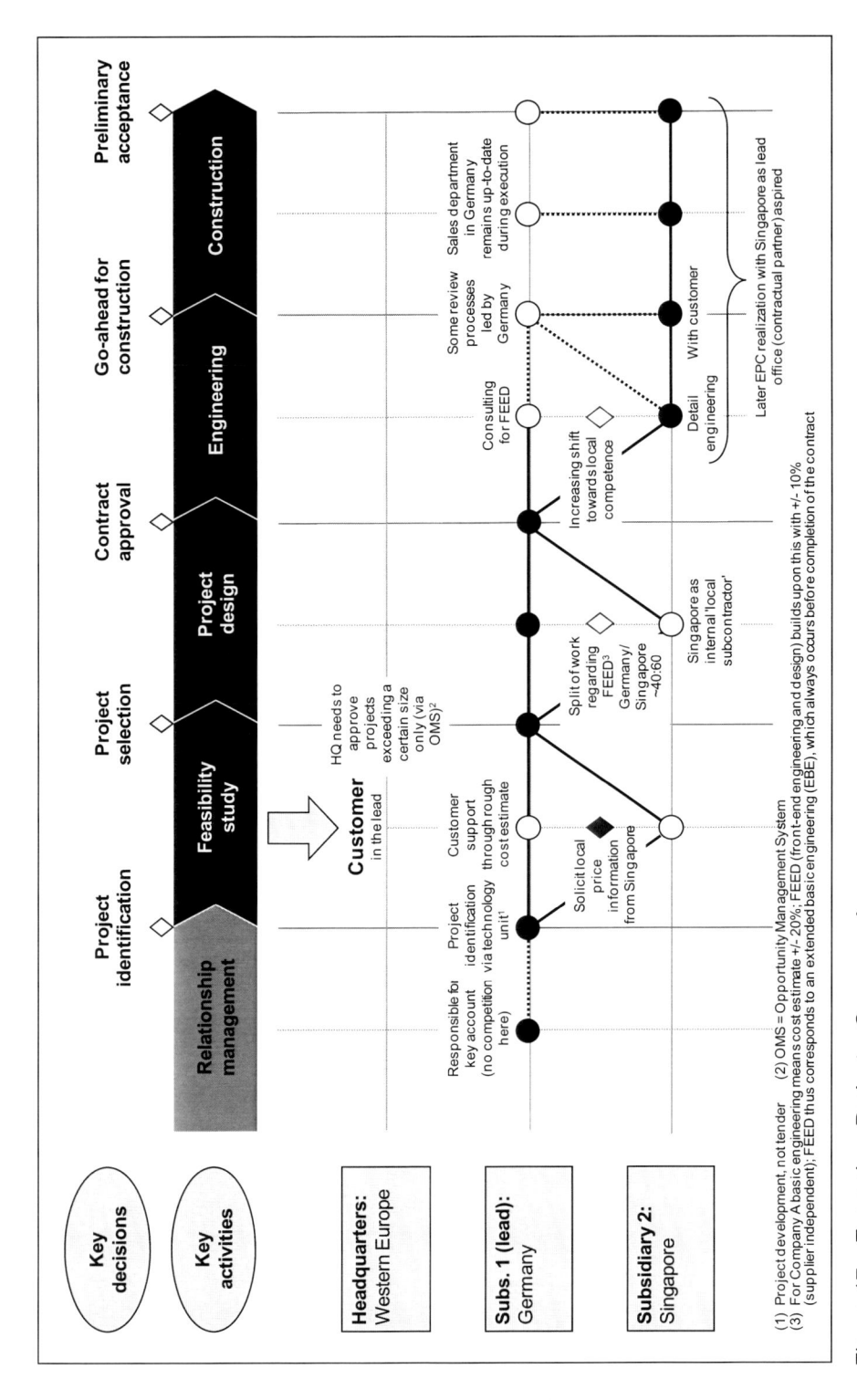

Figure 17: Exemplary Project – Company A

During the course of the project a continuous shift is taking place towards the local competence (or execution capability) in Singapore. In the project design phase the German subsidiary provided approximately 40% of the hours, whereas it would merely offer technical assistance in the detail engineering phase.[88] Prior to project execution the German subsidiary would lead some review processes but eventually the subsidiary in Singapore would operate self-sufficiently (P2). The example provides evidence of **subsidiary-led cooperation through a split of work**. Contracts are signed for the individual work packages, i.e. the German subsidiary is contractual partner for the FEED while the Singapore office would be contractually responsible for the EPC realization – provided that the customer decided to engage Company A's Singapore office for execution rather than a third-party provider. In the first part of the contract the Singapore office acts as subcontractor for the German subsidiary and in the second part of the contract the German subsidiary would offer consulting services as a subcontractor to the Singapore office (P3). There may then be an additional split of work by having the German subsidiary verify certain activities or drawings in this later phase (P1). The German subsidiary would continue to accompany the project not from a technical point of view but in terms of key account management.

Another form of cooperation (both through knowledge sharing and a split of work) manifests itself between the salesman and the proposal manager. The two prepare the commercial and technical offer in tandem, which works best if they are located in the same subsidiary. A local salesman is needed to coordinate the proposal, while key account management maintains the overall customer relationship. In view of follow-on projects, Sales continues to accompany the project as bystander – in large projects typically as a member of the bi-monthly steering committee (P2). Cooperation further extends itself to the interaction between proposal manager and project manager, the two ideally – yet rarely – being one and the same person (P3). Concerted action in preparing offers is important, i.e. being of one opinion and accepting or not accepting the same contract clauses (P2).

The project described above is regarded as typical in terms of its complex execution structure. The German subsidiary's experience and relationship with the licensee allows it to prepare a FEED more efficiently and pass it on to the respective project location. Simpler projects involve only one location, but typically the lead subsidiary maintains the customer relationship, and (detail) engineering is performed by a high-

---

[88] It should be noted that highly professional customers tend to approach plant engineering companies to discuss project realization only after having prepared their own feasibility study.

value center (P3).[89] Headquarters is only involved if it is a contracting party – it does not take on a superordinate coordinating role. Intersubsidiary cooperation is the result of subsidiary initiative; it is not explicitly supported by central structures or processes, although the so-called opportunity management system (OMS) does facilitate concerted action (P3). Such decentralization is indicative of the derived multinational strategic orientation.

To sum up, in Company A **headquarters-led cooperation is low** and **subsidiary-led cooperation is moderate.** The overall philosophy of cooperation is that technology and know-how come from a Western, say the German subsidiary, and the bulk of man hours are provided by or in a lower-cost country (P2). Performing individual work steps in different geographic locations is important for remaining competitive. In Company A there is limited central support for such cooperation; it is rather upon the lead subsidiary's initiative that multiple locations work together. Yet cooperation seldom seems to exceed the rather pragmatic level required by a specific project.

6.5.3 Discussion of Intersubsidiary Relationships

6.5.3.1 Review of the Propositions

Given that Company A shows features of both the multinational and the global type, a clear-cut evaluation of the propositions is difficult to achieve. In Table 10 the results for Company A are compared to the propositions that were developed in section 5.2 for MNCs with multinational and global strategic orientation, respectively. Company A's main feature of combined subsidiary-led competition and cooperation – i.e. subsidiary-led coopetition – is best reflected in project acquisition and execution model 4b (see section 4.3). Additional headquarters-led elements need to be recognized.

---

[89] There is a general attempt to reduce the overall costs of a project by having Western subsidiaries contribute engineering know-how and undertake the procurement of complicated components, while operational tasks are delegated to other locations. Detail engineering is typically carried out in so-called high-value (or low-cost) centers. In this case the latter do not compete with one another, but are chosen by the lead subsidiary based on competence, preference and previous experience (P1).

Types of intersubsidiary relationship		Multinational	Global	Company A	Key explanation
Competition	Headquarters-led	None	Low	Low	Some competition allowed for efficiency reasons
	Subsidiary-led	High	None	Moderate	Subsidiary independence increasingly being curtailed
Cooperation	Headquarters-led	None	Low	Low	Some central support of project-specific cooperation
	Subsidiary-led	Low	None	Moderate	International project business requires cooperation

Table 10: Review of Propositions for Company A – Expected and Actual Level of Intersubsidiary Competition and Cooperation

Since Company A's strategic orientation is described as multinational with global tendencies, one would expect results to combine elements of what is proposed for the two types of strategic orientation. And indeed – with the exception of subsidiary-led cooperation – all results for Company A deviate one notch from what is proposed for the multinational model towards what is proposed for the global model (possibly leading to identical values for Company A and the global model). Headquarters-led competition is expected to be non-existent in the multinational company and low in the global company. Company A features a low level of **headquarters-led competition**, given that some intersubsidiary competition is admitted for efficiency purposes (for example, between the German and the Czech subsidiary). **Subsidiary-led competition** in Company A is only moderate – and not high as expected for the multinational model – because global influences increasingly curtail subsidiary independence. Headquarters wishes to have a stronger say in which projects are pursued by which national unit and occasionally steps in to settle conflicts of interest between subsidiaries.

Its greater level of involvement has a similar impact on intersubsidiary cooperation: In Company A **headquarters-led cooperation** is low – rather than non-existent as proposed for the multinational model – since some central support for intersubsidiary cooperation is provided. For example, coordination during project acquisition is facilitated by a common sales database (the aforementioned OMS) and centrally summoned telephone conferences. By reaching a moderate level, merely **subsidiary-led cooperation** in Company A does not follow the identified pattern. When such cooperation is expected to be low in a multinational company and even non-existent in a global company, important particularities of the project business are neglected. The international scope of the plant engineering industry and the corresponding division of labor were emphasized in section 4.1. In order for the company as a whole to remain competitive, the lead subsidiary needs to involve its peers in other, mainly lower-cost countries. As Company A's project example has shown, both cooperation through knowledge sharing and cooperation through a split of work mainly result from subsidiary initiative. A moderate level of cooperation is not exceeded given that subsidiaries tend to cooperate on a project-specific basis only.

As noted above, Company A's hybrid strategic orientation makes it difficult to clearly confirm or reject the propositions developed in section 5.2. The case provides **broad support** for sub-propositions (a) headquarters-led competition, (b) subsidiary-led competition and (c) headquarters-led cooperation for both the multinational (1) and the global (2) model. On the other hand, there is a definite lack of support for sub-proposition (d) on subsidiary-led cooperation in both types of company.

6.5.3.2 Additional Influencing Factors

Although Company A's case does not permit a clear evaluation of the individual propositions, both interviewees explicitly acknowledged that independent subsidiary action comes along with competition (P1, P3) – thus supporting the overall proposition of strategic orientation constituting a key influencing factor for intersubsidiary relationships. They also propose additional influencing factors, which – similar to the determinants reviewed in section 3.5 – can be grouped into three broad categories: (1) **Individual** characteristics (personality/philosophy), (2) **internal** characteristics (organization/infrastructure), (3) **external** characteristics (industry/environment). These factors are summarized in Table 11.

At this point it should be noted that the allocation of determinants to categories is not always clear-cut. In this case, for example, 'management philosophy' is considered an individual trait because it refers to differences in attitude or style between managers who may or may not belong to the same firm. Management philosophy in Perlmutter's sense, however, characterizes the corporation as a whole and gives it a distinct profile. It would therefore represent a collective or internal feature (compare to subsection 3.3.3.2 and the footnote in section 2.5).

	Determinants of intersubsidiary relationships	Explanation / comment
Individual	Human / natural behavior	Egocentrism rather than altruism (P1)
	Personality	Sales representatives characterized by autonomy and a strong will to succeed; people who want to expose themselves to competition (P2) Same with cooperation: personality and commitment of individuals is key (P2)
	Management philosophy	Some try to manage and control more tightly than others (P1)
Internal	Incentive system	Bonus now depends more on group results and less on the performance of a single subsidiary or office (P1); enhances intersubsidiary cooperation rather than competition
	Relationship network	Internal network and quality of (personal) relationships is essential for intersubsidiary cooperation (P1)
	Organizational change	Distortions from a merger or acquisition, such as temporary overlaps in office responsibilities, for which a competent solution needs to be found (P2) Evolving markets and subsidiary competences; example Croatia: vitalization of its home turf and sudden ability to prepare self-contained offers (P2) Changing ownership structure(s) / M&A; centralization increases together with the relative importance of the engineeering unit within the combined entity (P2)
External	Market distortions	Changing customer ownership structures and business models, partly triggered by consolidation and new entrants from developing economies (P1, P2); engineering companies need to react by rearranging their internal responsibilities
	Customer behavior	Competition induced by preferring one subsidiary over another, e.g., due to contract language (P2) Cooperation triggered by explicitly demanding to enter into the contract with one subsidiary while reaping monetary benefits from contributions of another subsidiary (P2)

Table 11: Additional Influencing Factors for Intersubsidiary Competition and Cooperation – Company A

6.5.3.3 Developments and Their Managerial Implications

A key takeaway from the case study on Company A is that industry particularities – such as the international division of labor in plant engineering – need to be taken into account when evaluating contingencies related to intersubsidiary relationships. The developments that have taken place in Company A imply that in the current environment it is both difficult and undesirable for plant engineering companies to maintain complete subsidiary independence. Foreign subsidiaries need to cooperate to satisfy customer demands for state-of-the-art project execution at competitive prices. A certain level of internal competition may be tolerable to enhance efficiency, but it may neither go to the expense of the customer nor the company as a whole. In Company A, **centralization and formalization** have increasingly been used to curtail detrimental competitive practices, which were mainly facilitated by two developments: (1) uncertain responsibilities resulting from changing customer ownership structures and (2) capability enhancement of subsidiaries located in lower-cost countries. As is the case for Company A, stronger centralization can also be the result of a merger or acquisition. The new owner wishes to have more control over subsidiaries' activities and realizes the necessity of redefining responsibilities to eliminate redundancies upon integration. The traceable **shift in Company A's strategic orientation** from predominantly multinational to multinational with global tendencies reflects both changing industry requirements and a new management philosophy. Moreover, it constitutes an important step in the company's aspired transition towards the transnational model.

6.6 Empirical Findings on Company B

Company B, an international technology company operating in the field of plant contracting and process engineering, has recently been acquired by a leading industrial group, whose core business is withheld for confidentially reasons. The rationale of the complementary acquisition was for the new owner to accelerate growth by strengthening resources in existing markets and gaining access to new technologies. The integration doubles the size of the engineering unit and increases its geographic scope. Company B has its headquarters in Western Europe and maintains other important engineering centers in Eastern Europe, the United States, India and South Africa.

6.6.1 Strategic Orientation

Company B used to proclaim that headquarters was the heart of the company and that subsidiaries in India and Poland in particular served as extended workbenches, i.e. were only meant to produce cheap engineering hours (P4). This perception belongs to the past, however. Nowadays Company B tries to develop subsidiaries in their competencies and enhance their entrepreneurial spirit. This means giving them more responsibility by not only procuring engineering hours but assigning them entire work packages or projects (P4).

Company B is currently in a transition process from the global to the international model (P4). The company's strategic orientation used to be global, with centralized, global-scale operations and corporate strategy being defined at headquarters (P4). The goal now is to fully arrive at the international model, meaning that certain core competencies are left centralized while others are being decentralized. At the same time the focus from the periphery to the center is being loosened (P4, P5). The following illustrations show that Company B's strategic orientation can be regarded as being **international with global remainders**.

There are several **international characteristics** which emerged in the exploratory phase of the research and were confirmed in the official interviews. In terms of centralizing core competencies, Company B has taken the decision that the development of a particular technology is always bound to a single location – in most cases headquarters, although there are some international locations with proper competencies (P4). The reason for this allocation is to have better control over development. Company B further attempts to **set global standards** which are then **adjusted to local circumstances**. For example, headquarters provides so-called project execution procedures (PEPs), which are available to the entire organization. The lead subsidiary is responsible for adapting and implementing them on a project-specific basis (P4). Headquarters also has the task to set standards that allow the executing units to understand each other. This includes a centrally designed database that is replicated in the execution centers. Subsidiaries are advised to exercise discispline with respect to headquarters' requirements (P6).

By joining resources from multiple execution centers in a single, initially headquarters-based task force, knowledge is transferred from headquarters to the subsidiaries (P5). Being a key characteristic of the international model, such **knowledge transfer from the center to the periphery** is perceived as a question of trust. Headquarters not only has to feel confident that the subsidiary is capable of assuming certain tasks; it also has to accept the transfer risk and be convinced that the transferred knowledge is not used against headquarters itself (P4). Key informants in Company B observe that wherever this knowledge transfer has been implemented it works very well and is beneficial to the competitiveness of the company as a whole (P4). What is not regarded as being achieved yet – and the question is whether it is desirable at all – is that the subsidiaries interact perfectly amongst each other (P4).

Company B's mainly international strategic orientation can further be explicated by an **exemplary project** in India, which is described in more detail in the next subsection (P4): The project is not led by headquarters but by the Indian subsidiary. Basic engineering is carried out where the respective technological expertise is – in this case in South Africa and headquarters. Equipment is delivered partly from India and partly from South Africa. Tensions arise between India and South Africa regarding the scope of work packages and the interaction with the customer. Headquarters oversees but does not manage the process; it accompanies the project review process for international projects and gets involved to resolve conflicts. Within the 'coordinated federation' the Indian subsidiary – as a traditional execution center – is to do two things: (1) attract and conduct local business and (2) cooperate in international projects led by headquarters by producing engineering packages (the cost factor being crucial). The managing director in India is delegated from headquarters, but the rest of the organization is completely Indian (P4). In Company B parent knowledge and capabilities are used to develop overseas units, which may then undertake their own projects under their own management (P5).

As far as the relationship to the Indian subsidiary is concerned, it has proven useful for headquarters to keep a tight hold on the reins. This includes delegating a managing director from headquarters to the subsidiary. In the past, all attempts to lead the Indian subsidiary 'Indian style' have failed. Under headquarters control, however, operations need to be managed by a local director for acceptance purposes (P6).

Although certain projects are led by subsidiaries, headquarters is actively involved in **strategic leadership**, i.e. deciding in which direction to head or what not to do. It is not the case that subsidiaries lead the way and headquarters follows – on the contrary: project selection is primarily up to headquarters (P4). This is an international rather than a global characteristic, since strategy is not imposed, yet considerably coined by headquarters. Similarly, **headquarters coordinates** the process of assessing project risks (P4). This again is an international feature, since subsidiaries leverage headquarters' experience and competencies by presenting the projects of interest. Headquarters further determines the project setup, i.e. which partners collaborate in which manner. Although operational project execution is then delegated to the lead subsidiary (P4), headquarters basically controls all current projects in the engineering phase (P6). Provocatively said, Company B's core is at headquarters and the others are allowed to play along (P6). With confidence in subsidiary abilities being limited, many activities are still tightly controlled by headquarters.

When two subsidiaries compete for tasks, headquarters needs to take a particularly strong lead. Obviously headquarters will analyze the situation in detail and weigh risks and opportunities of any relocation. Subsidiaries have the chance to articulate their preferences and concerns, but eventually headquarters decides in a top-down manner and communicates its decision (P4). Or, as another interviewee puts it, questions such as where it is most reasonable to make profit have to be taken centrally; they cannot be taken by an affiliate (P6). In this respect Company B still has **elements of the global model**.

6.6.2 Intersubsidiary Relationships

6.6.2.1 Competition

One interviewee emphasizes that the situation in Company B cannot be termed 'competitive' but is more adequately described as **unpracticed collaboration** (P4). Rather than seeing themselves as part of an integrated whole (with the overall project success being the decisive component), subsidiaries still focus on their national success. As far as the aforementioned project in India is concerned, there is more of an interface problem than competition between subsidiaries (P4). The customer not only communicates with – or via – the lead subsidiary, but also directly with the subsidiary providing the technology, i.e. South Africa (P4). Although the customer contributed to the given project constellation (not least by signing contracts with multiple parties), he may find it disturbing to detect ruptures within the project and to have more than one contact person (P4).[90] Another interviewee prefers to speak of an execution philosophy that focuses on profit optimization rather than direct competition between units (P6).

Ultimately, however, national units do **compete for jobs or charters** – e.g., where basic engineering is performed, in Germany or Poland. Neither location wants to let go because whoever has to sacrifice tasks fears that they no longer have work to do (P4). Shifting work packages or (sub)projects to subsidiaries that were formerly treated as extended work benches increases the established subsidiaries' fear that the entire activity is increasingly being relocated (P4). Despite the inherent opportunities such a shift this spurs a sense of competition, which may also have positive implications (P4).

---

[90] As far as many international projects are concerned, it needs to be differentiated how the project is treated from an operational/strategic perspective versus a legal/tax perspective, i.e. where the actual project management is performed versus which contracts are signed (P4).

Conflicts are bound to arise given that Company B is not fully integrated yet. The vision is to have all national units perceive themselves as part of a whole, which possibly requires adapting the incentive schemes accordingly. Conflict is preprogrammed if each subsidiary tries to optimize its own profit-and-loss account (P&L) rather than achieving common project goals (P4). With its predominantly international strategic orientation, Company B is currently more a group of individual businesses, each pursuing its own interests rather than acting in favor of the collective (P4). As articulated in subsection 6.6.1, the strings therefore need to be pulled at headquarters (P4).

According to the manager of a reference project in Malaysia – which is described in the following subsection on cooperation – **competitive tensions between subsidiaries** exist. There is a rather high level of natural competitiveness between Company B's Indian subsidiary and headquarters. In 90% of the cases it is considered as being healthy, in 10% there seemed to be a definite will to prove somebody incompetent. These tensions also exist on an intersubsidiary level (P5). Particularly at the beginning of the respective project, there was a lot of sparring going on as to who wanted a bigger piece of the project. Various subsidiaries and headquarters signaled that they could do everything, but effectively they were already half-loaded – or in case of headquarters could not provide competitive man-hour rates. **Splitting work** among multiple locations was an essential element in designing the best possible execution concept for the best price. In the early phases of the project **intersubsidiary competition** was **for charters** rather than customers. With respect to relationship management a clear matrix of responsibility is drawn up, restricting competition for customers. Roles and responsibilities in project execution are also clearly defined: The subsidiary in Malaysia operates in South East Asia, the subsidiary in Poland operates in Eastern Europe and the subsidiary in India operates in India. The latter two also provide engineering services to headquarters. So if there were a project in Korea, for example, there would probably be some cooperative arrangement between the Malaysian subsidiary and one of its peers in South East Asia. Again, the best execution concept is aspired based on each subsidiary's resource loading and order-book intake as well as Company B's overall resource availability. Most importantly, there must be a clear understanding at the beginning of the project as to who is responsible for undertaking the various aspects of the work. Further along in the project there is no intersubsidiary competition, because the execution of certain items is awarded based on competency and expertise. In this project, it was not a valid option to have fired heaters be engineered in India rather than Poland (P5).

Last but not least it is recognized that Company B's **acquisition** has not enhanced competition. Given the complementarity of the transaction, there are very few overlaps, and 'crowding out' is hardly expected (P4).

Although it is perceived as human nature to be competitive (P5), the preceding discussion has shown that in Company B **headquarters-led competition is low** and **subsidiary-led competition is low** as well. Subsidiaries are sufficiently independent to develop a sense of competition and headquarters does not restrict it completely.

6.6.2.2 Cooperation

Intersubsidiary cooperation in Company B takes on different shapes depending on whether the project is a 'local' one, i.e. led independently by subsidiaries, or an 'international' one, where headquarters is directly involved and signs a contract (P6).

A coal gasification project in India serves as an example of a **'local' project**, or rather an international project not led by headquarters (P4).[91] Ideally the local organization leads such a project for legal, tax and cultural reasons, provided that it has the respective competence and experience. Headquarters may steer and control the process in the background, but in this case the Indian subsidiary coordinated the project from an operational point of view (P4). Given that such a complex project cannot be carried out as a one-man-show, the subsidiary needs to act in collaboration with headquarters and other participating parties. Although the local organization is responsible for managing the relationship with the customer, technical and commercial experts assist in sales meetings. Similarly, the general evaluation of whether or not to pursue a project is incumbent on the subsidiary, but it possibly needs to consult partners with respect to technical details of the feasibility study (P4). Both situations are examples of **subsidiary-led cooperation through knowledge sharing**.

In the example project cooperation took place between Company B's subsidiary in South Africa and a 50:50 joint venture between Company B and a global energy company (P6). The two acquired the project with a steel- and power-producing company in India together. Although the customer was based in India, the Indian subsidiary only accompanied the acquisition, given that South Africa and the joint

---

[91] For this example project no graphical illustration is included since it was not indicated as being 'typical' of Company B and therefore discussed in less detail than the subsequent 'international' project.

venture had the technological expertise. The project was acquired via project development (not an ITB) since the customer was overwhelmed by the technology and did not really know what he wanted (P6). Based on how the contract was structured, the customer contact was initially managed by South Africa and subsequently shifted to India. In this case it was more of an exception how the project was acquired, since subsidiaries have regional sales responsibilities. The feasibility study was carried out in South Africa, with participation by the Indian subsidiary on the cost side (P6).

Project selection is ultimately performed by headquarters. The project team – including the local representative – presents to a central committee, which then decides how to proceed (full approach, next substep, abort or the like). The subsidiary cannot choose which partner(s) it wishes to collaborate with – this decision is taken by headquarters (P4).[92] In the example project, South Africa completed the basic engineering package in cooperation with headquarters and the joint venture. With the whole workstream being very much subsidiary-led, headquarters was basically regarded as a supplier for certain sub-units only. The detail engineering contract was again handled separately – there was not even an umbrella contract (P6).

During **project execution**, India and South Africa communicated bilaterally, albeit not always harmoniously. South Africa performed the basic engineering for a particular package based on its own standards and perceptions. The result, however, did not meet the Indian subsidiary's expectations. At that point headquarters needed to interfere to decide who would rework the package so that the Indian subsidiary could continue with detail engineering. Headquarters is typically called upon in case of conflict, i.e. for **moderation or mediation** purposes (P4).

The above examples already show that **cooperation in 'local' projects** is both **headquarters-led (setup)** and **subsidiary-led (execution)**. Headquarters defines the split of work and the lead subsidiary coordinates it, deciding when knowledge exchange among peers is necessary or beneficial. In Company B, the Indian subsidiary in particular is increasingly taking on the responsibility for an entire project, involving other units but having headquarters take key decisions only. Centrally drafted project execution procedures (PEPs) specify not only how to communicate

---

[92] One of the interviewees pointed to cultural differences between India and the Western hemisphere, which may reinforce the headquarters-led nature of cooperation: While being enormously quick in doing parallel work, many Indians first have to get used to taking decisions (P6).

with the customer but how cooperation is organized internally (possibly even via a formal consortium agreement) (P4). Corporate management further has the right to say which sub-contracts a subsidiary has to give to which partner (P6).

Cooperation in **'international' projects** is even more **headquarters-led**. When asked for a 'typical' project, interviewees of Company B refer to a project that was undertaken for a leading oil and gas multinational in Malaysia (P5). The fact that this is such an 'international' project reflects the persistently strong role of the center. The project is rightly discussed in this subsection because it highlights the importance (and dominance) of **intersubsidiary cooperation**. Analogous to Company A, the project is visualized in Figure 18 and subsequently described. Again, the illustration is based on the project marketing models developed in section 4.3 and the legend introduced in Figure 12.

The project in Malaysia is regarded as typical for Company B because **decision making** is very much **headquarters-based** and **more than one subsidiary** is being dealt with (P5). Besides headquarters the subsidiaries involved were those in India, Poland and Malaysia. The Indian subsidiary did all of the detail engineering from a certain point onwards, Poland was involved for a small portion of the works, and Malaysia was mainly responsible for the onshore procurement of certain items and the construction management. Although the customer was Malaysian, the subsidiary in Malaysia did not play a leading role in the project. It contributed to the local relationship management but otherwise lacks the necessary size and competence. The project was driven and commercially managed by headquarters (P5).[93] In the following, the project's key activities are described with particular focus on the relationship between national units. The information was extracted from the interview with the responsible project manager (P5 unless noted otherwise).

---

[93] This is a common approach: In times where there are no specific projects, Company B uses its local organizations to maintain the customer relationship and to find out about potential projects. If an interesting business opportunity comes up, headquarters monitors and possibly pursues it, and the local subsidiary contributes to managing the customer relationship (P4).

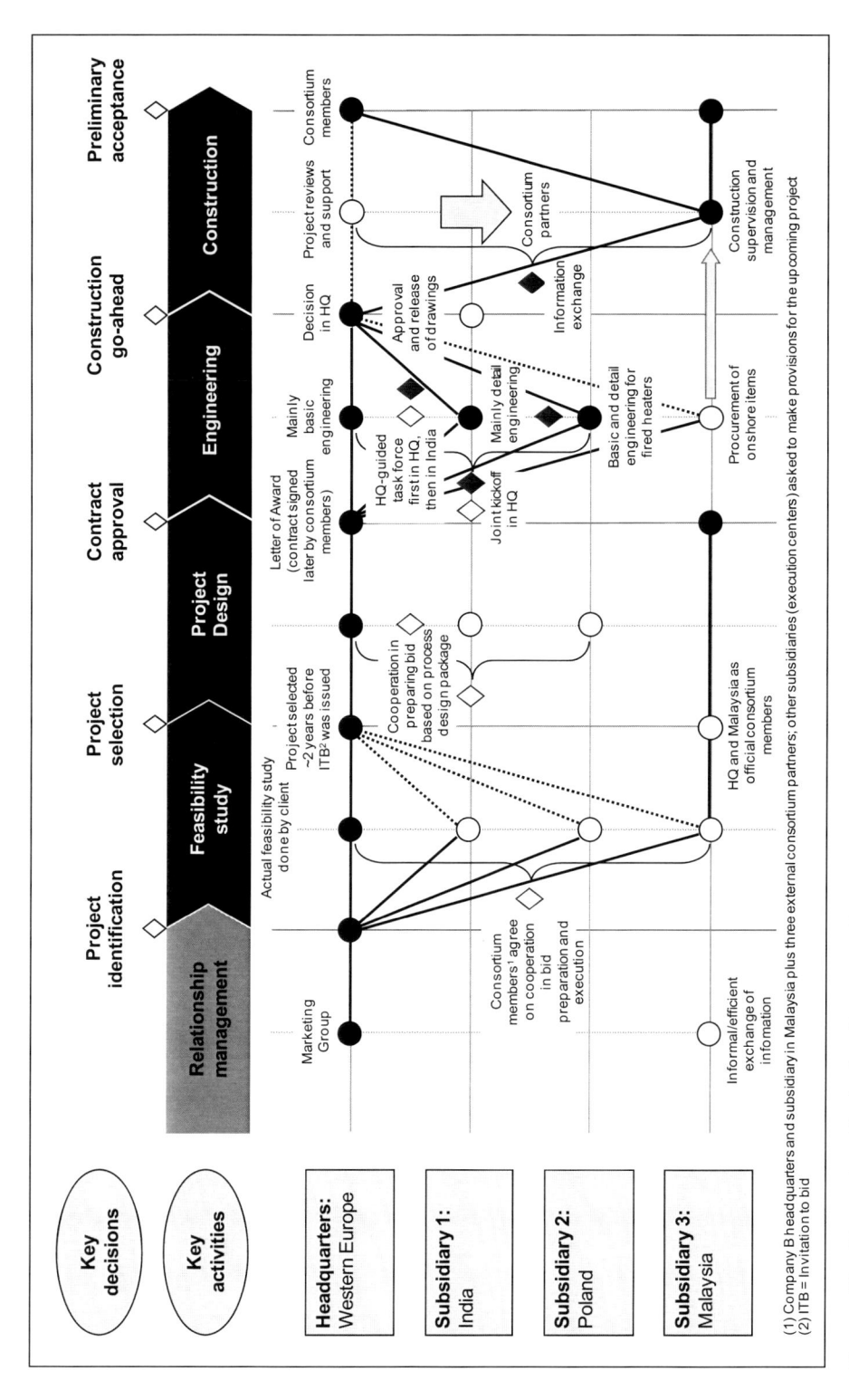

Figure 18: Exemplary Project – Company B

The **relationship** with the customer and the particular acquisition were mainly **managed** by headquarters, although Company B also utilized the personal relationship between Malaysia's managing director and the customer for an informal and efficient exchange of information. The invitation to bid (ITB) was prepared by a third party on behalf of the customer and took over two years to be completed. During this time, Company B's (corporate) marketing group was following the project and the company was positioning itself for undertaking it. A headquarters-based proposal manager was responsible for preparing the offer (P6). Before the project became effective, five partners (three of them external) entered into a consortium agreement. They agreed to work with each other in preparing the bid and finally executing the contract. In this phase (internal) cooperation was mainly between headquarters and the subsidiary in Malaysia. Execution centers were asked to make provisions for the upcoming project in a tertiary arrangement. Joining resources from all of the various centers is important not only to achieve the lowest technically acceptable price in a competitive bidding process. It was mainly due to this cost situation that India was included in the planning phase to perform the detail engineering (P6). In this early phase of the project there was mainly **headquarters-led cooperation through knowledge sharing**

The actual **feasibility study** was completed by the owner before the ITB was undertaken. Eventually headquarters received the ITB and thus officially took notice of the project. **Project selection**, however, had already taken place once Company B had found out about the project roughly two years earlier. Usually, with the ITB the company receives a FEED package. In this case, it was a process design package (pre-basic engineering) issued by a licensor, which had to be taken and detailed out into a basic engineering and then a detail engineering package. Headquarters cooperated with the execution centers to put the bid together. This is important so that the people who execute the work have intimate knowledge as to how the bid came about. Company B started with its actual works once it was awarded the contract and the project became effective.[94]

Basic engineering was undertaken in headquarters. Project management mobilized resources from India, Poland and the external consortium partners to headquarters, set up a task force and kicked off the project. To Company B it is very important to have all disciplines working together in one location. Subsidiaries are not just meant to **split work**, but the idea is to **transfer knowledge** from headquarters (or the

---

[94] Prior to contract signature risk board papers are drawn up and a risk board discusses the merits of executing the project.

respective knowledge base) to the execution centers (see subsection 6.6.1 on this characteristic of the international model). Once basic engineering was completed, the whole team, i.e. around ten lead engineers, transferred to India to execute the project with their Indian colleagues (also see P6).[95] In essence this was a top-down requirement by headquarters, which was viewed critically by the Indian subsidiary. Previous projects had shown how difficult it is for globally inexperienced lead engineers to cope with severely different perceptions of work. The project was quickly restructured so that an Indian lead engineer was made responsible for the local **detail engineering** and the headquarters-delegated engineers were subjected to him as a kind of task force (P6). De-facto detail engineering remains under the **guidance and control** of headquarters. The Indian subsidiary has its own management, but the overall direction is given by headquarters.[96] In the particular project, headquarters also designated the project manager, who is ideally located in the execution center where the bulk of the work is being undertaken. Constituting the pivotal point as to where and what decisions are being made, the project manager mediates between two disciplines if there is a conflict of interest.

The **go-ahead for construction** is given by headquarters. Although it is the respective execution center that releases drawings as they become available, the decision is taken by headquarters. Once approved by the engineering manager, drawings are issued to the site and construction begins. In the example project, the **construction** was physically carried out by one of the external consortium partners. The subsidiary in Malaysia was only responsible for the construction, supervision and management for Company B's portion; they were effectively resource suppliers (including the procurement of onshore items). Once the task force in India has closed down because detail engineering has largely been accomplished, coordination and cooperation (in the form of project reviews and support) takes place between headquarters and Malaysia.[97] Mechanical completion, pre-commissioning and commissioning follow; the preliminary acceptance is signed by all consortium members.

The above elaborations have shown that the execution of 'international' projects is mainly characterized by **headquarters-led cooperation through knowledge**

---

[95] It needs to be recognized that in order to reach tight deadlines there may be significant overlaps between the basic engineering, detail engineering and civil construction phases (P5).
[96] Within the Indian subsidiary cooperation between the headquarters-delegated managing director and the local director of operations is regarded as the key to success (P6).
[97] A headquarters-led project review takes place at least once a month. 'Local' projects are not controlled in this manner, which has positive implications for success, since headquarters interference is perceived as a lack of trust (P6).

sharing and a split of work, depending on the respective project phase. But subsidiaries also take the initiative to converse bilaterally. A few years ago, the Indian subsidiary gave an entire work package to Poland because it was fully loaded (P6). In the example project, the lead engineer in Poland – who completed the detail engineering of fired heaters remotely – coordinated directly with India, even visiting from time to time. Although headquarters is kept informed of the discussions taking place, cooperation has **subsidiary-led elements** here. Directing everything via a central point would be much too time-consuming and inefficient. Subsidiary-led cooperation occurs on a required basis, i.e. subsidiaries interact in order to make sure that the project is successful.

Cooperation between subsidiaries is determined by the entire process organization that is designed for a project. In order to minimize interfaces in the daily business, Company B – like several of its competitors – mainly tries to realize vertical cuts by making subsidiaries responsible for entire units or work packages. The Indian subsidiary, however, also performs horizontal elements (civil engineering) for all projects (P6). During execution, subsidiaries mainly cooperate through a split of work, given that each unit is supposed to complete its assigned work package independently. Knowledge sharing would only occur if they were really working together on a particular issue (P6).

Headquarters facilitates intersubsidiary cooperation by having all four execution centers linked via intranet and internet. With engineering now being undertaken in a 3D model, everyone is engineering at the same time in the same model. This is possible with migration of the model from various execution centers and time zones. Intersubsidiary cooperation is further supported by email and video-conferencing facilities. From a headquarters perspective securing communication channels is particularly important. The various locations need to understand what it is that was discussed and decided and how to implement these decisions. In projects where several subsidiaries collaborate it has proven useful to set up a joint task force and to have a project team that meets on a regular basis – possibly even relocating to one location for a certain period of time (e.g., the engineering and/or construction phase) (P4). At the kickoff meeting the project execution concept is presented to all members of the project team. By encouraging participants to ask questions in an interactive session, cooperation through knowledge sharing is encouraged. Project management defines the execution concept, philosophy, procedures and protocols very early in the process. The split of work between Company B's international locations is laid out in great detail.

When bringing together the findings from the two example projects – the one in India being led by the local subsidiary, the one in Malaysia by headquarters – it can be summarized for Company B that **headquarters-led cooperation is moderate** and **subsidiary-led cooperation is moderate** as well. Intersubsidiary cooperation takes place in all project phases, yet the dominance of a particular unit does not support high levels of either type of cooperation.

6.6.3 Discussion of Intersubsidiary Relationships

6.6.3.1 Review of the Propositions

As derived above, Company B's strategic orientation most closely resembles the international type, including a few elements of the global model. Consequently, the results for Company B are primarily compared to the propositions for MNCs with international strategic orientation (see section 5.2). In Table 12 the expectations for companies with global features are contrasted on a supplementary basis. Company B's main features of headquarters-led and subsidiary-led cooperation are best reflected in project acquisition and execution models 2a and 2b (see section 4.3). Select competitive elements argue in favor of a coopetitive model.

Types of intersubsidiary relationship		International	Global	Company B	Key explanation
Competition	Headquarters-led	Low	Low	Low	Some competition for project participation admitted
	Subsidiary-led	Low	None	Low	Competition as a function of subsidiary independence
Cooperation	Headquarters-led	Moderate	Low	Moderate	Cooperation promoted under headquarters control
	Subsidiary-led	Moderate	None	Moderate	Cooperation pursued on a project-specific basis

Table 12: Review of Propositions for Company B – Expected and Actual Level of Intersubsidiary Competition and Cooperation

A glance at Table 12 reveals that for all four types of intersubsidiary relationship, Company B yields support of the developed propositions. The expected and actual level of **headquarters-led competition** is low. Although headquarters determines the project setup and takes all major decisions, it admits some intersubsidiary competition for the participation in international projects. By 'upgrading' subsidiaries that formerly served as extended workbenches, headquarters spurs the remaining subsidiaries' fear of being marginalized. In the long run, subsidiaries may thus compete via the development of competencies. As far as a particular project is concerned, competition tends to be eliminated once the project setup is determined and execution begins.

Headquarters takes its decisions in view of the overall project success. Stronger integration rather than competition is regarded as being most conducive. Such integration would also continue to restrain **subsidiary-led competition**, the expected and actual level of which is low. In Company B – as a 'coordinated federation' – subsidiaries do not have the freedom to compete openly. Only if headquarters is willing to consider alternative project setups may they advertise their competencies. As long as the incentive scheme is oriented towards optimizing their own P&L, however, subsidiaries will try to position their national interests over the success of an international project. Their ability of doing so increases with the level of experience and competence they have gained by conducting local projects. By encouraging subsidiaries to pursue local business, headquarters enhances subsidiary independence, which in turn provides a platform for intersubsidiary competition.

In accordance with Company B's strategic orientation, however, headquarters continues to channel subsidiary activity by exerting leadership and control. Under this control, headquarters primarily supports intersubsidiary cooperation to enhance project success. Consequently, the expected and actual level of **headquarters-led cooperation** is moderate. In the project business, cooperation between national units is necessary to realize a competitive price point – and beneficial to leveraging dispersed competencies. Since headquarters is in charge of the project setup, it makes a strong effort to determine the ideal split of work. Given headquarters' dominant role in the process, the level of intersubsidiary cooperation it promotes remains moderate. This result extends to **subsidiary-led cooperation**, the expected and actual level of which is moderate as well. Despite the focus on their national markets, subsidiaries realize the benefits of cooperation with respect to local projects. It is in their own interest that local customers benefit from bringing together decentralized competencies on a project-specific basis. Subsidiaries' relative independence allows them to at least achieve a moderate level of subsidiary-led cooperation.

The above analysis shows that the case provides **support for all four sub-propositions** of the international (3) model: (a) low headquarters-led competition, (b) low subsidiary-led competition, (c) moderate headquarters-led cooperation and (d) moderate subsidiary-led cooperation. The aforementioned global influences do not seem to impact intersubsidiary relationships. Even if headquarters plays a very strong role, Company B's goal is not to restrict subsidiary-led relationships altogether. On the contrary, local initiatives are encouraged – as long as they are ultimately beneficial to the company as a whole. Also, as noted with respect to Company A, even a strong center realizes that intersubsidiary cooperation – both in terms of knowledge transfer and a split of work – is an essential feature of the international project business.

6.6.3.2 Additional Influencing Factors

The fact that Company B's remaining global characteristics hardly seem to impact its intersubsidiary relationships could also suggest that strategic orientation is not the only influencing factor. It is worth noting, however, that those interviewees in the position to assess the company's strategic orientation were openly confronted with its implied link to intersubsidiary relationships and at least implicitly supported it (P4, P6). The additional influencing factors mentioned can be attributed to two of the categories established with respect to Company A: (1) **Individual** characteristics and (2) **internal** characteristics. Merely external characteristics were not explicitly identified. Table 13 provides a summary of the suggested determinants.

Again it needs to be said that cultural elements, for example, may also concern the organization as a whole (e.g., in terms of cultural roots or corporate culture). In this case, however, the decisive factor is indeed the national culture of individuals (colleagues or customers). For the concept of trust, the reverse applies: although trust is eventually established between individuals, here it collectively refers to the confidence organizational units have in other units.

	Determinants of intersubsidiary relationships	Explanation / comment
Individual	Human / natural behavior	Human nature to want to be better than the next person (P5)
	Personality	Cooperation and competition are very much personality-driven; some people are more prone to challenging headquarters' decisions than others (P5)
	Expertise / qualifications	Getting a resolution on material issues is easier with a technically skilled project manager than with a purely commercially minded project manager (P5)
	Cultural background	Cooperation is oftentimes easier among people from the same country – here between Indians working on the construction site and an Indian consortium partner; there are significantly less coordination problems (P6) Cultural understanding as a basis of cooperation, e.g., recognizing different perceptions of time, multi-tasking relationships and power distances (P6)
Internal	Relationship network	Personal relationships play a huge part when designing the execution concept of a project – both in terms of competition and cooperation (P5) Use of bypass channels and personal feedback loops – particularly in the connection to the parent company – necessary to avoid the isolated development of a subsidiary (P6)
	Business model	In the Anglosaxon model – due to a historical lack of specialists – companies (mainly contractors) developed a high level of procedures, standards and process handbooks, which allow a horizontal mode of operation; Company B and its competitors focus on having subsidiaries execute vertical structures (P6)
	Organizational trust	Trust that the transferred knowledge is not being played off against the providing unit (P4) Trust in subsidiary capabilities; it is difficult to foster cooperation by requesting subsidiary personnel – e.g., Indians – to execute projects in headquarters (P6)

Table 13: Additional Influencing Factors for Intersubsidiary Competition and Cooperation – Company B

6.6.3.3 Developments and Their Managerial Implications

The above influencing factors can be expected to be of similarly dynamic nature as a company's strategic orientation and the related intersubsidiary relationships. In Company B developments are not only linked to the acquisition but also to market trends, corporate strategy and cultural aspects.

Interviewees explicitly confirm that changes have taken place upon the **acquisition** (P4, P6). The acquirer had signaled from day one on that – in accordance with his business model – he wishes to fully integrate the target. He currently disposes of a supply chain in each region that supports his core business, and this supply chain includes engineering services (P4). Prior to the acquisition, the plant engineering business, i.e. Company B, operated rather independently under a sort of holding structure. Although the combined company is currently in a transition phase, business parameters and management philosophy are bound to change dramatically. Despite the remaining uncertainties there have been severe managerial implications: several top managers have recently left the firm. It needs to be recognized that they had stepped in for a certain strategy and conviction, which can no longer be maintained.

The new owner is promoting integration by setting up joint teams and activities and aiming for a concerted standardization and optimization of plants (P4). These changes may very well have consequences for Company B's internal organization structures (P4). The role of the center, i.e. headquarters, is already changing substantially. In the acquiring company, engineering activities have always been rather decentralized, given that they were organized as a regional service rather than a central division. Apart from certain headquarters-led control hierarchies the regions are vastly independent (P6). This constellation reflects the prevailing business model; otherwise the investor represents a very centralized company, so that strategic decision making is expected to gradually shift to corporate headquarters. Company B's headquarters is then likely to move to the periphery, constituting a subsidiary of the combined company's worldwide engineering activities – or one subsidiary in the 'coordinated federation'. The implications of this development are ambiguous. On the one hand, it may enhance the horizontal cooperation and coordination between subsidiaries; on the other hand, European influence on North American business, for example, has already been curtailed (P4).

The overall business perspective has also changed since Company B has become an integral part of the acquirer. Building plants for an internal customer has the positive effect of receiving feedback on operations but also poses new challenges in terms of quality (P6). It remains to be seen which business lines will ultimately be created. It is up to these business lines to define global standards and to exercise conceptual control for projects that are executed in the regions (P6). The changes attributed to the acquisition are unlikely to significantly impact the relationship between Company B's subsidiaries because each of the latter has its own product and regional focus.

The above elaborations have shown that an acquisition can bring about significant strategic and organizational change, including subsidiary and managerial responsibilities. At the same time there are **market trends** that the company needs to follow irrespective of the acquisition. The industry evolves continuously and nowadays it is difficult for a project to be undertaken 100% from a Western European location. Companies need to optimize their costs while ensuring that they keep the level of competence in their various subsidiaries to a level that gives them a competitive edge. Since the industry cannot afford internal 'single-sourcing' anymore, intersubsidiary cooperation is expected to intensify (P5).

Intersubsidiary cooperation in Company B is further enhanced by the fact that subsidiaries formerly serving as extended workbenches now have much greater responsibility – and consequently greater self-esteem (P4). **'Upgrading' subsidiaries** is part of Company B's corporate strategy and as such independent of the acquisition. It has been Company B's goal to build up independent engineering units that are able to execute work packages independently and pursue business in their local market (P6). In one case, the Indian subsidiary had only accompanied the acquisition of a project, but once they decided to perform the entire detail engineering for the mandate they also took the lead in managing the customer relationship (P6). Headquarters has to recognize that technical knowledge is increasingly coming from outside, i.e. from the subsidiaries. Experience – bundled in headquarters – will no longer be able to displace subsidiary qualifications so easily (P6). This trend is only reinforced by the acquisition. The Indian subsidiary is expecting to receive more mandates from the new parent company, which enhances their contribution to the overall value creation (P6).

Last but not least it is necessary to respect **cultural elements** and act with caution when 'manipulating' strategic orientation and/or intersubsidiary relationships. Upon the acquisition it will be important to continue to respect cultural differences and the resulting customer preferences – e.g., for cultural proximity reasons the Polish subsidiary may be better positioned to serve a German customer than its Indian counterpart (P6). What remains to be seen is how long the engineering center in the U.S. can be maintained. In a global world the time difference to India becomes negligible – or at least manageable. Obviously, the interfaces between subsidiaries would further increase, with more work packages being offshored to execution centers.

Given the long-term nature of the plant engineering industry, a few years are a relatively short time for the mother-daughter relationship to change. Although subsidiaries have significantly enhanced their competencies, a certain level of distrust persists. In dealing with the Indian subsidiary, headquarters had to realize that it had made mistakes both on a cultural and an operational level. It was therefore a deliberate and – in retrospective – wise decision to move ahead slowly and carefully.

The case study on Company B has shown that intersubsidiary relationships vary according to the type of project, i.e. 'local' or 'international', and the related amount of headquarters control. Changes in these relationships may result from external effects – such as an acquisition – or internal strategic decisions – such as developing subsidiaries from extended workbenches to units capable of operating projects independently. Its differentiated approach to projects and subsidiary roles gives Company B a certain flexibility in responding to changing market conditions.

6.7 Empirical Findings on Company C

Company C is the plant engineering unit of a large industrial conglomerate and organizationally situated within one of its business segments. As a contractor with own technology it sells its experience in the chemicals sector in the form of plant engineering services using own or third-party licenses (P7, P8, P10). Its traditional focus is on selling technologies as plant engineer, i.e. providing engineering, procurement and construction (EPC) services, usually lump-sum turnkey (LSTK).[98] In addition, subsidiaries independently pursue regional EPC opportunities. In the medium term, Company C is expected to significantly expand its global EPC business, meaning that subsidiaries cooperatively execute projects that do not fit in with its proper product portfolio, oftentimes limited to engineering or procurement services (P7, P9). Company C has its headquarters in Western Europe and subsidiaries (or associates) with engineering competence in Europe, Africa, North Africa, North and South America, Asia and Australia.[99] In addition it maintains a small number of sales and project execution offices, which are mainly responsible for monitoring the local market (P7). At headquarters level, Company C is primarily divided into technology divisions. The global EPC business is managed as a separate business segment.

---

[98] Lump-sum refers to the payment of a fixed sum for the delivery; turnkey specifies that the scope of work includes the operational start-up of the facility.
[99] For confidentiality reasons regions rather than countries are referred to throughout the case study.

6.7.1 Strategic Orientation

When assessing Company C's current strategic orientation one initially has to differentiate between the technology business, regional EPC business and global EPC business. As suggested above, the difference between technology and EPC business is that the former is based on Company C's proper process engineering know-how, whereas the latter utilizes processes provided by a third party (clients, licensors or other) (P7). While the technology business is managed by headquarters – with subsidiaries providing support in terms of capacity, engineering hours and the like – regional EPC mandates are pursued independently by the subsidiaries (P7, P9, P10). As an important strategic pillar, Company C is currently developing its global EPC business, which from an organizational point of view means that all EPC activities are consolidated and coordinated in a separate business segment. Subsidiaries therefore have three distinct roles: (1) support the worldwide activities of Company C's technology division as extended workbenches, (2) pursue regional business as profit centers, including sales and marketing responsibilities, (3) participate in Company C's global EPC business (and global networking activities) (P9).[100]

As one interviewee states, the **technology business** – compared to the regional (and global) EPC business – is 100% centralized and thus corresponds to the **global** model (P9). Technology know-how is developed and retained at the center. Subsidiaries support global-scale operations as extended workbenches and thus assist in implementing headquarters strategies. The strong role of the center is illustrated by the fact that detail engineering is accompanied and controlled through the continuous or temporary presence of headquarters delegates in the respective subsidiary (P8).[101] As another human resource-related measure, Company C has planned to transfer its assessment center to the subsidiaries in order to ensure that the same employment criteria are used worldwide (P7). Aiming at standardization rather than leaving room for local adaptation, this is also a global (rather than an international) characteristic. Finally, personnel exchange or combination is being discussed – not in the project sense, i.e. a subsidiary in Asia does the detail engineering and headquarters sends in a lead engineer for control purposes, but

---

[100] Global networking includes resource management (i.e. optimization of capacity utilization within the group), development of operation centers and global engineering (i.e. harmonization of IT tools, procedures, personnel development, etc.) as well as support of strategic plans (i.e. definition of centers of competence, internationalization strategies, etc.).
[101] A few years ago Company C decided that for control purposes it preferred to have (close to) fully-owned subsidiaries only. The challenge now is to establish or ensure joint business model principles (P7).

within the line organization. A highly qualified Asian engineer could then be chosen as head of electrical engineering at headquarters level or vice versa (P7). Such measures would contribute to worldwide learning and integration and therefore reflect **transnational tendencies**. Up to now, however, knowledge sharing is mainly project-based and one-way – from headquarters to the subsidiaries (P7, P8). According to one interviewee, Company C should continue to develop particular subsidiaries in Europe and South America for smaller processes in order to decrease the workload of the engineering center in Asia (P8). This, too, is primarily a global (rather than an international) feature: Although knowledge is transferred to overseas units, the goal is not to decentralize competencies but to enable subsidiaries to implement headquarters' strategies.

With respect to the **regional EPC business** Company C clearly has a **multinational** strategic orientation. Subsidiaries are regarded as nationally self-sufficient and it is up to them to define and implement strategies for their regional market. As decentralized 'EPC units without proper technology' they have full profit and loss responsibility and – unless they really needed help – headquarters does not interfere with their local activities (P7, P9). That subsidiaries receive clearly defined work packages from headquarters is part of their business model. Most subsidiaries, however, would survive if they no longer had work to do for the centrally coordinated technology business. With either type of business it is difficult for subsidiaries to realize substantial growth. Quantum leaps may only be achieved by engaging in the global EPC business P10).

The declared goal for the **new business model** – which includes the global EPC business and global networking – is to arrive at the **transnational** model (P9).[102] In contrast to the international model, core competencies need not be centralized, it is just important to know where they are located. Rather than transferring knowledge from headquarters to subsidiaries, the global EPC business is about using the knowledge developed within individual units. The goal is to leverage local competencies such as the execution expertise for a certain type of plant or the project development expertise for a particular geographic market (P9). A roadmap was developed to show competence centers based on replication effects (rather than technology licensing) (P9).[103] The dispersed, interdependent and specialized

---

[102] The global EPC business is regarded as part of a new business model rather than a third strategic pillar because it incorporates – or amplifies – the regional EPC business. Subsidiaries will continue to pursue local market opportunities, but the goal is to enhance the linkages between them.
[103] It is recognized that a particular expertise may also be concentrated at headquarters level (P9).

configuration of capabilities is a distinct characteristic of the transnational company. National units make differentiated contributions to integrated worldwide operations. The headquarters-based Global Coordination Center aims at identifying and leveraging the respective competencies (P9), which is why the aspired role of the center is stronger than implied in Bartlett and Ghoshal's integrated network.[104] Headquarters takes a leading role in bringing subsidiaries together, allocating work packages and defining interfaces (P9). It also remains the core in terms of developing and protecting technology know-how (P10). Operational knowledge, on the other hand, is ideally developed jointly and shared worldwide. The expansion of the global EPC business is thus accompanied by a systematic approach to personnel development. The goal is to bring the best people of the group together rather than maintaining country-specific support programs (P9).

Important indicators of Company C's strategic orientation had already been collected in an explorative interview with the Head of Corporate Development of the conglomerate's relevant business segment. Historically, a strong parent company accepted orders (LSTK) and centrally executed projects. Subsequently, regional units were developed via greenfield investments or acquisitions in order to support headquarters and to serve the local market. Today, technology and process know-how are still bundled in the core unit. In the technology business headquarters deploys project managers internationally and provides global standards for efficiency purposes. Know-how is being transferred from headquarters to subsidiaries to promote worldwide learning. Company C's goal, however, is to arrive at a network organization with a multitude of small centers – or what the interviewee refers to as a 'polycentric system'. In this respect it is important that the necessary structures for implementation have been and are being created.[105] Developing regional engineering competence is important for responding to local particularities. In combination with global (and international) elements this feature of the multinational model becomes a characteristic of the transnational organization. The explorative interview revealed that top management is convinced of – and dedicated to – the network company both at the conglomerate and the divisional (i.e. Company C's) level.

In order not to let the assessment of the propositions get too fragmented it is necessary to reconcile the above findings and arrive at an **overall strategic**

---

[104] The second organizational measure taken by Company C concerns the introduction of a global steering committee. The latter meets every six to eight weeks to decide on projects, resource allocation, marketing approach and other strategic issues (P9).
[105] Including the definition of standard engineering procedures and detailed lists, i.e. exact definitions of what is to be passed on from basic to detail engineering.

orientation for Company C. In summary, Company C has significant global and multinational, as well as select international characteristics. Combining global competitiveness with multinational flexibility and worldwide learning is defined as the key strategic capability of the transnational company. When classifying Company C as a transnational company, this is currently the result of a sum-of-the-parts evaluation of its distinct project approaches. According to the interviewees, however, Company C has the explicit goal of becoming an integrated network, albeit it with a notably more dominant center than stipulated in Bartlett and Ghoshal's typology. Given the relative importance of the technology business, global elements already outweigh multinational ones today. Company C's strategic orientation is therefore summarized as **transnational with global preponderance**.

6.7.2 Intersubsidiary Relationships

6.7.2.1 Competition

Analogous to the assessment of Company C's strategic orientation, intersubsidiary relationships initially need to be described separately for the technology business, regional EPC business and global EPC business (or rather the new business model).

In the **technology business** there is hardly any competition between subsidiaries. Competition in the acquisition phase is restricted through pre-defined regional sales responsibilities, and in the execution phase headquarters decides on where engineering works are carried out based on a number of criteria: free capacity, size of the project, experience, and secondary factors such as (English) language skills (P8). There are also competence clusters according to the type of plant. Tensions do arise in that a South American subsidiary, for example, complains that the majority of engineering works are given to an Asian subsidiary, although the latter is already fully loaded. These sensitivities are understandable since subsidiaries are managed as profit centers. But certain smaller subsidiaries simply do not have the expertise (or the capacity) to complete the full detail engineering for highly complex projects (P8). The goal certainly is to make these subsidiaries competitive, but currently they are not on a par yet (P8). Product divisions prefer to rely on the long-standing and proven cooperation with the organization in Asia (P8). Intersubsidiary competition for charters may become an issue as new engineering centers are being added and existing ones upgraded. A recent preview of resources confirmed that divisions tend to choose Asia as execution center without considering alternative subsidiaries in Europe, North Africa or South America. Given the capacity constraints in Asia, divisions were urged to reconsider and restate their demand. The idea is that headquarters, i.e. the Global Coordination Center, would then assign work packages to subsidiaries based on the divisions' specifications (P9). Such resource management is part of the global networking initiative. To sum up, Company C's technology business is currently characterized by very **low headquarters-led competition** and **no subsidiary-led competition.**

The **regional EPC business** was not explicitly discussed with respect to intersubsidiary competition. Given that each unit focuses on its local market, however, interfaces are basically non-existent. All indications in the interviews suggest that there is **no headquarters-led competition** and **no subsidiary-led competition**. Interviewees did not describe any incidents where multiple subsidiaries were interested in the same business opportunity.

By definition, the aforementioned interfaces are created – and managed – through the **global EPC business**, where intersubsidiary competition is much more likely to occur. Constructive competition for charters is even desired (P9, P10). There is an example of a customer inquiry for a basic engineering package which headquarters was unable to fulfill with the given resources (P9, P10). After having analyzed the request, headquarters sent it out to all subsidiaries so that they could apply internally. Lastly there were two strong candidates – Australia and Africa – which left headquarters facing a dilemma. Given that this was the first time such an 'internal tender' was held, headquarters did not wish to lose either subsidiary. The decision for Australia was taken in coordination with both candidates, yet it did leave Africa displeased despite the use of clearly defined criteria (P9). As the interviewee states, being the referee in such a process is a difficult role to play. But allocating work packages to subsidiaries based on their capacity, competence, etc. is really how it should be. For competitive reasons, much of the engineering was eventually even completed by the Asian subsidiary, with select support by its Australian peers (P10). Although this example may not be completely typical of the global EPC business scheme, it does reflect the opportunities inherent in considering multiple subsidiaries as service providers.[106] In the global EPC business, intersubsidiary competition is for charters rather than customers, because headquarters is to be notified of all relevant projects and subsidiaries have clearly defined areas of responsibility (P10). Initial examples of the global EPC business show that it involves **moderate headquarters-led competition** but **no subsidiary-led competition.**

---

[106] As suggested previously, such allocation is also expected for technology projects, but currently divisional demands still tend to have a higher priority and enjoy preferential treatment (P9).

For Company C as a whole it can be stated that **headquarters-led competition is low** but on the rise, while **subsidiary-led competition does not exist**. In the technology business headquarters determines which subsidiary to involve in a top-down manner, and in the regional EPC business subsidiaries act independently with focus on their local market. It is in the global EPC business that headquarters encourage subsidiaries to compete for participation in worldwide projects.

6.7.2.2 Cooperation

The assessment of Company C's intersubsidiary cooperation again follows an initial differentiation of project types.

In **technology projects** there is a historical split of work between headquarters and subsidiaries as extended workbenches. The latter are assigned up to 50% of the hours related to internal activity (P7). In large, complex projects detail engineering can no longer be performed in headquarters due to a lack of manpower (P8). It is a well-practiced split of work between headquarters and subsidiaries that basic engineering is performed by headquarters and detail engineering is continued in Asia, South America or the like (P8). The resource issue is becoming increasingly more important for involving subsidiaries than the low-cost issue (P8). As the example of a project in Asia shows, intersubsidiary cooperation in the technology business is limited: Headquarters signed the contract with the customer and engaged several subsidiaries, including two in Asia, more or less as extended workbenches – and not in terms of a pre-defined strategic concept (P7). There was little need for bilateral interaction between subsidiaries.

The same is true for the project that Company C's interviewees chose for illustration purposes. Currently, a **'typical' project** for Company C is a **technology** one, involving headquarters, an engineering center and the plant location. This constellation applies to the engineering and procurement Company C is providing for a fertilizer complex in North Africa (P8). Although the project does not involve intersubsidiary, but only headquarters-subsidiary cooperation, it is discussed in this subsection, because it is important to understand Company C's traditional project business and the related split of work in order to assess – and value – the development of the global EPC business. Given that the project is not regarded as typical in terms of the contract constellation – an aspect which is not relevant for the underlying research issue – the usual steps leading up to contract approval are implied and described for illustration purposes.[107] This 'typical' project is outlined in Figure 19, which again follows the illustration of the project marketing models developed in section 4.3, and the respective legend introduced in Figure 12. In order to include some exemplary elements in the illustration, the legend is merely complemented by a grey circle representing an 'in similar projects possibly involved unit'.

In technology projects – as the name implies – the **acquisition** phase is initially driven by the sales manager of the respective technology division. If the customer is interested in a certain project or approaches Company C with a tender, an offer team or task force is set up, which includes an offer manager execution (ideally the later project manager) and an offer manager technical issues (ideally the later engineering manager). The complexity of the offer phase mainly depends on the novelty of the plant or project (P8).

In case of an ITB the central business development unit channels customer inquiries or the customer is familiar with Company C's organization and knows whom to contact directly (in the respective product division). Inquiries are usually obtained by headquarters, although subsidiaries – such as the one in Asia – do acquire projects and sell plants themselves (P8). Company C's sales organization includes both customer and regional responsibilities, and foreign sales offices (or subsidiaries) attend to their local markets (P8). Headquarters-subsidiary cooperation is determined by the matrix between customer/region and technology. Ultimately, however, profit responsibility lies with the technology division. In terms of project selection, the steering committee takes a bid/no-bid decision in divisional meetings with strong involvement of the respective engineering, procurement and construction managers (P8). The questions asked in this phase are comparable to a **feasibility study** (P8). Subsidiaries may possibly contribute their know-how if a completely new plant is concerned.

---

[107] Also, most projects are LSTK, with the responsibility for construction lying with the provider, not the customer (P8).

259

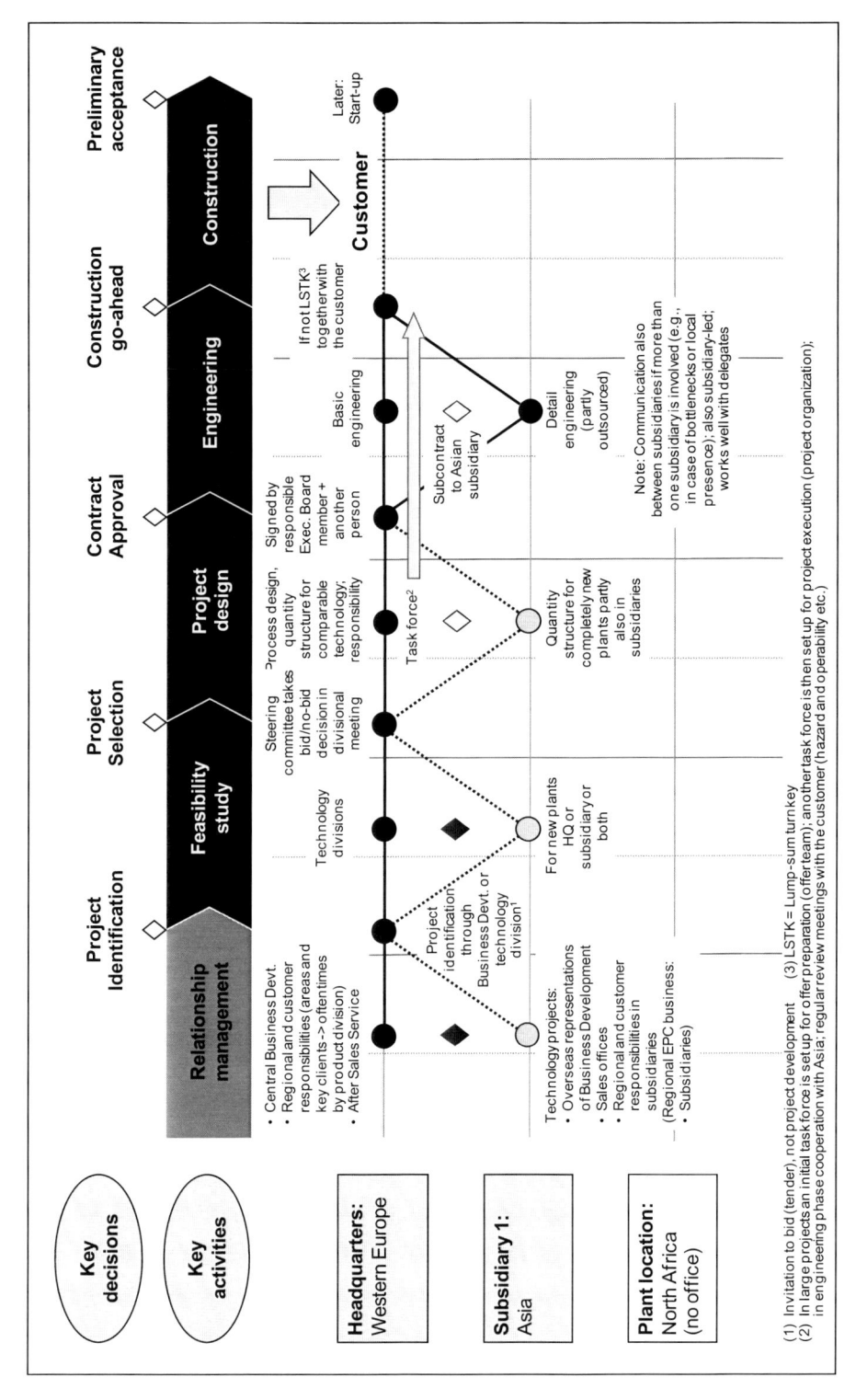

Figure 19: Exemplary Project – Company C (Technology)

Cooperation in **project design** may even result in a split of work: Process engineering is usually laid out by headquarters, whereas the quantity structure – particularly for new plants – may also be drawn up by a subsidiary. Ultimately, however, the sales manager in the respective – headquarters-based – technology division is responsible for ensuring that everything was calculated correctly (P8). The offer manager execution determines both the time schedule and the cooperation with (external) partners and subsidiaries (P8). Since it cannot be guaranteed that those managers preparing the offer will also be involved in project execution, a certain responsibility for completeness and correctness needs to be assumed within the line organization (P8). Consequently, there is a matrix organization between project management and line organization, i.e. the heads of the relevant technology divisions and business segments. Unless the project was acquired by a subsidiary, the contract is also signed by two headquarters representatives: the member of the Executive Board responsible for the respective technology division and whoever interacted most closely with the client (P8). If the customer agrees, subcontracts may then be given to subsidiaries.

The offer for the particular project in North Africa, which was largely based on an existing plant, was prepared by an offer team. When Company C won the bid, a task force was set up to lay out the details of the plant (P8). In the calculation phase it was already determined how the project would be executed, i.e. the project execution concept was outlined in the sense that a significant portion of detail engineering would be performed in Asia.[108] Consequently the calculation included the Asian hourly wage rate as well as travel costs for delegates (P8). Headquarters began with **basic engineering** and soon invited its Asian colleagues to join them as part of the task force. This early cooperation made it easier for the Asians to then take the basic (engineering) package and carry on the **detail engineering** in Asia on their own account (P8). During this phase of a project, regular review meetings with the customer are scheduled in his location of choice (i.e. headquarters, engineering center or location of the plant). The customer tends to be strongly involved in the course of the project – although he need not be since the ultimate responsibility lies with the provider (P8). Given that this particular contract is not LSTK, the go-ahead for construction is jointly given by headquarters and the customer – provided that the latter has made certain advance contributions (obtain official approvals, geological surveys, etc.). In cases where the customer does not choose to do the **construction** himself, Company C engages one or more subcontractors. They need to be

---

[108] Depending on where the respective suppliers (for software, large machinery, etc.) are located, certain elements of detail engineering remain with headquarters. Direct customer contact and the majority of procurement are also managed centrally (P8).

contacted early in order to make sure they are available and to include their unit rates in the calculation of the offer (P8).

With respect to **interunit cooperation**, it is important to note that Company C operates with the same tools (and releases) in headquarters and subsidiaries, and everyone is bound to the same quality manual (P8).[109] These standards, as well as clearly defined processes and expected outputs, ensure continuity and facilitate the transition from basic to detail engineering. A leased line between headquarters and the Asian subsidiary facilitates communication and enables the transfer of large amounts of data. Spatially separated engineers collaborate by means of 3D tools. Obviously these are tools and standards that are currently being used to support the collaboration between headquarters and subsidiaries but that could just as well be employed in the bilateral cooperation between subsidiaries. In most cases, however, headquarters determines and coordinates the split of work – even if more than one subsidiary is involved (P8).[110] For calculation purposes this needs to be done fairly early in the process, i.e. in the offer phase. Company C preferably tries to realize a **vertical split of work**, with subsidiaries being responsible for entire, clearly defined plant components. Cutting horizontally across these components – e.g., in terms of process engineering, plot and arrangement planning, and electrical engineering – would create unnecessary interfaces and require intense communication (P8, P10).

In the project in North Africa parts of detail engineering needed to be outsourced given that the Indian subsidiary was fully loaded (P8). The delegate principle may then be turned around by sending an Asian engineer to the respective execution office. In the example project the latter was an external partner, but cooperation may just as well occur between two of Company C's subsidiaries. The delegate then bridges the gap between two international locations and ensures bilateral communication. This is an example of **subsidiary-led cooperation through knowledge sharing**, since the initiative to send a delegate is taken by the subsidiary itself (albeit upon headquarters' recommendation). The determination of the split of work, however, remains headquarters-led (the main question being who has resources available) (P8). Another example of subsidiary-led cooperation is the

---

[109] The corporate quality manual forms the basis of and is slightly adapted to the specific project (P8).
[110] The interviewee provided the example of a project in Germany where detail engineering was performed partly in India and partly in Russia (P8). More than one subsidiary may be involved to overcome bottlenecks or ensure local presence. In countries where there are no subsidiaries it can occur that Company C opens and maintains a local office for one or more specific projects (P8).

historical relationship between Company C's subsidiaries in Asia and Africa, with Asia serving as extended workbench for Africa (P7).

In technology projects **headquarters-led cooperation is low** and **subsidiary-led cooperation is low** as well.

In the **regional EPC business** subsidiaries cooperate by necessity – both through a split of work and through knowledge sharing. Africa, for example, had to realize that it was losing important resources and know-how. Consequently management decided to give certain engineering packages to Asia and to build up the subsidiary's oil and gas business. Since they could not count on headquarters to help, they approached their sister company in Australia. Such initiatives are the exception, though, which is why in the regional EPC business **subsidiary-led cooperation is low**. Currently **headquarters-led cooperation is basically non-existent**, given that subsidiaries are left almost entirely up to themselves.

Company C's goal, however, is to move from select examples of intersubsidiary cooperation to executing projects in a large network. This is the objective of the global EPC business. The global EPC business takes the regional EPC business a step further by integrating subsidiary activities and – this is important to note – is pursued alongside the technology business. By involving multiple subsidiaries rather than relying on the bilateral cooperation between headquarters and one subsidiary, Company C can make optimal use of capacities and time (P10).[111] The following insights on the objectives and initial accomplishments of the global EPC business as well as their implications for intersubsidiary cooperation were mainly extracted from the interview with the responsible director (P9 unless otherwise noted).

For many years Company C did not manage to really join subsidiary activities together, each of them – as a profit center – having its proper interests and businesses. But, as one interviewee puts it, as long as subsidiaries 'revolve around some sun as disconnected planets' many opportunities will remain unexploited (P10). Although the idea of **leveraging the network of subsidiaries** is not new, the company has only recently begun to systematically expand and organizationally embed the global EPC business. Subsidiaries that can and would like to contribute to the global EPC business are now consolidated and coordinated in a new business segment. The global EPC business group brings subsidiaries together and assigns

---

[111] One interviewee figuratively refers to the global EPC business as 'rotation business', indicating that subsidiaries in different time zones are involved to perform work around the clock (P10).

roles and interfaces. The objective is to assemble the project like a puzzle in order to find the ideal solution in terms of technical expertise, execution expertise, regional know-how and – last but not least – competitiveness. By giving self-contained work packages to subsidiaries around the globe Company C can save both time and costs (P10).[112] Subsidiaries are largely enthusiastic about the global EPC business because it allows them to contribute their expertise to a project as equal partners rather than serving as extended workbenches (P10). The global EPC business not only provides them with an additional source of income, but also constitutes a means of hedging against market fluctuations (P10).

The prerequisite for having multiple subsidiaries work on a single project is that they have a common language, common rules and instructions. The end product needs to be a homogenous one, meaning that from an outside perspective it should not be recognizable where in the world a certain module was completed (P10). The common language is best reflected in an IT platform and the design principles (and tools) for the preparation of technical documents. Both are provided by headquarters and facilitate the **horizontal cooperation between subsidiaries** (P10).[113] In addition, a so-called 'interface manager' is necessary for coordination purposes (most likely a cost controller, procurement manager or the like, not an engineer). Coming from an international team of high potentials, his role is to move between subsidiaries and ensure communication and the adherence to predefined concepts.[114] Intersubsidiary cooperation is not just about a **split of work** but also about **knowledge sharing**, i.e. identifying and leveraging who knows what (P10). In any project the first question should be who has the necessary technological or rather operational know-how. Secondly it needs to be asked who is locally available, i.e. who is able to obtain the optimal local input (components, policies, etc.). Finally it remains to be asked who within Company C has the best resources to complete the bulk work (P10). Consequently, global EPC projects are not only about an ideal use of resources but also about an ideal use of knowledge – factual knowledge, local knowledge and knowledge of how to execute large projects (P10).

---

[112] Based on the awareness that engineers are most efficient (and effective) if employed in their home country, Company C's objective is to 'bring work to the people' and not the other way around (P9, P10).

[113] In its early phase, the global EPC business is about identifying and implementing the minimum amount of standards that are necessary for successful intersubsidiary cooperation. This includes, for example, a harmonization of locally established wordings and processes (P9).

[114] Candidates need to have strong intercultural management skills (P10).

Worldwide cooperation in sales is achieved through regular telephone conferences. Salesmen located in Company C's subsidiaries and offices exchange information on customers, partners, competitors and project-specific issues. **Knowledge sharing** is supported by sharing information of global projects in a database. This database constitutes the basis of the sales conference and, by enhancing transparency, allows headquarters to identify and initiate global EPC projects. Results are consolidated for the Global Steering Committee. Both approaches (telephone conference and database) are currently in the process of being intensified and institutionalized.

A large project in Africa serves as an early **example of the global EPC business** and can be contrasted with the technology project described above. At the time of the interviews the project setup was being planned, which is why the responsibilities suggested in Figure 20 are for illustration purposes only. Although the participating parties had not been finally specified, the project is included as a second 'typical' project of Company C because it reflects the essence of the global EPC business. The graphic representation contrasts local project identification and execution with central selection and structuring.

The customer interface is managed by the African subsidiary, technological expertise comes from one of the headquarters-based product divisions, and detail engineering is eventually completed in South America or Asia. One (basic) engineering package is also worked on in Australia and is likely to be transferred to Asia for cost reasons. This project embodies many aspects that are otherwise being discussed in theory, including the aforementioned harmonization of procedures and IT tools, as well as the development of a corporate identity. It is not fully representative of the aspired form of the global EPC business, however, given that its setup was initiated via **informal relationships** between the subsidiaries in Africa and Australia. Africa identified the project for a key client but had to realize that it was not able to manage a project of this size by itself.

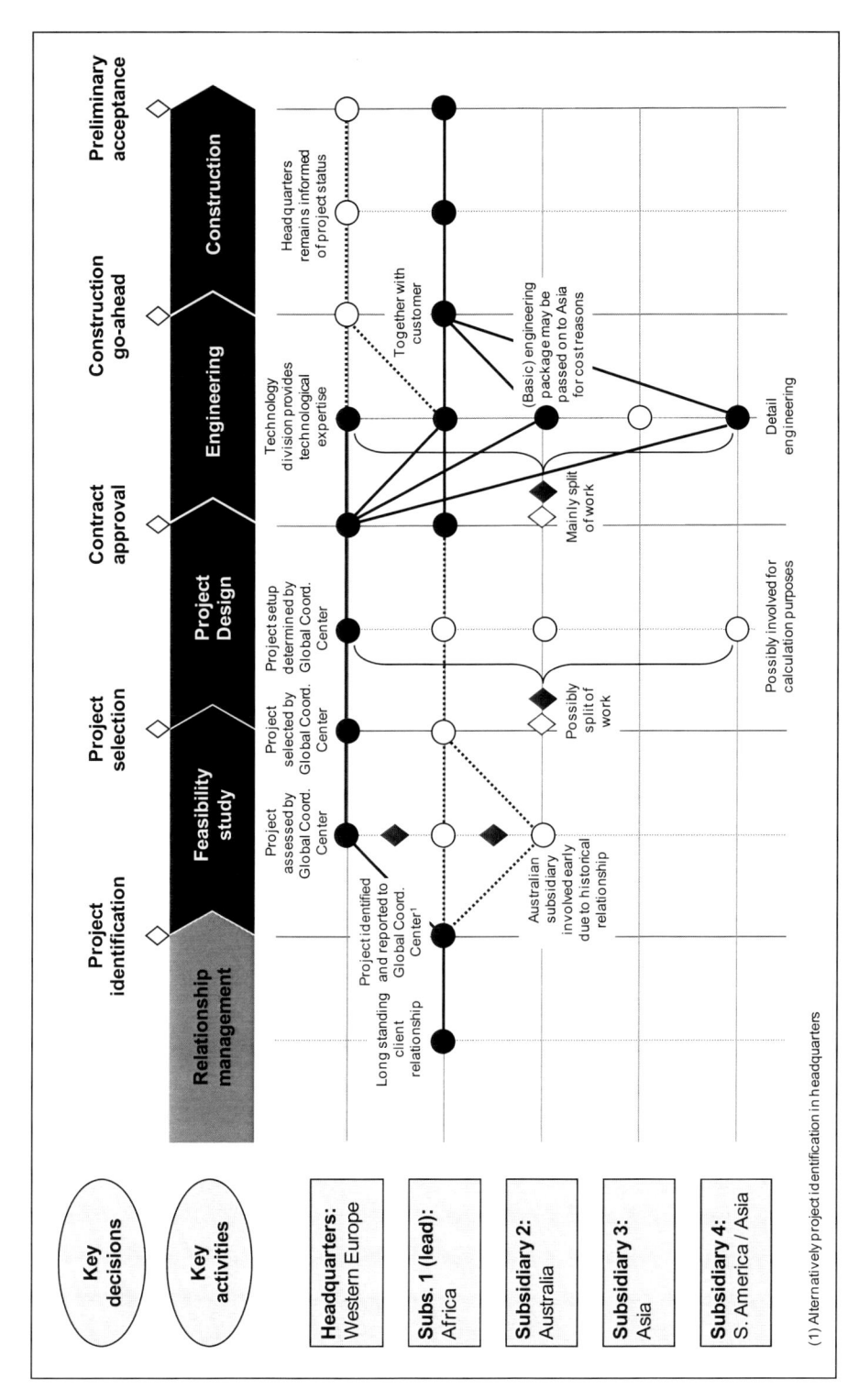

Figure 20: Exemplary Project – Company C (Global EPC Business)

Going forward, headquarters wishes to make sure that intersubsidiary cooperation is no coincidence but managed actively: Subsidiaries report a potential project, whereupon headquarters (i.e. the Global Coordination Center) reviews the reports, identifies the project as relevant to the global EPC business, speaks with the required parties and composes the project organization. Which subsidiary takes the lead in a particular project is ultimately decided by the Global Steering Committee (P7). The chosen unit then develops the acquisition and execution concept together with the Global Coordination Center. The latter is involved in assessing risks and may assist with certain key functions if necessary. For example, it could provide a suitable project manager or engage central procurement if necessary. The operational responsibility, however, lies with the subsidiaries (P7).

The above elaborations suggest that **intersubsidiary cooperation** in the global EPC business is very much **headquarters-led**. At times, a headquarters representative may need to be based on site in order to make sure that subsidiaries communicate. Besides bringing subsidiary expertise together, headquarters may also have to manage cultural aspects. Another key task is to make sure that resources are allocated to the benefit of the company as a whole and not based on the self-interest of a certain product division. A regular **information exchange** between national units is required, which differs from intersubsidiary knowledge sharing in that it has little to do with the content of a specific project. This is in fact part of Company C's global networking initiative, which includes both technology projects and the global EPC business. The global EPC business is primarily about a (project-specific) **split of work**, i.e. distributing and allocating work packages where they are most reasonably accomplished. In line with the transnational model (see subsection 6.7.1) this includes having a certain expertise within the group – such as the existing oil and gas expertise in Australia – and finding ways of leveraging it. The essential question is how this expertise can be brought to subsidiaries that are basically non-existent in revenue terms. Why not, for example, send an Asian to Europe for skill training? Up to now knowledge was mainly transferred by headquarters, i.e. headquarters-based engineers would be delegated to subsidiaries to tell them how things were done and demanded by headquarters. Systematically developing subsidiaries in their capabilities and contributions is also an important prerequisite for achieving an even workload (P9, P10).

Despite headquarters' coordinative role, **intersubsidiary cooperation** in the global EPC business may also be **subsidiary-led**. For example, if the Indian subsidiary identifies an interesting local market opportunity but cannot shoulder the workload, it may approach the Global Coordination Center for the allocation of additional resources (P10). The initiative to cooperate by **splitting work** is thus taken by the subsidiary, even if the resulting set-up is largely influenced by headquarters. In other occasions intersubsidiary cooperation is the result of historically grown relationships, e.g., when the Asian subsidiary works directly for its peer in Africa without interference of the parent company (P10).

As the above discussion has shown, the global EPC business is all about intersubsidiary cooperation. In this early stage, where processes are in the midst of being defined, **headquarters-led cooperation is moderate** and **subsidiary-led cooperation is moderate** as well. In the medium term, the Global Coordination Center wishes to fortify its role in managing global EPC projects while curtailing subsidiary initiatives that bypass central approval.

For the overall assessment of intersubsidiary cooperation in Company C it is recognized that the company is making a very strong effort of enhancing and leveraging its worldwide network of subsidiaries. Management not only has the vision of creating a truly global project organization but has already realized a number of concrete implementation steps – including the definition of new structures and processes. More than most of its competitors, Company C has the declared objective of including multiple subsidiaries in the execution of large projects – not least in order to pool competencies and serve the customer on a 24/7 basis. As a key element of Company C's growth strategy, the global EPC business is being given particular management attention and commitment. Although the approach is still in the set-up phase, it is thus justified to give it more weight in the overall assessment of intersubsidiary relationships than Company C's traditional project business.[115] In summary, it can be stated that in Company C **headquarters-led cooperation is moderate** but on the rise and **subsidiary-led cooperation is moderate** as well. These results can be related to the moderate levels of both types of cooperation in Company B, which differentiates between international projects led and not led by headquarters.

---

[115] Company C's traditional business – which as described above is composed of regional projects executed by a single subsidiary and technology projects executed in a bilateral relationship between headquarters and one subsidiary (P10) – will continue to be an important revenue driver.

6.7.3 Discussion of Intersubsidiary Relationships

6.7.3.1 Review of the Propositions

In section 5.2 it was recognized that the transnational model reflected a somewhat ideal state, which only few companies were coming close to realizing. As argued above, given its dedication to developing and leveraging its global network of subsidiaries, Company C can be seen as one of them – even if the different types of projects pursued by the company require some compromise in terms of classification. For the evaluation of the propositions it further needs to be considered that for the most part of its business Company C has chosen to maintain (or even enhance) the coordinative role of the center, which is why results on intersubsidiary relationships need to be related to a **transnational model with select global features**. Correspondingly, Table 14 contrasts the findings for Company C with the propositions developed in section 5.2 for MNCs with transnational and global strategic orientation. Company C's main features of headquarters-led and subsidiary-led cooperation are best reflected in project acquisition and execution models 2a and 2b (see section 4.3). They are complemented by incidents of headquarters-led competition.

	Types of intersubsidiary relationship	Transnational	Global	Company C	Key explanation
Competition	Headquarters-led	Moderate	Low	Low	Constructive competition desired in global EPC business
	Subsidiary-led	Moderate	None	None	Subsidiary autonomy in local business but no competition
Cooperation	Headquarters-led	High	Low	Moderate	Cooperation as a key element of global EPC business
	Subsidiary-led	High	None	Moderate	Cooperation as a key element of global EPC business

Table 14: Review of Propositions for Company C – Expected and Actual Level of Intersubsidiary Competition and Cooperation

As Table 14 reveals, the results for all four types of intersubsidiary relationship in Company C lie within the range of expectations for the transnational and the global model. **Headquarters-led competition** is found to be low rather than moderate as expected for the transnational company, because it is only selectively encouraged in the global EPC business. Rather than increasing worldwide efficiency, charter competition is used to enhance transparency on dispersed subsidiary capabilities. The example of an internal tender for the completion of engineering works has shown that headquarters may – but need not – include subsidiaries in finding the best solution. As suggested in section 5.2, intersubsidiary competition may be part of a flexible coordination process. In the technology business headquarters traditionally pursues a top-down allocation of responsibilities, but also reserves this right for the global EPC business. Expectations for the global company thus carry more weight than those for the transnational company.

The same is true for **subsidiary-led competition**, which is found to be non-existent rather than moderate as expected for the transnational organization. Given that subsidiaries are largely told what their responsibilities are, their ability to take initiative and compete for projects is limited. This is particularly the case for the technology business, but even in the regional EPC business subsidiaries are more or less bound to their assigned turf. Although one could imagine a situation where two or more subsidiaries are interested in seizing opportunities in untapped markets, this has apparently not occurred in Company C. Subsidiary-led competition in the global EPC business is constrained by the fact that headquarters wants to be in charge of setting up the project. In the global EPC business, subsidiaries explicitly do not compete for who gets to carry out the largest part of the project. Instead, they ask for (centrally coordinated) support from their peers for local projects that exceed their capacity and/or capabilities. Consequently, as the global EPC business gains ground, subsidiary-led competition for resources could become an issue, but this is not part of the research focus.

What is part of the research focus, however, is the indicated **headquarters-led cooperation** between subsidiaries. As argued above, this cooperation is found to be moderate in Company C, given management's dedication to the global EPC business. Headquarters-led cooperation does not reach the high levels expected for transnational companies because technology projects and the regional EPC business are characterized by subsidiary independence, and the global EPC business is not fully established yet. With respect to the global EPC business, not Company C's global features limit headquarters-led cooperation but rather the immaturity of the business.[116] Essential know-how is supposed to come from subsidiaries and a vertical split of project structures is aspired. Subsidiaries are currently in the process of further developing the specialized skills they can contribute to projects via knowledge sharing and a split of work.

---

[116] In global companies cooperation is not expected since essential know-how comes from headquarters and activities tend to be bundled in one location for efficiency reasons (compare to section 5.2).

Due to the expansion of the global EPC business, headquarters-led cooperation in Company C is on the rise, whereas **subsidiary-led cooperation** is intended to be curtailed. The latter is still moderate, given that some subsidiaries take the initiative to cooperate with their peers on an informal basis. In a transnational company, headquarters' role is seen in encouraging such interdependent relationships, which is why subsidiary-led cooperation is expected to be high (compare to section 5.2). In Company C, however, headquarters created a new coordination unit and the related processes to achieve these ends. With workflow planning being a central task, the presence of global elements becomes evident here. Headquarters limits subsidiaries' autonomy by defining their roles and responsibilities in the overall organization and in a specific project.

Given the described ambiguities in Company C's strategic orientation, it is particularly difficult to conclude whether or not the results support the propositions developed in section 5.2. The above analysis shows that the intersubsidiary relationships found in Company C can indeed be explained based on the MNC's strategic orientation. However, it also reveals that a **differentiated explanation** is needed for each category. All in all it can be maintained that the case is **reconcilable with sub-propositions** (a) headquarters-led competition, (b) subsidiary-led competition, (c) headquarters-led cooperation and (d) subsidiary-led cooperation for the transnational (4) in combination with the global (2) model.

6.7.3.2 Additional Influencing Factors

The interviewee most engaged in Company C's global EPC business initiative explicitly supported the proclaimed link between strategic orientation and intersubsidiary relationships (P9). The others at least implicitly agreed to it. Almost all of them suggest additional influencing factors, which fall into the three previously identified categories – (1) Individual characteristics (personality/philosophy), (2) internal characteristics (organization/infrastructure), (3) external characteristics (industry/environment) – and are summarized in Table 15.

In accordance with subsection 6.5.3, management philosophy is considered an individual characteristic since the interviewee explicitly referred to the ambitions of the present CEO. When management is treated collectively – as suggested in the second comment in Table 15 – its philosophy could also be regarded as an internal characteristic. The reverse applies to the relationship network, which is assigned to the 'internal' category because it refers to relationships that are established within the boundaries of the organization. This argumentation is in line with the overall research approach, although one could also put stronger emphasis on the fact that relationships actually connect individuals rather than units.

	Determinants of intersubsidiary relationships	Explanation / comment
Individual	Management philosophy	Present CEO pushed for realization of 24/7 concept (explorative interview)
		Level of subsidiary independence has been changing with firm management (P9)
Internal	Relationship network	Network important for analyzing and aligning business models within the company; worldwide company conference held once a year, which allows top managers to get to know each other and facilitates personal communication (P7)
		Personal contacts are oftentimes more effective than following rigid organizational structures; but also difficult if relationships are too informal (P9)
	Subsidiary size and (lack of) competence	Subsidiaries may be unable to compete for project participation if a certain volume and technical expertise is required; the same is true for English language skills (P8)
		Competition may also be constrained by historically grown cooperation patterns (P8)
	Organizational responsibilities	Competition in the acquisition phase is restricted through pre-defined regional sales responsibilities (P8)
External	Global market	Global competitiveness is only possible through cost reduction; globalization requires international presence (explorative interview). Both elements impact project structures
	Resource availability	Intersubsidiary relationships may be impacted by the access to engineers (explorative interview)
	Customer requirements	The customer has an influence on the units involved in a project by allowing or restricting that subcontracts are given to subsidiaries, or – vice versa – demanding a certain amount of local content, particularly in the form of supplies and construction services (P8)

Table 15: Additional Influencing Factors for Intersubsidiary Competition and Cooperation – Company C

6.7.3.3 Developments and Their Managerial Implications

In contrast to Companies A and B, which are both subject to an acquisition, Company C is largely promoting change on its own initiative. Its dedication to the global EPC business as a new pillar of its business model reflects a very progressive, forward-looking stance. Company C has realized that seizing business opportunities beyond the traditional technology business also requires a new strategic orientation. As outlined below, the developments related to the global EPC business can be viewed from different angles: (a) from a corporate perspective as part of a strategic trajectory, (b) from a subsidiary perspective as an enhancement of responsibilities, and (c) from a headquarters perspective in terms of implementing organizational change.

(a) In technology projects the operations center – i.e. project management, basic engineering and procurement – is headquarters-based. Individual work packages are given to subsidiaries, but the latter cannot live off of their role as extended workbenches. They always had to take the initiative and pursue local business opportunities, oftentimes resulting in the proportion of proprietary business significantly exceeding that of headquarters-assigned tasks – in terms of hours, not volume that is (P9). The logical sequence is that first subsidiaries serve as extended workbenches for the technology business, second they operate self-sufficiently as a contractor in their own market and third they 'export' or implement their acquired competencies internationally. The first two steps have a long history in Company C, so that now the company aims at securing large projects in untapped geographical markets by **joining subsidiary competencies** (P9).[117] The chosen growth path may be contrasted with two strategic alternatives: (1) Further increasing market share in product divisions by systematically upgrading existing technologies, which is difficult to achieve given the already high levels and (2) expanding the product portfolio by acquiring and developing new technologies, which is costly and non-trivial given that Company C already has a substantial coverage of technological growth areas. Consequently, Company C decided to grow through competencies and experience rather than technology. The declared goal is to enhance worldwide coverage in the global EPC business by bridging the gap between subsidiaries and optimizing the utilization of resources (P9).

(b) As illustrated above, in Company C subsidiaries have always been involved in large projects, basically serving as extended workbenches for engineering works. What is novel is that subsidiaries cooperate in the global EPC business based on a pre-defined strategic concept (P7). These developments are not least a response to increasing customer demand for local competence. In the future it will thus be

---

[117] In the past, subsidiary roles somewhat oscillated between extended workbench and independent contractor, depending on the prevailing management philosophy. But currently the tenor clearly is to give subsidiaries full responsibility for their local business (P9).

increasingly important to employ **vertical cuts**, i.e. subsidiaries assuming responsibility for individual parts or components of a plant (P7). Subsidiaries have distinct technical – not to be confused with technological – competencies, such as engineering, procurement, construction management. Ideally Company C can **mix and match these competencies** as appropriate for a given project, while being considerate of local particularities (P7). Subsidiaries appreciate the global EPC business effort, because they feel that their competencies and initiatives are being valued. Headquarters needs to take a coordinative role in this process, but experience has shown that 'dictating' subsidiaries what to do is not the way to success. As far as the global EPC business is concerned, subsidiaries need to be willing to contribute within the partnership (P9).

(c) From a headquarters perspective, promoting systematic intersubsidiary cooperation requires the establishment of corresponding structures and processes – and, most importantly, top management commitment. As one interviewee puts it, it is necessary to have a visionary and implementer to promote organizational change (P9). Company C has a clear vision of where they are heading in terms of the global EPC business, and management has already realized concrete **implementation steps**. The latter include anchoring the extended business model in the organization by setting up specific units/divisions and assigning responsibilities (P8). Company C is currently in the process of realigning its entire personnel development to this global model (P7).[118] Further organizational developments may be necessary, e.g., tackling the question of how to cover the European market if Company C has no engineering center there but the customer demands some form of local presence (P9). The expansion of the global EPC business may also require Company C to modify its reporting structures so that subsidiaries fall within the remits of the desired units. It will be difficult to fully eliminate conflicts given that subsidiaries participate in both the technology and the (global) EPC business. Company C will also have to define (budget) responsibilities of corporate functions versus business segments (P9).

Independent of the global EPC business, Company C aims at increasing cooperation between headquarters and subsidiaries by moving beyond the mere project focus. It is worth considering **vertical forms of cooperation** in Company C for two reasons: First, creating a more cooperative atmosphere may also have an impact on subsidiary behavior, and second, the employed modes of cooperation may possibly be transferred to the horizontal relationship between subsidiaries. Specifically,

---

[118] The term 'global' is not used in Bartlett and Ghoshal's sense here but rather colloquially as suggested by the interviewee.

Company C wishes to enhance transparency on employee qualifications within the line organization, i.e. between headquarters and subsidiaries, and to promote the exchange of best practices. Select employees from headquarters and subsidiaries cooperate on organizational projects such as benchmarking and optimizing quality management systems, business processes and IT tools (P7). This form of cooperation enhances mutual learning and contributes to lifting employees onto the same qualification levels. Headquarters may still like to believe that they are the only ones capable of performing certain tasks but this is no longer the case. Subsidiaries have professional and successful business models of their own, which are worth to be looked into by headquarters (P7) – and possibly exchanged among peers.

A main conclusion from the case study on Company C is that plant engineering companies can exploit market potential and hedge market risks by pursuing different project approaches in parallel. However, one needs to be aware that resource management then becomes increasingly complex. Even more than the previous case study on Company B, the above example has revealed how intersubsidiary relationships vary with the type of project (technology versus regional and global EPC business).

The case study further shows that there are companies that are well on the way of becoming a transnational company. At the same time it acknowledges that truly transnational companies are difficult to find in practice (compare to section 5.2). Although Company C – as well as most of its competitors – intuitively regard the integrated network as the ideal configuration, headquarters is still hesitant to loosen the reins. On the other hand, it may need to be recognized that the (large-scale) project business simply requires a certain degree of central coordination and that intersubsidiary cooperation will mainly be headquarters-led.

6.8 Empirical Findings on Company D

Company D is the engineering division of a Western European corporation. As a leading technology partner it is mainly dedicated to the planning, project development and construction of turnkey industrial plants. Its focus lies on plants for the production of hydrogen, oxygen and olefin as well as plants for natural gas treatment. Company D supports its parent company with the provision of plants for its core business, but is also directly and actively engaged in the market via its central product divisions and subsidiaries. The company is divided into five product divisions plus a number of functional departments such as engineering, research and development, contract management and procurement. It has fourteen subsidiaries (or execution centers) in Western Europe, the United States, India, China and Saudi Arabia, as well as a good half-dozen sales representatives, mainly in third countries. Company D's parent company has recently completed the acquisition of a key competitor; the impact on the engineering business is negligible, however.

6.8.1 Strategic Orientation

According to one interviewee, strategic orientation in Company D differs **by product line**: Some product lines are very centralized (corresponding to the global model), others only exist in subsidiaries (following the multinational model) and again others have a worldwide presence and are managed as an integrated network or a coordinated federation (P12). Since such an approach would even exceed the differentiated analysis of project types undertaken for Company C, a strong effort is made to arrive at an overall classification. Following this rationale, Company D's strategic orientation combines **elements of the multinational, international and global models**. In summary, it comes closest to the transnational model – of which it also has some distinct characteristics. The respective features are described below.

With respect to the **multinational** model, there are several reasons for Company D to build and maintain a strong local presence – particularly when supporting its parent company's sales activities in strategic growth markets such as the United States, India and China. Having headquarters export a turnkey plant is not reasonable (or feasible) due to tariffs, taxes, exchange rates, man-hour rates and capacity limitations. Local units need to have profound technical skills because travel costs would skyrocket if a headquarters-based expert would have to be called in every time. Last but not least, customer proximity is very important (P13). Plant engineering companies typically have few, but very large customers, which is why the locations where Company D chooses to found and develop subsidiaries depends on where these customers are – and lastly where the business is (P13).

An example of subsidiaries being nationally self-sufficient and pursuing local opportunities is that the subsidiary in China manufactures certain types of plants completely independently (P13). Interestingly, from a subsidiary perspective independence is thought to be relatively high as long as performance expectations are met. Each subsidiary tries to conduct its own business and has its specific task, even if the product is the same (P12). Headquarters, on the other hand, finds it has rather tight control of subsidiaries. Despite their independence they need to be fully integrated so that they know where to procure what at the best price or who has spare engineering capacities (P13).[119] Headquarters provides the rules and infrastructure, on the basis of which subsidiaries can act independently. It is their responsibility to ask for central support as necessary (P13). On a project-specific basis, however, a split of work may be imposed (and controlled) by headquarters, which argues in favor of a more centralized model.

International characteristics in Company D are existent but limited, given that unilateral knowledge transfer is explicitly not considered a key element (P13). In Company D 90% of know-how is said to be located at headquarters. For fear of losing this know-how, headquarters does not simply transfer it to subsidiaries but sells licenses (P13).[120] Arguing in favor of decentralized competencies, the so-called 'Global Business Manager' is (or should be) located where the respective product know-how is (P13).[121]

In line with the **global** model, all necessary standards in Company D – including plant safety – are defined and controlled by headquarters (P13). The (internal or external) customer should know what to expect no matter which subsidiary delivers the device (P12). The so-called 'management system' incorporates all procedures – i.e. which documents need to be received, edited and passed on in a given timeframe – and is rolled out to the subsidiaries. Besides following the same procedures, subsidiaries need to have the same tools such as engineering and administration software. In order to determine project yields, common cost control and, consequently, similar organization structures (e.g., for overhead allocation) are necessary. Headquarters basically has to pretend as if subsidiaries were fully integrated – and only situated in different locations (P13). Having locally remote units work with the same systems is not always easy given the different educational (and cultural) backgrounds (P13).

Further **standardizations**, including those related to computer systems, are promoted by the so-called 'Global Business Functions' (P12). Aiming at coordination rather than centralization, the latter may be regarded as an element of the transnational model. However, procedures and tools do constitute central guidelines rather than joint developments. **Central coordination** further extends to capacity

---

[119] This is an example of perception gaps between headquarters subsidiaries as suggested, for example, by Schmid/Daniel 2007; 2009.
[120] There are incidents of more informal know-how transfer, e.g., to India (P12).
[121] See the remainder of this subsection for an introduction to Global Business Functions and their managers.

management, e.g., between the two main furnace-producing subsidiaries. Global capacity planning for engineering is currently being rolled out; realizing even workloads is not only beneficial to the allocation of overhead (P13). Last but not least, decision making is relatively centralized if two units are unable to come to an agreement. The responsible board members mediate in cases of conflict (P13).

Beyond the combination of multinational, international and global elements, Company D shows incomplete characteristics of Bartlett and Ghoshal's **transnational** organization. Subsidiaries make differentiated contributions to integrated worldwide (project) operations, and the configuration of assets and capabilities is dispersed and specialized yet not necessarily interdependent. Differentiated subsidiary roles and the introduction of the Global Business Functions – which are meant to enhance coordination and interdependence – are discussed below. Finally it is worth noting that developing knowledge jointly also belongs to the goals of a learning organization such as Company D (P13).

Differentiated subsidiary roles are a characteristic of the transnational company. In Company D all subsidiaries have a proper self-understanding and try to position themselves based on technology, price or other competencies. Subsidiaries that have their own product, i.e. one that headquarters does not have, also have their own sales and project management activities. The German furnace-producing subsidiary, for example, allocates around 50% of its capacity to headquarters-led projects. China also executes local projects independently, whereas India is used almost exclusively as extended workbench. The intensity of headquarters control also varies by subsidiary: successful, i.e. profitable subsidiaries have much greater freedom (P12). While some subsidiaries have always been dependent on headquarters, others have historically enjoyed a high level of independence (P13).

Differences between acquired and organically grown subsidiaries are only seen by a headquarters representative – mainly for cultural reasons (P13). According to the subsidiary-level interviewee some subsidiaries differ from the majority given their specific product or manufacturing focus, and others set themselves apart through the role they fulfill within the MNC. The subsidiary in Saudi Arabia, for example, is engaged in local projects only, and the subsidiary in India is slowly outgrowing its role as extended workbench (P12).

Company D is currently undergoing considerable organizational change, with the recently established **Global Business Functions** facilitating central coordination. Strong growth – including many new subsidiaries – had left structures increasingly unclear. More and more subsidiaries were entrusted with tasks without knowing how everything would be organized (P12). The introduction of Global Business Functions is meant to bring some order into a network that was not designed systematically but grown organically. Just to give an example, air-separation plants are being engineered, procured and constructed in seven different subsidiaries: two in Germany and China, respectively, one in India, one in Great Britain and one in the United States (P12). These locations are of different size and have their own history, competencies and specializations. How they cooperate, however, was more or less unorganized (P12). The same is true for hydrogen plants and furnaces – both are manufactured in multiple locations. Although subsidiaries did let others know of their undertakings and exchanged knowledge on a technological level, no one was really in authority. In order to enhance efficiency, one person for each product (or region) was needed to bring activities together (P12).

As suggested above, the goal is to set **global standards** for engineering, process and environmental safety, plant components, document management, etc., and to make local structures (such as a subsidiary's archive) consistent, connectable and exchangeable. Global Business Functions are organized by product or task and are supposed to harmonize the different approaches as much as possible (P12). The manager or leader of these Global Business Functions need not be headquarters-based, although this is currently the case for all main product lines. There are products (or plants) that are only manufactured in one international location, so that the Global Business Manager then comes from this subsidiary (P13). Being responsible for the performance of his product, the Global Business Manager oversees the complete product lifecycle, from research and development, to sales, execution and after-sales service (P13). In order to optimize performance across locations he needs to ensure that everyone has the same communication channels and devices (P13).

Company D attempts to integrate subsidiary activities via these Global Business Functions. It is indeed more appropriate to speak of **integration** rather than centralization, since the Board of Directors does not necessarily plan to tighten the reins over entire subsidiaries. Such centralization would be difficult to achieve given that subsidiaries – as centers of competence – have product portfolios and also their own technologies (P12).[122] Headquarters did find, however, that particularly the smaller subsidiaries needed a geographically and technically close leadership, and facilitated more direct control via the introduction of Global Business Functions (P12).

---

[122] Most of Company D's subsidiaries indeed have multiple product lines (P12).

The **Global Business Manager** is responsible for ensuring that the same methods and procedures are employed on a worldwide basis – not as superior but as coordinator (P13). In order to preserve subsidiary commitment and autonomy, mediation is more important than giving top-down orders. Global Business Managers are meant to support subsidiaries in enhancing their (local) performance (P13). Although the goal is to coordinate activities without depriving subsidiaries of their profit responsibility and entrepreneurship, the optimum result needs to be with the project – and eventually with the company as a whole (P13). Headquarters summons an annual business strategy meeting to define subsidiary targets, which are then reviewed at the end of the year. Performance is linked to a bonus system that consequently rewards both subsidiary and corporate results (P13).

For subsidiaries these new structures mean that they have (at least) two reporting lines: one to the responsible member of the Board of Directors and one to the Global Business Manager (for the respective product and/or function). If subsidiaries have multiple product lines – such as the one in Germany – these reporting lines can become increasingly complex (P12).[123]

From a subsidiary perspective the concept does not seem completely clear yet, given that ultimately P&L responsibility – including capacity management – remains with the subsidiaries (P12). Historically, informal cooperation took place, which is obviously easier (and more promising) if the respective subsidiary is in the same location as headquarters. Given Company D's global presence, it needs to be acknowledged that worldwide interdependencies require a more formal approach to coordination. Currently, however, one problem seems to be that the Global Business Managers hardly communicate with each other and – given the lack of defined structures – the subsidiary finds itself facilitating such cooperation (P12). The interviewee refers to the example of a hydrogen plant, which involves components from multiple product lines (P12).

The interviews reveal that from a subsidiary perspective the introduction of Global Business Functions is seen somewhat critically. They are thought to bring back much control to headquarters (P12) rather than being perceived as a means of mediation (P13). Subsidiaries feel that they lose some of their independence when having to report to an interface manager. At the same time it is headquarters' support that enables subsidiaries to act upon their independence.

---

[123] The German subsidiary generates revenues with two main product divisions and on the free market (P12).

The above elaborations are best integrated by one interviewee himself, who proposes a fifth model besides the four types of MNC differentiated by Bartlett and Ghoshal – one which he believes is the 'real' model for large-scale plant engineering companies. He explains that his organization is very centralized concerning specific products but that subsidiaries interact as well. The latter make individual contributions to worldwide (project) operations, but headquarters executes central control and compiles a summary of costs (P13). The two interviewees at headquarters level refer to their proposed model as being 'transnational-global'. They find that in Bartlett and Ghoshal's transnational company the role of the center is too weak. It may also be the case that some subsidiaries are stronger than others (P13).

In accordance with Company C, Company D's strategic orientation is summarized as being **transnational with global preponderance**. Both companies are making strong efforts to arrive at an integrated network – albeit with a continuously strong center. Although several transnational features have not been brought to perfection yet, in both cases the concrete implementation steps need to be recognized. In this respect, what the global EPC business is for Company C, the Global Business Functions are for Company D.

For the subsequent analysis of intersubsidiary relationships it is important to note that although one headquarters-level interviewee prefers to speak of 'sister company' rather than subsidiary (P11), central product divisions are differentiated from decentral subsidiary activities. The identified strategic orientation underlines that headquarters does not perceive itself on an equal level with subsidiaries but does assume a leading role in large-scale projects.[124] This conclusion is explicitly supported by another interviewee – at least for the time being (P13). In ten to fifteen years' time – cycles in plant engineering are longer than in other industries – the situation may be a different one. Headquarters dominance can be expected to decrease as know-how distribution becomes more balanced among subsidiaries. The more independently subsidiaries can act based on the same systems etc., the more homogeneous knowledge structures will become.

---

[124] This leading role is illustrated in the example project presented in the next subsection.

6.8.2 Intersubsidiary Relationships

6.8.2.1 Competition

In Company D intersubsidiary competition is only an issue with respect to the planning and construction of furnaces (P11, P12). The furnace-producing subsidiaries have a special status because they provide a particular component to the plants that are designed and built by the product lines. Historically, there have been two units involved in this technology – a German and a U.S. subsidiary.[125] Responsibilities are assigned based on a **geographical split**: North and South America are served by the U.S. subsidiary, whereas Europe and the Middle East belong to the German subsidiary. In case of uncertainty (or unassigned territory) there are (written) **rules for decision making**: The first decision criterion is the country of construction; the second criterion is the country of order or the end customer. There are examples of projects involving the subsidiary that had an established relationship with the customer, although the plant was built in the other subsidiary's territory. The example project discussed below shows that the decision for one subsidiary or another need not always follow these rules. India does not normally belong to the classical U.S. market, but the U.S. subsidiary was involved in the predecessor project by chance. Competition was eliminated by simply replicating the proven project constellation (P11). Sometimes projects are handed over from one subsidiary to the other as circumstances change. This decision can either be subsidiary-led – and then marks a case of coopetition – or headquarters-led. In the latter case, the German subsidiary – due to its proximity to headquarters – is more likely to have to sacrifice a project to its U.S. peers than vice versa (P12).

One interviewee admits that the described duplication is not really adequate for a global player. Up to now Company D could afford such an approach, but having two locations manufacture the same product does not seem maintainable in the long run. Merging two firms engaged in the same activities is estimated to generate substantial profits (P11).

The defined regional responsibilities **restrain both headquarters-led and subsidiary-led competition for (external) customers**.[126] It may happen that a multinational customer accidentally, but not intentionally, places a request with both

---

[125] Another 'second degree' subsidiary in the U.S. produces small, standardized reformers – a field in which the German subsidiary is no longer active in.
[126] Or as one interviewee puts it, in principle the two subsidiaries compete with each other, but given their defined markets they currently do not harm each other (P12).

the German and the U.S. subsidiary. Company D, however, has been making a strong effort to enhance transparency on subsidiaries' territories. According to the managing director of the German subsidiary, up to now, they had never made the mistake that a customer received two offers.[127] Coordination takes place based upon goodwill rather than clearly defined structures (P12).

On an internal level, however, the same managing director does perceive a certain degree of competition between the German and the U.S. subsidiary – not least because the current dollar exchange rate treats his American peers favorably. These frictions are confirmed by headquarters (P13). Company D as an internal customer is not allowed to solicit competing bids from within the group, but although the product divisions know the assigned territories, they do not always observe the rules (P12). **Headquarters-led competition for charters** is supported by the fact that product divisions have a substantial database which allows them to compare offers and cost structures.[128] Depending on the underlying technology, parameters may vary significantly among subsidiaries. There have been recent initiatives from both headquarters and subsidiaries to enhance transparency and coordination (P12). Headquarters-led competition for charters could intensify with the introduction of Global Business Functions (compare to subsection 6.8.1), because central managers want to have a stronger say in who supplies the furnace (P12). Being responsible for the overall product – i.e. a specific type of plant – Global Business Managers are interested in procuring components such as furnaces at the lowest cost (P13).

Subsidiary-led competition for charters becomes an issue with respect to a third furnace-producing unit in Italy, which was founded as a licensee of the German subsidiary (P12). Meanwhile the division reports directly to Company D's headquarters and is thus on par with the German subsidiary. The latter can no longer determine which projects go to which location, but faces competition for business opportunities. This intersubsidiary competition would be for customers if it were not suppressed, i.e. converted into charter competition (compare subsection 2.4.1.3 for this rationale). As described above, historically there has been a geographical split between the German and the U.S. subsidiary, with a few 'free' countries where the two would come to an agreement. Given its newly acquired independence, the Italian subsidiary now wants a piece of the pie as well – preferably via access to the

---

[127] An interviewee at headquarters level points out that in the past it has indeed happened that two subsidiaries approached the same customer, which he considers to be fatal (P13).
[128] As suggested in subsections 2.4.1.3 and 2.4.1.4, the boundaries between intersubsidiary competition for charters and customers are somewhat blurred when internal customers are concerned. In both cases competition is settled by an internal decision.

German subsidiary's entire territory. The U.S. subsidiary understandably is not willing to give away any of its regional responsibilities. Italy is supposed to focus on a specific product segment, for which it has been assigned a third of the German subsidiary's territory. The rest is up to negotiation – which does not tend to pose any problems if there is enough work to do (P12). In general one can say that – with few exceptions – subsidiaries make a strong effort to solve conflicts of interest bilaterally; they are hesitant to involve the Board of Directors in such matters (P12). The latter is responsible for capacity management, however (P13).

The above illustration reveals that charter competition tends to become an issue when a new player is introduced to the group. The complementary acquisition of a Swiss company engaged in process heating systems resulted in little to no competition with the German subsidiary. But therefore the Swiss and the Italian furnace-producing subsidiaries entered into a conflict, because the Italians were not willing to provide an essential component to their Swiss peer – a component which the Swiss had discontinued to reduce overlaps within the MNC (P12). In a broad sense, **subsidiary-led competition for charters** thus finds its manifestation in a denial of cooperation. Subsidiaries then compete for the use of capacities.

Moving away from pure intersubsidiary relationships, there are observable elements of **competition between profit centers** on headquarters and subsidiary level. The fact that headquarters prefers to speak of its subsidiaries as 'sister companies' illustrates that the issue may also be relevant on an intersubsidiary level (P11). In general, conflicts are bound to arise when one unit provides the service but another unit gets paid for it. The interviewee mentions the example of India requesting headquarters' support in the procurement of a specific device but subsequently denying the corresponding budget transfer (P11). In order to defend their profit center, 'sister companies' may further try to take advantage of customer-requested changes by demanding a higher compensation or deadline extensions from headquarters (P11). Similarly, in the example project discussed below subsidiaries were not particularly cooperative in solving problems but referred to their defined work packages. Arguing that 'a copy is a copy', the U.S. subsidiary was inflexible in terms of including elements that were not part of the predecessor project (P11). Given that all client interaction went through project management (i.e. headquarters), such behavior makes coordination of a large project difficult.

To sum up, in Company D **headquarters-led competition is low** and **subsidiary-led competition is low** as well. Whereas competition for (external) customers is avoided completely, some charter competition is created by both headquarters and subsidiaries. Headquarters signals that it has certain freedom to choose between furnace-providing subsidiaries, and these subsidiaries themselves are confronted with clarifying responsibilities as established structures change. The significance of intersubsidiary competition in Company D needs to be put in perspective since it only concerns one particular type of product (or component).

6.8.2.2 Cooperation

Analogous to the previous three case studies, the example project for Company D is discussed in this subsection on cooperation. Company D contributed several hydrogen-manufacturing units to a very large refinery project for an Indian conglomerate in India. The project constellation – headquarters (in the lead), an engineering center (India) and a subsidiary with a specific technical competence (U.S.) – can be regarded as typical for Company D with respect to large, complex projects. According to one interviewee, in such projects a split of work makes sense (or is even necessary) in order to leverage competencies and minimize costs. In smaller projects headquarters-bound (or local) execution is preferable in order to avoid interface management and achieve short response times (P11). Subsidiaries such as China, Australia and the United States execute small local projects on their own, consulting headquarters only in case of some complex matter.

It needs to be recognized that a 'typical' project for Company D is one that not necessarily involves any intersubsidiary relationships. On the contrary, it is the interaction between headquarters and one or more subsidiaries that differentiates a large from a small or a complex from a simple project. Nevertheless, it is valuable to discuss the example project in this subsection on intersubsidiary cooperation, considering that headquarters often speaks of subsidiaries as 'sister companies' and thus adopts a balanced rather than a hierarchical perspective. Also, the infrastructure provided to facilitate subsidiaries' contribution to centrally coordinated projects may very well support horizontal cooperation between subsidiaries. In Figure 21 the project is illustrated in the style of the project marketing models developed in section 4.3, again based upon the legend introduced in Figure 12. Incidents of true intersubsidiary relationships are subsequently discussed.

285

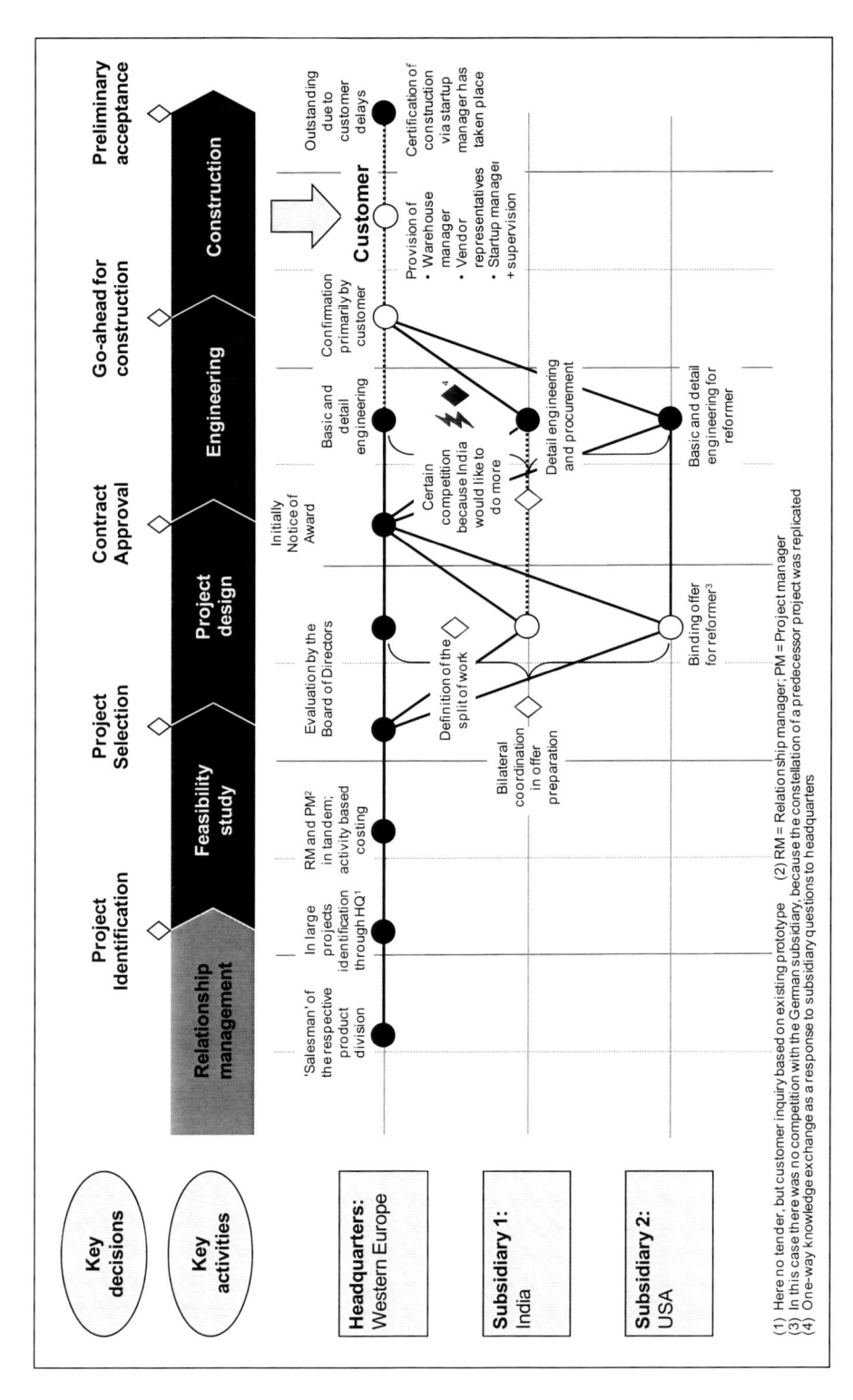

Figure 21: Exemplary Project – Company D

In the example project, the **customer relationship** was managed by the salesman in the respective product division, i.e. hydrogen plants (P11). Sales responsibilities are organized by product division, not key accounts. Therefore, it is not unlikely to occur that one division has an established relationship with a customer, but the latter is directed to another division when inquiring about a different product. In this case there was no tender, given that the customer approached Company D based on a predecessor project. The larger the project, the more important it is to include experienced project managers to provide information and support. This project manager already supports the salesman in the (pre-)acquisition phase in order to define and limit risks (P11).[129] One has the commercial and process know-how, the other execution and practical skills. Both prepare the offer together, although collaboration is not always easy given their diverging interests (P11).[130] As argued above, projects of significant size cannot be covered by subsidiaries with a low capital base, but need to be coordinated by headquarters due to financing, liability and warranty issues (P11). Ultimately all P&Ls are consolidated at group level.

The salesman and the project manager conduct the **feasibility study** together. The latter includes verifying whether the plant is actually deliverable in the ambitious timeframe demanded by the customer, consulting large engineering companies in this respect and developing a new concept for a key component (P11). It is necessary to picture the technical and commercial implications early in the process – i.e. prior to basic engineering – in order to give the customer the requested fixed price. Internal experts are asked to perform a shortcut calculation on the additional effort and activity-based costing is conducted to determine the dimensions of the plant. The rough cost estimate provided by the technical departments together with the activity-based costing constitutes the basis of a serious cost calculation. Additional input comes from cost controlling as well as commercial and construction departments (P11). Prior to the Notice of Award (NoA) Company D only performs so-called 'acquisition engineering'. An NoA is comparable to an LoI and practically marks the beginning of project execution; the customer still needs to clarify commercial details before issuing the official purchase order. If the NoA is found to have the quality of a serious mandate, the project manager will mobilize his team and

---

[129] It seems more adequate to speak of a salesman rather than a relationship manager because client interaction is primarily product-/project-bound.
[130] In the past such collaboration was not promoted, resulting in mutual accusations once the project was supposed to be executed as sold (P11).

begin the basic engineering works.[131] Deferring basic engineering until after the contract has been awarded is necessary in order to economize on resources (P11).

So far, the entire activity seems to have taken place at headquarters. The latter, however, does not assume sole responsibility for such a large project if it intends to involve subsidiaries in the process. A **split of work** between headquarters and subsidiaries already takes place in the offer phase. In the project example, the U.S. subsidiary was asked to provide a cost estimate for the reformer they were going to provide analogous to the predecessor project.[132] The resulting cost estimate is incorporated in the binding offer to the client. In case of renegotiations (e.g., regarding price) the respective subsidiary is consulted directly. Close coordination with subsidiaries is necessary in order to avoid conflicts in subsequent project phases (P11).

Similarly, headquarters defined the split of work with India in the **project design** phase. India agreed to provide a specific engineering package at a certain offer price. Subsidiaries tend to take advantage of such a situation by not offering the lowest possible price and headquarters ultimately has to shoulder the acquisition costs (P11). Such behavior can be seen as the result of each subsidiary having its own P&L. Consequently, headquarters treats subsidiaries as subcontractors in the sense that on the basis of their offer they are fully responsible for their respective package. In case of miscalculation they have to deal with time- and cost-related consequences and possibly carry liquidated damages (P11). Including subsidiaries in the acquisition phase is important for submitting a competitive offer.

In the example project, the split of work followed the structures which had proven advantageous in the predecessor project, not least because they corresponded to subsidiaries' competencies. It would have been a waste of resources not to leverage the existing knowledge and technology. For the same reason it was clear from the beginning that the reformer would be provided by the U.S. subsidiary (P11) (also see subsection on competition). A split of work between headquarters and subsidiaries already takes place in the acquisition phase in that both parties prepare initial estimates and calculations for their contribution to the project. The head of divisional sales together with the head of the respective product division verify the resulting

---

[131] The procedure may be a different one depending on cultural circumstances. The interviewee notes that in collaborating with the Chinese he has never begun a project before the official contract was signed (P11).
[132] Steam reformers are the key component of process technology plants in the chemical and petrochemical industry. They convert methane (and other hydrocarbons in natural gas) into hydrogen and carbon monoxide by reaction with steam over a nickel catalyst.

offer and consult the Board of Directors. The number and intensity of reviews depends on the size of the project. The contract is then signed on the basis of the NoA, which already includes basic elements such as price, delivery period and payment terms.

The majority of **basic engineering** is carried out at headquarters. When approaching the **detail engineering phase** the workload increasingly shifts to India (P11). In general one can say that most of the 'intelligence' comes from headquarters (i.e. activity-based costing, industrial engineering, etc.), whereas the less creative engineering work is completed in India. This is not meant to degrade the Indian subsidiary, but has simply proven most reasonable. Performing standard engineering works at headquarters level would have been much too expensive (P11). Headquarters deposits its basic engineering documents in an online documentation center so that the Indian subsidiary has permanent access to them.[133] In the example project, the Indians updated their model based on this platform, completed detail engineering according to their defined scope of work and initiated procurement. In a **headquarters-led split of work** the Indian subsidiary also carried out select elements of basic engineering. They further asked to be considered with respect to other apparatuses and took the initiative to propose that a certain analysis needed to be performed, which they themselves were incapable of conducting. Although headquarters decided to maintain the originally planned split of work, the latter proved to have some **subsidiary-led elements**.

As far as knowledge sharing is concerned, headquarters has a pronounced interest in enhancing the Indian subsidiary's qualifications – simply because headquarters is too expensive for carrying out certain work steps. Transferring experience and know-how, however, is not accomplished from one day to another. At the same time headquarters is hesitant to give away its process technology know-how, because this is the company's core asset (P11). From a bottom-up perspective, the Indian subsidiary does approach headquarters with select questions on materials, security, or process technology (P11).

When all engineering works were completed, the customer initiated **construction**. Given the enormous size of the project this was a strategically planned undertaking – and, as one interviewee puts it, an exceptional achievement (P11). During construction, Company D provided warehouse managers that took over the materials

---

[133] Exchanging work in progress via the internet is most efficient because subsidiaries can work in a time-delayed manner (P13).

receiving and sent in both internal and external experts to supervise the construction and (pre-)commissioning of key devices. This included a start-up manager who was responsible for the entire plant (P11). Construction has been confirmed to the start-up manager, but the obligatory performance test is still outstanding due to customer delays.[134] The final acceptance will ultimately be signed by headquarters (P11).

As indicated in the introduction to the example project, it is important to note that the described forms of cooperation do not concern the relationship between subsidiaries but between headquarters and subsidiaries.[135] Nevertheless, they illustrate the opportunities and challenges of involving (multiple) subsidiaries in headquarters-led projects and mark some central elements of the large-scale project business.

Direct **intersubsidiary cooperation** is addressed with the managing director of the furnace-producing German subsidiary, who points out that historically such cooperation took place by coincidence. Interaction depended on who knew whom – and on whether this person happened to have time. In some subsidiaries the related structures and processes were more clearly defined than in others (P12). The newly established Global Business Functions are meant to organize such cooperation. A product-related Global Business Manager has to coordinate the activities of all subsidiaries engaged in the respective product – no matter how dispersed they may be. Although the respective Global Business Manager could also be based in one of the subsidiaries, central coordination of intersubsidiary cooperation gives it **headquarters-led elements**. Headquarters not only provides the infrastructure that is necessary for cooperation but also dictates which procedures to use in a split of work (P13). It directs subsidiaries where to go for procurement or construction, although the decision with whom to cooperate is ultimately taken where the project responsibility lies (P13). Promoting networking and know-how transfers is regarded as necessary so that everyone has the same knowledge and tools.[136] Unlike in Company C, where the goal of the global EPC business is to have subsidiaries cooperatively execute projects, for Company D's headquarters intersubsidiary cooperation is not an end in itself.

---

[134] Given the project scope, the customer had set other priorities, but everything was paid for (P11).
[135] Or cooperation may even be completely headquarters-bound, as reflected in the tandem between salesman and project manager (P11).
[136] For example, the U.S. subsidiary must be able to easily contact its peers in China or India to inquire whether the procurement of certain components and/or services is cheaper in these locations. Only locals know the respective contract specifics, delivery periods and quality standards.

Despite the perceived – and previously described – competition between the furnace-producing subsidiaries in Germany and the United States, the responsible managing directors do communicate with each other. In biweekly telephone conferences they exchange information on customer inquiries, review offer lists and plan new business with respect to capacities, customer relationships and subsidiary preferences. Identifying the least costly product for both internal and external customers requires intense cooperation. In an effort **supported by headquarters**, the two subsidiaries are currently planning to set up a project to compare price and cost structures and to determine whether one of the two locations is systematically cheaper – although it was already difficult to align the scope (if not the content) of their supplies (P12). The latter was undertaken in an effort initiated by the German subsidiary's managing director, who at the time was a (headquarters-based) project manager. Meanwhile **cooperation** in this particular case shifted to being mainly **subsidiary-led**. Knowledge sharing is further enhanced by the fact that the two managing directors are members of each others' boards.

On an operational level, **subsidiary-led cooperation through knowledge sharing** has two elements: First, furnace-producing subsidiaries align their activities from a technical point of view in order to find the best solution and to maintain common product standards. Technical cooperation is very close and may include elements such as joint procurement. Second, subsidiaries cooperate in offer preparation to avoid double offers (P12).

In very large projects, such as those requiring multiple heaters, subsidiaries may also cooperate through a split of work (P12). Given the inherent competition between furnace-producing subsidiaries, such mutual support needs to be well organized (P12). **Subsidiary-led cooperation through a split of work** also characterizes the relationship between the furnace-supplying subsidiary and the subsidiary responsible for the design and construction of the remaining plant. Here, an exact definition of the field of activity – both content- and space-wise – is important. Independent of large projects, the German furnace-producing subsidiary has offshored certain engineering works to its Indian colleagues and contributes to know-how transfer through training (P12). It is not uncommon for one subsidiary to serve as extended workbench for another subsidiary (P13).

Although the example project included hardly any elements of intersubsidiary (competition and/or) cooperation, Company D's interviewees did provide some evidence for its existence. **Headquarters-led cooperation is moderate**, with Global Business Managers increasing transparency on subsidiary interfaces. Just because

Global Business Managers have worldwide product responsibility they do not necessarily have to promote intersubsidiary cooperation. This is the difference to Company C's global EPC business. The infrastructure they provide supports it, though. **Subsidiary-led cooperation is moderate** as well. Although furnace-providing subsidiaries enjoy a special status due to their common product, it needs to be acknowledged that they have been making a strong effort of aligning their activities – and that their cooperation outweighs competition. The overall level of subsidiary autonomy allows them to take such initiatives.

6.8.3 Discussion of Intersubsidiary Relationships

6.8.3.1 Review of the Propositions

As derived above, Company D's strategic orientation does not correspond to one specific model but – in analogy to Company C – is best summarized as **'transnational with global preponderance'**. According to the interviewees, their company represents a fifth model – 'transnational-global' (P13) – rather than some intermediate level towards a pure transnational organization. Again, the decision for a strong center has been a deliberate one. Consequently, the empirical findings on intersubsidiary relationships need to be compared to the propositions developed in section 5.2 for MNCs with transnational and global strategic orientation. A summary is included in Table 16, which underlines that also for this last case a clear-cut evaluation is not possible. Company D's main features of headquarters-led and subsidiary-led cooperation are best reflected in project acquisition and execution models 2a and 2b (see section 4.3). Again, select competitive elements are suggestive of a coopetitive model.

Types of intersubsidiary relationship		Transnational	Global	Company D	Key explanation
Competition	Headquarters-led	Moderate	Low	Low	Incidents of competition with respect to a particular product
	Subsidiary-led	Moderate	None	Low	Some competition for product-related responsibilities
Cooperation	Headquarters-led	High	Low	Moderate	Global Business Functions facilitate cooperation
	Subsidiary-led	High	None	Moderate	Cooperation initiated by subsidiaries as necessary

Table 16: Review of Propositions for Company D – Expected and Actual Level of Intersubsidiary Competition and Cooperation

As illustrated by Table 16, the results for Company D deviate one notch from what is expected for the transnational model towards what is expected for the global model (leading to one identical value for Company D and the global model). While **headquarters-led competition** is expected to be moderate in the transnational company, it is found to be low in Company D. Select competitive elements are merely introduced to the relationship between subsidiaries dedicated to a specific product line, i.e. the planning and construction of furnaces. These subsidiaries hold a special position due to the duplication of activities. In contrast to Company C, competition is mainly admitted for efficiency purposes (determining the least costly product) rather than to enhance transparency on subsidiary competencies. Headquarters' goal is not necessarily to find the best solution together with competing subsidiaries. It prefers to be involved only in severe cases of conflict; ideally subsidiaries come to an agreement themselves.

The same autonomy applies to **subsidiary-led competition**, which is also expected to be moderate in the transnational company, but is low in Company D. Again, the one example of such competition is that between furnace-producing subsidiaries in Germany, the U.S., Italy and, potentially, Switzerland. These subsidiaries would actually compete for customers but they themselves realize that they have to come to an agreement on (geographic) responsibilities before approaching a customer. Competition for customers is thus converted into competition for charters. Irrespective of its origin, competition is found to be low in Company D because it applies to a very small set of subsidiaries only. This constellation underlines that in a transnational company the demand for cost efficiency limits duplication.

Headquarters-led cooperation between subsidiaries is moderate in Company D versus high in transnational companies. Historically, headquarters was mainly interested in coordinating subsidiaries involved in centrally managed projects. By providing the necessary systems, tools and procedures the newly established Global Business Functions facilitate cooperation – both through knowledge sharing and a split of work. Most technological know-how, however, still comes from headquarters and few subsidiaries could replace this central know-how. Their specializations and expertise need some more time to develop.

Subsidiary-led cooperation takes place as required. Subsidiaries prefer to interact bilaterally rather than involving headquarters for coordination purposes. Most of the projects Company D is involved in do not require significant intersubsidiary cooperation, because headquarters assumes the leading role. The example of furnace-producing subsidiaries, however, has shown that cooperation becomes an issue when a common product calls for coordination or a subsidiary offshores engineering works to one of its peers in low-cost countries. In general, Company D's subsidiaries are sufficiently independent to take such initiatives.

The fact that Company D's strategic orientation does not match one of Bartlett and Ghoshal's pure types impedes a clear-cut evaluation of the propositions developed in section 5.2. The above analysis has shown, however, that the company's intersubsidiary relationships may very well be explained by elements of its strategic orientation and that they come very close to what is expected for the transnational organization. By proposing a fifth model when being confronted with the suggested link between strategic orientation and intersubsidiary relationships, interviewees implicitly support the proclaimed contingency. Despite the identified deviations, the results for Company D are **reconcilable with sub-propositions** (a) headquarters-led competition, (b) subsidiary-led competition, (c) headquarters-led cooperation and (d) subsidiary-led cooperation for the transnational (4) in combination with the global (2) model. Speaking of a 'support' of the propositions would not be adequate, though.

6.8.3.2 Additional Influencing Factors

Besides recognizing that strategic orientation has an impact on how MNC units interrelate, interviewees in Company D make references to additional influencing factors. These were not as explicitly addressed and related to subsidiaries as in some of the other cases, but they are certainly worth a brief summary. As illustrated in Table 17, influencing factors can again be grouped into three categories: (1) Individual characteristics (personality/philosophy), (2) internal characteristics (organization/infrastructure), (3) external characteristics (industry/environment).

The rationale for treating management philosophy as an individual characteristic has already been outlined in subsections 6.5.3 and 0. Again only a certain facet of the concept is addressed, namely the managerial preference for an internal supplier. This time trust is also regarded as a personal (rather than organizational) feature, given that the interviewee explicitly speaks of people, not units.

	Determinants of intersubsidiary relationships	Explanation / comment
Individual	Management philosophy	Management attitude towards (internal) procurement from one of two competing subsidiaries (P12)
	Personal trust	Based on a long-standing history with the company, people know and trust each other and do not suspect that their counterpart wants to harm them (P13)
Internal	Incentive system	Cooperation is supported by a bonus system that rewards both subsidiary and MNC performance (P13); it cannot be the goal to achieve a stellar result on subsidiary level but a suboptimal result on corporate level
	International growth strategy	Cultural differences between acquired and organically grown subsidiaries (P13)
	Subsidiary product similarity / diversity	The German subsidiary, for example, has little to do with its Chinese colleagues because the latter are involved in completely different products (P12)
	Relationship network	Cooperation depends on who knows whom (P12); it is enhanced through personnel exchange and trust (P13)
	Infrastructure	Cooperation requires a common language; have subsidiaries make use of the same communication channels and devices (P13)
External	Exchange rates	Customers – both internal and external – prefer to buy from a subsidiary with a weaker currency) (P12, P13)
	Customer preferences	Customer preference for one (in this case furnace-producing) subsidiary or another are the ultimate driver (P13)

Table 17: Additional Influencing Factors for Intersubsidiary Competition and Cooperation – Company D

6.8.3.3 Developments and Their Managerial Implications

The most important developments in Company D which could be extracted from the interviews are related to two main topics: First, the evolution of furnace-producing subsidiaries as an epitome of **entrepreneurial units**, and second, the introduction of **Global Business Functions** as a means of systematically enhancing coordination and integration. The subsection concludes with some general learnings and takeaways.

The focus on subsidiaries engaged in the planning and constructing of furnaces is justified because the competitive aspect is most relevant there. Internal and external growth has left several international locations manufacturing the same product – although it is questionable whether such a constellation will be maintainable in the long run given the inherent synergy potential (P11). For the time being however, **intersubsidiary competition** persists due to the duplication of activities. As discussed in the previous subsection, it has even been intensified through changing reporting lines. Consequently, the question is how this competition should be managed. Historically, furnace-producing subsidiaries used to be rather independent. Headquarters hardly interfered with their activities and relationships, and in case of conflict competing subsidiaries had the ambition to arrive at a bilateral solution. Not only is it likely that such an agreement on (geographic) responsibilities becomes more difficult when there is less overall work to do (P12). Subsidiary independence is also expected to change with the introduction of Global Business Functions. These developments show that intersubsidiary competition is bound to evolution, and that managerial decisions can affect it in the one or other direction.

The Global Business Functions were introduced upon thorough consideration in order to coordinate the product-related activities of subsidiaries. Cooperation used to be informal and erratic (P12). These functions can be expected to enhance both **cooperation and competition between subsidiaries** engaged in the same product. On the one hand, new structures and platforms for cooperation are being established. On the other hand, Global Business Managers want to have a higher involvement in which unit provides the component (i.e. the furnace).

In general, it needs to be recognized that Global Business Functions enhance coordination but not necessarily bilateral cooperation between subsidiaries. Given that the Global Business Manager has worldwide product responsibility, he may have an interest in pooling information rather than promoting its exchange. A common infrastructure, however, facilitates such cooperation. Company D is fairly advanced in the development of the respective systems, tools and procedures – and its own development towards a learning network (P13).

It is worth noting that in comparison with Company C, the Global Business Functions represent a coordinating device, not a new business area such as the global EPC business. The two case studies show that there are different means of institutionalizing cooperation between subsidiaries.

On a more general level the interviews in Company D revealed that headquarters needs to make a continued effort to **balance coordination and control with subsidiary independence and entrepreneurship**. It has to succeed in conveying subsidiaries that the Global Business Functions are a means of mediation and integration rather than centralization. This is an important aspect for managers. Subsidiaries' initiative and willingness to learn can only be maintained by not dictating everything from above (P13).

At the same time, it is headquarters' declared goal to keep up its dominant position in the (network) organization. A key takeaway from the case study on Company D is that it may be necessary to define a fifth model of strategic orientation for the large-scale project business. Representing an integrated network with a strong center and possibly less balanced subsidiary contributions, this model can be called 'transnational-global' (P13). A very similar tendency has already been identified by and for Company C. The overall trend, however, goes towards subsidiaries being fortified by gaining experience and know-how. In ten to fifteen years' time headquarters may no longer hold such a dominant position in the network and may itself face competition from subsidiaries, e.g., for project management (P13).

To conclude this subsection on developments, it is worth noting that Company D enjoys the benefit of mainly having grown organically, i.e. not having been affected by an overall merger or acquisition (P13).[137] There is no imposed culture or strategic orientation; there are no resulting overlaps or integration problems. Managers who have to deal with such external effects may be more restricted in terms of implementing organization change.

6.9 Summary and Implications

The empirical study underlined the managerial relevance of the topic and provided profound insights into the relationships between subsidiaries. The interviews with key decision makers in four leading large-scale engineering companies showed that in this particular industry the question of how MNC units – and subsidiaries in particular – interrelate is of utmost importance. They confirmed that a company's strategic orientation has a considerable impact on how subsidiaries compete and/or cooperate.

---

[137] The parent company's acquisition of a key competitor has had basically no impact on the engineering division.

Taking up the two elements of the case studies, this section provides a brief summary and cross-case discussion of the findings on strategic orientation (subsection 6.9.1) and intersubsidiary relationships (subsection 6.9.2).

6.9.1 Strategic Orientation

The **applicability of Bartlett and Ghoshal's typology** of multinational companies was corroborated in that it was well received and understood by managers, who self-typed their companies based on the proposed characteristics. Some interviewees initially associated the integrated network with more erratic interunit relationships; others immediately identified it as the most desirable form of organization. The personal interview situation permitted discussing and clarifying such issues, thus enhancing the validity of the empirical classifications.

An important finding from the case studies was that it is difficult to determine a clear-cut strategic orientation for MNCs. At least in the large-scale plant engineering industry **hybrid types** seem to be more common. Of the four companies investigated, one was classified as multinational with global elements, one as international with global remainders, and two as transnational with global preponderance. The fact that elements of all four types of MNC could be found in practice adds to the quantitative investigations of the typology, which were reviewed in subsection 5.1.2. At the same time it needs to be highlighted that all four companies have global elements which complement their basic strategic orientation. This result can be attributed to the particularities of the large-scale project business, where some form of central coordination seems to be important. Recall from section 4.1 that MNCs in the plant engineering industry are thought to be driven by the simultaneous demands for global efficiency, national responsiveness and worldwide learning.

In his matrix on internationalization strategies Meffert ascribes the plant engineering industry both high globalization and high localization advantages (Meffert 1986: 694; 1990: 98; compare to section 4.1). The discrepancy between Meffert's assessment and the results from the case studies may be explained from two different angles: First, the companies investigated may not be capable of delivering such a balanced response to industry requirements (yet). In their original investigation Bartlett and Ghoshal found companies with very different strategic positions, not necessarily reflecting the dominant industry characteristics (for example, Bartlett/Ghoshal 1998: 15, 23). The better the fit between industry requirements and company capabilities, however, the more successful a company is likely to be in the marketplace (also see Kutschker/Schmid 2006: 293).[138] Administrative heritage may be one reason for a company's inability to respond to the new strategic demands of its operating environment (Bartlett/Ghoshal 1998: 39-40). Second, Meffert's classification, which lacks both clearly defined criteria and empirical investigation, may require further exploration – and possibly modification.

6.9.2   Intersubsidiary Relationships

6.9.2.1 Review of the Propositions

Altogether, the empirical findings were in line – or at least reconcilable – with the propositions developed for the respective types of MNC. For each case it was demonstrated how and why results lie within the spectrum of expectations for the two relevant types. The prevailing ambiguities in strategic orientation, however, make it difficult – or inappropriate – to speak of a confirmation of the propositions. Bartlett and Ghoshal's typology has proven as a useful framework for investigation, but it needs to be realized that its parsimony does not capture the complexity of the large-scale plant engineering industry. The same is true for the example project(s) discussed for each company. Table 18 recalls the propositions as a condensed version of Table 9.

Types of intersubsidiary relationship		Multinational	Global	International	Transnational
Competition	Headquarters-led	None	Low	Low	Moderate
	Subsidiary-led	High	None	Low	Moderate
Cooperation	Headquarters-led	None	Low	Moderate	High
	Subsidiary-led	Low	None	Moderate	High

Table 18: Summary of Propositions – Expected Level of Competition and Cooperation by Type of MNC

---

[138] Compare that with respect to Perlmutter's EPRG profile, the relationship between a particular orientation and corporate success is seen as depending on individual firm characteristics such as resources, objectives and market position (Schmid/Machulik 2006: 255 with reference to Wind et al. 1973: 22).

The limited number of cases also makes it difficult to draw conclusions on **consistency**. Only Companies C and D can be attributed to the same type of MNC, although they are pursuing different approaches in their realization of an integrated network with a strong center. Except for a small discrepancy with respect to subsidiary-led competition – which is non-existent in Company C and low in Company D – results for the two companies indeed overlap. As Table 19 reveals, full consistency is found for Companies B and D, which are quite different in terms of their strategic orientation, though. In fact, it needs to be recognized that results are fairly similar across all four companies, particularly when looking at headquarters-led competition (low) and subsidiary-led cooperation (moderate).

Types of intersubsidiary relationship		Company A	Company B	Company C	Company D
		Multinational with global tendencies	International with global remainders	Transnational with global preponderance	Transnational with global preponderance
Competition	Headquarters-led	Low	Low	Low	Low
	Subsidiary-led	Moderate	Low	None	Low
Cooperation	Headquarters-led	Low	Moderate	Moderate	Moderate
	Subsidiary-led	Moderate	Moderate	Moderate	Moderate

Table 19: Summary of Results – Actual Level of Competition and Cooperation by Company

A glance at Table 19 further shows that – irrespective of the origin of the relationship – there is a clear **dominance** of low levels for intersubsidiary competition and moderate levels for intersubsidiary cooperation. This constellation seems to be characteristic of the large-scale plant engineering industry: Whereas world-spanning cooperation has become indispensable for the successful planning and execution of multi-million-dollar projects, intersubsidiary competition is only admitted selectively and constitutes a much lesser issue. Interestingly, the results on subsidiary-led competition show the greatest variance: One company reaches a moderate level, two reach a low level, and in the fourth company such competition is non-existent. The fact that no company reaches a high level is not surprising, given the potentially detrimental effects of interunit competition. With respect to cooperation, explanations for a lack of high levels can be extracted from the case studies: First, cooperation tends to occur on a rather pragmatic, project-specific level only. Second, one or two units typically dominate the process, impeding network-like cooperation. And third, strategic and organizational initiatives for enhancing intersubsidiary cooperation are currently underway but have not been completed yet. In conclusion, it can be said that both types of intersubsidiary relationships were – and continue to be – worth an investigation.

The case studies illuminated many different aspects and manifestations of the phenomenon, and the condensed presentation of the results should not hide its complexity. Both the propositions and the employed frameworks provided structure to the investigation and helped focus interviews on the main research questions. These frameworks included the project acquisition and execution models developed in section 4.3. Given that intersubsidiary cooperation is accompanied by competitive elements in all four companies, **intersubsidiary coopetition** results as the predominant type of relationship. Since they had been designed as parsimonious representations of (potential) intersubsidiary relationships, it is not surprising that the models in their purest form were not found in practice. In retrospect, one modification to the models would be appropriate, which has little impact on intersubsidiary relationships, though: Besides reflecting headquarters' responsibility regarding key decisions, they should incorporate its oftentimes leading role in basic engineering. Based on the findings of the case studies, the fictitious case example presented in the introduction may also appear somewhat exaggerated. Having multiple subsidiaries compete for participation in a project has turned out to be one valid scenario but certainly not the norm. However, the example is deliberately maintained as a 'teaser' to the topic.

Before concluding the review of the propositions, one last question merits discussion: Is there a unidirectional or possibly a reciprocal relationship between strategy and structure, i.e. between an MNC's strategic orientation and its intersubsidiary relationships?[139] The **direction of the strategy-structure-link** was already addressed in the context of the contingency approach in subsection 3.4.4 and with respect to the I-R framework in subsection 5.1.1. It has also been relevant to the elaboration of the propositions in section 5.2. The case studies have provided evidence that certain interdependencies between the two concepts do exist, but that the proposed contingency cannot simply be reversed. In fact, there are some constellations where the reciprocity seems to work, and others where it appears unconvincing. For example, in Company B intersubsidiary cooperation indeed leads to mutual (or worldwide) learning, which constitutes the key strategic capability of an

---

[139] Recall from subsection 5.1.2 that Bartlett and Ghoshal assume a company's strategic orientation to influence the configuration and coordination of its international activities. This logic was extended to intersubsidiary relationships as one expression of a company's structural configuration.

international company. In Company A, intersubsidiary competition results from subsidiary autonomy, which is an expression of a multinational strategic orientation; it is quite difficult, however, to conceptualize such competition as enhancing local responsiveness. The most obvious reciprocity is reflected by Companies C and D, which foster intersubsidiary cooperation in their development towards a transnational organization. This is not surprising given that the TNO itself is characterized by – or defined as – an integrated network. Although cooperation is the more prominent concept with respect to internal networks (compare to subsections 3.3.3 and 5.1.2), a reverse link need not be limited to cooperative relationships. Headquarters-led charter competition, for example, may be introduced to enhance transparency on dispersed subsidiary capabilities. Such competition implies a balance between central coordination and subsidiary independence, which is a characteristic of the transnational company. Last but not least, it was found that the international project business requires a certain level of cooperation between MNC units worldwide. Bartlett and Ghoshal argue that a company's strategic capabilities ideally match the respective industry requirements (compare to subsection 5.1.2).

The above examples show that it may be possible to draw select conclusions regarding a company's strategic orientation based on its intersubsidiary relationships. Overall, however, it needs to be recognized that strategic orientation is the 'greater' of the two concepts, meaning that – by definition – it comprises elements of structural configuration. Since intersubsidiary competition remains largely unaddressed in Bartlett and Ghoshal's typology (see subsection 5.1.2), it may have to be treated differently from intersubsidiary cooperation. Another differentiation is suggested between the ongoing development towards a specific model and a steady-state, i.e. having reached the aspired strategic orientation. In order to become transnational, for example, fostering some form of intersubsidiary cooperation will be essential. Once an MNC has at least come close to realizing this orientation, intersubsidiary cooperation can be regarded as a key characteristic.

More generally speaking, intersubsidiary competition and cooperation are thought of expressing a certain strategic orientation without actually entailing it. It is headquarters' stance towards subsidiaries (reflected in its strategic orientation) that allows or promotes intersubsidiary competition and/or cooperation. The fact that it takes some kind of platform for intersubsidiary relationships to be realized on also argues in favor of treating them as a dependent variable.

To sum up, a certain **reciprocity or interrelatedness** between an MNC's strategic orientation and its intersubsidiary relationships cannot be ruled out, but the supremacy of the proposed contingency is confirmed. MNCs may utilize competition and, most notably, cooperation between subsidiaries to support or implement a particular strategic orientation, but it is not possible to draw up an equivalent set of logically derived propositions. A good 'fit' between structure, strategy and environmental demands is believed to drive superior performance (Bartlett/Ghoshal 1998: 60).

6.9.2.2 Additional Influencing Factors

Although interviewees explicitly or implicitly supported the implied link between an MNC's strategic orientation and its prevailing intersubsidiary relationships, the fact that the developed propositions could not be explicitly confirmed (or rejected) gives rise to the question of whether other influencing factors should be considered. In anticipation of this issue – and underlining the complexity of the topic – three groups of additional influencing factors were extracted from the interviews: (1) Individual characteristics (personality/philosophy), (2) internal characteristics (organization/ infrastructure) and (3) external characteristics (industry/environment). The theoretical and practical relevance of these factors remains to be investigated. Such an attempt would exceed the scope of this research, but the mere compilation of potential determinants that were articulated in the interviews paves the way for future research. It can be regarded as one of the advantages of qualitative research that it may promote unexpected or additional insights, which in this case can be taken up by other scholars. It will certainly be necessary to further analyze, classify and corroborate the suggested determinants, which is why the current review is kept very brief.

Without addressing each of the empirically derived factors, some general **comparisons** may be drawn with the **literature review on influencing factors** presented in section 3.5. What strikes most in this respect is that individual characteristics were completely neglected in previous contributions on the topic. It sounds convincing, however, that the personality, expertise and philosophy of management have an impact on their stance towards and, consequently, their support of intersubsidiary competition and/or cooperation. Other than that, similar categories of determinants were identified: Environmental determinants concern the industry as a whole, whereas organizational determinants affect select MNCs. As explained in section 3.6, many (internal) aspects related to strategy and structure were merged in the concept of strategic orientation. While IB scholars further point to the specifics of knowledge and (other) resources[140], they are merely joined by the interviewees in drawing attention to subsidiary characteristics. Before investigating additional influencing factors in practice, a combined list from both sources should be compiled. The determinants extracted from the interviews further need to be differentiated according to their impact on competition and/or cooperation. Finally, one aspect that was highlighted in section 3.5 should be considered with respect to the influencing factors suggested by the interviewees: Infrastructural elements such as communication platforms and incentive systems should rather be perceived as means of facilitating or promoting intersubsidiary relationships.

6.9.2.3 Developments and Their Managerial Implications

As far as the third research question is concerned, the interviews reveal that both a company's strategic orientation and its intersubsidiary relationships are subject to continuous evolution. The changes that have taken – and are currently taking – place are either bound to a particular company or concern the industry as a whole. In case of **'individual' developments** the trigger is oftentimes some external effect, such as a merger or acquisition. As illustrated by the examples of Companies A and B, the acquired company may face historically strong(er) centralization, a new management philosophy and/or the need to realize synergies by eliminating redundancies or realigning the business model. Organizational change may also be induced by deliberate management decisions, which may or may not be the response to changing industry requirements. Management may choose to leverage subsidiaries' existing competencies or to 'upgrade' select subsidiaries, giving them greater responsibility and confidence. As included in the examples of Companies C and D, it may also introduce additional units or functions for interface management. All of these measures reflect a certain strategic orientation and have an impact on intersubsidiary relationships. Taking the results of this study to a higher level, it is worth noting that these implications also apply to industries other than plant engineering (compare to the objective formulated in section 1.3).

The **'collective' developments** identified in the interviews are necessarily more bound to the large-scale plant engineering industry. Here, the overall trend goes towards more intersubsidiary cooperation and less intersubsidiary competition.

---

[140] Examples are the tacitness and context-specificity of knowledge as well as the mobility of resources (all Cerrato 2006), but also the fungibility and retrogression of unit capabilities (Birkinshaw/Lingblad 2005 and Luo 2005, respectively).

Cooperation between subsidiaries in multiple countries is becoming a must to satisfy customer demands for state-of-the-art project execution at competitive prices – and with a certain amount of local content. As reflected in the example projects, all of the companies investigated are enhancing the integration and qualification of low-cost (or high-value) centers in India, South East Asia or the like. It also needs to be recognized, however, that as subsidiaries develop capabilities and know-how they are more likely to enter into competition with each other. Interviewees agree that although such competition may enhance efficiency, it may not go to the expense of the company as a whole. In terms of strategic orientation, some centralization and formalization is found to be necessary, not only to leverage and coordinate subsidiary competencies but also to curtail or avoid detrimental competitive practices.

In order to meet the challenges of balancing coordination and control with subsidiary independence and entrepreneurship, the overall trend goes towards the realization of a network organization with a strong center; the transnational model is unlikely to be found in its purest form. Getting back to the objectives formulated for the third research question (see section 1.4), a good 'fit' can be identified between this **'transnational-global' model** and the desired combination of high cooperation and low competition between subsidiaries. The case studies have shown that in practice there is still scope for enhancing intersubsidiary cooperation, given that none of the companies were found to have reached a 'high' level yet. How and to which extent MNCs in the large-scale plant engineering industry continue to develop in this direction remains to be seen.

When reviewing developments it also has to be considered that there is a **broad range of products and projects** that need differentiated treatment. Projects vary in scope from study to lump-sum turnkey, and from subsidiary-led ('regional EPC business' or 'local') to headquarters-led ('technology' or 'international'). Unsurprisingly, the larger and more complex a project is, the higher headquarters' involvement and the more structured intersubsidiary relationships tend to be. As reflected in the case studies, MNCs pursue different types of projects in parallel – both in order to seize opportunities and to hedge risks. The classifications of an MNC's strategic orientation and its intersubsidiary relationships can therefore only represent an aggregation of individual projects. Moving from a descriptive to a normative statement, it has to be recognized that there is not just one successful type of strategic orientation but that it may vary with the types of project an MNC pursues as well as its strategic goals. The same is true for intersubsidiary relationships.

From an academic point of view, the empirical study has provided support of Bartlett and Ghoshal's underlying proposition that an MNC's strategic orientation can change – for all or some parts of the business (for example, Bartlett/Ghoshal 1998). In terms of managerial implications it needs to be recognized that the **development towards an aspired model** requires concrete implementation steps. The two companies that have come closest to the transnational model (Companies C and D) are those that have taken specific structural and procedural measures to achieve integration: Company C has set up the Global Coordination Center, and Company D established Global Business Functions. Eventually the respective organization may be able to function as an integrated network without receiving such support. Important for promoting the necessary organizational change is to achieve management buy-in and commitment at both headquarters- and subsidiary-level. At this point it is worth noting that Companies C and D – unlike Companies A and B – are unaffected by a merger or acquisition. Without being able to investigate this supposition, there are reasons to believe that strategic independence is beneficial to the successful development towards a transnational company.

The above takeaways appear similarly valid for **other industries**. When analyzing and initiating strategic and organizational developments, however, the respective industry characteristics need be taken into account. For the plant engineering industry these are its long-term nature and resulting 'stickiness'.

7 Contributions, Limitations and Implications for Future Research

This research departed from the observation of a particular phenomenon: The (foreign) subsidiaries of MNCs in the plant engineering industry may not only cooperate but also compete with one another. An introductory case example served as a 'teaser' to investigate how and why MNCs operating in the same industry differ in terms of their intersubsidiary relationships. It was soon realized that the existing IB literature provides little insight into the horizontal relationships between MNC subsidiaries – the focus has always been more on the vertical relationship between headquarters and subsidiaries as well as on subsidiary roles. Significant groundwork was thus needed to allow for a systematic investigation of the phenomenon – both in terms of developing a conceptual framework for analyzing intersubsidiary relationships and in terms of identifying a suitable theoretical basis for explaining them. Eventually, a contingency approach was adopted, attributing different manifestations of intersubsidiary relationships to the MNC's strategic orientation. In order to follow the call for more consideration of intersubsidiary relationships in empirical investigations (Ghoshal/Bartlett 1990: 620; Harzing/Noorderhaven 2006: 212), the theoretical framework was linked back to the specific industry and functional focus, i.e. project marketing of plant engineering companies. Case studies based on interviews in four leading large-scale plant engineering companies contributed to the 'rich description' of an under-researched phenomenon and confirmed that an MNC's strategic orientation has a considerable impact on how subsidiaries compete and/or cooperate. Although findings need to be mirrored against industry particularities, they allow some transcending conclusions to be drawn.

The academic contributions and managerial implications of this research are reviewed below (sections 7.1 and 7.2, respectively), followed by a critical assessment of its limitations and an identification of avenues for future research (section 7.3).

7.1 Contributions to IB Research

This in-depth investigation of intersubsidiary relationships contributes to a holistic view of the MNC by complementing existing IB research on headquarters-subsidiary relationships and subsidiary roles. It not only draws attention to the internal manifestations of competition, cooperation and coopetition, but also provides actionable frameworks for analyzing and explaining them (see subsections 7.1.1 and

7.1.2, respectively). It can further be shown that this research adds to the literature on plant engineering and project marketing (subsection 7.1.3) and that the empirical study has made some important achievements (subsection 7.1.4).

7.1.1 Analyzing Intersubsidiary Relationships

Chapter 2 of this study laid the conceptual foundation for **analyzing** intersubsidiary relationships. Based on a definition and delineation of key terms, a classification scheme for intersubsidiary relationships was developed. Competition and cooperation were first broken down into their origins (headquarters-led and/or subsidiary-led) and then differentiated according to their objects (competition for resources, charters and/or customers; cooperation through resource sharing, knowledge sharing and/or a split of work). A diligent literature review not only supports the qualified choice of categories but also constitutes the first comprehensive discussion of intersubsidiary relationships.[141] Particularly intrafirm competition has not received the deserved attention in IB literature yet (compare Birkinshaw/Lingblad 2005: 684). On an academic level, the resulting framework is helpful for structuring the ideas and findings from previous research and for guiding future research. It encourages IB scholars to further investigate the duality of intersubsidiary competition and cooperation as requested by Walley (2007: 25). The derived classification scheme is applicable to a great variety of settings and is by no means limited to investigations in a particular industry (such as plant engineering) or function (such as project marketing).

7.1.2 Explaining Intersubsidiary Relationships

Chapter 3 was dedicated to **explaining** how and why MNCs operating in the same industry differ in terms of their intersubsidiary relationships. It was openly recognized that finding a suitable theoretical foundation for the phenomenon in question poses a significant challenge. Against this background it is understandable that those IB scholars who have addressed intersubsidiary relationships have largely refrained from assuming a clear, if any, theoretical position (most importantly Luo 2005). In this study, relevant theoretical perspectives were identified by taking the inventive approach of analyzing the benefits and drawbacks of intersubsidiary relationships. To

---

[141] The only other contribution on intersubsidiary coopetition is provided by Luo (2005), albeit in a more condensed form.

date, the resulting evaluation of transaction cost economics, the resource-based view and network approaches seems to be the only theoretical discussion on interunit (or intersubsidiary) competition and cooperation.[142] Even though – or just because – none of these three pillars (or any of the identified complementary perspectives) were found sufficiently powerful for explaining intersubsidiary relationships in their entirety, the analysis offers IB scholars a high level of transparency – and 'food for thought'.

Eventually, a contingency approach was adopted in the attempt to explain different manifestations of intersubsidiary competition and/or cooperation via the existence of certain influencing factors. This path has been followed by other IB scholars, whose ideas were incorporated in the resulting contingency framework (Li/Ferreira 2003; Birkinshaw/Lingblad 2005; Luo 2005; Li et al. 2007). In Chapter 5, theoretically sound propositions were developed on the expected link between a company's strategic orientation (operationalized via Bartlett and Ghoshal's typology of MNCs) and its intersubsidiary relationships. By including the empirical investigation of the propositions, this research goes beyond the scope of previous studies on determinants of intersubsidiary relationships (with the exception of Zhao/Luo 2005, who empirically explore the antecedents of intersubsidiary organizational knowledge sharing). Again, the proposed framework is transferable to other – industry and/or functional – research settings. The propositions on the link between an MNC's strategic orientation and the relationships between its subsidiaries can similarly be used as a starting point for investigations in other industries and functions.

7.1.3 Industry and Functional Insights

Given that the empirical study was going to be conducted with a particular industry and functional focus, it was necessary to provide a solid introduction to the specific research setting, i.e. **project marketing** in **plant engineering** companies. In pursuit of this objective, an obvious research gap on the internal issues of project marketing was identified in Chapter 4. By addressing the question of how the supplier is set up internally, this research complements the literature on project marketing, which is mostly dedicated to external business relationships and transactions (compare, most prominently, contributions by INPM and IMP researchers, such as Günter/Bonaccorsi 1996; Skaates/Tikkanen 2003 and Håkansson 1982; Håkansson/Snehota 1995).

---

[142] As illustrated in section 3.3.5, Cerrato makes an attempt to link the configuration of each type of internal market suggested by Birkinshaw (2001b) to a particular research stream (Cerrato 2006). He does not, however, try to identify an all-encompassing theory or framework.

On a more general level, the discussion contributes to clarifying and integrating the various concepts used within the – mainly German-speaking – literature on the marketing process of large industrial projects (Backhaus/Günther 1976; Engelhardt 1977; Bretschneider 1980; Blessberger 1981; Schwanfelder 1989; Heger 2000; Königshausen/Spannagel 2004; Backhaus/Voeth 2007) – and compensates for some of the lack of Anglo-Saxon contributions. A 'phase-differentiated approach' to project marketing was chosen for tracing and illustrating intersubsidiary relationships (compare to Diller/Ivens 2006; Diller/Ivens 2007). The compiled overview of the project acquisition and execution process currently seems to present the most comprehensive yet concise of its kind. It integrates components of various academic publications and was verified with industry experts. Finally, alternative project marketing models were developed by combining this process view with the intersubsidiary relationships outlined in Chapter 2. These simplified models make intersubsidiary relationships more tangible and support a systematic approach to their (empirical) analysis.

7.1.4 Empirical Insights

The concluding **empirical study** has four major achievements: First, it provided insights into the practices of multinational plant engineering companies and revealed different manifestations of intersubsidiary competition and cooperation. Second, it proved the applicability of the classification scheme, which guided the investigation and served as a basis for discussion with managers. Third, it provided for the exploration of the propositions on the link between an MNC's strategic orientation and its intersubsidiary relationships. And fourth, it complemented quantitative studies on the existence of alternative strategic orientations by investigating Bartlett and Ghoshal's typology via qualitative case studies. The ability to discuss orientations with managers reduced the risk of misclassifying organizations and enhanced the validity of the findings.

It can be regarded as a result in itself that a clear-cut determination of **strategic orientation** was not possible in any of the cases. The finding is not completely surprising given that Bartlett and Ghoshal themselves recognize that even within a single company, the needs for global integration and national differentiation vary by business, function, task and geography (Bartlett/Ghoshal 1987b; 1998: 111). Similarly, Perlmutter speaks of the EP(R)G mix, recognizing that in a certain company multiple orientations can simultaneously prevail to a varying extent and in different combinations (Perlmutter 1969a: 14).[143] For both concepts the fact that companies can evolve from one archetype to the next (without following any deterministic sequence) further suggests that intermediate or hybrid forms are likely to prevail (for a graphical illustration of the transition to the transnational see Bartlett 1986: 377; for a visualization of the "directions of multinationalism" see Heenan/ Perlmutter 1979: 21). Nevertheless, working with a limited number of archetypes facilitates a structured research approach (compare Schmid/Machulik 2006 on the prominence of Perlmutter's archetypes in IB literature). The fact that a pure transnational company was not among the identified types although the large-scale plant engineering industry seems best classified as such was already addressed in subsection 6.9.1: Alternative explanations may be found in a lack of (current) MNC capabilities – not least due to the company's administrative heritage – or a potential misclassification of the industry. Given that the case studies provided significant evidence of the simultaneous needs for globalization, localization and worldwide learning in the marketing of large international projects, it appears to be the companies' responses that may need further development and/or adaptation.

The empirical study did, however, reveal that elements of all four types of MNC could be found in practice – even within a single industry. A multitude of combinations is possible when conceptualizing globalization, localization and worldwide learning as the axes of a three-dimensional space (compare to the discussion in subsection 5.1.2.1). Although the described ambiguity impeded a clear confirmation or rejection of the propositions, the impact of strategic orientation on intersubsidiary relationships was ascertained. By including both headquarters' and subsidiaries' perspective, the interviews provided a balanced view on the discussed issues (on perception gaps between headquarters and subsidiaries see, for example, Schmid/Daniel 2007; 2009). They further yielded a number of additional (internal and external) influencing factors for intersubsidiary relationships, which may be explored in subsequent research projects (compare to subsection 6.9.2). Based on the developments that have taken place over time, conclusions could be drawn regarding the suitability (and possibly the success) of alternative strategic orientations and/or intersubsidiary relationships. While it can be stated that there is no single best approach, clear tendencies towards a network model with a strong center could be identified for the large-scale plant engineering industry (assessments of the transferability of results to

---

[143] Empirical investigations of the EPRG orientations, however, are largely outstanding (compare to the future avenues for IB research proposed by Schmid/Machulik 2006: 257).

other industries occur where appropriate throughout this chapter). This leads over to the managerial implications of this research.

7.2 Managerial Implications

On the part of MNC management, this research contributes to an enhanced understanding of how subsidiaries actually and/or possibly interrelate. Managers are provided with an awareness of the spectrum of opportunities related to intersubsidiary competition and cooperation, and, consequently, with an informed basis for decision making. The managerial implications of both the conceptual and empirical part of this research are outlined below (subsections 7.2.1 and 7.2.2, respectively).

7.2.1 Conceptual Elements

The derived **classification scheme** offers MNC managers – irrespective of their industry affiliation – a framework for systematically assessing the strategic options they have in designing and governing intersubsidiary relationships. Managers at both headquarters and subsidiary level are encouraged to reflect upon the role they (can) play in shaping these relationships.

The introductory analysis in Chapter 3 offers a starting point for weighing the **benefits and drawbacks** of intersubsidiary competition and cooperation. Managers may want to base their decision whether to leverage or curtail certain intersubsidiary relationships on these grounds. It is important for MNC managers to understand the opportunities, costs and risks associated with different kinds of intersubsidiary relationships – as well as their potential determinants.

The literature review in section 3.5 provides initial insights on the **influencing factors** of competition and cooperation between subsidiaries. The proposed link between an MNC's strategic orientation and its intersubsidiary relationships is expected to be of particular interest to managers when taken to an empirical level. It then serves as a basis for discussing real action parameters.[144] But already the conceptual

---

[144] When conducting organizational research it needs to be recognized that researchers and practitioners have different frames of reference (see Shrivastava/Mitroff 1984). Certain theoretical questions are of limited interest to managers, who are primarily concerned with strategy development and problem solving.

examination of **strategic orientation** in Chapter 5 encourages managers to reflect upon the positioning of their company (and function) and to evaluate whether they have chosen the most adequate response to the prevailing industry requirements. The interviews revealed that managers appreciated the confrontation with a clear delineation of multinational, global, international and transnational strategic orientation, as proposed by Bartlett and Ghoshal's typology. Interviewees admitted that these terms were often used interchangeably within their organization, which tended to create confusion in discussions. These comments show that managers are very much interested in the practical implications of academic contributions and underline the importance of the empirical investigation. Given their general applicability, the conceptual elements of the study should be of similar value to managers from other industries.

7.2.2 Empirical Findings

The results of the **empirical study** are valuable for managers assessing their strategic and organizational action parameters. Besides revealing alternative constellations of intersubsidiary relationships in the plant engineering industry, the case studies disclose different strategies for managing them. In both respects it is difficult to make normative statements, i.e. determine which alternative(s) work(s) best. Nevertheless, certain trends can be observed, such as the attempt to balance integration with control. Seemingly progressive companies are developing towards a network model with a strong center. **Industry-transcending** insights include that concrete implementation steps are necessary to bring about such a shift in strategic orientation. They provide managers with examples of organizational measures that can be used to enhance integration, such as the introduction of group- or company-wide coordination units. Management commitment and perseverance have proven indispensable for promoting organizational change.

Although many of the empirical findings are relevant beyond the boundaries of one industry, the case studies do offer some particular benefits to managers involved in the project marketing activities of large-scale **plant engineering** companies. The case studies reveal that these companies face the same – or at least very similar – opportunities and challenges. Based on the empirical evidence, managers can position – or benchmark – their companies in relation to select, albeit undisclosed peers. Ideally managers constantly review their positioning against evolving industry trends and the strategic responses taken by their competitors. Based on the discussion of recent developments, this research demonstrates that strategic orientation and intersubsidiary relationships are bound to change and reinforces management's role in accompanying this transformation. Rich descriptions allow managers unfamiliar with the plant engineering industry to understand and assess the prevailing particularities and to possibly transfer findings to their specific setting. Certain parallel trends and developments are likely to be found in other industries.

7.3 Limitations and Implications for Future Research

It needs to be recognized that despite its valuable contributions to IB research and management practice, this research also has its limitations. Several of the concessions made to keep this research project manageable point to promising avenues for future research. One can distinguish between conceptual issues concerning the adopted perspectives and frameworks (subsection 7.3.1) and methodological issues related to the empirical study (subsection 7.3.2).

7.3.1 Conceptual Issues

From a conceptual angle, the **classification scheme** for intersubsidiary relationships is not exhaustive. Although the categories included were based on an informed choice, it would be possible to focus on other or additional elements of relationships. Recall from subsection 4.2.3 that Håkansson and Snehota, for example, propose to analyze (business) relationships according to their structural and process characteristics as well as the effects they produce (Håkansson/Snehota 1995: 5-10, 25-28). The fact that no such classification scheme existed prior to this research reinforces the objective of reducing complexity by focusing on a few central elements. Departing from the classification scheme, the research focus could be amplified by including resources as objects of competition and cooperation.

The **contingency framework** focuses on strategic orientation as the independent variable and intersubsidiary relationships as the dependent variable. Although strategic orientation was identified as the most comprehensive and presumably most important influencing factor (compare to suggestions by Li/Ferreira 2003: 76-77; Birkinshaw/Lingblad 2005: 680-681; Luo 2005: 77-80, 87; Zhao/Luo 2005), there may very well be other intervening variables. Both the literature review conducted in section 3.5 and the case studies presented in Chapter 6 provide compilations of such potential determinants. So far very few authors have adopted a balanced view on intersubsidiary competition and cooperation. Whereas Birkinshaw and Lingblad (2005) focus on the determinants of intrafirm competition, Zhao and Luo (2005) investigate factors affecting knowledge transfer, as one object of interunit cooperation. Merely Li and Ferreira (2003), Luo (2005) and Cerrato (2006) look into the drivers of coopetition between MNC subsidiaries. Going forward further effort should be made to take a holistic approach to intersubsidiary relationships – either by clearly differentiating between relevant (sets of) influencing factors or, preferably, by identifying factors that can explain both types of relationship. In this respect it could be particularly interesting to study the effects of management philosophy, relationship networks and incentive systems – although one should continue to differentiate between influencing factors and means of implementation. On a conceptual level, the deteminants identified in this research may need to be regrouped and systematically related to existing work.

With respect to the contingency framework is further seems noteworthy that – apart from a brief discussion in section 6.9 – there is little consideration of the interplay or reverse link between the two variables. The extent to which intersubsidiary relationships may impact an MNC's overall strategic orientation remains to be clarified. Alternative conceptualizations of strategic orientation may prove useful for investigating the effects of intersubsidiary competition and cooperation.

Moving beyond the contingency framework, future research could extend the effort of finding a substantial **theoretical explanation** for cross-company differences in intersubsidiary relationships – even if an extensive review has not yielded any promising path yet. The explanatory power of transaction cost economics, the resource-based view and network approaches – among others – has been found to be limited. TCE represents a top-down approach to organizing activities within firms, which mainly provides an explanation for headquarters-led (versus subsidiary-led) relationships (compare to subsections 3.3.1.2 and 3.3.1.3). In contrast, the RBV – a firm-level theory applicable to the subsidiary level – emphasizes the objects of competition and cooperation (compare to subsections 3.3.2.2 and 3.3.2.3). Network approaches include the linkages between actors as a core concept, but provide little insight into their horizontal manifestations (compare to subsections 3.3.3.2 and 3.3.3.3). Although all three perspectives can shed light on select aspects of intersubsidiary competition and cooperation, none of them are able to explain why MNCs operating in the same industry differ in terms of the relationships between their subsidiaries. Despite the limited applicability of the reviewed theories (or approaches), it cannot be ruled out that there may be some other theoretical perspective – possibly from neighboring disciplines such as social psychology – that is able to shed light on the phenomenon. So far, only Deutsch's (1949) 'theory of cooperation and competition' has been considered in this respect (see subsection 3.3.4). It could be an enriching approach for IB researchers to cooperate with social psychologists in this respect.

As a last conceptual issue it is worth noting that the parsimony of the developed **project acquisition and execution models** reflects a deliberate – and desired – reduction of complexity. At the same time, these models underline the industry-specific character of this research. A particular industry (and function) was chosen in order to control for complexity and to begin with extracting the very essence of an under-researched phenomenon. Since the underlying conceptual frameworks (classification scheme and contingency-based propositions) were designed to be relevant and applicable to other industries, additional insights could be gained from broadening the research setting. This would not only allow further corroborating the empirical relevance of the concepts but would yield more industry-specific and, ideally, industry-transcending insights.

7.3.2 Methodological Issues

In the **empirical** study, Bartlett and Ghoshal's typology of MNCs was used as an independent variable. By looking into the project marketing activities of plant engineering companies, this research accounted for the fact that **strategic orientation** may vary by function. In the case analysis, further differentiations by project type were undertaken as appropriate, but eventually an aggregated view – or average classification – was required for evaluating the propositions. The resulting types of strategic orientation fall short of reflecting this project-related diversity. Future research may wish to adopt an even more differentiated view on strategic orientation, possibly reflecting this level of detail in the propositions.

Speaking of detail, it was impossible – or inappropriate – to discuss each and every characteristic of Bartlett and Ghoshal's typology in the interviews with top-level managers. Respondents were fairly quick in coming to a conclusion regarding the positioning of their company and, once challenged, their assessment had to be respected. These limitations are not meant to reduce the validity of the results, given that interviewees were very much in positions to reliably self-type their company.[145]

---

[145] In general, perceiving one's organization to be of a certain type does not mean that it actually reveals all the characteristics normatively prescribed to it (Leong/Tan 1992: 462).

To combine the best of both worlds, future research could complement interviews by (quantitative) surveys in order to address the characteristics of strategic orientation more systematically. This suggestion extends to the **investigation of the propositions**. Now that profound insights were provided into an under-researched phenomenon the empirical study could be continued on a more condensed basis. The dilemma, however, will remain: the more senior respondents are, the less time they have to spare on details.

Irrespective of a quantitative supplement to this research, it could be insightful to extend the **case studies** to other MNCs in the plant engineering industry and beyond to see whether some kind of pattern emerges. With a selection of four companies it is difficult to represent all four types of strategic orientation – although the output of this research was already relatively broad in this respect. At the same time, consistency cannot be determined since there are no more than two same types. This drawback leads to the general problem of generalization in qualitative research, which was addressed in subsection 6.2.2. Including MNCs from other industries would allow shedding light on a great variety of different constellations, thus contributing to the comprehensive understanding of intersubsidiary competition and cooperation.

Future research could also include more subsidiaries per company and possibly explore some bilateral relationships in detail. The discussion of typical projects allowed investigating how subsidiaries interrelate without having to speak with all of them (which would have gone far beyond the scope of this research). Nevertheless, the research would certainly benefit from incorporating subsidiaries' first-hand experiences and to capture **multiple interaction patterns**. Perception gaps, such as those suggested to exist between headquarters and subsidiaries, e.g., with respect to subsidiary roles (see Schmid/Daniel 2007; 2009), may very well characterize different subsidiaries' assessment of the relationship with their peers. Just to give an example: Whereas an MNC's German subsidiary may find the relationship with its Indian counterpart to be very cooperative, the Indian subsidiary may perceive subtle, or even considerable, competitive pressures. In this research the approach to avoiding significant discrepancies has been to include a somewhat unbiased or superordinate headquarters and/or functional perspective. It could also be interesting to examine which roles subsidiaries within and across MNCs play based on the combination of competition and cooperation with their peers (see subsection 3.5.3 for a typology proposed by Luo 2005).[146]

Finally, it is worth noting that the case studies only have a single point of reference. Interviewees have spoken about the past, present and future but little evidence is obtainable for the described developments. **Longitudinal studies** on the evolution of strategic orientation and intersubsidiary relationships would allow a more qualified assessment of their performance and long-term success – although these constructs will remain difficult to measure.

---

[146] Luo differentiates between aggressive demanders, silent implementers, ardent contributors and network captains, all of which he positions in a 2x2 matrix of high and low competition and cooperation (Luo 2005: 80-84).

Appendices

Appendix I: Overview of Interviews

Company A	P1	Interview with the Managing Director of Company A's German subsidiary
	P2	Interview with the Director Business Development Sales of Company A's German subsidiary
	P3	Follow-up interview with the Director Business Development Sales of Company A's German subsidiary
Company B	P4	Interview with the Executive Board member responsible for Operations and Engineering at Company B
	P5	Interview with a Project Director at Company B
	P6	Interview with the Managing Director of Company B's Indian subsidiary
Company C	P7	Interview with the Head of Corporate Center at Company C
	P8	Interview with the Head of Project Management Division at Company C
	P9	Interview with the Director Global EPC Business at Company C
	P10	Interview with the Vice Chairman of the Board and Managing Director of Company C's Asian subsidiary
Company D	P11	Interview with a Project Manager at Company D
	P12	Interview with the Managing Director of one of Company D's German subsidiaries
	P13	Interview with the Spokesman of the Board of Directors and the Director of Controlling at Company D

Appendix II: Interview Guideline

0 Opening

Dissertation project: "Competition and Cooperation between Foreign Subsidiaries" (possibly take into account national subsidiaries)

Goal is to *describe* and *explain* intersubsidiary relationships; suggested link between a company's strategic orientation and the relationship between its subsidiaries

Empirical investigation / case studies in the plant engineering industry; begin with headquarters, then interview subsidiary managers

Personal background / objectives

Confidentiality / anonymity of data and results; use for academic purposes only

Duration of interview / permission to record

1   General Information

(To be filled in ex ante)

    Name of company: _____

    Division (if applicable): _____

    Name of interviewee: _____

    Title of interviewee: _____

    HQ or subsidiary: _____

    Location of interview: _____

    Date of interview: _____

    Duration of interview (ex post): _____

    Comments: _____

    _____

Q   Which recent developments or particularities would you like to highlight with respect to your company / division / position?

[Note: Direct the questions towards specific issues based on company information and prior knowledge: implications from a recent merger or acquisition, internal restructuring, change of interviewee's role within the company, etc.]

2 Intersubsidiary Relationships

N Notes / guidelines:

- Please describe the situation *as is*. References to an aspired state are appreciated but should be stated explicitly

- If not already specified ex ante: To facilitate our discussion, please try to think of a *typical large-scale project* in your organization [subsidiary managers: consider referring to the same project as headquarters; otherwise please provide an explanation for your preference]; do not hesitate to point out (and if possible explain) deviations in other projects

- Please relate your answers to the *project acquisition and execution* process. Technology / R&D and operations / service are not investigated as part of this research

[Note: show and explain overview of process steps here; possibly introduce template]

2.1 Project Characteristics

N Notes / guidelines:

- Please provide information on the chosen project if you have not yet done so

[Note: ask interviewee to provide project information ahead of interview for preparatory purposes; otherwise ask for written information to be provided during / after the interview]

Q Please provide some information on the reference project you have chosen and which you consider as typical or exemplary for your organization [only once per project].

a) Description / type of project

b) Client (if possible)

c) Location

d) Project size (capacity / contract value)

e) Scope of services and supplies

f) Project development or tender

g) Award date

h) Start-up date (actual or planned)

i) Project highlights (if applicable)

2.2 Intersubsidiary Competition and Cooperation

N Notes / explanation:

- Subsidiaries can compete for *customers* and *charters*. Competition for resources is *not* in the focus of this research

- Subsidiaries can cooperate through *knowledge sharing* and a *split or work*. Cooperation through resource sharing is *not* in the focus of this research

- Depending on their origin, intersubsidiary competition and cooperation can be either *headquarters-led* or *subsidiary-led*

[Note: explain contents / objects of competition and cooperation here (see below); show classification scheme for visualization]

⚡ Competition for (external) customers

= competition for winning and pursuing large-scale projects in the market place (via project development or tender participation)

Example: Two subsidiaries interested in developing a project or participating in a tender approach the same customer.

⚡ Competition for (internal) charters

= competition for actively participating in and assuming responsibility for certain businesses (product and market arenas) within the organization

Example: Two subsidiaries interested in serving the same customer or participating in a tender try to convince headquarters (or each other) of their distinct abilities and qualification.

◆ Cooperation through knowledge sharing

= cooperation by exchanging (market-, customer-, technology- or process-related) information or know-how

Example: Two subsidiaries share information on customer preferences or know-how on basic engineering.

◇ Cooperation through a split of work

= cooperation by carrying out distinct functions or dividing up work packages

Example: Two subsidiaries contribute to different phases of a project, e.g., design and engineering – and realize / experience their interdependence.

Q Let us go through the project acquisition and execution process step-by-step. For each activity / decision, could you please answer the following questions?

   a) Which units, i.e. headquarters / subsidiaries, are involved? (as leading or participating unit)

   b) Which information and feedback flows occur between these units? (primary or optional flows)

   c) How do subsidiaries compete and / or cooperate? (see notes / explanation above)

   d) Is the depicted intersubsidiary competition / cooperation headquarters- or subsidiary-led? [should be coherent with information flows]

e) What are the rules or procedures for managing the depicted intersubsidiary competition / cooperation?

f) Is the depicted intersubsidiary competition / cooperation of temporary or permanent nature?

2.3 Dynamic Aspect

Q Which important changes in the relationships between your company's (foreign) subsidiaries have taken (or are taking) place over time? What have been / could be the reasons for this development?

3 Strategic Orientation

N Notes / guidelines:

- Please describe the situation *as is*. References to an aspired state are appreciated but should be stated explicitly

- Please try to assign your *company* (in case of divisions your *division*) to one of the four archetypes. In case of an intermediate position please provide additional information

- Please highlight any *substantial* product-related, functional or task-related differences. E.g., does strategic orientation vary for different types of plants, between project marketing and technology / R&D, between project acquisition and execution, or between engineering and procurement?

[Note: explain characteristics of B/G's four archetypes based on the overview and highlight differences in a neutral manner]

With respect to the illustrations of structural configuration:

- Headquarters are depicted at the center of each model, subsidiaries at the periphery
- Dotted and solid lines represent weak and strong interunit ties, respectively
- The color of the boxes illustrates the units' relative importance in strategic and operational decision making (ranging from black = strong position over grey to white = weak position)

3.1 Company Type

Q Let us take a look at Bartlett and Ghoshal's typology of multinational companies. Which of the four archetypes most closely resembles your company / division?

a) Multinational

b) Global

c) International

d) Transnational

3.2 Dynamic Aspect

Q Which important changes in your company's strategic orientation have taken (or are taking) place over time? What have been / could be the reasons for this development?

4 Influencing Factors

N Notes / guidelines:

- Please reflect on what influences the type of relationship (competition, cooperation, coopetition or independence) between the (foreign) subsidiaries in *your* company / division

- Try to consider why *your* company / division may differ from others in the industry

4.1 Strategic Orientation

Q In how far do you think your company's strategic orientation (summarized as local responsiveness, global efficiency, worldwide learning or a combination of all) influences the type of relationship that prevails between its (foreign) subsidiaries?

[Note: do not to lead interviewee in a certain direction; examples for backup only]

Examples:

- Is subsidiary-led competition driven by national independence?

- Is headquarters-led competition driven by the quest for global efficiency?

- Are headquarters- and subsidiary-led cooperation driven by the desire to leverage knowledge?

4.2 Other Factors

Q In your opinion, which (other) factors account for / contribute to the intersubsidiary relationship depicted earlier?

[Note: do not lead interviewee in a certain direction; examples for backup only]

Examples:

- Historical development / events (e.g., tradition)
- Firm characteristics (e.g., governance, organization structure)
- International strategy (e.g., growth strategy, target markets)
- Management characteristics (e.g., philosophy, expertise, personal preferences)
- Subsidiary characteristics (e.g., competencies, initiatives, similarity, age)
- Project characteristics (e.g., size, scope, technology)
- Market characteristics (e.g., customer devt. / demands, competitive pressures)
- Industry characteristics (e.g., maturity)
- Business environment (e.g., uncertainty)
- [Reward system (e.g., management incentives) -> means of implementation]

5   Closing

Thank you for your time and support

Any (additional) comments / questions?

References for follow-up interviews in (other) subsidiaries?

Next steps / option to clarify open issues

Share results once dissertation completed

References

Aaker, David A./Mascarenhas, Briance (1984): The Need for Strategic Flexibility. In: Journal of Business Strategy. Vol. 5, No. 2, 74-82.

Adenfelt, Maria/Lagerström, Katarina (2006): Knowledge Development and Sharing in Multinational Corporations: The Case of a Centre of Excellence and a Transnational Team. In: International Business Review. Vol. 15, No. 4, 381-400.

Allen, Robert E. (ed., 1990): The Concise Oxford Dictionary of Current English. Clarendon Press, Oxford.

Allers, Tyark (2002): Internationalisierung aus der Sicht eines deutschen Großanlagenbau-Unternehmens. In: Krystek, Ulrich/Zur, Eberhard (eds.): Handbuch Internationalisierung. Globalisierung – eine Herausforderung für die Unternehmensführung. Springer, Berlin, 361-371.

Amit, Raphael/Schoemaker, Paul J.H. (1993): Strategic Assets and Organizational Rent. In: Strategic Management Journal. Vol. 14, No. 1, 33-46.

Andersson, Ulf/Forsgren, Mats (2000): In Search of Centre of Excellence: Network Embeddedness and Subsidiary Roles in Multinational Corporations. In: Management International Review. Vol. 40, No. 4, 329-350.

Argyres, Nicholas/Zenger, Todd (2007): Are Capability-Based Theories of Firm Boundaries Really Distinct from Transaction Cost Theory? Academy of Management Best Paper Proceedings, Philadelphia.

Arndt, Sven W./Kierzkowski, Henryk (2001): Fragmentation: New Production Patterns in the World Economy. Oxford University Press, Oxford.

Arnold, David/Birkinshaw, Julian/Toulan, Omar (2001): Can Selling Be Globalized? The Pitfalls of Global Account Management. In: California Management Review. Vol. 44, No. 1, 8-20.

Arrighi, Giovanni/Drangel, Jessica (1986): The Stratification of the World-Economy: An Exploration of the Semiperipheral Zone. In: Review (Fernand Braudel Center). Vol. 10, No. 1, 9-74.

Arrow, Kenneth J. (1964): Control in Large Organizations. In: Management Science. Vol. 10, No. 3, 397-408.

Axelrod, Robert (1984): The Evolution of Cooperation. Basic Books, New York.

Axelsson, Björn/Easton, Geoffrey (1992): Industrial Networks: A New View of Reality. Routledge, London.

Backhaus, Klaus/Günther, Bernd (1976): A Phase-Differentiated Interaction Approach to Industrial Marketing Decisions. In: Industrial Marketing Management. Vol. 5, No. 5, 255-270.

Backhaus, Klaus/Köhl, Thomas (1999): Claim-Management im internationalen Anlagengeschäft. In: Hübner, Ulrich/Ebke, Werner F. (eds.): Festschrift für Bernhard Großfeld zum 65. Geburtstag. Verlag Recht und Wirtschaft, Heidelberg.

Backhaus, Klaus/Voeth, Markus (2004): Besonderheiten des Industriegütermarketing. In: Backhaus, Klaus/Voeth, Markus (eds.): Handbuch Industriegütermarketing. Gabler, Wiesbaden.

Backhaus, Klaus/Mühlfeld, Katrin (2005): Strategy Dynamics in Industrial Marketing: a Business Types Perspective. In: Management Decision. Vol. 43, No. 1, 38-55.

Backhaus, Klaus/Voeth, Markus (2007): Industriegütermarketing. 8th Ed. Vahlen, München.
Backhaus, Klaus/Aufderheide, Detlef/Späth, Georg-Michael (1994): Marketing für Systemtechnologien – Entwicklung eines theoretisch-ökonomisch begründeten Geschäftstypenansatzes. Schäffer-Poeschel, Stuttgart.
Backhaus, Klaus/Büschken, Joachim/Voeth, Markus (2003): Internationales Marketing. 5th Ed. Schäffer-Poeschel, Stuttgart.
Baliga, B.R./Jaeger, Alfred M. (1984): Multinational Corporations: Control Systems and Delegation Issues. In: Journal of International Business Studies. Vol. 15, No. 2, 25-40.
Bamberger, Ingolf/Wrona, Thomas (1996a): Der Ressourcenansatz im Rahmen des Strategischen Management. In: Wirtschaftswissenschaftliches Studium. Vol. 25, No. 8, 386-391.
Bamberger, Ingolf/Wrona, Thomas (1996b): Der Ressourcenansatz und seine Bedeutung für die Strategische Unternehmensführung. In: Zeitschrift für betriebswirtschaftliche Forschung. Vol. 48, No. 2, 130-153.
Banki, Karin/Jung, Hans-Herrmann/Paschold, Reinaldo (2006): Erfolgsfaktoren der "Best Performance" im Maschinen- und Anlagenbau. VDMA-Verlag, Frankfurt am Main.
Bansard, Denis/Cova, Bernard/Salle, Robert (1993): Project Marketing: Beyond Competitive Bidding Strategies. In: International Business Review. Vol. 2, No. 2, 125-141.
Barner-Rasmussen, Wilhelm/Björkman, Ingmar (2005): Surmounting Interunit Barriers. Factors Associated with Interunit Communication Intensity in the Multinational Corporation. In: International Studies of Management and Organization. Vol. 35, No. 1, 28-46.
Barney, Jay (1991): Firm Resources and Sustained Competitive Advantage. In: Journal of Management. Vol. 17, No. 1, 99-120.
Barney, Jay (1996): The Resource-Based View of the Firm. In: Organization Science. Vol. 7, No. 5, 469-469.
Barney, Jay (1999): How a Firm's Capabilities Affect Boundary Decisions. In: Sloan Management Review. Vol. 40, No. 3, 137-145.
Barney, Jay (2001a): Resource-based Theories of Competitive Advantage: A Ten-Year Retrospective on the Resource-Based View. In: Journal of Management. Vol. 27, No. 6, 643-650.
Barney, Jay (2001b): Is the Resource-Based "View" a Useful Perspective for Strategic Management Research? Yes. In: Academy of Management Review. Vol. 26, No. 1, 41-56.
Barney, Jay/Wright, Mike/Ketchen, David J. Jr. (2001): The Resource-Based View of the Firm: Ten Years after 1991. In: Journal of Management. Vol. 27, No. 6, 625-641.
Barrmeyer, Martin C. (1982): Die Angebotsplanung bei Submission. LIT-Verlag, Münster.
Bartlett, Christopher A. (1986): Building and Managing the Transnational: The New Organizational Challenge. In: Porter, Michael E. (ed.): Competition in Global Industries. Harvard Business School Press, Boston, 367-401.
Bartlett, Christopher A./Ghoshal, Sumantra (1986): Tap your Subsidiaries for Global Reach. In: Harvard Business Review. Vol. 64, No. 4, 87-94.
Bartlett, Christopher A./Ghoshal, Sumantra (1987a): Managing Across Borders: New Strategic Requirements. In: Sloan Management Review. Vol. 28, No. 4, 7-17.

Bartlett, Christopher A./Ghoshal, Sumantra (1987b): Managing Across Borders: New Organizational Responses. In: Sloan Management Review. Vol. 29, No. 1, 43-53.
Bartlett, Christopher A./Ghoshal, Sumantra (1988): Organizing for Worldwide Effectiveness: The Transnational Solution. In: California Management Review. Vol. 31, No. 1, 54-74.
Bartlett, Christopher A./Ghoshal, Sumantra (1993): Beyond the M-Form: Toward a Managerial Theory of the Firm. In: Strategic Management Journal. Vol. 14, Winter Special Issue, 23-46.
Bartlett, Christopher A./Ghoshal, Sumantra (1998): Managing Across Borders: The Transnational Solution. 2nd Ed. Harvard Business School Press, Boston.
Bartlett, Christopher A./Ghoshal, Sumantra/Birkinshaw, Julian (2004): Transnational Management. Text, Cases, and Readings in Cross-Border Management. 4th Ed. McGraw-Hill, Boston.
Bartlett, Christopher A./Ghoshal, Sumantra/Beamish, Paul W. (2007): Transnational Management. Text, Cases, and Readings in Cross-Border Management. 5th Ed. McGraw-Hill, Boston.
Bartmess, Andrew/Cerny, Keith (1993): Building Competitive Advantage through a Global Network of Capabilities. In: California Management Review. Vol. 35, No. 2, 78-102.
Beersma, Bianca/Hollenbeck, John R./Humphrey, Stephen E./Moon, Henry/Conlon, Donald E. (2003): Cooperation, Competition, and Team Performance: Towards a Contingency Approach. In: Academy of Management Journal. Vol. 46, No. 5, 572-590.
Belz, Christian/Zupancic, Dirk (2007): Key Account Management "revisited". In: Büschken, Joachim/Voeth, Markus/Weiber, Rolf (eds.): Innovationen für das Industriegütermarketing. Schäffer-Poeschel, Stuttgart, 249-271.
Bendt, Antje (2000): Wissenstransfer in multinationalen Unternehmen. Gabler (mir-Edition), Wiesbaden.
Bengtsson, Maria/Kock, Sören (1999): Cooperation and Competition in Relationships Between Competitors in Business Networks. In: Journal of Business & Industrial Marketing. Vol. 14, No. 3, 178-193.
Bengtsson, Maria/Kock, Sören (2000): "Coopetition" in Business Networks – to Cooperate and Compete Simultaneously. In: Industrial Marketing Management. Vol. 29, No. 5, 411-426.
Berndt, Ralph/Fantapié Altobelli, Claudia/Sander, Matthias (2003): Internationales Marketing-Management. 2nd Ed. Springer, Berlin.
Birkinshaw, Julian (1996): How Multinational Subsidiary Mandates Are Gained and Lost. In: Journal of International Business Studies. Vol. 27, No. 3, 467-495.
Birkinshaw, Julian (1997): Entrepreneurship in Multinational Corporations: The Characteristics of Subsidiary Initiatives. In: Strategic Management Journal. Vol. 18, No. 3, 207-229.
Birkinshaw, Julian (2001a): Strategies for Managing Internal Competition. In: California Management Review. Vol. 44, No. 1, 21-38.
Birkinshaw, Julian (2001b): Entrepreneurship in the Global Firm: Enterprise and Renewal (Strategy). Sage, London.
Birkinshaw, Julian/Morrison, Allen J. (1995): Configurations of Strategy and Structure in Subsidiaries of Multinational Corporations. In: Journal of International Business Studies. Vol. 26, No. 4, 729-753.

Birkinshaw, Julian/Fry, Nick (1998): Subsidiary Initiatives to Develop New Markets. In: Sloan Management Review. Vol. 39, No. 3, 51-61.

Birkinshaw, Julian/Hood, Neil (1998a): Introduction and Overview. In: Birkinshaw, Julian/Hood, Neil (eds.): Multinational Corporate Evolution and Subsidiary Development. Macmillan/St. Martin's Press, Houndmills, Basingstoke, New York, 1-19.

Birkinshaw, Julian/Hood, Neil (1998b): Multinational Subsidiary Evolution: Capability and Charter Change in Foreign-owned Subsidiary Companies. In: Academy of Management Review. Vol. 23, No. 4, 773-795.

Birkinshaw, Julian/Lingblad, Mats (2001): Making Sense of Internal Competition: Designs for Organisational Redundancy in Response to Environmental Uncertainty. Paper submitted to the Academy of Management Review, December 2001.

Birkinshaw, Julian/Hood, Neil (2001): Unleash Innovation in Foreign Subsidiaries. In: Harvard Business Review. Vol. 79, No. 3, 131-137.

Birkinshaw, Julian/Lingblad, Mats (2005): Intrafirm Competition and Charter Evolution in the Multibusiness Firm. In: Organization Science. Vol. 16, No. 6, 674-686.

Birkinshaw, Julian/Hood, Neil/Jonsson, Stefan (1998): Building Firm-Specific Advantages in Multinational Corporations: The Role of Subsidiary Initiative. In: Strategic Management Journal. Vol. 19, No. 3, 221-241.

Birkinshaw, Julian/Toulan, Omar/Arnold, David (2001): Global Account Management in Multinational Corporations: Theory and Evidence. In: Journal of International Business Studies. Vol. 32, No. 2, 231-248.

Björkman, Ingmar/Barner-Rasmussen, Wilhelm/Li, Li (2004): Managing Knowledge Transfer in MNCs: The Impact of Headquarters Control Mechanisms. In: Journal of International Business Studies. Vol. 35, No. 5, 443-455.

Blessberger, Roland (1981): Projektbezogene Arbeitsorganisation im Großanlagenbau. Verband wissenschaftlicher Gesellschaften Österreichs, Wien.

Bonoma, Thomas V. (1985): Case Research in Marketing: Opportunities, Problems, and a Process. In: Journal of Marketing Research. Vol. 22, No. 2, 199-208.

Bourgeois III, L. Jay (1981): On the Measurement of Organizational Slack. In: Academy of Management Review. Vol. 6, No. 1, 29-39.

Brandenburger, Adam M./Nalebuff, Barry J. (1996): Co-opetition. Currency Doubleday, New York.

Bretschneider, Klaus (1980): Strukturentwicklungen zur Akquisition im Großanlagenbau. Rheinisch-Westfälische Technische Hochschule Aachen.

Brown, Steven P./Cron, William L./Slocum, John W. Jr. (1998): Effects of Trait Competitiveness and Perceived Intraorganizational Competition on Salesperson Goal Setting and Performance. In: Journal of Marketing. Vol. 62, No. 4, 88-98.

Brown, Warren B. (1969): The Impact of a Dynamic Task Environment: A Study of Architectural Engineering Firms. In: Academy of Management Journal. Vol. 12, No. 2, 169-177.

Brühl, Rolf/Buch, Sabrina (2006): Einheitliche Gütekriterien in der empirischen Forschung? – Objektivität, Reliabilität und Validität in der Diskussion. Working Paper, No. 20, ESCP-EAP European School of Management Berlin, Berlin.

Buckley, Peter J./Casson, Mark C. (1976): The Future of the Multinational Enterprise. Macmillan, London, Basingstoke.

Buckley, Peter J./Carter, Martin J. (1999): Managing Cross-Border Complementary Knowledge. In: International Studies of Management & Organization. Vol. 29, No. 1, 80-104.
Buckley, Peter J./Carter, Martin J. (2000): Knowledge Management in Global Technology Markets: Applying Theory to Practice. In: Long Range Planning. Vol. 33, No. 1, 55-71.
Buckley, Peter J./Carter, Martin J. (2002): Process and Structure in Knowledge Management Practices of British and US Multinational Enterprises. In: Journal of International Management. Vol. 8, No. 1, 29-48.
Buckley, Peter J./Carter, Martin J. (2003): Governing Knowledge Sharing in Multinational Enterprises. In: Management International Review. Vol. 43, No. 3, 7-25.
Burgelman, Robert A. (1991): Intraorganizational Ecology of Strategy Making and Organizational Adaptation Theory and Filed Research. In: Organization Science. Vol. 2, No. 3, 39-262.
Burgelman, Robert A. (1994): Fading Memories: A Process Theory of Strategic Business Exit in Dynamic Environments. In: Administrative Science Quarterly. Vol. 39, No. 1, 24-56.
Burns, Tom/Stalker, George M. (1961): The Management of Information. Tavistock, London.
Burrell, Gibson/Morgan, Gareth (1979): Sociological Paradigms and Organisational Analysis. Heinemann, London.
Burt, Ronald S. (1983): Distinguishing Relational Contents. In: Burt, Ronald S./Minor, Michael J. (eds.): Applied Network Analysis. A Methodological Introduction. Sage, Beverly Hills, 35-74.
Burt, Ronald S. (1992): Structural Holes: The Social Structure of Competition. Harvard University Press, Cambridge.
Büschken, Joachim/Voeth, Markus/Weiber, Rolf (2007): Aktuelle und zukünftige Forschungslinien für das Industriegütermarketing. In: Büschken, Joachim/Voeth, Markus/Weiber, Rolf (eds.): Innovationen für das Industriegütermarketing. Schäffer-Poeschel, Stuttgart, 3-20.
Caldwell, Bruce J. (1991): Clarifying Popper. In: Journal of Economic Literature. Vol. 29, 1-33.
Cerrato, Daniele (2006): The Multinational Enterprise as an Internal Market System. In: International Business Review. Vol. 15, No. 3, 253-277.
Chakravarthy, Balaji S./Perlmutter, Howard V. (1985): Strategic Planning for a Global Business. In: Columbia Journal of World Business. Vol. 20, No. 2, 3-10.
Chamberlain, Edward Hastings (1968): The Theory of Monopolistic Competition. Harvard University Press, Cambridge.
Chandler, Alfred D. (1962): Strategy and Structure: Chapters in the History of the American Industrial Enterprise. MIT Press, Cambridge.
Chandler, Alfred D. (1990): Scale and Scope. The Dynamics of Industrial Capitalism. Harvard University Press, Cambridge.
Chapman, Malcolm/Gajewska-De Mattos, Hanna/Antoniou, Christos (2004): The Ethnographic International Business Researcher: Misfit or Trailblazer? In: Marschan-Piekkari, Rebecca/Welch, Catherine (eds.): Handbook of Qualitative Research Methods for International Business. Edward Elgar, Cheltenham, Northampton, 287-305.
Charmaz, Kathy (2006): Constructing Grounded Theory. Sage, London, Thousand Oaks, New Delhi.

Child, John (1970): More Myths of Management Organizations? In: Journal of Management Studies. Vol. 7, 376-390.
Child, John (1972): Organizational Structure, Environment and Performance: The Role of Strategic Choice. In: Sociology. Vol. 6, 1-22.
Clarke, Adele E./Friese, Carrie (2007): Grounded Theorizing Using Situational Analysis. In: Bryant, Antony/Charmaz, Kathy (eds.): The SAGE Handbook of Grounded Theory. Sage, London, New Delhi, Thousand Oaks, Singapore, 363-397.
Cohen, Wesley, M./Levinthal, Daniel A. (1990): Absorptive Capacity: A New Perspective on Learning and Innovation. In: Administrative Science Quarterly. Vol. 35, No. 1, 128-152.
Conner, Kathleen R./Prahalad, Coimbatore K. (1996): A Resource-based Theory of the Firm: Knowledge Versus Opportunism. In: Organization Science. Vol. 7, No. 5, 477-501.
Cook, Karen S. (1977): Exchange and Power in Networks of Interorganizational Relations. In: Sociological Quarterly. Vol. 18, No. 1, 62-82.
Cook, Karen S./Emerson, Richard M. (1984): Exchange Networks and the Analysis of Complex Organizations. In: Bacharach, Samuel B. /Lawler, Edward J. (eds.): Research in the Sociology of Organizations. Vol. 3. JAI Press, Greenwich, 1-30.
Cool, Karel O./Dierick, Ingemar/Szulanski, Gabriel (1997): Diffusion of Innovations Within Organizations: Electronic Switching in the Bell System, 1971-1982. In: Organization Science. Vol. 8, No. 5, 543-559.
Copulsky, William (1976): Cannibalism in the Marketplace. In: Journal of Marketing. Vol. 40, No. 4, 103-105.
Corbin, Juliet/Strauss, Anselm (1990): Grounded Theory Research: Procedures, Canons and Evaluative Criteria. In: Qualitative Sociology. Vol. 13, No. 1, 3-21.
Corbin, Juliet/Strauss, Anselm (2008): Basics of Qualitative Research: Techniques and Procedures for Developing Grounded Theory. 3rd Ed. Sage, Thousand Oaks, London, New Delhi, Singapore.
Corsten, Hans/Corsten, Hilde (2000): Projektmanagement. Oldenbourg, München, Wien.
Cova, Bernard/Salle, Robert (2005): Six Key Points to Merge Project Marketing into Project Management. In: International Journal of Project Management. Vol. 23, No. 5, 354-359.
Cova, Bernard/Salle, Robert (2007): Introduction to the IMM Special Issue on 'Project Marketing and the Marketing of Solutions'. A Comprehensive Approach to Project Marketing and the Marketing of Solutions. In: Industrial Marketing Management. Vol. 36, No. 2, 138-146.
Cova, Bernard/Ghauri, Pervez/Salle, Robert (2002): Project Marketing: Beyond Competitive Bidding. John Wiley & Sons, Chichester.
Cray, David (1984): Control and Coordination in Multinational Corporations. In: Journal of International Business Studies. Vol. 15, No. 2, 85-98.
Creswell, John W. (1994): Research Design: Qualitative and Quantitative Approaches. Sage, Thousand Oaks.
Crookell, Harold (1986): Specialisation and International Competitiveness. In: Etemad, Hamid/Dulude, Louise Séguin (eds.): Managing the Multinational Subsidiary: Response to Environmental Changes and to Host Nation R&D Policies. Croom Helm, London, 102-111.

Cyert, Richard M./March, James G. (1963): A Behavioral Theory of the Firm. Prentice Hall, Englewood Cliffs.
Daft, Richard L. (1983): Organization Theory and Design. West, St. Paul.
Dagnino, Giovanni Battista (2002): Coopetition Strategy. A New Kind of Interfirm Dynamics for Value Creation. Paper presented at the EURAM Second Annual Conference – "Innovative Research in Management", Stockholm, May 9-11.
Daniels, John D./Cannice, Mark V. (2004): Interview Studies in International Business Research. In: Marschan-Piekkari, Rebecca/Welch, Catherine (eds.): Handbook of Qualitative Research Methods for International Business. Edward Elgar, Cheltenham, Northampton, 185-206.
Davidson, William H./Haspeslagh, Philippe (1982): Shaping a Global Product Organization. In: Harvard Business Review. Vol. 60, No. 4, 125-132.
Davis, Peter S./Pett, Timothy L. (2002): Measuring Organizational Efficiency and Effectiveness. In: Journal of Management Research. Vol. 2, No. 2, 87-97.
Denzin, Norman K./Lincoln, Yvonna S. (2005): Introduction: The Discipline and Practice of Qualitative Research. In: Denzin, Norman K./Lincoln, Yvonna S. (eds.): The Sage Handbook of Qualitative Research. 3rd Ed. Sage, Thousand Oaks, London, New Delhi, 1-41.
Deutsch, Morton (1949): A Theory of Co-operation and Competition. In: Human Relations. Vol. 2, No. 2, 129-152.
Devinney, Timothy M./Midgley, David F./Venaik, Sunil (2000): The Optimal Performance of the Global Firm: Formalizing and Extending the Integration-Responsiveness Framework. In: Organization Science. Vol. 11, No. 6, 674-695.
Diller, Hermann/Ivens, Björn S. (2007): Prozessorientiertes Industriegütermarketing. In: Büschken, Joachim/Voeth, Markus/Weiber, Rolf (eds.): Innovationen für das Industriegütermarketing. Schäffer-Poeschel, Stuttgart, 479-498.
Diller, Herrmann/Ivens, Björn Sven (2006): Process Oriented Marketing. In: Marketing-Journal for Research and Management. Vol. 2, No. 1, 14-29.
DiMaggio, Paul J./Powell, Walter W. (1983): The Iron Cage Revisited: Institutional Isomorphism and Collective Rationality in Organizational Fields. In: American Sociological Review. Vol. 48, No. 2, 147-160.
Donaldson, Lex (1985): In Defense of Organization Theory: A Reply to the Critics. Cambridge University Press, Cambridge.
Döring, Hilmar (1998): Kritische Analyse der Leistungsfähigkeit des Transaktionskostenansatzes. Universität Göttingen, Göttingen.
Dowling, Michael/Lechner, Christian (1998): Kooperative Wettbewerbsbeziehungen: Theoretische Ansätze und Managementstrategien. In: Die Betriebswirtschaft. Vol. 58, No. 1, 86-102.
Dowling, Michael/Roering, William/Carlin, Barbara/Wisnieski, Joette (1996): Multifaceted Relationships Under Coopetition: Description and Theory. In: Journal of Management Inquiry. Vol. 5, No. 2, 155-167.
Doz, Yves L. (1976): National Policies and Multinational Management. Unpublished doctoral dissertation. Harvard Business School, Boston.
Doz, Yves L. (1980): Strategic Management in Multinational Companies. In: Sloan Management Review. Vol. 21, No. 2, 27-46.
Doz, Yves L./Prahalad, Coimbatore K. (1984): Patterns of Strategic Control Within Multinational Corporations. In: Journal of International Business Studies. Vol. 15, No. 2, 55-72.

Doz, Yves L./Prahalad, Coimbatore K. (1991): Managing DMNCs: A Search for a New Paradigm. In: Strategic Management Journal. Vol. 12, No. 4, 145-164.

Doz, Yves L./Bartlett, Christopher A./Prahalad, Coimbatore K. (1981): Global Competitive Pressures and Host Country Demands: Managing Tensions in MNCs. In: California Management Review. Vol. 23, No. 3, 63-74.

Dunning, John H. (1980): Towards an Eclectic Theory of International Production: Some Empirical Tests. In: Journal of International Business Studies. Vol. 11, No. 1, 9-31.

Dyer, Jeffrey H./Singh, Harbir (1998): The Relational View: Cooperative Strategy and Sources of Interorganizational Competitive Advantage. In: Academy of Management Review. Vol. 23, No. 4, 660-679.

Easton, Geoffrey/Araujo, Luis (1986): Networks, Bonding and Relationships in Industrial Markets. In: Industrial Marketing and Purchasing. Vol. 1, No. 1, 8-25.

Easton, Geoffrey/Araujo, Luis (1989): The Network Approach: An Articulation. In: Hallén, Lars/Johanson, Jan (eds.): Networks of Relationships in International Industrial Marketing. Advances in International Marketing. Vol. 3. JAI Press, Greenwich, 97-119.

Easton, Geoffrey/Araujo, Luis (1992): Non-economic Exchange in Industrial Networks. In: Axelsson, Björn/Easton, Geoffrey (eds.): Industrial Networks: A New View of Reality. Routledge, London.

Ebers, Mark (1992): Organisationstheorie, situative. In: Frese, Erich (ed.): Handwörterbuch der Organisation. 3rd Ed. Poeschel, Stuttgart, 1817-1838.

Edwards, Tony/Kuruvilla, Sarosh (2005): International HRM: National Business Systems, Organizational Politics and the International Division of Labour in MNCs. In: International Journal of Human Resource Management. Vol. 16, No. 1, 1-21.

Egelhoff, William G. (1982): Strategy and Structure in Multinational Corporations: An Information Processing Approach. In: Administrative Science Quarterly. Vol. 22, No. 3, 435-458.

Ehemann, Petra (2007): Die Autonomie von Landesorganisationen bei der Marktbearbeitung: Determinanten, Auswirkungen und State of Practice. Deutscher Universitäts-Verlag, Wiesbaden.

Eisenhardt, Kathleen (1989): Building Theories from Case Study Research. In: Academy of Management Review. Vol. 14, No. 4, 532-550.

Eisenhardt, Kathleen M./Galunic, Charles D. (2000): Coevolving. At Last, a Way to Make Synergies Work. In: Harvard Business Review. Vol. 78, No. 1, 91-101.

Engelhardt, Werner Hans (1977): Grundlagen des Anlagen-Marketing. In: Engelhardt, Werner Hans/Laßmann, Gert (eds.): Anlagen-Marketing. Zeitschrift für betriebswirtschaftliche Forschung. Special Edition 7. Westdeutscher Verlag, Opladen, 9-37.

Fang, Tony (2006): Book review: Coopetition in International Business. In: International Business Review. Vol. 15, No. 4, 436-438.

Fehr, Ernst/Fischbacher, Urs (2002): Why Social Preferences Matter – The Impact of Non-Selfish Motives on Competition, Cooperation and Incentives. In: Economic Journal. Vol. 112, No. 478, C1-C33.

Felsenthal, Dan S. (1980): Applying the Redundancy Concept to Administrative Organizations. In: Public Administration Review. Vol. 40, No. 3, 247-252.

Fengler, Jörg (1996): Konkurrenz und Kooperation in Gruppe, Team und Partnerschaft. Pfeiffer, München.

Filiatrault, Pierre/Lapierre, Jozée (1997): Managing Business-to-Business Marketing Relationships in Consulting Engineering Firms. In: Industrial Marketing Management. Vol. 26, No. 2, 213-222.
Fisher, Joseph/Govindarajan, Vijay (1992): Profit Center Manager Compensation: An Examination of Market, Political and Human Capital Factors. In: Strategic Management Journal. Vol. 13, No. 3, 205-217.
Fiske, Alan P. (1991): Structures of Social Life: The Four Elementary Forms of Human Relations. The Free Press, New York.
Flick, Uwe (1996): Psychologie des technisierten Alltags. Soziale Konstruktion und Repräsentation technischen Wandels. Westdeutscher Verlag, Opladen.
Flick, Uwe (2006): An Introduction to Qualitative Research. 3rd Ed. Sage, London.
Flick, Uwe (2007): Qualitative Sozialforschung. Eine Einführung. Rowohlt, Reinbek bei Hamburg.
Fong, Cher-Min/Ho, Hua-Lun/Weng, Liang-Chieh/Yang, Kai-Peng (2007): The Inter-subsidiary Competition in an MNE: Evidence from the Greater China Region. In: Canadian Journal of Administrative Sciences. Vol. 24, No. 1, 45-57.
Forsgren, Mats/Johanson, Jan (1992): Managing in International Multi-Centre Firms. In: Forsgren, Mats/Johanson, Jan (eds.): Managing Networks in International Business. Gordon and Breach, Philadelphia, 19-31.
Foss, Nicolai Juul/Pedersen, Torben (2000): Organizing Knowledge Processes in the Multinational Corporation: An Introduction. In: Journal of International Business Studies. Vol. 35, No. 5, 340-349.
Franko, Lawrence G. (1976): The European Multinationals. A Renewed Challenge to American and British Big Business. Harper & Row, London, New York, Hagerstown, San Francisco.
Frese, Erich (1985): Marktinterdependenzen in Unternehmungen der Investitionsgüterindustrie als organisatorisches Problem. Ergebnisse einer empirischen Untersuchung. In: Zeitschrift für betriebswirtschaftliche Forschung. Vol. 37, No. 4, 267-290.
Frese, Erich (1992): Organisationstheorie: Historische Entwicklung, Ansätze, Perspektiven. 2nd Ed. Gabler, Wiesbaden.
Frese, Erich (2005): Grundlagen der Organisation. Entscheidungsorientiertes Konzept der Organisationsgestaltung. 9th Ed. Gabler, Wiesbaden.
Frese, Erich/Lehmann, Patrick (2002): Der koordinierte Weg zum Kunden – Konzeption einer strategiekonformen Vertriebsorganisation. In: Böhler, Heymo (ed.): Marketing-Management und Unternehmensführung. Festschrift für Richard Köhler. Schäffer-Poeschel, Stuttgart, 505-546.
Fritz, Carl-Thomas (2006): Die Transaktionskostentheorie und ihre Kritik sowie ihre Beziehung zum soziologischen Neo-Institutionalismus. Peter Lang, Frankfurt am Main.
Fudenberg, Drew/Tirole, Jean (1991): Game Theory. MIT Press, Cambridge.
Galbraith, Jay (2001): Building Organizations Around the Global Customer. In: Ivey Business Journal. Vol. 66, No. 1, 17-24.
Galbraith, Jay R. (1973): Designing Complex Organizations. Addison-Wesley, Reading.
Galunic, Charles D./Eisenhardt, Kathleen M. (1996): The Evolution of Intracorporate Domains: Divisional Charter Losses in High-technology, Multidivisional Corporations. In: Organization Science. Vol. 7, No. 3, 255-282.

Gates, Stephen R./Egelhoff, William G. (1986): Centralization in Headquarters-Subsidiary Relationships. In: Journal of International Business Studies. Vol. 17, No. 2, 71-92.

Gereffi, Gary/Humphrey, John/Sturgeon, Timothy (2005): The Governance of Global Value Chains. In: Review of International Political Economy Vol. 12, No. 1, 78-104.

Geser, Hans (1992): Towards an Interaction Theory of Organizational Actors. In: Organization Studies. Vol. 13, No. 3, 429-451.

Ghauri, Pervez (2004): Designing and Conducting Case Studies in International Business Research. In: Marschan-Piekkari, Rebecca/Welch, Catherine (eds.): Handbook of Qualitative Research Methods for International Business. Edward Elgar, Cheltenham, Northampton, 109-124.

Ghauri, Pervez/Grønhaug, Kjell (2005): Research Methods in Business Studies: A Practical Guide. 3rd Ed. FT Prentice Hall, Harlow.

Ghauri, Pervez/Cateora, Philip (2005): International Marketing. 2nd Ed. McGraw-Hill, Maidenhead.

Ghoshal, Sumantra (1987): Global Strategy: An Organizing Framework. In: Strategic Management Journal. Vol. 8, No. 5, 425-440.

Ghoshal, Sumantra/Bartlett, Christopher A. (1988): Creation, Adoption, and Diffusion of Innovations by Subsidiaries of Multinational Corporations. In: Journal of International Business Studies. Vol. 19, No. 3, 365-388.

Ghoshal, Sumantra/Nohria, Nitin (1989): Internal Differentiation Within Multinational Corporations. In: Strategic Management Journal. Vol. 10, No. 4, 323-337.

Ghoshal, Sumantra/Bartlett, Christopher A. (1990): The Multinational Corporation as an Interorganizational Network. In: Academy of Management Review. Vol. 15, No. 4, 603-625.

Ghoshal, Sumantra/Moran, Peter (1996): Bad for Practice: A Critique of the Transaction Cost Theory. In: Academy of Management Review. Vol. 21, No. 1, 13-47.

Ghoshal, Sumantra/Korine, Harry/Szulanski, Gabriel (1994): Interunit Communication in Multinational Corporations. In: Management Science. Vol. 40, No. 1, 96-110.

Gleich, Ronald/Müller, Michael/Kämmler, Andrea/Staudinger, Michael (2005): Managementherausforderungen im Großanlagenbau. In: Zeitschrift für wirtschaftlichen Fabrikbetrieb. Vol. 100, No. 4, 182-186.

Gnyawali, Devi R./Singal, Manisha/Mu, Shaohua "Carolyn" (2007): Inter-subsidiary Collaboration for Knowledge: A Conceptual Model. Academy of Management Best Paper Proceedings. Philadelphia.

Govindarajan, Vijay/Gupta, Anil K. (2001): The Quest for Global Dominance. Jossey-Bass, San Francisco.

Grant, Robert M. (1991): The Resource-Based Theory of Competitive Advantage: Implications for Strategy Formulation. In: California Management Review. Vol. 33, No. 3, 114-135.

Griffin, Abbie/Hauser, John R. (1996): Integrating R&D and Marketing: A Review and Analysis of the Literature. In: Journal of Product Innovation Management. Vol. 13, No. 3, 191-251.

Grosse, Robert (1996): International Technology Transfer in Services. In: Journal of International Business Studies. Vol. 27, No. 4, 781-800.

Grunwald, Wolfgang (1982): Konflikt – Konkurrenz – Kooperation: Eine theoretisch-empirische Konzeptanalyse. In: Grunwald, Wolfgang/Lilge, Hans-Georg (eds.): Kooperation und Konkurrenz in Organisationen. Haupt, Bern, Stuttgart, 50-96.

Grunwald, Wolfgang/Lilge, Hans-Georg (1982): Kooperation und Konkurrenz in Organisationen. Haupt, Bern, Stuttgart.

Guba, Egon G./Lincoln, Yvonna S. (1981): Effective Evaluation: Improving the Usefulness of Evaluation Results Through Responsive and Naturalistic Approaches. Jossey-Bass, San Francisco.

Guba, Egon G./Lincoln, Yvonna S. (1989): Fourth Generation Evaluation. Sage, Newbury Park.

Guba, Egon G./Lincoln, Yvonna S. (2005): Paradigmatic Controversies, Contradictions, and Emerging Confluences. In: Denzin, Norman K./Lincoln, Yvonna S. (eds.): The Sage Handbook of Qualitative Research. 3rd Ed. Sage. Thousand Oaks, London, New Delhi, 191-215.

Günter, Bernd (1979): Das Marketing von Großanlagen. Strategieprobleme des Systems Selling. Duncker & Humblot, Berlin.

Günter, Bernd/Bonaccorsi, Andrea (1996): Project Marketing and Systems Selling – in Search of Frameworks and Insights. In: International Business Review. Vol. 5, No. 6, 531-537.

Gupta, Anil K. (1987): SBU Strategies, Corporate SBU-Relations, and SBU Effectiveness in Strategy Implementation. In: Academy of Management Journal. Vol. 30, No. 3, 477-500.

Gupta, Anil K./Govindarajan, Vijay (1986): Resource Sharing Among SBUs: Strategic Antecedents and Administrative Implications. In: Academy of Management Journal. Vol. 29, No. 4, 695-714.

Gupta, Anil K./Govindarajan, Vijay (1991): Knowledge Flows and the Structure of Control Within Multinational Corporations. In: Academy of Management Review. Vol. 16, No. 4, 768-792.

Gupta, Anil K./Govindarajan, Vijay (2000): Knowledge Flows Within Multinational Corporations. In: Strategic Management Journal. Vol. 21, No. 4, 473-496.

Gupta, Anil K./Becerra, Manuel (2003): Impact of Strategic Context and Inter-unit Trust on Knowledge Flows Within the Multinational Corporation. In: McKern, Bruce (ed.): Managing the Global Network Corporation. Routledge, London, 23-39.

Håkansson, Håkan/Östberg, Claes (1975): Industrial Marketing: An Organizational Problem? In: Industrial Marketing Management. Vol. 4, No. 2/3, 113-123.

Håkansson, Håkan/Snehota, Ivan (1995): Developing Relationships in Business Networks. Routledge, London, New York.

Håkansson, Håkan (1982): International Marketing and Purchasing of Industrial Goods. An Interaction Approach. John Wiley & Sons, Chichester.

Halal, William E. (1994): From Hierarchy to Enterprise: Internal Markets Are the New Foundation of Management. In: Academy of Management Executive. Vol. 8, No. 4, 69-83.

Halal, William E./Geranmayeh, Ali/Pourdehnad, John (1993): Internal Markets. Bringing the Power of Free Enterprise Inside Your Organization. John Wiley & Sons, New York.

Hall, David J./Saias, Maurice A. (1980): Strategy Follows Structure! In: Strategic Management Journal. Vol. 1, No. 2, 149-163.

Hamel, Gary (1991): Competition for Competence and Interpartner Learning Within International Strategic Alliances. In: Strategic Management Journal. Vol. 12, No. 4, 83-103.
Hamel, Gary/Doz, Yves L./Prahalad, Coimbatore K. (1989): Collaborate with Your Competitors – and Win. In: Harvard Business Review. Vol. 67, No. 1, 133-139.
Hammersley, Martyn/Gomm, Roger/Foster, Peter (2000): Case Study and Theory. In: Gomm, Roger/Martyn, Hammersley/Foster, Peter (eds.): Case Study Method: Key Issues, Key Texts. Sage, London, Thousand Oaks, New Delhi.
Hansen, Morten T. (1999): The Search-Transfer Problem: The Role of Weak Ties in Sharing Knowledge Across Organization Subunits. In: Administrative Science Quarterly. Vol. 44, No. 1, 82-111.
Harbison, Frederick/Myers, Charles A. (1959): Management in the Industrial World. An International Analysis. McGraw-Hill, New York, Toronto, London.
Harris, Ira C./Ruefli, Timothy W. (2000): The Strategy/Structure Debate: An Examination of the Performance Implications. In: Journal of Management Studies. Vol. 37, No. 4, 587-603.
Harrison, Jeffrey S./Hitt, Michael A./Hoskisson, Robert E./Ireland, R. Duane (2001): Resource Complementarity in Business Combinations: Extending the Logic to Organizational Alliances. In: Journal of Management. Vol. 27, No. 6, 679-690.
Harzing, Anne-Wil (2000): An Empirical Analysis and Extension of the Bartlett and Ghoshal Typology of Multinational Companies. In: Journal of International Business Studies. Vol. 31, No. 1, 101-120.
Harzing, Anne-Wil (2004): Strategy and Structure of Multinational Companies. In: Harzing, Anne-Wil/Van Ruysselveldt, Joris (eds.): International Human Resource Management. Sage, London, 33-64.
Harzing, Anne-Wil/Noorderhaven, Niels G. (2006): Knowledge Flows in MNCs: An Empirical Test and Extension of Gupta & Govindarajan's Typology of Subsidiary Roles. In: International Business Review. Vol. 15, No. 3, 195-214.
Hedlund, Gunnar (1986): The Hypermodern MNC – A Heterarchy? In: Human Resource Management. Vol. 25, No. 1, 9-35.
Hedlund, Gunnar/Rolander, Dag (1990): Actions in Heterarchies – New Approaches to Managing the MNC. In: Bartlett, Christopher A./Doz, Yves L./Hedlund, Gunnar (eds.): Managing the Global Firm. Routledge, London, 15-46.
Heenan, David A./Perlmutter, Howard V. (1979): Multinational Organization Development. Addison-Wesley, Reading.
Heger, Günther (2000): Marketing im Anlagengeschäft. Fernstudienagentur des FVL. Berlin.
Helm, René (2004): Vertrieb im Systemgütergeschäft. Gestaltungsparameter für eine Vertriebskonzeption. Deutscher Universitäts-Verlag, Wiesbaden.
Hennart, Jean-François (1993a): Control in Multinational Firms: the Role of Price and Hierarchy. In: Westney, D. Eleanor/Ghoshal, Sumantra (eds.): Organization Theory and the Multinational Corporation. Macmillan, London, 157-181.
Hennart, Jean-François (1993b): Explaining the Swollen Middle: Why Most Transactions Are a Mix of Market and Hierarchy. In: Organization Science. Vol. 4, No. 4, 529-547.
Hennart, Jean-François (2001): Theories of the Multinational Enterprise. In: Rugman, Alan M./Brewer, Tom (eds.): The Oxford Handbook of International Business. Oxford University Press, London, 127-150.

Hill, Charles W. L./Hoskisson, Robert E. (1987): Strategy and Structure in the Multiproduct Firm. In: Academy of Management Review. Vol. 12, No. 2, 331-341.
Hill, Charles W. L./Hitt, Michael A./Hoskisson, Robert E. (1992): Cooperative vs. Competitive Structures in Related and Unrelated Diversified Firms. In: Organization Science. Vol. 3, No. 4, 501-521.
Hillebrand, Bas/Biemans, Wim G. (2003): The Relationship Between Internal and External Cooperation: Literature Review and Propositions. In: Journal of Business Research. Vol. 56, No. 9, 735-743.
Hintze, Martin (1998): Betreibermodelle bei bautechnischen und maschinellen Anlagenprojekten: Beurteilung und Umsetzung aus Auftraggeber- und Projektträgersicht Ferber. Gießen.
Hirsch, Fred (1976): Social Limits to Growth. Routledge & Kegan Paul, London.
Hirshleifer, Jack (1982): Evolutionary Models in Economics and Law: Cooperation Versus Conflict Strategies. In: Rubin, Paul H. (ed.): Research in Law and Economics. Vol. 4. JAI Press, Greenwich, London, 1-60.
Hodgson, Geoffrey M. (2002): The Legal Nature of the Firm and the Myth of the Firm-Market Hybrid. In: International Journal of the Economics of Business. Vol. 9, No. 1, 37-60.
Holm, Ulf/Pedersen, Torben (2000): The Emergence and Impact of MNC Centres of Excellence: A Subsidiary Perspective. Macmillan, London.
Holtbrügge, Dirk (2005): Configuration and Co-ordination of Value Activities in German Multinational Corporations. In: European Management Journal. Vol. 23, No. 5, 564-575.
Holton, Judith A. (2007): The Coding Process and Its Challenges. In: Bryant, Antony/Charmaz, Kathy (eds.): The SAGE Handbook of Grounded Theory. Sage, London, New Delhi, Thousand Oaks, Singapore, 265-289.
Homans, George Caspar (1973): Social Behavior: Its Elementary Forms. Routledge & Kegan Paul, London.
Hopf, Christel/Schmidt, Christiane (1993): Zum Verhältnis von innerfamilialen sozialen Erfahrungen, Persönlichkeitsentwicklung und politischen Orientierungen. Dokumentation und Erörterung des methodischen Vorgehens in einer Studie zu diesem Thema. Institut für Sozialwissenschaften der Universität Hildesheim, Hildesheim.
Hoskisson, Robert E./Hill, Charles W. L./Kim, Hicheon (1993): The Multidivisional Structure: Organizational Fossil or Source of Value? In: Journal of Management. Vol. 19, No. 2, 269-298.
Hussey, Jill/Hussey, Roger (1997): Business Research. A Practical Guide for Undergraduate and Postgraduate Students. Palgrave, Houndmills, Basingstoke, Hampshire, New York.
IMP Group (2007): About the IMP Group. Website of IMP Group. URL: http://www.impgroup.org/about.php (13/11/2007).
Jansen, Stephan A./Schleissing, Stephan (2000): Konkurrenz und Kooperation. Interdisziplinäre Zugänge zur Theorie der Co-opetition. Metropolis, Marburg.
Johanson, Jan/Vahlne, Jan-Erik (1977): The Internationalization Process of the Firm – A Model of Knowledge Development and Increasing Foreign Market Commitments. In: Journal of International Business Studies. Vol. 8, No. 1, 25-34.

Johanson, Jan/Mattson, Lars-Gunnar (1987): Interorganisational Relations in Industrial Systems: A Network Approach Compared with a Transaction Cost Approach. In: International Studies of Management & Organization. Vol. 17, No. 1, 34-48.

Johnson, David. W./Johnson, Roger T. (1989): Cooperation and Competition: Theory and Research. Interaction Book Company, Edina.

Johnson, Julius H. Jr. (1995): An Empirical Analysis of the Integration-Responsiveness Framework: U.S. Construction Equipment Industry Firms in Global Competition. In: Journal of International Business Studies. Vol. 26, No. 3, 621-635.

Johnson, Michael P. (1982): Social and Cognitive Features of the Dissolution of Commitment to Relationships. In: Duck, Steve (ed.): Personal Relationships 4: Dissolving Personal Relationships. Academic Press, New York, 51-73.

Jost, Peter-Jürgen (2001): Die Spieltheorie in der Betriebswirtschaftslehre. Schäffer-Poeschel, Stuttgart.

Kalnins, Arturs (2004): Divisional Multimarket Contact Within and Between Multiunit Organizations. In: Academy of Management Journal. Vol. 47, No. 1, 117-145.

Kalra, Ajay/Shi, Mengze (2001): Designing Optimal Sales Contests: A Theoretical Perspective. In: Marketing Science. Vol. 20, No. 2, 170-193.

Kanter, Rosabeth Moss (1982): The Middle Manager as Innovator. In: Harvard Business Review. Vol. 60, No. 4, 95-105.

Kaplinsky, Raphael (2004): Spreading the Gains from Globalization: What Can Be Learned from Value-Chain Analysis? In: Problems of Economic Transition. Vol. 47, No. 2, 74-115.

Katz, Daniel and Kahn, Robert L. (1978): The Social Psychology of Organizations. John Wiley & Sons, New York.

Kelle, Udo (2000): Computergestützte Analyse qualitativer Daten. In: Flick, Uwe/von Kardoff, Uwe/Steinke, Ines (eds.): Qualitative Forschung – Ein Handbuch. 2nd Ed. Rowohlt, Hamburg.

Kelle, Udo (2007): The Development of Categories: Different Approaches in Grounded Theory. In: Bryant, Antony/Charmaz, Kathy (eds.): The SAGE Handbook of Grounded Theory. London, New Delhi, Thousand Oaks, Singapore, 192-213.

Kelle, Udo/Kluge, Susann (1999): Vom Einzelfall zum Typus. Leske & Budrich, Opladen.

Kern, Manfred (1979): Klassische Erkenntnistheorien und moderne Wissenschaftslehre. In: Raffée, Hans/Abel, Bodo (eds.): Wissenschaftstheoretische Grundfragen der Wirtschaftswissenschaften. Vahlen, München, 11-27.

Khanna, Tarun/Gulati, Ranjay/Nohria, Nitin (1998): The Dynamics of Learning Alliances: Competition, Cooperation, and Relative Scope. In: Strategic Management Journal. Vol. 19, No. 3, 193-210.

Kieser, Alfred (1989): Organisationsstruktur, empirische Befunde. In: Macharzina, Klaus/Welge, Martin K. (eds.): Handwörterbuch Export und Internationale Unternehmung. Poeschel, Stuttgart, 1574-1590.

Kieser, Alfred (2002): Der Situative Ansatz. In: Kieser, Alfred (ed.): Organisationstheorien. 5th Ed. Kohlhammer, Stuttgart, 169-198.

Kieser, Alfred/Kubicek, Herbert (1992): Organisation. 3rd Ed. Walter de Gruyter, Berlin, New York.

Kirk, Jerome/Miller, Marc (1986): Reliability and Validity in Qualitative Research. Sage, Beverly Hills.
Kirsch, Werner/Kutschker, Michael/Lutschewitz, Hartmut (1980): Ansätze und Entwicklungstendenzen im Investitionsgütermarketing: Auf dem Wege zu einem Interaktionsansatz. 2nd Ed. Poeschel, Stuttgart.
Klaus, Erich (2002): Vertrauen in Unternehmensnetzwerken – Eine interdisziplinäre Analyse. Deutscher Universitäts-Verlag, Wiesbaden.
Kobrin, Stephen J. (1991): An Empirical Analysis of the Determinants of Global Integration. In: Strategic Management Journal. Vol. 12, No. 4, 17-31.
Kogut, Bruce/Zander, Udo (1992): Knowledge of the Firm, Combinative Capabilities, and the Replication of Technology. In: Organization Science. Vol. 3, No. 3, 383-397.
Kogut, Bruce/Zander, Udo (1993): Knowledge of the Firm and the Evolutionary Theory of the Multinational Corporation. In: Journal of International Business Studies. Vol. 24, No. 4, 625-645.
Köhl, Thomas (2000): Claim-Management im internationalen Anlagengeschäft: Nachforderungspotentiale und deren Realisierung in unterschiedlichen Vertragsverhältnissen. Gabler, Wiesbaden.
Kohn, Alfie (1986): No Contest: The Case Against Competition. Houghton Mifflin, Boston.
Königshausen, Horst/Spannagel, Frieder (2004): Marketing im internationalen Anlagenbau. In: Backhaus, Klaus/Voeth, Markus (eds.): Handbuch Industriegütermarketing. Gabler, Wiesbaden, 1123-1142.
Kuckartz, Udo (2007): Einführung in die computergestützte Analyse qualitativer Daten. 2nd Ed. Verlag für Sozialwissenschaften, Wiesbaden.
Kuckartz, Udo/Grunenberg, Heiko/Dresing, Thorsten (eds., 2007): Qualitative Datenanalyse: computergestützt. Methodische Hintergründe und Beispiele aus der Forschungspraxis. Verlag für Sozialwissenschaften, Wiesbaden.
Kuhn, Thomas S. (1962): The Structure of Scientific Revolutions. 2nd Ed. University of Chicago Press, Chicago.
Kutschker, Michael/Schmid, Stefan (1995): Netzwerke internationaler Unternehmungen. Discussion Paper, No. 64, Katholische Universität Eichstätt, Ingolstadt.
Kutschker, Michael/Schmid, Stefan (2006): Internationales Management. 5th Ed. Oldenbourg, München, Wien.
Kutschker, Michael/Schurig, Andreas/Schmid, Stefan (2002): Centers of Excellence in MNCs. An Empirical Analysis from Seven European Countries. In: Larimo, Jorma (ed.): Current European Research in International Business. Vol. 86. Vaasan Yliopiston Julkaisuja, Vaasa, 224-245.
Lado, Augustine A./Boyd, Nancy G./Hanlon, Susan C. (1997): Competition, Cooperation, and the Search for Economic Rents: A Syncretic Model. In: Academy of Management Review. Vol. 22, No. 1, 110-141.
Lagerström, Katarina/Andersson, Maria (2003): Creating and Sharing Knowledge Within a Transnational Team – The Development of a Global Business System. In: Journal of World Business. Vol. 38, No. 2, 84-95.
Landau, Martin (1969): Redundancy, Rationality, and the Problem of Duplication and Overlap. In: Public Administration Review. Vol. 29, No. 4, 346-358.
Lane, Peter J./Lubatkin, Michael (1998): Relative Absorptive Capacity and Interorganizational Learning. In: Strategic Management Journal. Vol. 19, No. 5, 461-477.

Lawrence, Paul R./Lorsch, Jay W. (1967): Organization and Environment. Managing Differentiation and Integration. Harvard University Press, Boston.

Lehmann, Patrick (2002): Interne Märkte: Unternehmungssteuerung zwischen Abwanderung und Widerspruch. Gabler, Wiesbaden.

Leong, Siew Meng/Tan, Chin Tiong (1992): Managing Across Borders: An Empirical Test of the Bartlett and Ghoshal [1989] Organizational Typology. In: Journal of International Business Studies. Vol. 24, No. 3, 449-464.

Lerner, Allan W. (1987): There Is More Than One Way to Be Redundant. In: Administration and Society. Vol. 18, No. 3, 334-359.

Levine, Sol/White, Paul E. (1961): Exchange as a Conceptual Framework for the Study of Interorganizational Relationships. In: Administrative Science Quarterly. Vol. 5, No. 4, 583-601.

Levy, Sidney M. (1996): Build, Operate, Transfer: Paving the Way for Tomorrow's Infrastructure. John Wiley & Sons, New York.

Lewis, Helen Block (1944): An Experimental Study of the Role of the Ego in Work. I. The Role of the Ego in Cooperative Work. In: Journal of Experimental Psychology. Vol. 34, No. 2, 113-127.

Li, Dan/Ferreira, Manuel Portugal (2003): Technology Transfer Within MNEs: An Investigation of Inter-subsidiary Competition and Cooperation. Paper presented at the 4th IB Research Forum at Temple University, Philadelphia, March 29.

Li, Dan/Ferreira, Manuel Portugal/Serra, Fernando (2007): Technology Transfer Within MNEs: An Investigation of Inter-subsidiary Competition and Cooperation. globADVANTAGE Working Paper, No. 1, Instituto Politécnico de Leiria, Leiria.

Lindskold, Sven (1982): Die Entwicklung von Vertrauen, der GRIT-Ansatz und die Wirkung von konziliantem Handeln auf Konflikt und Kooperation. In: Grunwald, Wolfgang/Lilge, Hans-Georg (eds.): Kooperation und Konkurrenz in Organisationen. Haupt, Bern, Stuttgart, 241-273.

Ling, Yan/Floyd, Steven W./Baldridge, David C. (2005): Toward a Model of Issue-Selling by Subsidiary Managers in Multinational Organizations. In: Journal of International Business Studies. Vol. 36, No. 6, 637-654.

Lockau, Ina (2000): Organisation des Global-Account-Management im Industriegütersektor. Erich Schmidt, Berlin.

Luo, Xueming/Slotegraaf, Rebecca J./Pan, Xing (2006): Cross-Functional "Coopetition": The Simultaneous Role of Cooperation and Competition Within Firms. In: Journal of Marketing. Vol. 70, No. 2, 67-80.

Luo, Yadong (2004): Coopetition in International Business. Copenhagen Business School Press, Copenhagen.

Luo, Yadong (2005): Toward Coopetition Within a Multinational Enterprise: A Perspective from Foreign Subsidiaries. In: Journal of World Business. Vol. 40, No. 1, 71-90.

Luo, Yadong (2007): A Coopetition Perspective of Global Competition. In: Journal of World Business. Vol. 42, No. 2, 129-144.

Machlup, Fritz (1980): Knowledge: Its Creation, Distribution and Economic Significance. Princeton University Press, Princeton.

Mahnke, Volker/Pedersen, Torben/Venzin, Markus (2005): The Impact of Knowledge Management on MNC Subsidiary Performance: The Role of Absorptive Capacity. In: Management International Review. Vol. 45, Special Issue (2), 101-119.

Mahoney, Joseph T. (2001): A Resource-based Theory of Sustainable Rents. In: Journal of Management. Vol. 27, No. 6, 651-660.

Makadok, Richard (2001): Toward a Synthesis of the Resource-Based and Dynamic Capability Views of Rent Creation. In: Strategic Management Journal. Vol. 22, No. 5, 387-401.

Mandják, Tibot/Veres, Zoltán (1998): The D-U-C Model and the Stages of the Project Marketing Process. Proceedings of the 14th Annual IMP Conference, Turku.

March, James G./Simon, Herbert A. (1958): Organizations. John Wiley & Sons, New York.

Marschan-Piekkari, Rebecca/Reis, Cristina (2004): Language and Languages in Cross-cultural Interviewing. In: Marschan-Piekkari, Rebecca/Welch, Catherine (eds.): Handbook of Qualitative Research Methods for International Business. Edward Elgar, Cheltenham, Northampton, 224-243.

Marschan-Piekkari, Rebecca/Welch, Catherine/Penttinen, Heli/Tahvanainen, Marja (2004): Interviewing in the Multinational Corporation: Challenges of the Organisational Context. In: Marschan-Piekkari, Rebecca/Welch, Catherine (eds.): Handbook of Qualitative Research Methods for International Business. Edward Elgar, Cheltenham, Northampton, 244-263.

Marschan, Rebecca (1996): New Structural Forms and Inter-unit Communication in Multinationals. The Case of KONE Elevators. Helsinki School of Economics and Business Administration.

Marshall, Catherine/Rossman, Gretchen B. (2006): Designing Qualitative Research. 4th Ed. Sage, London.

Martinez, Jon I./Jarillo, J. Carlos (1989): The Evolution of Research on Coordination Mechanisms in Multinational Corporations. In: Journal of International Business Studies. Vol. 20, No. 3, 489-514.

Mason, Charlotte H./Milne, George R. (1994): An Approach for Identifying Cannibalization Within Product Line Extensions and Multi-Brand Strategies. In: Journal of Business Research. Vol. 31, No. 2/3, 163-170.

Matsuo, Makoto (2005): The Role of Internal Competition in Knowledge Creation. An Empirical Study in Japanese Firms. Peter Lang, Bern.

Mattson, Lars-Gunnar (1973): Systems Selling as a Strategy on Industrial Markets. In: Industrial Marketing Management. Vol. 3, No. 2, 107-120.

May, Mark A./Doob, Leonard W. (1937): Cooperation and Competition. Social Science Research Council Bulletin, No. 25, New York.

McCann, Joseph E./Ferry, Diane L. (1979): An Approach for Assessing and Managing Inter-unit Interdependence. In: Academy of Management Review. Vol. 4, No. 1, 113-119.

McGaughey, Sara L. (2004): 'Writing It Up': The Challenges of Representation in Qualitative Research. In: Marschan-Piekkari, Rebecca/Welch, Catherine (eds.): Handbook of Qualitative Research Methods for International Business. Edward Elgar, Cheltenham, Northampton, 529-530.

McKenna, R.F. (1975): A Description of the Organizational Interfaces of the Formal and Informal Systems. In: Industrial Management. Vol. 17, No. 11, 1-6.

Mead, Margaret (1937): Co-operation and Competition Among Primitive Peoples. McGraw-Hill, New York.

Meffert, Heribert (1986): Marketing im Spannungsfeld von weltweitem Wettbewerb und nationalen Bedürfnissen. In: Zeitschrift für Betriebswirtschaft. Vol. 56, No. 8, 689-712.

Meffert, Heribert (1990): Implementierungsprobleme globaler Strategien. In: Welge, Martin K. (ed.): Globales Management. Erfolgreiche Strategien für den Weltmarkt. Poeschel, Stuttgart, 93-115.
Meffert, Heribert (2000): Marketing. Grundlagen marktorientierter Unternehmensführung. Konzepte – Instrumente – Praxisbeispiele. 9th Ed. Gabler, Wiesbaden.
Meier, Andreas (1997): Das Konzept der transnationalen Organisation: Kritische Reflexion eines prominenten Konzeptes für die Führung international tätiger Unternehmen. Verlag Barbara Kirsch, München.
Meuser, Michael/Nagel, Ulrike (2002): ExpertInneninterviews – vielfach erprobt, wenig bedacht. Ein Beitrag zur qualitativen Methodendiskussion. In: Bogner, Alexander/Littig, Beate/Menz, Wolfgang (eds.): Das Experteninterview. Leske & Budrich, Opladen, 71-95.
Michaelis, Elke (1985): Organisation unternehmerischer Aufgaben – Transaktionskosten als Beurteilungskriterium, Peter Lang, Frankfurt am Main.
Miles, Matthew B./Huberman, A. Michael (1994): Qualitative Data Analysis: An Expanded Sourcebook. 2nd Ed., Sage, Thousand Oaks, London, New Delhi.
Miller, Danny (1983): The Correlates of Entrepreneurship in Three Types of Firms. In: Management Science. Vol. 29, No. 7, 770-791.
Millman, Tony F. (1996): Global Key Account Management and Systems Selling. In: International Business Review. Vol. 5, No. 6, 631-645.
Minbaeva, Dana B./Pedersen, Torben/Björkman, Ingmar/Fey, Carl F./Park, Hyeon Jeong (2003): MNC Knowledge Transfer, Subsidiary Absorptive Capacity, and HRM. In: Journal of International Business Studies. Vol. 34, No. 6, 586-599.
Mintzberg, Henry (1979): The Structuring of Organizations: A Synthesis of the Research. Prentice Hall, Englewood Cliffs.
Möller, Kristian K./Wilson, David T. (1995): Business Marketing: An Interaction and Network Perspective. Kluwer, Boston.
Monteiro, L. Felipe/Arvidsson, Niklas/Birkinshaw, Julian (2008): Knowledge Flows Within Multinational Corporations: Explaining Subsidiary Isolation and Its Performance Implications. In: Organization Science. Vol. 19, No. 1, 90-107.
Moore, Karl/Birkinshaw, Julian (1998): Managing Knowledge in Global Service Firms: Centers of Excellence. In: Academy of Management Executive. Vol. 12, No. 4, 81-92.
Moran, Peter/Ghoshal, Sumantra (1996): Value Creation by Firms. In: Academy of Management Proceedings. 41-45.
Morgan, Gareth (1979): Response to Mintzberg. In: Administrative Science Quarterly. Vol. 24, No. 1, 137-139.
Mougeot, Michel/Naegelen, Florence (2005): Designing a Market Structure When Firms Compete for the Right to Serve the Market. In: Journal of Industrial Economics. Vol. 53, No. 3, 393-416.
Mudambi, Ram/Navarra, Pietro (2004): Is Knowledge Power? Knowledge Flows, Subsidiary Power and Rent-Seeking Within MNCs. In: Journal of International Business Studies. Vol. 35, No. 5, 385-406.
Müller, Michael/Stroh, Volker (2007): Claimsmanagement im Anlagenbau. In: VDMA Nachrichten. Vol. 86, No. 7, 82-84.
Murphy, William H./Dacin, Peter A. (1998): Sales Contests: A Research Agenda. In: Journal of Personal Selling & Sales Management. Vol. 18, No. 1, 1-16.

Murphy, William H./Dacin, Peter A./Ford, Neil M. (2004): Sales Contest Effectiveness: An Examination of Sales Contest Design Preferences of Field Sales Forces. In: Journal of the Academy of Marketing Science. Vol. 32, No. 2, 127-143.

N.N. (1978): Großanlagenbau: Vertriebsstrategie und ihre Kosten. In: Absatzwirtschaft. Vol. 21, No. 3, 36-44.

Nadler, David A./Tushman, Michael L. (1999): The Organization of the Future: Strategic Imperatives and Core Competencies for the 21st Century. In: Organizational Dynamics. Vol. 28, No. 1, 45-60.

Nahapiet, Janine/Ghoshal, Sumantra (1998): Social Capital, Intellectual Capital, and the Organizational Advantage. In: Academy of Management Review. Vol. 23, No. 2, 242-266.

Narver, John C./Slater, Stanley F. (1990): The Effect of a Market Orientation on Business Profitability. In: Journal of Marketing. Vol. 54, No. 4, 20-35.

Nault, Barrie R./Vandenbosch, Mark B. (1996): Eating Your Own Lunch: Protection Through Preemption. In: Organization Science. Vol. 7, No. 3, 342-358.

O'Donnell, Sharon Watson (2000): Managing Foreign Subsidiaries: Agents of Headquarters, or an Interdependent Network? In: Strategic Management Journal. Vol. 21, No. 5, 525-548.

Ortmann, Günther/Sydow, Jörg (2001): Strukturationstheorie als Metatheorie des strategischen Managements – Zur losen Integration der Paradigmenvielfalt. In: Ortmann, Günther/Sydow, Jörg (eds.): Strategie und Strukturation. Strategisches Management von Unternehmen, Netzwerken und Konzernen. Gabler, Wiesbaden, 421-447.

Osterloh, Margit (1998): Unternehmensinterne Märkte: Je mehr, desto besser? In: Glaser, Horst/Schröder, Ernst F./Werder, Axel v. (eds.): Organisation im Wandel der Märkte. Festschrift zum 60. Geburtstag von Erich Frese. Gabler, Wiesbaden, 287-315.

Ouchi, William G. (1980): Markets, Bureaucracies and Clans. In: Administrative Science Quarterly. Vol. 25, No. 1, 129-141.

Ouchi, William G./Van de Ven, Andrew H. (1980): Antitrust and Organization Theory. In: Williamson, Oliver E. (ed.): Antitrust Law and Economics. Houston, 291-311.

Parker, Glenn M. (1994): Cross-Functional Teams. Jossey-Bass, San Francisco.

Peng, Mike W. (2001): The Resource-based View and International Business. In: Journal of Management. Vol. 27, No. 6, 803-829.

Penrose, Edith T. (1959): The Theory of the Growth of the Firm. Basil Blackwell, Oxford.

Perlmutter, Howard V. (1965): L'Entreprise Internationale – Trois Conceptions. In: Revue Economique et Sociale. Vol. 23, No. 2, 151-165.

Perlmutter, Howard V. (1969a): The Tortuous Evolution of the Multinational Corporation. In: Columbia Journal of World Business. Vol. 4, No. 1, 9-18.

Perlmutter, Howard V. (1969b): Some Management Problems in Spaceship Earth: The Megafirm and the Global Industrial Estate. In: Academy of Management Proceedings. 59-87.

Petry, Thorsten (2006): Netzwerkstrategie. Deutscher Universitäts-Verlag, Wiesbaden.

Pfeffer, Jeffrey/Sutton, Robert I. (2000): The Knowing-Doing Gap: How Smart Companies Turn Knowledge into Action. Harvard Business School Press, Boston.

Phelps, Nicholas A./Fuller, Crispian (2000): Multinationals, Intracorporate Competition, and Regional Development. In: Economic Geography. Vol. 76, No. 3, 224-243.
Picot, Arnold (1982): Transaktionskostenansatz in der Organisationstheorie: Stand der Diskussion und Aussagewert. In: Die Betriebswirtschaft. Vol. 42, No. 2, 267-284.
Pihl, Håkan (2003): A New Organisational Form in Multinational Enterprises: From M-form to W-form. Working Paper Series 2003:10, Kristianstad University, Kristianstad.
Pinto, J.K. and Rouhiainen, P.K. (2001): Building Customer-Based Project Organizations. John Wiley & Sons, New York.
Plinke, Wulff (2000): Grundlagen des Marktprozesses. In: Kleinaltenkamp, Michael/Plinke, Wulff (eds.): Technischer Vertrieb: Grundlagen des Business-to-Business Marketing. 2nd Ed. Springer, Berlin, Heidelberg, 3-98.
Popper, Karl R. (1934): Logik der Forschung. Springer, Wien.
Popper, Karl R. (1972): Objective Knowledge: An Evolutionary Approach. Clarendon Press, Oxford.
Porter-Roth, Bud (2002): Request for Proposal: A Guide to Effective RFP Development. Addison-Wesley, Boston.
Porter, Michael (1980): Competitive Strategy. Techniques for Analyzing Industries and Competitors. The Free Press, New York.
Porter, Michael E. (1986a): Changing Patterns of International Competition. In: California Management Review. Vol. 28, No. 2, 9-40.
Porter, Michael E. (1986b): Competition in Global Industries: A Conceptual Framework. In: Porter, Michael E. (ed.): Competition in Global Industries. Harvard Business School Press, Boston, 15-60.
Powell, Walter W. (1990): Neither Market nor Hierarchy: Network Forms of Organization. In: Research in Organizational Behavior. Vol. 12, 265-336.
Prahalad, Coimbatore K. (1975): The Strategic Process in a Multinational Corporation. Unpublished doctoral dissertation. Harvard Business School, Boston.
Prahalad, Coimbatore K./Doz, Yves L. (1987): The Multinational Mission: Balancing Local Demands and Global Vision. The Free Press, New York.
Pugh, Derek S. (1981): The Aston Program Perspective: The Aston Program of Research. Retrospect and Prospect. In: Van de Ven, Andrew/Joyce, William (eds.): Perspectives on Organization Design and Behavior. John Wiley & Sons, New York, 155-166.
Pugh, Derek S./Hickson, David J. (1971): Eine dimensionale Analyse bürokratischer Strukturen. In: Mayntz, Renate (ed.): Bürokratische Organisation. Kiepenheuer & Witsch, Köln, 82-93.
Pugh, Derek S./Hickson, David J./Hinings, Christopher R./Turner, Christopher (1968): Dimensions of Organization Structure. In: Administrative Science Quarterly. Vol. 13, No. 1, 65-105.
Putnam, Linda L./Mumby, Dennis K. (1993): Organizations, Emotion and the Myth of Rationality. In: Fineman, Stephen (ed.): Emotion in Organizations. Sage, London, 36-57.
Randøy, Trond/Li, Jiatao (1998): Global Resource Flows and MNE Integration. In: Birkinshaw, Julian/Hood, Neil (eds.): Multinational Corporate Evolution and Subsidiary Development. Macmillan/St. Martin's Press, Houndmills, Basingstoke, New York, 76-101.

Rank, Olaf N. (2003): Formale und informelle Organisationsstrukturen: Eine Netzwerkanalyse des strategischen Planungs- und Entscheidungsprozesses multinationaler Unternehmen. Gabler (mir-Edition), Wiesbaden.

Rapp, Matthias J. (2004): Das Ertragsgesetz im Anlagenbau. Beiträge zum Industrieanlagenbau. VDMA, Frankfurt am Main.

Reichardt, Charles S./Cook, Thomas D. (1979): Beyond Qualitative versus Quantitative Methods. In: Cook, Thomas D./Reichardt, Charles S. (eds.): Qualitative and Quantitative Methods in Evaluation Research. Sage, Beverly Hills, 7-32.

Rindfleisch, Aric/Heide, Jan B. (1997): Transaction Cost Analysis: Past, Present, and Future Applications. In: Journal of Marketing. Vol. 61, No. 4, 30-54.

Ring, Peter Smith/Van De Ven, Andrew H. (1994): Developmental Processes of Cooperative Interorganizational Relationships. In: Academy of Management Review. Vol. 19, No. 1, 90-118.

Robbins, Stephen P. (1990): Organization Theory. Structure, Design, and Applications. 3rd Ed. Prentice Hall, Englewood Cliffs, New Jersey.

Rosenstiel, Lutz von (1993): Kommunikation und Führung in Arbeitsgruppen. In: Schuler, Heinz (ed.): Lehrbuch Organisationspsychologie. Huber, Bern, 321-351.

Roth, Kendall/Morrison, Allen J. (1990): An Empirical Analysis of the Integration-Responsiveness Framework in Global Industries. In: Journal of International Business Studies. Vol. 21, No. 4, 541-564.

Roth, Kendall/Morrison, Allen J. (1992): Implementing Global Strategy: Characteristics of Global Subsidiary Mandates. In: Journal of International Business Studies. Vol. 23, No. 4, 715-735.

Rugman, Alan M. (1981): Inside the Multinationals: The Economics of Internal Markets. Columbia University Press, New York.

Rugman, Alan M. (1996): The Theory of Multinational Enterprises. Edward Elgar, Cheltenham.

Rugman, Alan M./Douglas, Sheila (1986): The Strategic Management of Multinationals and World Product Mandating. In: Etemad, Hamid/Dulude, Louise Séguin (eds.): Managing the Multinational Subsidiary: Response to Environmental Changes and to Host Nation R&D Policies. London, Croom Helm, 90-101.

Rugman, Alan M./Verbeke, Alain (1992): A Note on the Transnational Solution and the Transaction Cost Theory of Multinational Strategic Management. In: Journal of International Business Studies. Vol. 23, No. 4, 761-771.

Rugman, Alan M./Verbeke, Alain (2001): Subsidiary-Specific Advantages in Multinational Enterprises. In: Strategic Management Journal. Vol. 22, No. 3, 237-250.

Rugman, Alan M./Verbeke, Alain (2003): Extending the Theory of the Multinational Enterprise: Internalization and Strategic Management Perspectives. In: Journal of International Business Studies. Vol. 34, No. 2, 125-137.

Rumelt, Richard P. (1974): Strategy, Structure, and Economic Performance. Harvard University Press, Boston.

Schewe, Gerhard (1998): Strategie und Struktur. Eine Re-Analyse empirischer Befunde und Nicht-Befunde. Mohr/Siebeck, Tübingen.

Schiller, Thomas (2000): Kompetenz-Management für den Anlagenbau: Ansatz, Empirie und Aufgaben. Gabler, Wiesbaden.

Schlegelmilch, Bodo B./Chini, Tina Claudia (2003): Knowledge Transfer Between Marketing Functions in Multinational Companies: A Conceptual Model. In: International Business Review. Vol. 12, No. 2, 215-232.

Schmid, Stefan (1994): Orthodoxer Positivismus und Symbolismus im internationalen Management – Eine kritische Reflexion situativer und interpretativer Ansätze. Discussion Paper, No. 49, Katholische Universität Eichstätt, Ingolstadt.

Schmid, Stefan (1996): Multikulturalität in der internationalen Unternehmung. Konzepte – Reflexionen – Implikationen. Gabler (mir-Edition), Wiesbaden.

Schmid, Stefan (2003): How MNCs Can Upgrade Foreign Subsidiaries: A Case Study from Central and Eastern Europe. In: Stüting, Heinz-Jürgen/Dorow, Wolfgang/Claassen, Frank/Blazejewski, Susanne (eds.): Change Management in Transition Economies: Integrating Corporate Strategy, Structure and Culture. Palgrave/Macmillan, Houndmills, Basingstoke, New York, 273-290.

Schmid, Stefan (2004): The Roles of Foreign Subsidiaries in Network MNCs – A Critical Review of the Literature and Some Directions for Future Research. In: Larimo, Jorma/Rumpunen, Sami (eds.): European Research on Foreign Direct Investment and International Human Resource Management. Vol. 112. Vaasan Yliopiston Julkaisuja, Vaasa, 237-255.

Schmid, Stefan (2005): Kooperationen: Erklärungsperspektiven interaktionstheoretischer Ansätze. In: Zentes, Joachim/Swoboda, Bernhard/Morschett, Dirk (eds.): Kooperationen, Allianzen und Netzwerke. Grundlagen – Ansätze – Perspektiven. 2nd Ed. Gabler, Wiesbaden.

Schmid, Stefan/Bäurle, Iris (1994): Die Transnationale Organisation. In: WISU – Das Wirtschaftsstudium. Vol. 23, No. 12, 991-993.

Schmid, Stefan/Kutschker, Michael (2003): Rollentypologien für ausländische Tochtergesellschaften in Multinationalen Unternehmungen. In: Holtbrügge, Dirk (ed.): Management Multinationaler Unternehmungen. Festschrift zum 60. Geburtstag von Martin K. Welge. Physika/Springer, Heidelberg, 161-182.

Schmid, Stefan/Schurig, Andreas (2003): The Development of Critical Capabilities in Foreign Subsidiaries: Disentangling the Role of the Subsidiary's Business Network. In: International Business Review. Vol. 12, No. 6, 755-782.

Schmid, Stefan/Daub, Matthias (2005): Service Offshoring Subsidiaries – Towards a Typology. Working Paper, No. 12, ESCP-EAP European School of Management Berlin, Berlin.

Schmid, Stefan/Machulik, Mario (2006): What Has Perlmutter Really Written? A Comprehensive Analysis of the EPRG Concept. In: Larimo, Jorma/Rumpunen, Sami (eds.): Internationalization and Management of Foreign Operations. Vol. 130. Vaasan Yliopiston Julkaisuja, Vaasa, 248-283.

Schmid, Stefan/Kretschmer, Katharina (2006): Performance Evaluation of Foreign Subsidiaries – A Contingency Framework. Working Paper, No. 18, ESCP-EAP European School of Management Berlin, Berlin.

Schmid, Stefan/Daniel, Andrea (2007): Are Subsidiary Roles a Matter of Perception? A Review of the Literature and Avenues for Future Research. Working Paper, No. 30, ESCP-EAP European School of Management Berlin, Berlin.

Schmid, Stefan/Daub, Matthias (2007): Embeddedness in International Business Research – The Concept and Its Operationalization. Working Paper, No. 23, ESCP-EAP European School of Management Berlin, Berlin.

Schmid, Stefan/Maurer, Julia (2008): Relationships Between MNC Subsidiaries – Towards a Classification Scheme. Working Paper, No. 35, ESCP-EAP European School of Management Berlin, Berlin.

Schmid, Stefan/Daniel, Andrea (2009): Subsidiary Roles, Perception Gaps and Conflict – A Social Psychological Approach. In: Schmid, Stefan (ed.): Management der Internationalisierung. Festschrift zum 65. Geburtstag von Michael Kutschker. Gabler, Wiesbaden, 183-202.

Schmid, Stefan/Grosche, Philipp (2009): Konfiguration und Koordination von Wertschöpfungsaktivitäten in internationalen Unternehmen – Ein kritischer Beitrag zum State-of-the-Art. Working Paper, No. 48. ESCP-EAP European School of Management Berlin, Berlin.

Schmid, Stefan/Kretschmer, Katharina (2010): Performance Evaluation of Foreign Subsidiaries – A Review of the Literature and a Contingency Framework. In: International Journal of Management Reviews, Vol. 12, No. 3, 219-258.

Schmid, Stefan/Maurer, Julia (2011): Relationships Between MNC Subsidiaries – Opening a Black Box in the International Business Field. In: Schmid, Stefan (ed.): Internationale Unternehmungen und das Management ausländischer Tochtergesellschaften. Gabler (mir-Edition), Wiesbaden, 53-83.

Schmid, Stefan/Bäurle, Iris/Kutschker, Michael (1998): Tochtergesellschaften in international tätigen Unternehmungen – Ein "State-of-the-Art" unterschiedlicher Rollentypologien. Discussion Paper, No. 104, Katholische Universität Eichstätt, Ingolstadt.

Schmid, Stefan/Bäurle, Iris/Kutschker, Michael (1999): Ausländische Tochtergesellschaften als Kompetenzzentren. Ergebnisse einer empirischen Untersuchung. In: Kutschker, Michael (ed.): Management verteilter Kompetenzen in multinationalen Unternehmungen. Gabler (mir-Edition), Wiesbaden, 99-126.

Schmid, Stefan/Schurig, Andreas/Kutschker, Michael (2002): The MNC as a Network – A Closer Look at Intra-Organizational Flows. In: Lundan, Sarianna M. (ed.): Network Knowledge in International Business. Edward Elgar (Series New Horizons in International Business), Cheltenham, Northampton, 45-72.

Schoch, Rolf (1969): Der Verkaufsvorgang als sozialer Interaktionsprozess. Schellenberg, Winterthur.

Schreyögg, Georg (2003): Organisation. Grundlagen moderner Organisationsgestaltung. 4th Ed. Gabler, Wiesbaden.

Schwanfelder, Werner (1989): Internationale Anlagengeschäfte. Anbieterkonsortium – Projektabwicklung – Projektcontrolling. Gabler, Wiesbaden.

Schweiger, David M./Atamer, Tugrul/Calori, Roland (2003): Transnational Project Teams and Networks: Making the Multinational Organization More Effective. In: Journal of World Business. Vol. 38, No. 2, 127-140.

Scott, W. Richard (2003): Organizations: Rational, Natural, and Open Systems. 5th Ed. Prentice-Hall, Englewood Cliffs.

Selltiz, Claire/Wrightsman, Lawrence S./Cook, Stuart W. (1976): Research Methods in Social Relations. 3rd Ed. Holt, Rinehart & Winston, New York.

Shrivastava, Paul/Mitroff, Ian I. (1984): Enhancing Organizational Research Utilization: The Role of Decision Makers' Assumptions In: The Academy of Management Review. Vol. 9, No. 1, 18-26.

Siebel, Ulf R. (2001): Handbuch Projekte und Projektfinanzierung. C.H. Beck, München.

Sim, A. B. (1977): Decentralized Management of Subsidiaries and Their Performance. In: Management International Review. Vol. 17, No. 2, 45-52.

Skaates, Maria Anne/Tikkanen, Henrikki (2000): Focal Relationships and the Environment of Project Marketing: A Literature Review with Suggestions for Practitioners and Future Research. Proceedings of the 16th Annual IMP Conference, Bath.

Skaates, Maria Anne/Tikkanen, Henrikki (2003): International Project Marketing: An Introduction to the INPM Approach. In: International Journal of Project Management. Vol. 21, No. 7, 503-510.

Smith, Clagett G. (1966): A Comparative Analysis of Some Conditions and Consequences of Intra-Organizational Conflict. In: Administrative Science Quarterly. Vol. 10, No. 4, 504-529.

Smith, Ken G./Carroll, Stephen J./Ashford, Susan J. (1995): Intra- and Interorganizational Cooperation: Toward a Research Agenda. In: The Academy of Management Journal. Vol. 38, No. 1, 7-23.

Snow, Charles C./Hambrick, Donald C. (1980): Measuring Organizational Strategies: Some Theoretical and Methodological Problems. In: Academy of Management Review. Vol. 5, No. 4, 527-538.

Sorenson, Olav (2000): Letting the Market Work for You: An Evolutionary Perspective on Product Strategy. In: Strategic Management Journal. Vol. 21, No. 5, 577-592.

Staber, Udo (2000): Steuerung von Unternehmensnetzwerken: Organisationstheoretische Perspektiven und soziale Mechanismen. In: Sydow, Jörg/Windeler, Arnold (eds.): Steuerung von Netzwerken – Konzepte und Praktiken. Westdeutscher Verlag, Opladen, Wiesbaden, 58-87.

Staubach, Stefan (2005): Effektiver Einsatz interner Verrechnungspreise. Eine Untersuchung aus organisationstheoretischer Sicht. Hampp, Mering.

Steinke, Ines (1999): Kriterien qualitativer Forschung, Ansätze zur Bewertung qualitativ-empirischer Sozialforschung. Juventa, Weinheim, München.

Steinke, Ines (2004): Gütekriterien qualitativer Forschung. In: Flick, Uwe/von Kardorff, Ernst/Steinke, Ines (eds.): Qualitative Forschung. Ein Handbuch. 3rd Ed. Rowohlt, Reinbek bei Hamburg.

Stopford, John M./Wells, Louis T. (1972): Managing the Multinational Enterprise. Organization of the Firm and Ownership of the Subsidiaries. Basic Books, New York.

Strauss, Anselm (1987): Qualitative Analysis for Social Scientists. Cambride University Press, Cambridge.

Strauss, Anselm (1991): Grundlagen qualitativer Sozialforschung – Datenanalyse und Theoriebildung in der empirischen soziologischen Forschung. Fink, München.

Stroh, Volker (2006): Bilanz und Perspektiven des deutschen Industrieanlagenbaus. Speech held at the Conference "Anlagenbau der Zukunft. Wettbewerbsvorteile im Anlagenbau realisieren – Zukunftsszenarien und Erfahrungsberichte", Magdeburg, March 2-3.

Struthoff, Ralf (1999): Führung und Organisation von Unternehmensnetzwerken. Vandenhoeck und Ruprecht, Göttingen.

Szulanski, Gabriel (1996): Exploring Internal Stickiness: Impediments to the Transfer of Best Practice Within the Firm. In: Strategic Management Journal. Vol. 17, Winter Special Issue, 27-43.

Taggart, James H. (1997): Autonomy and Procedural Justice: A Framework for Evaluating Subsidiary Strategy. In: Journal of International Business Studies. Vol. 28, No. 1, 51-77.

Thibaut, John W./Kelley, Harold H. (1959): The Social Psychology of Groups. John Wiley & Sons, New York.
Thompson, Grahame/Frances, Jennifer/Levacic, Rosalind/Mitchell, Jeremy (1991): Markets, Hierarchies and Networks: The Coordination of Social Life. Sage, London.
Thompson, James D. (1960): Organizational Management of Conflict. In: Administrative Science Quarterly. Vol. 4, No. 4, 389-409.
Thompson, James D. (1967): Organizations in Action: Social Science Bases of Administrative Theory. McGraw-Hill, New York.
Thorelli, Hans B. (1986): Networks: Between Markets and Hierarchies. In: Strategic Management Journal. Vol. 7, No. 1, 37-51.
Tichy, Noel M./Tushman, Michael L./Fombrun, Charles (1979): Social Network Analysis for Organizations. In: Academy of Management Review. Vol. 4, No. 4, 507-519.
Toyne, Brian/Nigh, Douglas (eds., 1997): International Business: An Emerging Vision. University of South Carolina Press, Columbia.
Tsai, Wenpin (2000): Social Capital, Strategic Relatedness and the Formation of Intraorganizational Linkages. In: Strategic Management Journal. Vol. 21, No. 9, 925-939.
Tsai, Wenpin (2002): Social Structure of "Coopetition" Within a Multiunit Organization: Coordination, Competition and Intraorganizational Knowledge Sharing. In: Organization Science. Vol. 13, No. 2, 179-190.
Tsai, Wenpin/Ghoshal, Sumantra (1998): Social Capital and Value Creation: The Role of Intrafirm Networks. In: Academy of Management Journal. Vol. 41, No. 4, 464-476.
Türk, Klaus (1989): Neuere Entwicklungen in der Organisationsforschung: Ein Trend Report. Enke, Stuttgart.
Turner, Ian/Henry, Ian (1994): Managing International Organisations: Lessons from the Field. In: European Management Journal. Vol. 12, No. 4, 417-431.
Ullrich, Christian (2004): Die Dynamik von Coopetition. Möglichkeiten und Grenzen dauerhafter Kooperation. Deutscher Universitäts-Verlag, Wiesbaden.
Van de Ven, Andrew/Poole, Marshall Scott (1995): Explaining Development and Change in Organizations. In: The Academy of Management Review. Vol. 20, No. 3, 510-540.
Van Lange, Paul A. M./De Dreu, Carsten K. W. (2003): Soziale Interaktion: Kooperation und Wettbewerb. In: Stroebe, Wolfgang/Jonas, Klaus/Hewstone, Miles (eds.): Sozialpsychologie: eine Einführung. 4th Ed. Springer, Berlin.
VDMA (2007): Anhaltender Auftragsboom – Neue Herausforderungen. Lagebericht 2006. VDMA, Frankfurt am Main.
VDMA (2008): Portrait of the VDMA's Large Industrial Plant Manufacturers Group. Website of VDMA. URL: http://www.vdma.org/wps/portal/Home/en/Branchen/ L/AGAB/Uber_uns/Profil/AGAB_20070306_Art_en_Portrait_Large_Indutrial_Pl ant_Manufactuers_Group?WCM_GLOBAL_CONTEXT=/wps/wcm/connect/Ho me/en/Branchen/L/AGAB/Ueber_uns/Profil/AGAB_20070306_Art_en_Portrait _Large_Industrial_Plant_Manufacturers_Group (04/03/2008).
VDMA, Arbeitsgemeinschaft Großanlagenbau (2006): Großanlagenbau mit Auftragsrekord – Standortpolitischer Handlungsdruck bleibt. Lagebericht 2005. VDMA, Frankfurt am Main.

Venaik, Sunil/Midgley, David F./Devinney, Timothy M. (2002): An Empirical Examination of the Characteristics of the Integration-Responsiveness Pressures. Paper presented at the Annual Meeting of the Academy of International Business, San Juan (Puerto Rico), June 28 - July 1.

Verbeke, Alain/Yuan, Wenlong (2005): Subsidiary Autonomous Activities in Multinational Enterprises. In: Management International Review. Vol. 45, Special Issue (2), 31-52.

Walley, Keith (2007): Coopetition. In: International Studies of Management & Organization. Vol. 37, No. 2, 11-31.

Walton, Richard E./Dutton, John M. (1969): The Management of Interdepartmental Conflict: A Model and Review. In: Administrative Science Quarterly. Vol. 14, No. 1, 73-84.

Walton, Richard E./Dutton, John M./Cafferty, Thomas P. (1969): Organizational Context and Interdepartmental Conflict. In: Administrative Science Quarterly. Vol. 14, No. 4, 522-542.

Weber, Robert Philip (1990): Basic Content Analysis. Sage, Newbury Park, London, New Delhi.

Weigelt, Keith/Camerer, Colin (1988): Reputation and Corporate Strategy: A Review of Recent Theory and Applications. In: Strategic Management Journal. Vol. 9, No. 5, 443-454.

Weise, Peter (1997): Konkurrenz und Kooperation. In: Held, Martin (ed.): Normative Grundfragen der Ökonomik. Campus, Frankfurt am Main.

Weitzman, Eben A. (2000): Software and Qualitative Research. In: Denzin, Norman K./Lincoln, Yvonna S. (eds.): Handbook of Qualitative Research. 2nd Ed. Sage, London, 803-820.

Welge, Martin K. (1980): Management in deutschen multinationalen Unternehmungen. Ergebnisse einer empirischen Untersuchung. Poeschel, Stuttgart.

Welge, Martin K./Holtbrügge, Dirk (2006): Internationales Management. Theorien, Funktionen, Fallstudien. 4th Ed. Schäffer-Poeschel, Stuttgart.

Wengler, Stefan (2006): Key Account Management in Business-to-Business Markets. Gabler, Wiesbaden.

Werder, Axel v. (1999): Argumentation Rationality of Management Decisions. In: Organization Science. Vol. 10, No. 5, 672-690.

Wernerfelt, Birger (1984): A Resource-Based View of the Firm. In: Strategic Management Journal. Vol. 5, No. 2, 171-180.

White, Roderick E./Poynter, Thomas A. (1989): Achieving Worldwide Advantage with the Horizontal Organization. In: Business Quarterly. Vol. 54, No. 2, 55-60.

White, Roderick E./Poynter, Thomas A. (1990): Organizing for World-wide Advantage. In: Bartlett, Christopher A./Doz, Yves L./Hedlund, Gunnar (eds.): Managing the Global Firm. Routledge, London, 95-113.

Wildemann, Horst (1997): Koordination von Unternehmensnetzwerken. In: Zeitschrift für Betriebswirtschaft (ZfB). Vol. 67, No. 4, 417-439.

Williamson, Oliver E. (1975): Markets and Hierarchies: Analysis and Antitrust Implications. The Free Press, New York.

Williamson, Oliver E. (1981): The Economics of Organization: The Transaction Cost Approach. In: The American Journal of Sociology. Vol. 87, No. 3, 548-577.

Williamson, Oliver E. (1999): Strategy Research: Governance and Competence Perspectives. In: Strategic Management Journal. Vol. 20, No. 12, 1087-1108.

Williamson, Oliver E./Ouchi, William G. (1981): The Markets and Hierarchies and Visible Hand Perspective. In: Van de Ven, Andrew/Joyce, William F. (eds.): Perspectives on Organization Design and Behavior. John Wiley & Sons, New York, Chichester, Brisbane, Toronto, Singapore, 347-370.

Wimmer, Peter/Neuberger, Oswald (1982): Das Organisationsklima im Lichte kooperativen und konkurrierenden Verhaltens. In: Grunwald, Wolfgang/Lilge, Hans-Georg (eds.): Kooperation und Konkurrenz in Organisationen. Haupt, Bern, Stuttgart, 189-211.

Wind, Yoram/Douglas, Susan P./Perlmutter, Howard V. (1973): Guidelines for Developing International Marketing Strategies. In: Journal of Marketing. Vol. 37, No. 2, 14-23.

Windsperger, Josef (1996): Transaktionskostenansatz der Entstehung der Unternehmensorganisation. Physica-Verlag, Heidelberg.

Windsperger, Josef (1997): Beziehung zwischen Kontingenz- und Transaktionskostenansatz der Organisation. In: Journal für Betriebswirtschaft. Vol. 47, No. 4, 190-202.

Windsperger, Josef (1998): Ungelöste Probleme der Transaktionskostentheorie. In: Journal für Betriebswirtschaft. Vol. 4, No. 5/6, 266-276.

Woodward, Joan (1958): Management and Technology. H.M. Stationary Office, London.

Woodward, Joan (1965): Industrial Organisation: Theory and Practice. Oxford University Press, London.

Yin, Robert K. (2003): Case Study Research: Design and Methods. 3rd Ed. Sage, Thousand Oaks.

You, Jong-Il/Wilkinson, Frank (1994): Competition and Co-operation: Toward Understanding Industrial Districts. In: Review of Political Economy. Vol. 6, No. 3, 259-278.

Young-Ybarra, Candace/Wiersema, Margarethe (1999): Strategic Flexibility in Information Technology Alliances: The Influence of Transaction Cost Economics and Social Exchange Theory. In: Organization Science. Vol. 10, No. 4, 439-459.

Young, Stephen/Tavares, Ana Teresa (2004): Centralization and Autonomy: Back to the Future. In: International Business Review. Vol. 13, No. 2, 215-237.

Zack, Michael H. (1999): Managing Codified Knowledge. In: Sloan Management Review. Vol. 40, No. 4, 45-58.

Zander, Udo/Kogut, Bruce (1995): Knowledge and the Speed of the Transfer and Imitation of Organizational Capabilities. An Empirical Test. In: Organization Science. Vol. 6, No. 1, 76-92.

Zentes, Joachim/Swoboda, Bernhard/Schramm-Klein, Hanna (2006): Internationales Marketing. Vahlen, München.

Zhao, Hongxin/Luo, Yadong (2005): Antecedents of Knowledge Sharing with Peer Subsidiaries of Other Countries: A Perspective from Subsidiary Managers in a Foreign Emerging Market. In: Management International Review. Vol. 45, No. 1, 71-97.

Zwerling, Stephen (1980): The Dynamics of Domain Negotiation: The National Science Foundation and the Geographic Distribution of Research Awards. In: Public Administration Review. Vol. 40, No. 4, 351-358.

GABLER RESEARCH

„mir-Edition"
Hrsg./Eds.: Andreas Al-Laham, Johann Engelhard,
Michael Kutschker, Klaus Macharzina, Michael-Jörg Oesterle,
Stefan Schmid, Martin K. Welge, Joachim Wolf
zuletzt erschienen:

Alexander Bode
Wettbewerbsvorteile durch internationale Wertschöpfung
Eine Untersuchung deutscher Unternehmen in China
2010. XXIV, 293 S., 77 Abb., 16 Tab., Br. € 59,95
ISBN 978-3-8349-2085-0

Andrea Daniel
Perception Gaps between Headquarters and Subsidiary Managers
Differing Perspectives on Subsidiary Roles and their Implications
2010. XXIV, 300 S., 43 Abb., 18 Tab., Br. € 59,95
ISBN 978-3-8349-2071-3

Julia Maurer
Relationships between Foreign Subsidiaries
Competition and Cooperation in Multinational Plant Engineering Companies
2011. XXIV, 355 S., 21 Abb., 19 Tab., Br. € 59,95
ISBN 978-3-8349-3191-7

Stefan Schmid (Hrsg.)
Internationale Unternehmungen und das Management ausländischer Tochtergesellschaften
2010. XII, 386 S., 74 Abb., Br. € 59,95
ISBN 978-3-8349-2598-5

Philipp Seidel
Internationale Unternehmen, Gesellschaft und Verantwortung
Eine Kritik der Managementwissenschaft als Bezugsrahmen
2011, XXX, 498 S., 26 Abb., 25 Tab., Br. € 69,95
ISBN 978-3-8349-3094-1

Änderungen vorbehalten. Stand: August 2011.
Erhältlich im Buchhandel oder beim Verlag.
Gabler Verlag . Abraham-Lincoln-Str. 46 . 65189 Wiesbaden . www.gabler.de

GABLER